# The Way of Mary

## *Maryam, Beloved of God*

Mercy and truth are met together;
righteousness and peace have kissed each other.
Truth shall spring out of the earth;
and righteousness shall look down from heaven.
Truly, the Lord shall give that which is good;
and our earth shall yield her fruit.

[Bible, Psalms of David 85:11–13]

And the angel having come in, said unto her:
"Hail, full of grace, the Lord is with thee:
blessed art thou amongst women."

[Bible, Gospel of Luke 1:28]

*And remember when the angels said, "O Mary!*
*Truly God has chosen you and purified you—*
*chosen you above all the women of all the worlds."*

[Quran, *Surah al-'Imran* 3:42]

## *Enthusiasm for*
## The Way of Mary, Maryam, Beloved of God

Revered across the family of Abraham and Sarah, adored as Miriam, Mary, Maryam, Madre Maria, there is no other single figure who so universally serves to lift up the weary heart of the world, blessing us with lovingkindness and infusing us with hope. With her signature blend of sublime wisdom and grounded scholarship, beloved Sufi teacher Camille Helminski offers a penetrating and life-giving transmission of Maryam as guide to the awakening of the soul, during a time when we need her most.

~ **Mirabai Starr**, author of *God of Love* and *Wild Mercy*

I have read numerous books on the Holy Mother in Her many guises: Kali, Chochma, Sarada Devi, Shechinah, Avalokiteshvara, and of course Mary, but none was as striking, profound, and potentially heart-transforming as Camille Helminski's *The Way of Mary*. This book, steeped in wisdom, is a book to be savored. I cannot recommend it more highly.

~ **Rabbi Rami Shapiro**, author of *The Divine Feminine in Biblical Wisdom Literature*

What beautiful blessedness: the wise and gentle heart of Mary mirrored in the wise and gentle heart of Camille Helminski.

~ **The Rev. Dr. Cynthia Bourgeault**, author of *The Wisdom Jesus* and *The Meaning of Mary Magdalene*

I would like to thank Camille Hanim for bringing us Hazreti Meryem's fragrance full of patience, compassion, mercy, and knowing. Camille Hanim has done a great service to humanity by writing this book—the fact that she quotes from the Bible, the Quran and the *Masnavi* is very important in terms of realizing that all paths lead to the One. Even though the paths are different, the destination is the same.

~ **Esin Celebi Bayru**, 22nd generation granddaughter of Mevlana Jalaluddin Rumi; Vice President, International Mevlana Foundation

Camille Helminski's *The Way of Mary* is a lovely and welcome addition to the deep dialogue of the spirit shared between Muslims and Christians.

The Qur'an uses the exact same verb to talk about Mary being "chosen and purified" as that of the most common honorific for the Prophet Muhammad, *Mustapha*. Indeed, one could say that there is a close association between Mary and Muhammad, in that the former receives God's Word (Jesus) into her pure womb, and the latter God's Word (the Qur'an) into his luminous heart. Deeply rooted in the Qur'an and the Sufi tradition, *The Way of Mary* is a beautiful way of accessing the rich waters of life that are shared across our tradition, and is highly recommended to all spiritual seekers.

~ **Omid Safi**, Professor of Islamic Studies at Duke University;
Founder, Illuminated Courses and Tours

This priceless book is a treasure trove of precious insights, heartfelt poetry, sacred verses and meticulous scholarship. These elements exquisitely woven into twelve chapters uniquely and profoundly enrich our mind, purify our heart and exalt our soul. Our beings feel deeply grateful to be graced and blessed by beauty and a rare taste of the sacred.

~ **Imam Jamal Rahman**, Interfaith Community Sanctuary

This is a remarkable book, both a scholarly investigation and a treasure of meditative devotion. Camille Helminski moves back and forth between the differing but related stories of Maryam in the Quran, and Mary in the Christian New Testament, considering both texts in sensitive scholarly detail, from her Conception to the end of Beloved Maryam's life. But the spirit of the book is a loving tribute to Maryam/Mary, evoking the perfume of this Blessed Mother through Camille's deep devotion and love. As a longtime lover of Sufism and now Christian Catholicism, I marvel at Camille's capacity to consider Maryam/Mary in such depth with honor to both these rich streams of wisdom.

~ **Sara K. Winter**, Ph.D., Former Faculty Member,
Antioch University, Los Angeles

Camille Hamilton Adams Helminski's book *The Way of Mary* is a beautifully written and researched account of a holy woman of significance to the three Abrahamic religions. She artfully weaves together accounts of Mary's life from the Christian and Islamic traditions. Having been deeply immersed in Hinduism for most of my life, I knew little about Mary. But I feel deeply the importance today of bringing to the fore accounts of the lives and teachings of the female Masters from all traditions. And so through this narrative, I was pleased to meet Mary and learn of her complete devotion to and absorption in the Divine Reality. There are many beautiful metaphors in the book but one of the most touching and relevant today is the account of Mary during the travails of childbirth reaching out to a palm tree for strength. In this mutual exchange, she revives a withered branch and it becomes fruitful, while the tree grants her the strength she needs to endure the pain of childbirth. How appropriate this metaphor is for us today, as we seek to birth a new, ecological and dharmic civilization. It is perhaps our battered nature that can give us the strength and wisdom we need for this endeavor.

~ **Dena Merriam**, Founder & Convener, The Global Peace Initiative of Women; author, *The Untold Story of Sita*

*The Way of Mary, Maryam, Beloved of God* is an incredible offering of holy wisdom, scholarship, poetry, art, and song that brings Beloved Mary to life as a multidimensional Woman of God. Within these pages her story seems fresh, even new. For anyone unfamiliar with Mary this book is a rich introduction. Beloved Mary's story in the Torah, Psalms, Gospel, Quran, and other sources is interwoven to carry us on a journey from her pre-birth to after-death, thus offering a holistic view of her continuum, allowing the reader a deeper sense of the Beloved Lady, and quite possibly a deeper sense of Self in relation to this Love story.

~ **Aliya Kocamis**, Member, the Threshold Society

Bless our beloved companion Camille for bringing together these wondrous, deeply moving, and inspiring accounts of the Blessed Virgin as recorded by the People of the Book. Muslims regard her as the highest woman of all Creation and as an example of how to BE for men and women alike. Through her gentle and beautiful prose and poetry, Camille—who herself radiates the Marian presence—has conveyed a special guidance to us all by fleshing out our knowledge of Blessed Mary in this exquisitely illustrated and precious volume. Truly a treasure!!

~ **Virginia Gray Henry**, Director, Fons Vitae Publishing

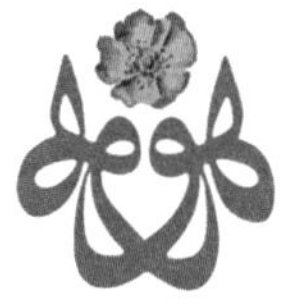

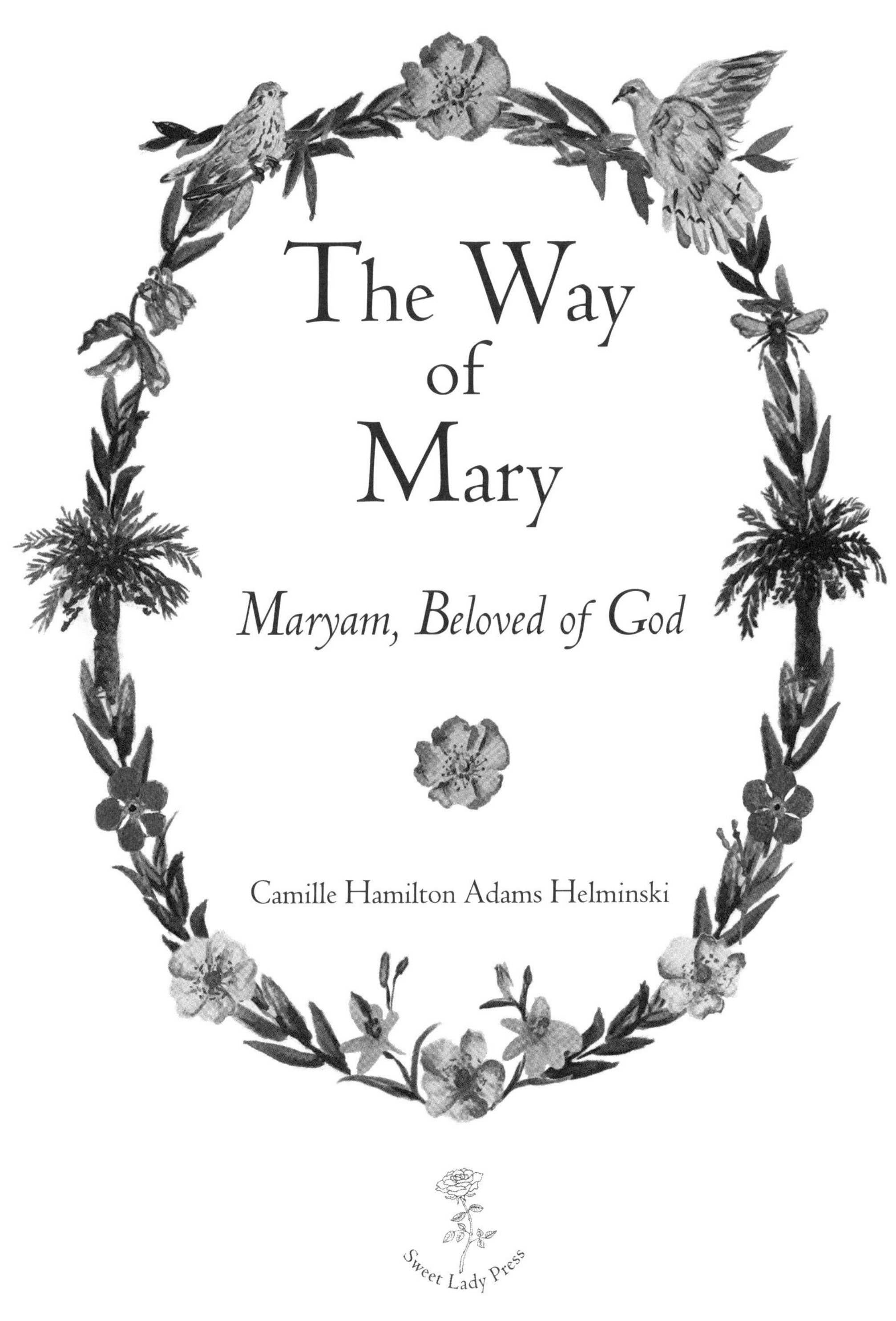

# The Way of Mary

## *Maryam, Beloved of God*

Camille Hamilton Adams Helminski

Sweet Lady Press

First edition published 2021
by Sweet Lady Press,
an imprint of Threshold Books



Hardcover ISBN: 978-0-9396602-6-1
Paperback ISBN: 978-0-9396604-2-1
E-book ISBN: 978-0-9396604-4-5

10 9 8 7 6 5 4 3 2 1



For continuation of copyright credits see "Illustrations," p. 455.

Library of Congress Control Number: 2021941750

Typeset by Daniel Thomas Dyer.

Printed and bound in Slovenia by GPS Group.

Threshold Books
Louisville, London, Istanbul

www.sweetladypress.com
www.sufism.org

# Table Of Contents

# *Author's Preface*

*In the Name of the Infinitely Compassionate and Infinitely Merciful One*

Offered here is a devotional journey with Beloved Mary through the stages of the soul, within the remembrance of the passages of her dear life. Rather than a "reading about" it is our hope and prayer that it might be a "being with," as in the Christian tradition of *Lectio Divina* and the immersion by heart with the Quran of the Islamic tradition, so that these pages—regarding her life from both traditions, founded as they are within the Jewish traditions of Moses and Miriam and Aaron, and the ancient tradition of Oneness in Beauty and Most Generous Love, that has supported human beings for so very long—might bring blessing for any heart drawn to journey with Beloved Mary in Spirit.

The mystic poet, Jalaluddin Rumi, reminds us of the vastness of the treasures of God, continually being bestowed:

> God's treasure houses are many, and God's knowledge is vast. If a person reads *one* Quran knowledgeably, why should he or she reject any *other* Quran?

> I once said to a Quran reader, "The Quran says: *Say, If the sea were ink to write the words of my Lord, verily the sea would fail, before the words of my Lord would fail* [*Surah al-Kahf* 18:109]. Now for fifty drams of ink one can write out the whole Quran. This is but a symbol of God's knowledge; it is not the whole of His knowledge. If a druggist put a pinch of medicine in a piece of paper, would you be so foolish as to say that the whole of the drugstore is in this paper? In the time of Moses, Jesus, and others, the Quran existed; that is, God's Word existed; it simply wasn't in Arabic." This is what I tried to make that Quran reader understand, but when I saw that it was having no effect on him I left.
>
> It is said that during the time of the Apostle, the Companions who memorized a chapter or half a chapter of the Quran were deemed extraordinary and were objects of admiration—this was because they "devoured" the Quran.[1]

They "devoured" and were nourished by their immersion in the Word of Spirit. It is the hope of this heart that this offering of *The Way of Mary, Maryam, Beloved of God* might be of support in traversing journeys of presence along with Beloved Mary—in a shared retreat process among friends, or simply as spiritual companionship for an individual heart along the way of this human journey of the soul.

As one journeys through these twelve stations of her life, one might choose to reflect with a particular passage of scripture or poetry in the following manner:

1. Read the poem, out loud if possible, three times.
2. Abide with the phrase or sentence that touches you.
3. Ask yourself what relevance or application this has to yourself, to your journey in this moment.
4. Sit within the afterglow of these reflections and open yourself to whatever new insight or message the Divine might have for you.
5. If you choose, keep a journal of insights and reflections along "The Way of Mary."

---

[1] Mevlana Jalaluddin Rumi, *Fihi ma Fihi*, available in English as *Signs of the Unseen*, translated by Wheeler Thackston, (Boulder, CO: Shambhala Publications, 1994). See pp. 85–86 (adapted here by the author).

Since earliest childhood, Beloved Mary has been with this heart, and I am so grateful for her loving presence that has flowed through all the days of my life. Through companionship within her loving light, radiating from the Light of our Most Loving Source, many openings of heart can occur.

I am so deeply grateful for so many hearts who have welcomed this endeavor and assisted in this birthing. An endless number of souls stretching around the horizons, only a few is it possible to name here, but all are remembered with deepest gratitude. A special thanks goes to Hamida Battla, dearest friend of so many years, such a devoted soul, whose love of Bibi Maryam and yearning of spirit has called forth more fully this unfolding; to Muneeb Choudry, dear friend of heart, such a stalwart support in so many ways; may God bless them both abundantly. And much gratitude to our dear daughter Cara and her husband Jimmy, who share such a love of Beloved Mary, with special gratitude for Cara's beautiful rendering of the presence of Beloved Mary, Maryam, for the chapter of the Annunciation, and the "Blessings of Nature" *vesica pisca* of our frontispiece; and to our dear friend Beth Hin for her eternal companionship. Much gratitude flows to the early readers of this work who have encouraged the journey by heart: Saimma and Daniel Dyer, Aliya Kocamis, with deepest thanks for her very gracious reading and suggestions, and for those of Matthew Wright and Shakira Debra Shatoff; to Tazeen Dhunna, Fatimah Ashrif, Donia Fahim, Uzma and Siema Taj, and Amira Abd El-Khalek; to Mary Ann Brussat, to Heydieh Soroush and A. Helwa, to Andy Gaus, to George Witterschein, to Sara Winter and Khadim Chishti, and to our dear friend Rabbi Rami Shapiro. With much gratitude to Rauf and Zakiyah Gharib for the blessed provision of the photograph of Beloved Mary's oratory, and to Fatima Terradon Iler for her gracious and timely assistance and that of her sister Marianne Saint George in transcribing the music of the "Songs of Love" in the Appendix (and to Celil Refik Kaya who first assisted in the transcription of "The Song for the Virgin Mary"). Abundant gratitude to my dear husband Kabir, for his support and patient companionship through all my journeyings in other realms, and for his expert assistance and that of Daniel and Saimma Dyer in bringing this book into manifest form.

We remember and express our deep gratitude to our Shaikh Suleyman Hayati Dede of the Way of Mevlana Jalaluddin Rumi, to Hazrati Mevlana and Hazrati Shams of Tabriz, to Beloved Muhammad, to Beloved Maryam, ever-present, and her beloved son, Jesus, to dear Miriam, Moses, and Aaron; may great peace and blessings be with all of them and with all the prophets and saints, illuminated beings and songbirds of the soul, friends of Spirit along the way who have shared their light, their wisdom, and songs of joy and encouragement.

With special gratitude to friends and mentors of the Way in Turkey, land of the abode of Mevlana Jalaluddin Rumi, for their hospitality of heart and all that has been shared of spirit that has become an integral part of this one's being and may in moments be reflected from this heart through this journey with Beloved Mary—to Refik Algan, to Metin Bobaroglu, to Hoca Cahit Goskan, to Turgot and Avidye Koca, and to Hasan Lutfi Shushud, masterful conveyor of the insights and blessings of the Khwajagan, the Masters of Wisdom of Central Asia, and also to Dr. Asad Ali of Damascus, Syria; and much gratitude to the family of beloved Mevlana, Celalettin Celebi and his dear wife, Guzide, and their children, Faruk Hemdem Celebi and his sister Esin Celebi Bayru, and the unfolding generations, may they all continue to carry the light of the Beloved into this world.

With deep gratitude, also, to my own dear parents, Mimi and Lee Adams, my beloved sisters, Marian and Anne, and our dear sons, Matthew and Shams and their beloved unfolding families. Within our early "interfaith" family (half Baptist, half Episcopalian), our mother, Mimi, from Episcopalian (and Presbyterian) roots was vividly alive with the exuberance of life, an artist in spirit, and our father, Lee, from Baptist (and Quaker) roots was a man of deep faith who revealed to us the miracles of creation through his being and his art for which I am eternally grateful; both of them were renowned environmentalists striving, until their sudden passing in 1971, to safeguard this beautiful creation for future generations. We are grateful to Donna Clarke of the Riverside Baptist Church of Jacksonville, Florida, for her very kind assistance in providing a reproduction of the *Presentation to the Shepherds* nativity painting by our father (the introductory illustration for Chapter Six) that was commissioned by the church and still abides in the Baptist church sanctuary; and gratitude also to the National Audubon Society for allowing the reproduction of our father's *Iris* painting from the series of fifty wildflower identification cards he painted for them not long before he passed from this earth.

Of the translations of Mevlana Jalaluddin Rumi offered here, most are translations accomplished with Kabir from various volumes of our work together over many years; other collaborations are noted. The passages from the Quran included are either from *The Light of Dawn, Daily Readings from the Holy Quran*, an offering from this heart, or adapted versions based on the foundational work of Muhammad Asad's *The Message of the Qur'an*, or the translation of Abdullah Yusuf Ali. Passages from the Bible are incorporated from the King James Version (with adjustment of "thee" to "you," etc., in some occurrences), from the Douay-Rheims Bible, or the English Standard Version (ESV), the New International Version (NIV), or from the *The Unvarnished Gospels* and *The Unvarnished New Testament* translated by Andy Gaus. We are so grateful for all the labors of so many hearts who have journeyed in this Way before us to enable the sharing of the passages included.

As the journey with Beloved Mary through these moments of blessing was unfolding, many questions of context arose, engendering supportive notes that developed so greatly it became apparent that it was best to place a portion of the longer notes at the end of the main text, in an "Extended Context Notes" completion section, the notes being in relation to the text like the mirror leaf of an emerging dicotyledon, or mirrored hands, open together in prayer. We hope that this will allow you, dear reader, easier journeying with the text and, also, provide further context that might assist in opening moments of meaning along the journey with Beloved Mary, such a heart-open-doorway to Truth and to Love, may God's great peace and abundant blessings continually rain upon and through her.

Along the journey of unfolding this text with Beloved Mary, one of the stories we met that we had not yet encountered, long beloved in the Christian tradition, is that of a yearning within the heart of Jesus arising when he was a child—when looking up into his dear mother's eyes, the longing came to his heart that others in the future might be able, also, to see the deep beauty of his beloved mother's heavenly blue eyes. The inspiration came to him to touch her eyes and then to wave his small hand over the earth, and as he did so clusters of forget-me-nots emerged. These little blue flowers that love to live close to sustaining water, came to also be known as "Mother Mary's eyes." May we not forget her beautiful companionship, her loving glance, and come to see through her eyes the glories of the Divine Reality present here within everything, every being of this amazing Creation. As it says in the Quran, *Wazhkur Maryam*, "Remember, chant, be in presence with Mary."[2]

We ask forgiveness for any errors within this offering, and pray that it might be of nourishment for hearts in this journey of the soul from-with-toward-within Our One Source, the Most Gracious Beloved:

*"O our Sustainer!*
*Cause us to enter upon whatever we may do in a true and sincere way,*
*and cause us to complete it in a true and sincere way,*
*and grant us, out of Your Grace, sustaining strength!"*[3]

We ask Beloved Mary to accompany us and to lend to us her light, while we discover more fully our own—the radiant Light of the Divine Reality that permeates and illumines all that is.

*In the "houses" which God has allowed to be raised*
*so that His/Her name shall be remembered in them,*
*there are those who praise His/Her limitless glory*
*morning and evening—*
*those whom neither business nor striving after gain*
*can turn from the remembrance of Divine Reality,*
*and from constancy in prayer, and from charity:*
*who are filled with awe*
*of the Day on which all hearts and eyes will be transformed,*
*who only hope that God will bestow upon them recompense*
*in accordance with the best of their actions,*
*and give them even more out of His/Her blessing:*
*for God grants sustenance to whom He/She wills,*
*beyond all reckoning.*
[Quran, *Surah an-Nur, "The Light,"* 24:36–38]

With much love and greetings,
heart to heart,
Camille

# Introduction

## *Twelve Stars of Blessing*

*Truly, those who have faith and do the deeds of wholeness and reconciliation the Infinitely Compassionate will endow with love.*
[Quran, *Surah Maryam*, 19:96]

*Bow in worship and draw near!*
[Quran, *Surah al-'Alaq* 96:19]

The being of Beloved Mary weaves together all three of the Abrahamic traditions in a Sea of Divine Love, surging from within her being. The variations of her name indicate her universal story: the name "Mary" of Latin and Greek origin, "Maria," carries the meaning of "Mistress of the Sea," and has come to be honored, also, as carrying the meaning of "Star of the Sea" (*Stella Maris*),[1] the shining Light of guidance. "Mary," as she is known in the Western Christian tradition, is also a variation

---

[1] Around 800 CE, hymns of greeting to the Virgin Mary were composed including "*Ave Maris Stella*" ("Hail Star of the Sea"); this beloved song later became the hymn for Christian Vespers services in the "Office of the Virgin," still lovingly celebrated today.

of the Hebrew "Miriam," in honor of the Hebrew prophetess, elder sister of Moses and Aaron, of the Virgin Mary's ancestral lineage. Remembrance of dear Miriam brings to heart the resonance of beloved Jewish traditions of devoted engagement in "listening" to God. As a young Jewish woman, Beloved Mary, who was devoted to the Temple at such an early age, would have been continually immersed in such practice, in bowing before God. She is recognized as being of those *who draw near, close, within the Presence of God*, as we are encouraged, also, to do, in the second of the two Quranic verses that open this Introduction (the mirrored pair of 19:96 and 96:19, mirrored in number and in meaning). Within the Islamic tradition, Beloved Mary is much revered, as "Bibi Maryam," "Hazrati Maryam," "Maryam," or "Mary," Beloved Mother of Jesus. Jesus is known by his Arabic name in the Quran, "Isa"; within the Quran he is, also, as he is in the Christian tradition, spoken of as the "Word of God."[2]

And the virgin's name was Mary.
[Bible,[3] New Testament, Gospel of Luke 1:27]

---

[2] The Quran, *Surah al-'Imran* 3:45.

[3] The original New Testament of the Bible was written in Greek; the Old Testament, which formed around the Hebrew Torah—the "Pentateuch" (five books of Moses)—was written mostly in Hebrew, with a few sections in Aramaic. The Torah would have been a source of great nourishment for Beloved Mary. Both the Torah and the Gospel are recognized in the Quran as "a light" and bright guidance:

*Step by step He has sent down to you this Book,*
*setting forth the truth which confirms whatever remains of earlier revelations:*
*for it is He who earlier bestowed from on high the Torah and the Gospel,*
*as a guidance to humankind,*
*and it is He who has bestowed the standard for discernment.*
[Quran, *Surah al-'Imran* 3:3–4]

*Truly, it is We who bestowed from on high the Torah,*
*in which there was guidance and light.*
*On its strength did the prophets, who had surrendered themselves unto God,*
*deliver judgment unto those who followed the Jewish faith;*
*and so did the [early] men of God and the rabbis,*
*inasmuch as some of God's writ had been entrusted to their care;*
*and they bore witness to its truth.*
[Quran, *Surah al-Maida* 5:44]

*And I have named her Mary.*
[Quran, *Surah al-Imran* 3:36]

Another possible meaning of "Mary," derived from the Hebrew "Miriam," is both "strong" and "wished-for child." "Miriam"[4] may, also, originally have been an Egyptian name, derived in part from *mry*, "beloved," or *mr*, "love." Some say the name "Mary" could be derived from the Egyptian *mar* ("to love") combined with the Hebrew *Ya* (YHWH), and so conveying the meaning "one loving the Lord" or "one loved by the Lord." Beloved Mary, Mother of Jesus, is such an example for all of us of one intensively devoted to her Lord, immersed in Love.

The passages of Beloved Mary's life radiate blessing to all of us when we hold them close in remembrance. St. John, the beloved disciple of Jesus, beheld a magnificent vision of a radiant, pregnant woman: "A great sign appeared in heaven—a woman clothed with the sun, with the moon beneath her feet, and a crown of twelve stars upon her head."[5] Many consider this to be a representation of Mother Mary. One might witness the passages of her life as twelve stars of blessing. The number twelve itself awakens many streams of remembrance: the twelve tribes of Israel nourished from the twelve streams that emerged with the blessing of Miriam's well,[6] the twelve

---

[4] The story of Miriam, and her mother, Jochebed, and her father, Amran (Imran) (Bible, Exodus 6:20), is a great inspiration for Christians, even as it is for Jews and for Muslims. The first "longed for child" of her devoted parents, Miriam was able through her God-given strength and clarity to protect her brother Moses from harm and assuage her mother's heart. Beloved Mary would have known her story well. See Quran, *Surah al-Qasas*, "The Story," 28: 3–13, in Extended Context Notes in Appendix, Introduction, 1.

[5] See Bible, Revelation 12:1–2.

[6] After Moses, with the support of Aaron and Miriam, led his people through the Red Sea towards the Promised Land, while they were wandering in the wilderness, water was provided for them through the blessing of Miriam and a rolling rock under her auspices which burst forth with a fountain of water for the people as they journeyed. She would take her staff and draw a channel in the sand for water to flow to each of the twelve tribes of Israel. After her death, the water stopped, and it was this same rock that Moses then struck and from which water poured forth for the tribes' sustenance. Moses is mentioned in the Quran many times with great reverence, e.g.: *For, indeed, We vouchsafed unto Moses the divine writ and caused apostle after apostle to follow him* [Quran, *Surah al-Baqarah* 2:87].

sons of Ishmael,[7] the twelve moons (or months) of the lunar or solar year, the twelve celestial signs of the zodiac, all circling round this "Queen of Heaven," she who was so deeply immersed in prayer, night and day. We are reminded, also, of the twelve apostles or "disciples" of Jesus, deeply devoted to this beloved Mother, she who is known as the "Rose of Sharon,"[8] the most graceful blossom of the Rose Garden of Love.[9]

Beloved Mary is mentioned only a few times in the Bible, very briefly in the Gospels of the New Testament. Many of the stories of her early life that come to us through the Christian heritage come to us through the Protoevangelium of James, the "Infancy Gospel" of James, from around the second century CE, containing stories from before her conception until Jesus's birth. Further details of her life were gathered together in the first full biography of the Virgin Mary, *The Life of the Virgin* attributed to the monk, Maximus the Confessor (580–662 CE).[10]

Many Christians are unaware that within the Quran, revealed through the heart of the Prophet Muhammad in the seventh century CE, there is a whole chapter (*Surah Maryam*) named after Beloved Mary that contains the story of the Virgin birth of Jesus; she is the only woman mentioned by name in the Quran and is mentioned much more often in the Quran than in the New Testament, remembered in verses revealed throughout the

---

[7] See Bible, Genesis 25:13–16 and, also, Genesis 17:

> But as for Ishmael, I have heard thee: behold I have blessed him,
> and will make him fruitful, and will multiply him exceedingly;
> twelve princes shall he beget, and I will make him a great nation.
> [Bible, Genesis 17:20]

[8] Rose of Sharon, "Althea" ("with healing power"): *Hibiscus syriacus*—of the family of *hibiscus* (indicating "delicate beauty")—this drought-tolerant "rose," whether white, pink, or lavender is deeply vibrant red at heart. Within the Bible, the "Rose of Sharon" symbolizes beauty, especially in the "Song of Solomon" where it is a symbol for the beauty of the Beloved of King Solomon.

[9] Beloved Mary is often identified with a rose, as the mystical rose among thorns, she who radiates healing grace and fragrant blessing amidst the sorrows of the world.

[10] *The Life of the Virgin* attributed to the monk Maximus the Confessor has been newly translated into English by Stephen Shoemaker from the Old Georgian translation (from the tenth century) of the now, apparently lost, Greek original manuscript of the sixth century. See *The Life of the Virgin—Maximus the Confessor*, Stephen Shoemaker (New Haven: Yale University Press, 2012).

early years of Islam both in Mecca and Medinah. Her story accompanied Muhammad and was of solace to those of faith who gathered with him, as it continues to be today.

In the early centuries of Christianity, the fullness of the life of the Virgin Mary was remembered with prayers of five joys, and later, with prayer passages of seven joys and seven sorrows, and still later, in the evolving "rosary"[11] prayers, as decades. These "decades," were formed as clusters of ten prayers which include recitations of ten "Hail Mary" prayers punctuated every ten recitations by the Lord's Prayer, which is very similar in meaning and structure to the *Fatiha*, the first *surah* of the Quran.[12] In the Catholic "Franciscan Crown" form of the rosary, the seven joys remembered begin with the moment of Annunciation of the birth of Jesus and complete with Beloved Mary's Ascension to Heaven. We have adapted the remembrance of her life to twelve passages or "stations" of experience (*maqams*), in resonance with the twelve stars of blessing often depicted as

---

[11] See p. 363 of this text.

[12] The *Fatiha*, the quintessential prayer of Islam, often referred to as the "seven oft-repeated verses":

*In the Name of God, the Infinitely Compassionate and Infinitely Merciful:*
*All praise belongs to God, Cherisher and Sustainer of all worlds,*
*the Infinitely Compassionate, the Infinitely Merciful,*
*Ruler on the Day of Recognition.*
*You alone do we worship; You alone do we ask for help.*
*Guide us on the straight path,*
*the path of those who have received Your Grace,*
*not the path of those who have brought stringency upon themselves,*
*nor of those who wander astray.*
[Quran, *Surah al-Fatiha*, "The Opening," 1:1–7]

The Lord's Prayer, the quintessential prayer of Christianity:

Our Father which art in Heaven, Hallowed be Thy Name.
Thy kingdom come, Thy will be done, in earth as it is in Heaven.
Give us this day our daily bread,
and forgive us our debts [our trespasses, our errors],
as we forgive our debtors.
And lead us not into temptation, but deliver us from evil:
for Thine is the Kingdom,
and the Power, and the Glory, forever. Amen.
[Bible, Gospel of Matthew 6:9–13]

surrounding her in radiance, beginning with the moment of the gift of her own birth to her mother, Anna. We open each *maqam* with a corresponding Quranic remembrance. Along this journey, we will see how the remembrance of these stations, these stars of heart, in the Christian tradition and in the Islamic tradition are parallel in inspiration as they offer guidance through the being of Beloved Maryam, she who was ever abiding in Love.

One of the most beautiful verses of encouragement in the Quran, verse 19:96, resides within the closing passages of *Surah Maryam*:

*Truly, those who have faith*
*[and keep their connection with the Source of Life,*
*trusting in the Generous Beneficence of Bestowal]*
*and do rightful deeds of wholeness and reconciliation*
*[the natural outflowing of that connection],*
*the Infinitely Compassionate will endow with Love,*
*[so that we also, as Beloved Maryam, might abide in Love].*
[Quran, *Surah Maryam* 19:96]

## *Mother of the Community (Umm al-Ummah)*

O Mother of the Community,
your robe is blue with stars,
because you shield us
under the heavens
filled with light from your heart,
that Heart that knows us,
each and everyone,
in our deepest beauty
and the strength of your love.
O Creator, with such depth
You have formed us!
How is it possible
that we can hold such space,
and can listen to songs
from ancient journeys,
and journeys
that still have not yet begun?
O Mary, you knew,
and you know,
these beauties—
our Lord has shown you.
Stand with us by heart,
enwrap us with your cloak,
until we, too, are strong enough
to come forth,
to work in the ways
of our Lord.
In all humility,
we wait upon the Word,
the willing, surging,
from deep within us

to master and muster
all the forces of Your Love
that are always guarding us
and uplifting our hearts,
O Infinitely Compassionate One,
O Allah!
You rain down Your Stars
to give us light to ride upon
as we return,
for You have promised
that we will all be gathered
in the Day—
Your Light will be so bright
that all shadows will melt away
and, brilliant in Your Love,
we will know ourselves to be nothing,
but You,
as together with the emanations
of the Angels we will sing,
every particle vibrating
with Your Name,
*Ya Rahman*, *Ya Rahim*,[1]
O You who birth us,
embrace us,
and enfold us into
Your Vast and Everlasting Love.

---

[1] *Ya Rahman*, O Infinitely Compassionate One, *Ya Rahim*, O Infinitely Merciful One.

## I. FIRST STAR OF BLESSING

## *The Gift of the Conception of Mary to Anna, She Who Had Been Barren*

# *The Gift of the Conception of Mary to Anna, She Who Had Been Barren*

The Virgin Mary's mother, Anna, "Hannah," or "Anne," is remembered in the Quran in the moments of her dedication of the fruit of her womb to God:

*Behold, God chose Adam, and Noah, and the House of Abraham,*
*and the House of 'Imran for the sake of all worlds, offspring, one of the other.*[1]
*And God was All-Hearing, All-Knowing*
*when a woman of 'Imran*[2] *said, "Lord, I vow to you what is in my womb,*

---

[1] "[This is] an allusion not merely to the physical descent of those prophets but also to the fact that all of them were spiritually linked with one another and believed in one and the same fundamental truth. . . . The [prophets mentioned] here circumscribe, by implication, all the prophets mentioned in the Quran inasmuch as most of them were descendants of two or more of these patriarchs. The House of 'Imran comprises Moses and Aaron [and Miriam], whose father was 'Imran (the Amram of the Bible), and Aaron's descendants, the priestly caste among the Israelites—thus including John the Baptist, both of whose parents were of the same descent (cf. the reference, in Luke 1:5, to John's mother Elisabeth as one 'of the daughters [descendants] of Aaron'), as well as Jesus, whose mother Mary—a close relation of John—is spoken of elsewhere in the Quran (19:28), as a 'sister [related descendant] of Aaron'): in both cases embodying the ancient Semitic custom of linking a person's or a people's name with that of an illustrious forebear. The reference to the House of 'Imran serves as an introduction to the stories of Zachariah, John, Mary, and Jesus." Excerpted from Muhammad Asad, *The Message of the Qur'an* (London: The Book Foundation, 2003), p. 71.

[2] Revealed in Medinah, the name of this *surah*, "The House of 'Imran," was derived from the references, in verses 33 and 35, to this common origin of a long line of prophets, beginning with Moses, Aaron, and Miriam, the three children of 'Imran and Jochebed. Miriam was the eldest, some say by six years, prior to Aaron, who was also, it is said, six years older than their younger brother, Moses. They are mentioned together in the Bible, in Numbers 26:59: "The name of Amram's wife was Jochebed, a descendant of Jacob and Leah,

*dedicated for Your special service, so accept this of me;*
*truly, you are the All-Hearing, the All-Knowing."*
[Quran, *Surah al-'Imran* 3:33–35]

We remember that a possible meaning of Beloved Mary's name, from the Hebrew of "Miriam," is "wished-for child." In the Quran, Mary is referred to as a descendant (sometimes translated as "daughter") of 'Imran—Amran, father of Miriam, Aaron, and Moses—and she is also referred to as related to Aaron (a "sister" of his descent), reminding us again of her holy ancestral lineage.[3]

---

who was born to the Levites in Egypt. To Amram she bore Aaron, Moses, and their sister Miriam."

3
For I brought you up out of the land of Egypt,
and redeemed you out of the house of servants;
and I sent before you Moses, Aaron, and Miriam.
[Bible, Micah 6:4]

After the exodus from Egypt (thirteenth century BCE), only Aaron and his descendants served as priests in the Jewish rites. All high priests were Levites (descended from Levi, son of Jacob and Leah) through Aaron. Only the high priest could enter the Most Holy inner sanctuary, once a year on the Day of Atonement (Yom Kippur). Other Levites of the lineage of David, who served as priests to care for the tabernacle would rotate through the year in service. Zachariah would have served there in this way. In the Gospel of Matthew 1:1, as well as other verses in the New Testament, Jesus is spoken of as "Jesus, son of David," referring to this line of blessing. In the Talmud (*Sotah* 11b) it mentions that because Miriam assisted her mother Jochebed in saving the Jewish babies in Egypt, Miriam merited that King David's line should descend from her. Some commentators indicate Miriam was a grandmother to King David by mentioning how she is called Ephrath, after her husband Caleb nursed her back to health following an almost fatal illness in her youth, and that King David is known as the son of a certain Ephrathite. See the Bible, I Samuel 17:12: "Now David was the son of an Ephrathite named Jesse."

Also see the Bible, Micah 5:2 for the emergence of the Messiah (through Beloved Mary descended from King David, out of Ephrathah, also known as Bethlehem):

But thou, Bethlehem Ephrathah,
though you be little among the thousands of Judah,
yet out of you shall he come forth unto me that is to be ruler in Israel;
whose goings forth have been from of old, from everlasting.

It was after the children of Israel left Egypt in the Exodus that God indicated the opening of the Hebrew priesthood through Aaron. To confirm the blessing

Miriam is the first female referred to in the Torah as a prophet of the Jewish people,[4] and by the time of the birth of beloved Mary (Maryam), it seems that more than a third of the female Jewish children were blessed with some form of her name in remembrance of this strong woman of Spirit. Even as a small child, Miriam had counseled her parents with wisdom, prophesying that her mother would give birth to a son who would free their people from bondage. Later, following Pharaoh's decree of the destruction of children, and her parents' subsequent divorce—to avoid such a fate for a child—it was Miriam who encouraged her parents to remarry. It soon became apparent that Moses had already been conceived. Miriam's courage was steadfast in support of her brothers, her people, her whole family, her faith, standing for the just fruition of Love.

Beloved Mary's mother, Anna, a descendant of 'Imran, had been longing for a child; she and her husband, Joachim, as he is known in the Bible, had grown old without the blessing of children being granted to them. Some say that one day, Anna was watching a bird feeding its young and the wish arose especially strongly in her heart for a child, for whom she ardently prayed, making the vow that should she be gifted with a child she would dedicate the child, whom she anticipated to be a boy, to the Temple in service to God. However, God saw fit to grant her a girl, and Anna named her "Mary," perhaps in instinctive recognition of the "Sea of Grace" she would be for all humanity. It is beautiful to remember that the name "Mary" has within it this meaning of "sea" (*mar*), from the Latin,[5] and in remembrance of Miriam, who helped to save her people, guiding them with Moses and Aaron, through the Red Sea:

---

of the priesthood, Moses gathered a rod from the leader of each tribe and placed the twelve rods in the meeting tent overnight. When they returned to the tent in the morning, Aaron's rod had blossomed and ripe almonds had already emerged from it (see the Bible, Numbers 17:8). Care of the Most Holy sanctuary, where the Ark of the Covenant was sheltered, was thereafter the responsibility of Aaron and his descendants.

[4] See Torah, Exodus 15:20. (The books of the Torah, the books of Moses, are, also, the first five books of the Bible: Genesis, Exodus, Leviticus, Numbers, and Deuteronomy, which were originally written in Hebrew.)

[5] Saint Louis-Marie de Montfort reflected: "God the Father gathered all the waters together and called them the seas *(maria)*. He gathered all His graces together and called them Mary (Maria)." See St. Louis-Marie de Montfort, *True Devotion to Mary* (London: Catholic Way Publishing, 2013), Part One, p. 23.

Then Miriam the prophetess, the sister of Aaron,
took a tambourine in her hand,
and all the women went out after her with tambourines
and dancing.
[Bible (ESV), Exodus 15:20]

The Arabic version of the name, "Maryam," likewise, from ancient times brings to us the awareness of water and the sense of nourishment and guidance that flows to all of us when we open to receive it.

The announcement of the gift of a child was brought to Beloved Mary's parents by angels, even as later to Beloved Mary herself news is granted. Though blessed and prosperous in many other ways, this blessing of a child was late coming to Hannah[6] and Joachim. In the text of Pseudo Matthew (based on the Protoevangelium of James)[7] Joachim is portrayed as a wealthy owner of flocks who generously gave a third of his income "to orphans, the widows, the strangers, and the poor,"[8] kept a third for himself and his wife, and gave the remaining third to the priests of the Temple. He had been only twenty when he married Anna, a descendant of Aaron, and some say of King David as well, and yet by the age of forty, still, this man devoted to the ways of God and his dear wife had not been granted the blessing of a child. A priest of the Temple taunted him with their lack of fruitfulness, which among Jews of that time would have been seen as quite a disgrace: "God has not blessed you so as to give you seed in Israel!" (Pseudo Matthew 2:1). Ashamed, Joachim fled from the Temple. It seems the priests had forgotten the deprivation of earlier patriarchs of the Jewish community and the sudden blessing that had come to them of a child granted during their old age, even as to Abraham and Sarah when, it is said, they were almost a hundred years old. In his distress, Joachim turned to the desert. It is related in the Protoevangelium of James, that

---

[6] "Hannah," the Hebrew variant of "Anne," or "Anna," may also be spelled as "Hana" in Arabic and has the meaning of "gracious," "full of grace." Traditionally in Islam, the mother of Beloved Mary is remembered as "Hana bint Faqudh."

[7] Pseudo Matthew and the Protoevangelium of James are among the apocryphal Gospels that were written during the second century CE; they filled in other details that were not included in the canonical Gospels, but which became a part of the Christian tradition over the centuries.

[8] Pseudo Matthew1:1.

Joachim spent forty days in the desert in prayer, remembering the grace bestowed upon Abraham and hoping from the depths of his heart for a similar blessing.

Many of the prophets spent time in the desert, in soul-searching inquiry and prayer. We are reminded of Jesus wandering forty days in the wilderness and of Muhammad being cared for as a small child by his wet-nurse, Halima, among the Bedouins, and later in retreat in the outer hills of Mecca, under the stars. In these times of isolation within such an open expanse, the soul in reflection can soar. Realm upon realm may open.

While Joachim was in the desert, tending his flocks, an angel visited him to tell him of the coming of a child. Meanwhile, Hannah had retreated to the garden in her distress and hearing the song of sparrows looked up to see them in their nests with their young in the shelter of a laurel tree, as related by Zamakshari in his *Kashshaf*.[9] While Joachim was yearning in the desert, Hannah was at home, yearning in the garden:

I am not likened unto the beasts of the earth,
for even the beasts of the earth are fruitful before You, O Lord.
Woe unto me, unto what am I likened?
[Protoevangelium of James 3:2]

And yet the song of the birds inspired her heart, and under the guardianship of the laurel trees, their ever-greenness conveying the blessing of the perpetuity of Life and of Love, a message reached her. It is related that, as with Joachim, an angel messenger came to Hannah, also, to tell her that

---

[9] See Zamakshari, *Kashshaf* I, 141–42. The laurel tree (*laurus nobilis*) is also known as the sweet bay (see illustration in heading of this chapter). The evergreen laurel was woven as a wreath of honoring by the ancient Greeks, especially for winners of the Phythian games, competitions originally in music. It is known as a symbol of Divine Wisdom and its scent encourages illumination, inspiring creativity. This noble laurel lends a sweet fragrance and protection to cloth stored with it, and the purifying scent can clear our abodes; because of its healing and fragrant properties it has also long been a basis of flavors for sustaining soups and stews (especially chicken or chickpea). Perhaps the next time we place a bay leaf into a pot of soup we will remember Saint Anne and the depth of her prayer, and increase our own prayers for wellbeing for family, for loved ones, to be inspired and nourished by all that we might be enabled to share in sustenance, sustaining the generations of life unfolding.

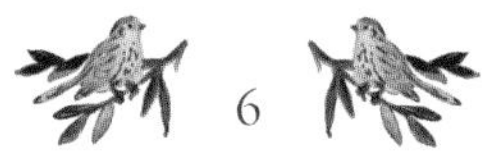

she would bear a child and that her "seed shall be spoken of throughout the world."[10]

Joachim returned, and Hannah met him joyfully at the gate to the city, where they shared with each other the blessing each had received. Some say the priests then became so impressed with these holy messages regarding the impending birth that they entrusted to Joachim the sacred drinking vessel of Abraham from the Ark of the Covenant.

A pure soul, gifted to aging parents, Mary was promised to the Temple, to devotion to God, even before she was born, and she herself came to be referred to as the "Ark of the Covenant," the bearer of holy wisdom, mother of the most pure "Word," Jesus (Isa). The miraculous story of her birth is acknowledged by verses in the Quran, even as it is spoken of in Christianity. Al-Tabari, one of the most renowned Islamic historians (839–923 CE), records mention of Beloved Mary's mother, Hannah. The great-great-great-grandson of Prophet Muhammad, Jafar as-Sadiq (702–765 CE), the revered mystic and scholar, also describes the birth of Beloved Mary in detail as it is recorded in the traditions. According to one of his narrations, God informs Beloved Mary's father through an angel that He will grant him a boy who will heal the leper and the blind and raise the dead by Divine permission. When he then told his beloved wife, Hannah, of this intimation, she assumed she would give birth to a boy.

And yet God, in His Infinite Wisdom, saw fit to grant Hannah a girl child who would be the purest of mothers, for the birthing of that holy son gifted in healing. When still in her mother's womb, Beloved Mary was dedicated to the Temple, before anyone knew that she would be a girl, and yet the Quran reminds us God knew:

*When [Hannah] gave birth she said,*
*"My Lord, I have given birth to a female child—*
*and God knew best what she had brought forth—*
*for a boy could never be like this girl—*
*and surely, I have named her Maryam,*
*and truly I seek refuge for her and her offspring from Satan, the accursed."*
*And Allah received her with gracious acceptance*
*and caused her to grow in beautiful purity*

---

[10] Protoevangelium of James 4:1.

*under the protection of Zakariyyah.*
[Quran, *Surah al-'Imran,* 3:35–37]

Muslims are very familiar with the stories of Abraham, of Moses, of Zachariah and Elizabeth, of Beloved Mary and Jesus, whose stories are all related with honor in the Quran. Even though a single chapter, or *surah,* of the Quran is named specifically for Beloved Mary (*Surah Maryam,* containing the core of her story and that of Zachariah), threads of her story are woven throughout the Quran, from the earliest chapters, that were revealed in Mecca, to the later verses, revealed in Medina. Such an honor is not given to Beloved Mary even in the Holy Bible—there is no chapter or "book" of the Bible named for her, and she is mentioned in it only a very few times, in the Gospels.

Yet among Christians, especially within the Catholic faith, Beloved Mary has been deeply honored for centuries. This is so much so that in recent centuries, when one may have heard reference to the "Immaculate Conception," though many might assume what is being referred to is the conception of Jesus (Isa) within the womb of Beloved Mary, actually, it is the conception of Beloved Mary, herself, being honored, as one who was by Divine decree created pure of any sin, a Divine gift to devoted parents, a pure vessel for the reception of a pure son.

As Maria Agreda, a Spanish Christian mystic, wrote:

> Her [Mary's] entire being was made to shine forth the Divinity; for since the Divine Word was to issue from the bosom of the eternal Father to descend to that of Mary, He provided for the greatest possible similarity between the mother and the Father."[11]

> It is said: like begets like—just as the water partakes of the qualities of the minerals through which it flows—and although the birth of Christ originated in the Divinity, yet it also partook of the conditions of the mother as far as was possible. She, therefore, would not have been suitable for the concurrence with the Holy Spirit in this conception, in which only the activity of the man was wanting, if she had not been endowed with perfections corresponding to those of the humanity of Christ.[12]

---

[11] Venerable Mary of Agreda, *The Mystical City of God,* translated by Piscar Marison (Charlotte, NC: TAN Books, 2009), p. 222.
[12] Ibid., p. 210.

Within the Islamic faith, though the Virgin Mary is held in the highest regard as the purest of human beings, together with her son, the "Word" of God, it is understood that human beings in our origin are all created with pure *fitrah* ("original nature"), that we are all intrinsically pure as created by God. There is no tenet of original sin, but it is recognized that in our wanderings in this earthly world we gather heaviness in our individuation (and are often misled by the raw desires of the ego, the "promptings of Satan"), become forgetful, and must work to re-purify our hearts and clear our souls to attune to our original Source and the guidance that is always offered. For Muslims, Beloved Mary is the pre-eminent example of one who stayed true to her original, pure nature, through prayer and sacrifice, "making sacred" every act and word, devoted, surrendered in Love, from whose example we can learn to turn to be with the "breath" of God in every moment. It is interesting to note that in Arabic the word for "self" or "soul"—*nafs*—is feminine, indicating the receptive stance of the soul before its Creator, its Cherisher and Teacher, its Beloved Lord, acknowledging the connection with the Source of Life through which it is nurtured.

Though Anna would have discerned the strong spirit of this precious child she carried in her womb and might have had intimations by heart of what gender this baby might be, still, until the birth she would not have known. What a surprising moment for her to gaze into the face of this dear infant newly arrived into her arms and recognize that this child whom she had dedicated to the Temple happened to be a girl; traditionally only male children were so dedicated in service. Even so, Hannah had made a vow to her Lord, so she held Beloved Mary close in prayer and love until she was just old enough to manage for herself. And then Hannah took her most precious little one to devote her to the Temple, to the Holy Sanctuary, where she might grow up in "nearness," devoted to the Source of her being.

*And keep your connection and remain conscious of God,*
*that you might attain felicity.*
[Quran, *Surah al-'Imran* 3:200]

## *Gardens upon Gardens*

Gardens upon gardens
arise
in our minds,
in our hearts,
and fall from our fingertips
when You smile
in us,
You who are the promise
of fecundity,
the Sun
and the rain of Grace.

Unbeknownst,
someone slept,
until You awakened her
with a kiss.

Coming into herself,
she recognized You
as the Source
of all that exists—

trees and toads, roads,
stars and angels,
every means of flowering
and fruitfulness
from the watery earth
and its fair hills
reaching
to return
the kiss

of Your
extravagance;

pastures purified
of our transgressions
turn again to green,

and soft syllables
of our Love
whispered across the aeons
make a nest in Nearness
we can, once again, call Home.

# II. SECOND STAR OF BLESSING

## *Within the Sanctuary*

# *Within the Sanctuary*

*This is part of the tidings of the Unseen,*
*beyond the reach of your perception,*
*which We reveal to you:*
*for you were not with them when they threw reeds*
*to know which of them should be the guardian caregiver of Maryam,*
*and you were not with them when they contended with one another about it.*
[Quran, *Surah al-'Imran* 3:44]

When the right moment arrived, and Anna knew it to be the moment, she brought her dear daughter, Beloved Mary, to the Temple to dedicate her for Temple services. According to the Protoevangelium of James, Beloved Mary (Maryam) was three years old. The story is told of her slipping away from her mother and immediately striding up the stairs of the Temple; she did not look back, so readily eager and ineluctably drawn was she to the Holy Sanctuary.

> But she stole away from them,
> so small, slipping from their grasp
> to enter her destiny, which was loftier than the temple
> and already surpassed the edifice in perfection.
>
> ~ Rainer Maria Rilke[1]

All the priests of the Temple then vied to be the guardian and caretaker of this luminous child. They cast lots with reeds to see to whom this honor would fall. Several Islamic scholars relate that this casting of reeds took

[1] Rainer Maria Rilke, excerpt from "The Presentation of Mary in the Temple", *The Life of the Virgin Mary.* As quoted by Jacques Duquesne in *Salve Regina, The Story of Mary* (Paris: Éditions Flammarion, 2006), p. 22. Rainer Maria Rilke, a Bohemian-Austrian poet of the German language (1875–1926), was greatly influenced by Islam. He indicated that the angels of his masterwork, the *Duino Elegies*, were inspired by the angels as rendered in the traditions of Islam.

place at the River Jordan. The reeds thrown by the other priests sank. The reed of Zachariah remained afloat; it followed the current of the water to the sea. In this, they all witnessed a clear sign, and so Zachariah, her maternal uncle, the husband of her mother's sister, Elizabeth,[2] was chosen to accompany young Mary on her journey of Spirit, to be her guardian while she would live in consecration to the Most Holy Temple. The Quran, too, speaks of how from an early age she spent much time alone in the sanctuary (*mihrab*), and describes, also, how she was attended devotedly by Zachariah (Zakariyyah).

The Holy of Holies, the most profound sanctuary within the Temple, was hidden by a veil separating the outer realm of this world and the hidden realm within. The inner realm was the realm of God and the angels. Priests who served in the Temple, clothed in white linen and barefoot, passed back and forth in service through the outer areas of the Temple, in their prayer and movement and song, continually integrating earth and Heaven. Beloved Mary, immersed in her devotions in her sanctuary, joined both within herself. Many Christians feel that verses from the Psalms of David, are portents of her beautiful spirit so attuned to her Lord:

God is in the midst of her, and she shall not be moved:
God shall help her, and that right early.
[Bible, Psalms of David 46:5]

Sing to the Lord a new song; sing to the Lord, all the earth.
Sing to the Lord, bless His Name.
[Bible, Psalms of David 96:1–2]

Mary, who was raised as a devoted Jewish practitioner, would have known the Psalms of David well and rejoiced with the recitation of passages such as these:

O come, let us sing unto the Lord:
let us make a joyful noise to the rock of our salvation.
Let us come before His Presence with thanksgiving,
and make a joyful noise unto Him with psalms.
[Bible, Psalms 95:1–2]

---

[2] It is mentioned in both early Christian and Muslim sources that Elizabeth was the sister of Mary's mother, Hannah (St. Anne or Anna).

Make a joyful noise unto the Lord, all you lands.
Serve the Lord with gladness: come before His presence with singing.
Know you that the Lord He is God:
it is He that hath made us, and not we ourselves;
we are His people, and the sheep of His pasture.
Enter into His gates with thanksgiving,
and into His courts with praise:
be thankful unto Him, and bless His Name.
For the Lord is good; His mercy is Everlasting;
and His Truth endures to all generations.
[Bible, Psalms 100]

In her purity, her beauty of Spirit, her natural inclination to be intimately in prayer with her Lord, she has come to be known and honored especially by Christians and Muslims as "full of grace," the pre-eminent exemplar of surrendered devotion to God. In the opening of the Protoevangelium of James, Mary is called "the Temple of the Holy Spirit," the "City of God," of which glorious things are spoken,[3] the "Paradise of the Tree of Life." She has come to be known among Christians as, herself, the "Ark of the Covenant," holding the promise of God and the deepest wisdom. She is lauded as the "pure enclosed garden" of the Beloved that is spoken of in the "Song of Songs" of Prophet Solomon, of whose lineage through David, it is said that Jesus is descended.[4]

A garden enclosed is my sister, my spouse;
a spring shut up, a fountain sealed.
Thy plants are an orchard of pomegranates, with pleasant fruits;
camphire, with spikenard, Spikenard and saffron;
calamus and cinnamon, with all trees of frankincense;
myrrh and aloes with all the chief spices;
a fountain of gardens, a well of living waters,

---

[3] See the Bible, Psalms 87:3: "Glorious things are said of thee, O city of God."
[4] Joseph, his father in earthly lineage, was of the lineage of King David, just as Mary, herself, it is said was descended from King David, Prophet of God, and the priestly line of Aaron. Jesus is referred to as "the son of David," several times in the Gospels.

and streams from Lebanon.
Awake O north wind; and come thou south;
blow upon my garden, that the spices thereof may flow out.
[Bible, Song of Songs 4:12–16][5]

In this beautiful Canticle of Canticles (the "Song of Songs"), the voice of Spirit refers to His bride as the "enclosed garden." This "enclosed garden" has come to be understood as a description of Mary's holy virginity ("enclosed"), as though she herself is the new Garden of Eden, radiant with the Divine Presence. When the second Song of Songs of the Old Testament declares, "I am the Rose of Sharon, and the Lily of the valleys,"[6] it is also understood by Christians to be referring to Mary, this radiant woman of God.

In the writings of St. Bridget we find an intimate meditation on the Virgin Mary, "Our Lady," as the Mystic Rose, *Rosa Mystica.*[7] St. Bridget (Brigid) relates how there was a time when she was quite downcast because the enemies of Spirit seemed so powerful, and Mary came to her and told her to remember the rose among thorns:

"The rose," Mary told her, "gives a fragrant odor;
it is beautiful to the sight, and tender to the touch,
and yet it grows among thorns—inimical to that beauty and tenderness.
So may, also, those who are mild, patient, and beautiful in virtue,
be put to the test among adversaries."

St. Bridget could see that though the rose has such a welcoming fragrance, is beautiful to gaze upon, and is so soft to the touch, yet it grows and flourishes among prickly thorns with no pleasing scent. She understood from Mary's instruction that the good and virtuous, even though they may be gentle in their patience, beautiful in their virtues, and sweetly fragrant in their good efforts, still, cannot become perfected except amid difficulties.

---

[5] *The Song of Songs which Is Solomon's,* illustrated and illuminated by Valenti Angelo for the members of the Heritage Club (New York: The Heritage Press, limited edition, 1935), p. 13.

[6] Bible, Song of Songs of Solomon 2:1.

[7] See *The Prophecies and Revelations of Saint Bridget (Birgitta) of Sweden,* Book 1, Chapter 22.

Since the fifteenth century, Franciscan practitioners (Christian followers of St. Francis) have prayed a cycle of prayer known as the "Crown Rosary" in remembrance of the "Seven Joys of the Blessed Virgin Mary." The story is told of a young Franciscan friar who was particularly devoted to Mary and loved to pray the rosary of "Hail Mary's" every day. One day, he was called to come for the evening meal but asked pardon to complete his rosary offering first, which had been delayed. The superior granted his request. After some time, when he did not appear in the dining hall, two other friars were sent to call him. When they entered his room they beheld him kneeling before a vision of the Virgin Mary accompanied by two angels. They stood transfixed, witnessing how as he voiced each recitation in honor of Mary, a rose opened from his mouth and the angels carried it to her, until little by little a whole garland of roses crowned her head as she smiled upon him.

In the fifteenth and sixteenth centuries, Carthusians[8] promoted the idea of sacred mysteries associated with the rose symbol and rose gardens as symbols of Mary. Many of the paintings of the Virgin Mary depict her within a rose garden, or with rose garlands around her, or conveying roses to the devoted near her.

In Muslim countries of the East, the rose has long been a source of inspiration and a metaphor for the truest heart of Beauty. The purest rose gathered for the making of essential rose oil—for which it takes 10,000 pounds of petals to distill a single pound of oil—is the *rosa damascena*, the "Rose of Damascus." For centuries, it has been known worldwide for its therapeutic fragrance and healing qualities. In Persian *ghazals* (poetic odes), it is the beauty of the rose that elicits the longing song of the nightingale. The grace of the Rose engenders the call of the lover, even as is the experience of the mystic whose heart is opened to call out in awe when contemplating the Beauty of God. Shabistari's *Rose Garden of Mystery* (*Gulshan i Raz*) and Saadi's *Rose Garden* (*Gulistan*) are renowned as gatherings of poetic reflections in gratitude and praise of the Beloved. So well-recognized has the poetry of such lovers of God become that the aphorisms of

---

[8] Carthusians are Christian practitioners inspired by St. Bruno of Cologne (mystic of the eleventh century) who was especially devoted to Mary and encouraged immersion in contemplation, that one might live as unceasingly as possible in the light of the love of God, through purity of heart, remembering that "Blessed are the pure in heart, for they shall see God" (Bible, Gospel of Matthew 5:8).

Saadi were even woven into children's stories of Kentucky in the 1930's. One such saying from Saadi—"Thy alchemist contentment be."[9]—reflects a saying of Imam Ali: "If trials are met with contentment and patience they are a constant blessing, and if blessings are devoid of gratitude they are an ever-present trial."[10] Another of the great mystic poets so well-loved today, Mevlana Jalaluddin Rumi, encourages us to wonder what God said to the rose that caused it to bloom in such full fragrance and beauty.

That which God said to the rose,
and caused it to laugh in full-blown beauty,
He said to my heart,
and made it a hundred times more beautiful.
[*Mathnawi* III: 4129]

Beloved Mary, open and listening to God's inspiration, bloomed with deepest grace. We recognize in Mary the perfect archetype of the mystic of Islam, in full surrender to the enlivening "Word" of God.

*And Allah [God] received her with gracious acceptance*
*and caused her to grow in beautiful purity . . .*
[Quran, *Surah al-'Imran* 3:37]

---

[9] See "The Desert of Waiting" in Anne Fellows Johnston, *The Little Colonel in Arizona* (part of the "Little Colonel" series) (New Orleans, Louisiana: Pelican Publishing Company, 2000), pp. 139–61. Also excerpted in Camille Helminski (ed.), *The Book of Character* (London: The Book Foundation, 2004), pp. 110–122.

[10] Islamic mystics recommend this practice: "Keep God as your companion in every state," so that through the Light of the Beloved's Presence we might be guided aright and that within the Presence of the Beloved, we might rest "content," returning, moment by moment, into that Presence, pleased (*radiyah*) and well-pleasing (*mardiyah*).

*On the Day of Reckoning God will say:*
*"Today, their truthfulness shall benefit*
*all who have been true to their word.*
*Theirs shall be gardens through which running waters flow,*
*there to dwell beyond the count of time;*
*well-pleased is God with them,*
*and well-pleased are they with Him: this is the ultimate success."*
[Quran, *Surah al-Maida* 5:119]

She grew up in the Temple, with luminous grace; another of the meanings of "Mary" is "illuminator." In her turning inward, in service and in prayer, through her mother's consecration (*muharrar*) of her dear being to God, she was emancipated within Truth (*al-Haqq*). As Jafar as-Sadiq described: "[*Muharrar* means] in emancipation from the bondage of the world (*dunya*) and its people. [It] means, I have vowed to You what is in my womb as a sincere servant (*'abd*) to You, not in servitude to any created being [including her own self (*nafs*)]."[11]

Al-Qushayri, commenting on Mary's state said: "God (*al-Haqq*), all glory be to Him in His pre-eminent wisdom, has emancipated this one from the bondage of being preoccupied with all appearances (*wujuh*) and states (*ahwal*)."[12]

Both Christian tradition and Islamic tradition describe how Mary would remain for hours in her prayer chamber. Immersed in worship and prayer, even as it is said of the Prophet Muhammad, she would be standing in prayer until her feet were swollen. And as the Prophet Muhammad responded when asked why, she might, also, have answered, "Should I not be a grateful servant?" Among the passages of the Psalms that she might have sung in offering is this one:

Have mercy on me, Lord,
for I call to you all day long.
Bring joy to your servant, Lord,
for I put my trust in you.
You, Lord, are forgiving and good,
abounding in love to all who call to you.
[Bible (NIV), Psalms 86:3–5]

Maximus, in his biography of Mary, relates a passage from the Psalms that he feels speaks of her:

---

[11] Jafar as-Sadiq, "Le Tafsîr Mystique attributé à Ǧa'far Sâdiq," Mélanges de l'Université Saint Joseph, 43, 1968, p. 192, as cited by Kristin Zahra Sands, *Sufi Commentaries on the Qur'an in Classical Islam* (New York: Routledge Studies in the Quran, 2000), p. 98.

[12] Al-Qushayri, *Lata'if al-isharat* (Cairo: Dar al Kutub al 'Arabi, 1968–71), vol.1, p. 249, as cited by Kristin Zahra Sands, *Sufi Commentaries on the Qur'an in Classical Islam*, op. cit., p. 98.

All the glory of the king's daughter is within.
[Bible, Psalms 45:13]

He notes that "her virtues reveal not only inner riches, but also incomprehensible riches of the Holy Spirit whose abundance and beauty are inexpressible."[13]

The Protoevangelium describes how she "received food from the hand of an angel."[14] Food given to her by the priests she would distribute to the poor. When Zachariah would visit her in her sanctuary, he would find her already provided with food—food of a surprising kind:

*Whenever Zachariah visited her in the sanctuary,*
*he found her provided with food. He would ask,*
*"O Mary, from where did this come to you?"*
*She would answer: "It is from God;*
*see how God grants sustenance to whom He/She wills,*
*beyond all reckoning."*
[Quran, *Surah al-'Imran* 3:37]

This passage of the Quran is often seen inscribed over the *mihrab* (the prayer niche indicating the direction toward which one turns for the ritual prayer) in many mosques. This *ayat* (verse or "sign") regarding Beloved Mary reminds us of her deep receptivity within the sanctuary, some time before the visit of the Angel Gabriel. Blessed Mary, in her complete immersion in prayer, is such an example for us of one who was profoundly receptive to Spirit, awaiting the arrival of the sustaining gifts of her Lord in every moment.

It is said that the Prophet Zachariah marveled at this miraculous food—in the middle of winter, fresh fruit of summer! The great grandson of the Prophet Muhammad, Imam Jafar as-Sadiq, narrates that when she had grown to be a young woman, she would enter the sanctuary and cover herself so that no one saw her, but that when Zachariah would enter to tend to her care, he would find her already provided for, with summer fruits in winter and winter fruits in summer. One might, also, understand this as the fruits of the spirit. In the midst of the duress of cold constriction, the

---

[13] Maximus the Confessor, *The Life of the Virgin*, op. cit., p. 42.
[14] Protoevangelium 8:1.

cheering fruits of summer, of the season of fullness were provided, and in the duress of the burning heat of summer, the refreshing fruits of winter—whether in contraction or expansion, her heart was soothed and sustained by her Lord. Zachariah was amazed, even Zachariah, himself of prophetic stature, one sincerely devoted to his Lord, marveled!

As Al-Nisaburi relates it:

> He found her with food, that is to say from the openings of the Unseen (*futuhat al-ghayb*) that God feeds the elect of His servants who spend the night with Him, not with themselves nor creation, just as the Prophet said, "I spend the night with (*'inda*) my Lord feeding me and giving me to drink."[15]

As the Quran reminds us, sustenance is pouring towards us from our Sustainer; truly, in worship is our sustenance!

*Yet go on reminding: for reminding benefits the faithful.*
*And I have created the invisible beings and human beings*
*only that they may worship Me.*
*No sustenance do I require of them*
*nor do I require that they should feed Me.*
*For God is the Giver of All Sustenance,*
*the Lord of All Power, the Eternally Steadfast.*
[Quran, *Surah adh-Dhariyat* 51:55–58]

*On the earth are signs for those with inner certainty,*
*just as within your own selves: will you not then see?*
*And in heaven is your sustenance*
*and all that which you are promised.*
*Then by the Sustainer of heaven and earth, this is the Truth—*
*as true as the fact that you are able to speak.*
[Quran, *Surah adh-Dhariyat* 51:20–23]

---

[15] Al Nisaburi, *Ghara'ib al-Qur'an wa ragha'ib al furqan*, Cairo: Mustafa al-Babi al-Halabi, 1962–70, vol. 3, p. 186, as cited by Kristin Zahra Sands, in *Sufi Commentaries on the Qur'an in Classical Islam*, op. cit., p.102. "I pass the night with my Lord—*He gives me to eat and to drink* [Quran, *Surah ash-Shu'ara* 26:79]." A *hadith*—recorded saying of Prophet Muhammad (peace and blessings be upon him).

It is interesting to note that both the Gospel of Luke (1:5–23) in the Bible and the chapter of the Quran named for Mary, *Surah Maryam*, begin with Zachariah's story,[16] with his own yearning for a child, for someone to continue to represent his lineage of righteous love of God, the lineage of Jacob. It would seem that his prayer was inspired by witnessing the being of Mary, precious child of his wife's sister, from the years of seeing her pure devotion, the depth of her prayer, and the miraculous provision she received from her Lord.[17]

*In the secrecy of his heart, he prayed: "O my Sustainer!*
*Feeble have become my bones, and my head glistens with grey.*
*But never yet, O my Lord, has my prayer unto You remained unanswered.*
*Bestow, then, upon me, out of Your grace, the gift of a successor*
*who will be my heir as well as an heir [to the dignity] of the House of Jacob;*
*and make him, O my Sustainer, well-pleasing to You!"*
*[Thereupon the angels called out unto him:[18]] "O Zachariah!*

---

16 *Surah Maryam* begins with relating the story of Zachariah's yearning and the arrival of John (Yahya). At its core, the *surah* conveys the story of beloved Mary and the birth of Jesus, and then it wraps back to earlier revelations with mention of Abraham and Moses and with awareness of the angels as messengers and the continual guidance that comes to us, reminding:

*And God endows those who avail themselves of [His] guidance*
*with an ever-deeper consciousness of the right way;*
*and good deeds, the fruit whereof endures forever,*
*are, in your Sustainer's sight, of far greater merit [than any worldly goods],*
*and yield far better returns.*
[Quran, *Surah Maryam* 19:76]

17 See also:

*In that self-same place, Zachariah prayed unto his Sustainer, saying:*
*"O my Sustainer! Bestow upon me [too], out of Your grace,*
*the gift of goodly offspring; for You, indeed, hear all prayer."*
[Quran, *Surah al-'Imran* 3:38]

18 See also:

*Thereupon, as he stood praying in the sanctuary, the angels called out unto him:*
*"God sends you the glad tiding of [the birth of] John,*
*who shall confirm the truth of a Word from God, and outstanding be among men,*
*and utterly chaste, and a prophet from among the righteous."*
[Quran, *Surah al-'Imran* 3:39]

*We bring you the glad tiding of [the birth of] a son whose name shall be John.*
*[And God says,] 'Never have We given this name to anyone before him.'"*[19]
*He exclaimed: "O my Sustainer!*
*How can I have a son when my wife has always been barren*
*and I have become utterly infirm through old age?"*
*Answered [the angel]: "Thus it is; your Sustainer says, 'This is easy for Me—*
*even as I have created you aforetime out of nothing.'"*
[Quran, *Surah Maryam* 19:3–9]

As Mevlana Jalaluddin Rumi relates it in his discourses:

> "O Lord," said Zachariah, "since you grant all requests, I, too, have a desire. Give me a son who will be a friend to You. Let him be familiar with You without my having to urge him, and let him concern himself with acts of worship and obedience to You." And God did bring John into being after his father had become weak and bent with age and after his mother, too, who had not given birth in her youth, suddenly experienced menstruation and became pregnant.
>
> You may thus realize that all that is a pretext revealing God's power; that everything is from Him and that with Him is the Command (*'Amr*). The faithful know Who behind this wall is informed of our every condition and Who sees us even though we do not see Him. For one who is faithful, this much is certain. [20]

Similarly, in the Gospel of Luke of the Bible, the story of Zachariah and his wife and the gift of John is related just before the moment of the Annunciation of the birth of Jesus to Beloved Mary is conveyed. In awareness of Beloved Mary and her devotion within the sanctuary, Zachariah called upon God with heart-felt prayer, and yet his response to the gracious news from his Lord through Gabriel is incredulity. It seems his individual intellect was quite active, and so silence is gifted to him as the remedy, as a sign, that he might immerse in the reality of God's Grace.

---

[19] As Muhammad Asad mentions in his commentary, "The name *Yahya* (John) signifies 'he shall live,' i.e., he will be spiritually alive and will be remembered forever; and the fact that God Himself had chosen this name for him was a singular distinction, equivalent to a Divine promise." See *The Message of the Qur'an.*
[20] *Fihi ma Fihi*, Discourse 45, *Signs of the Unseen*, op. cit., pp. 181–82 (adapted by the author).

Zachariah is rendered mute for three days, as it is related in the Quran; in the Bible his silence endures until Elizabeth is delivered. To share the news of their child, Zachariah writes his name on a tablet: Yahya (John)! The community is surprised that this child will not be named after his father. Just as, in older age, Hannah and Joachim's prayer for a child was answered in Beloved Mary, Zachariah's prayer is answered in the gift of news of the arrival of a son, "Yahya," "he shall live," named by God. "John," "the living one," becomes the one who opens the way for the "Word" of Jesus, son of Mary. Miracles abound!

Just as in the early days of Moses and Aaron and Miriam when the Tabernacle (tent of meeting) provided an intimate place of meeting with God, the Temple had been established as a sacred space for the meeting of God and the human being.

The priests then brought the ark of the Lord's covenant
to its place in the inner sanctuary of the temple,
the Most Holy Place, and put it beneath the wings of the cherubim.
The cherubim spread their wings over the place of the ark
and covered the ark and its carrying poles.
These poles were so long that their ends, extending from the ark,
could be seen from in front of the inner sanctuary,
but not from outside the Holy Place . . .
There was nothing in the ark
except the two tablets that Moses had placed in it at Horeb,
where the Lord made a covenant with the Israelites
after they came out of Egypt.
The priests then withdrew from the Holy Place.
All the priests who were there had consecrated themselves,
regardless of their divisions.
All the Levites who were musicians—Asaph, Heman, Jeduthun,
and their sons and relatives—
stood on the east side of the altar,
dressed in fine linen and playing cymbals, harps and lyres.
They were accompanied by one hundred and twenty priests
sounding trumpets.
The trumpeters and musicians joined in unison
to give praise and thanks to the Lord.
Accompanied by trumpets, cymbals and other instruments,

the singers raised their voices
in praise to the Lord and sang: "He is good; His love endures forever."
Then the temple of the Lord was filled with the cloud,
and the priests could not perform their service because of the cloud,
for the glory of the Lord filled the Temple of God.
[Bible (NIV), II Chronicles 5:7–14]

Throughout rabbinic literature, the *Shekhinah*, the transformational Presence of God, is comprehended as of feminine aspect and is referred to as intensively manifest in the Tabernacle, within the Temple in Jerusalem. The glory of Sophia, or Holy Wisdom, also of feminine aspect, emanates from this Holy Presence, as a dear rabbi friend of ours says, like the flowing of the ocean or the glittering of a diamond:

> The sages of the Talmud called it *Bat Kol*,[21] the Daughter's Voice, and understood it to be the voice of God. . . . I understand it to be the voice of *Chochma/Sophia*, Mother Wisdom, who is to God what flowing is to an ocean and glittering is to a diamond.[22]
>
> Listening to Her voice draws us nearer to Her. Listening to Her voice we hear ourselves invited to sit at Her table and enjoy the meal She has prepared for us,[23] a meal empowering us to create a world rooted in justice, compassion, and humility.[24]

---

[21] *Bat Kol*: "An ancient rabbinic euphemism for the Voice of God. The 'daughter' is *Chochma/Sophia*, Lady Wisdom, the first manifesting of God and the Mother of all the living."

"Chochma/Sophia is the original happening of YHVH and 'the fashioner of all things' [Wisdom of Solomon 7:22]. *Targum Yonatan*, a second century Aramaic translation of the Hebrew Torah, renders the first word of Genesis not as the Hebrew *bereishit*—'in the beginning'—but as the Aramaic *b'chuchmata*—'through *Chochma*'. Chochma emerges from No-thingness as a manifesting of the unformed and unnamed YHVH. [Job 28:12] As the Psalmist put it, 'You [YHVH] made all things through Chochma;' [Psalm 104:24] and as King Solomon taught, 'Chochma enlivens all reality.' [Ecclesiastes 7:12]"

We are encouraged to: "Keep watch for Me at every gate, wait for Me at every door" (The Gospel of Sophia 4:300). From *The Gospel of Sophia, the Good News of Mother Wisdom,* edited and annotated by Rabbi Rami Shapiro, p. 9; 11; 33.

[22] Ibid., p. 7.

[23] Bible, Proverbs 9:1–6.

[24] Bible, Micah 6:8.

Now, within the Temple, where the Ark of the Covenant had once been sheltered, within her sanctuary, was Mary, the "receptive vessel of God's Wisdom," listening deeply within her heart and receiving such nourishment!

In the Islamic tradition, *sakinah*, the Arabic equivalent of *shekhinah*, similarly signifies the Peace inspiring Presence of God. In the Quran it is spoken of as being sent by God in support for the heart, bringing illumination. This felt Presence, conveying "tranquility" is mentioned in *Surah al-Baqara, Surah at-Tawba* and *Surah al-Fath.*[25] Through continual immersion in prayer, one might say, Mary was suffused with *sakinah* and guarded within herself the *sirr al-rubiibiyya* (the secret of divine Godhead).

*"And God bestows His dominion upon whom He wills:*
*for God is Infinite, All-Knowing."*
*And their prophet [Samuel continued to speak] to them:*
*"Behold, it shall be a sign of dominion that the Ark*[26] *will come to you*
*endowed by your Sustainer with tranquility [sakinah, inner peace]*
*and with all that is enduring*
*in the angel-borne heritage left behind by the House of Moses*
*and the House of Aaron.*[27]

---

[25] See Quran: 2:248; 9:26; 9:40; 48:4; 48:18; 48:26.

[26] Lit., "that there will come to you the Ark of the Covenant (*tabut*)" (which has also been understood by Baydawi, Zamakshari, and Ibn al Athir as having the additional meaning of 'heart'). See Asad, *The Message of the Qur'an.*

The Ark of the Covenant mentioned in the Old Testament, a highly-ornamented chest guarded by angelic presences, carried the Tablets of the Laws of Moses, and radiated immense energy, just as a righteous heart might also carry these commandments and be of powerful action in this world.

[27] Lit., "and the remainder of that which the House of Moses and the House of Aaron left behind (*baqiyyah*), borne by the angels."

As Muhamamd Asad comments in *The Message of the Qur'an*, "Lit., 'and the remainder of that which the House of Moses and the House of Aaron left behind, borne by the angels. The expression 'borne by the angels' or 'angel-borne' is an allusion to the God-inspired nature of the spiritual heritage left by those two prophets; while the 'remainder' (*baqiyyah*) denotes that which is 'lasting' or 'enduring' in that heritage."

In the spiritual stages of purification of the soul, as one dies to the urges of the commanding self (*nafs al-ammarah*), one passes through annihilation of the self (*fana*) and becomes enduring in the Loving Presence of God (*baqa*); then one

*In this indeed is a sign for you if you are of the faithful."*
[Quran, *Surah al-Baqarah* 2:247–48]

The angels are carrying this heritage of Love towards us, continually. Mary was of those who bowed in recognition, immersing in the tranquility of that remembrance, a radiant heart honoring that covenant of Love.

As we are reminded in *Surah ar-Rad*:

*He guides to Himself all who turn to Him—*
*those who have faith*
*and whose hearts find satisfaction in the remembrance of God—*
*truly in the remembrance of God, hearts find tranquility*
*[alaa bi zhikrillahi tatma'innul qulub].*
[Quran, *Surah ar-Rad* 13:28]

The Quran speaks of Mary with numerous titles of honor recognizing her devotion. In *Surah al-Maida* ("The Feast," 5:75), she is referred to as *Siddiqah*, "she who confirms the truth," or "she who is completely and sincerely faithful." Derived from *Surah al-'Imran* (3:43),[28] Mary is referred to as *Sajidah*, "she who prostrates to God in worship." The motion of *sujud*, the prostration in prayer, is considered by some Muslims to be partly derived from Mary's instinctive practice of prostrating in awe before the Presence of God, with hands, knees, and forehead all connecting with the ground. Mary is also known as *Rakiah*, "she who bows down,"[29] as *Tahirah*, "she who was purified," as *Mustafia*, "she who was chosen (twice)": *O Mary! God has chosen you and purified you, and again He has chosen you above all women of all nations of the worlds.*[30] In *Surah at-Tahrim* (66:12), she is also called *Qanitah*, "wholeheartedly devout—she who is in constant surrender to the Divine, absorbed in prayer."

---

is moved in true alignment with His Will, rather than being distracted by one's own limited personal desires and wanderings, which have dissolved and faded away.

[28] *O Mary! Worship your Lord devoutly: prostrate yourself* (Quran, *Surah al-'Imran* 3:43).

[29] *And bow with those who bow* (Quran, *Surah al-'Imran* 3:43). Some say the *ruku* position of the *salah* ritual prayer also derives from her practice as well as that offered by the Prophet Muhammad in the way he was instructed by Archangel Gabriel on the Night Journey (*al-Isra'*).

[30] *Surah al-'Imran* 3:42.

*And Mary, the daughter of 'Imran, who guarded her chastity.*
*Then We breathed therein Our Spirit,*
*and she confirmed the Words of her Lord and His Books;*
*and she was one of the wholeheartedly devout.*
[Quran, *Surah at-Tahrim* 66:12]

The songs of David, for Christians, foretell the beautiful fruitfulness of this sacred earth of Mary:

Mercy and truth are met together;
righteousness and peace have kissed each other.
Truth shall spring out of the earth;
and righteousness shall look down from heaven.
Truly, the Lord shall give that which is good;
and our earth shall yield her fruit.
[Bible, Psalms 85:11–13]

Mary instinctively knew how to turn to her Lord in complete surrender to His/Her instructive Wisdom conveyed through the Light of Grace that engenders new life. She turned to the East, the place of sunrise, of illumination within the heart, and enwrapped herself in God's numinous Presence.

*And remember [zhikr] in the book, Maryam—*
*see how she withdrew from her family to a place in the east*
*and placed a veil [hijab] to seclude herself from them.*
[Quran, *Surah Maryam* 19:16–17]

Ruzbihan al-Baqli, an Iranian Islamic mystic of the twelfth century, offers us a beautiful reflection on Mary's intimacy with God, in recognition of her intrinsic spirituality as the purest of souls intimately trained by *Haqq* (the Real).

> The true indication here [of Surah Maryam 19:16] is that the essence of Mary is the essence of the holy *fitrah* (primordial soul nature). And her essence was trained by "the Real", by the light of intimacy. And in all of her respirations (every breath) she was *majdhuba*[31] by the attribute

[31] One intensely attracted by the attraction of God (*jadhb*).

of the closeness and intimacy to the Source of Divine Illumination. She became constantly in a state of spiritual vigilance (*muraqaba*) for the manifestation of the illumination of the World of Sovereignty (*jabarut*) from the point of the rising place of spiritual orientation (*mashriq*) in the realm of the Kingdom (*malakut*). And she withdrew from the world through spiritual resolve (*himma*) of the highest category, characterized by the Light of the Unseen. And she approached the rising-places (*mashriq*) of the Illumination of the Essence (*dhat*), and she inhaled the Attributes—fragrances from the Eternal World without beginning (*'alam al-azal*). And the gift reached her—the communion with the Pre-Eternal (*azaliyya*). And the Illumination of the witnessing of the Eternal (*mushahadat al-qidamiyya*) shone upon her. And when she experienced the vision of the illumination of the Manifestation of Eternity, Its Lights flashed, and Its Secrets reached her spirit (*ruh*), and her spirit became impregnated with the Divine Secret, and she became the bearer of the glorious Word and the light of the spirit of the Most High. And when her state became magnified with the reflection of the beauty of the Illumination of Eternity upon her, she concealed herself out of fear [of people] and withdrew [from them] with the 'bridegroom' of the Reality (*al-haqiqa*).[32]

In the purity of her heart, beloved Maryam was prepared; one might say the Names or Attributes of God of *Al-Quddus* (The Most Holy and Pure), *Al-Wadud*, (The Infinitely Loving), and *An-Nur* (The Light) were already brightly illuminating her heart. Her abode was within the abode of God; it was there she rested, there she found refuge.

---

[32] Ruzbihan al-Baqli, 'Ara'is II, 7, excerpt as quoted by Aliah Schleifer in *Mary the Blessed Virgin of Islam* (Louisville, KY: Fons Vitae, 1997), p. 91.

## *Under the Mantle of the Beloved's Veil*[1]

Stay close,
under the mantle of Your veil;
*hijab*
is not meant
for everyone,
but Mary drew herself
aside
into Your Sanctuary
beyond the intimations
of family,
that she might know
Your Heart.

Opened wide
her heart was,
where no one saw,
not even
Zachariah.

Fruits of love
spring
fully formed
from the Garden
of Your Love,
even in the cold
of winter.

---

[1] Excerpt from *A New World*, "Songs of the Soul" series, Camille Hamilton Adams Helminski (forthcoming from Sweet Lady Press).

Come close,
and closer still
behind the veil
of this existence,
where Prophets gather
in the orchard
to hear
Your discourse
coursing through
the ears of their hearts,
as they bend
to the Ground
of Your Being
and catch Your vibration
through their feet,
their limbs,
and hair
cascading in rivulets
down into this atmosphere.

Glories, Glories,
Ever-Abiding.
Hosanna![2]
*Hu*, Ana,[3]

---

[2] "Hosanna!" is a cry of help, seeking divine aid in the Jewish tradition, and a cry of praise and honor in the Christian tradition. It was chanted by the multitudes in greeting to Jesus when he was entering Jerusalem on what is known as Palm Sunday (the week before Easter), when he was welcomed with the waving of palms (sustainers of life, offerings of peace). "Hosanna!" is sometimes understood as having the meaning of "Hallelujah!"

See the Bible, Gospel of Matthew 21:9: "Hosanna to the Son of David! Blessed is he who comes in the name of the Lord! Hosanna in the highest heaven!"

The Hebrew root words indicating a cry for help are found in Psalm 118:25: "Save us, we pray, O Lord!"

[3] *Hu*, Ana conveys the greetings of God (*Hu*, the pronoun of Divine Presence) to the Mother (Ana), held in the Highest Presence. In Islam, the "Mother of the Book" (*Ummu al-Kitab*) is the Source from which the Divine Word flows forth. See the Quran, *Surah ar-Rad* 13:39: *With Him is the Mother of the Book [the source of all revelation].*

in the Highest,
*Subhanallah,*
*Ya Rabb al-Alameen!*
*Ya Sami,*
*Ya Alim,*
*Ya Basir.*[4]

[4] *Subhanallah* ("Glory be to God"), *Ya Rabb al-Alameen!* ("Sustainer of All Worlds!"), *Ya Sami* ("O You Who are All-Hearing"), *Ya Alim* ("O You Who are All-Knowing"), *Ya Basir* ("O You Who Are All-Seeing").

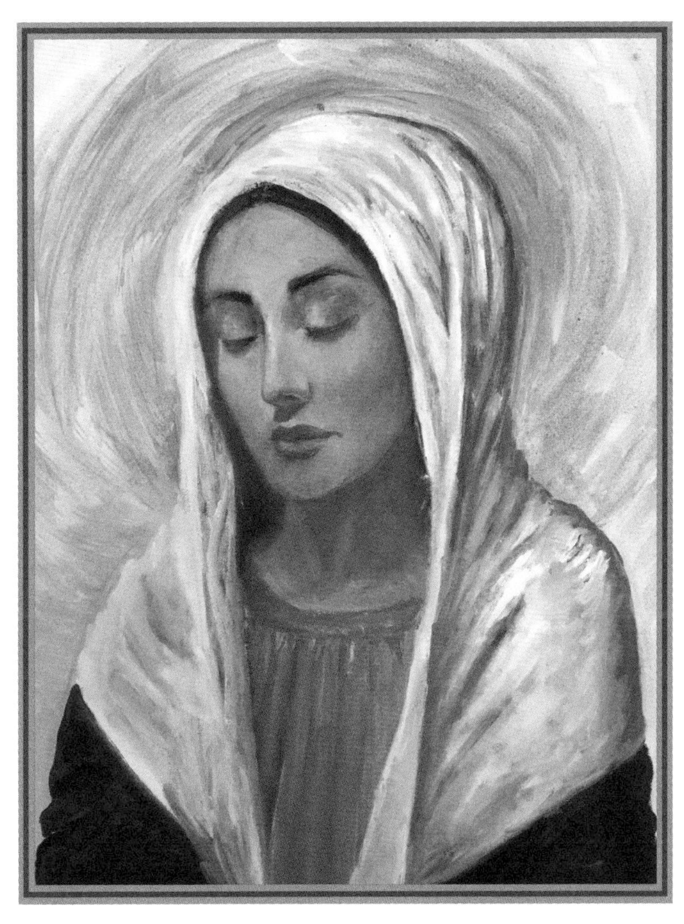

# III. THIRD STAR OF BLESSING

## *Annunciation of the Word*

# *Annunciation of the Word*

*Remember when the angels said, "O Mary!*
*Truly, Allah*[1] *gives you the good news of a Word from Him*
*whose name is Messiah,*[2] *Jesus, son of Mary,*
*honored in this world and the world to come,*
*and he is of those nearest to Allah.*
*He shall speak to people from his cradle, and as a grown man,*
*and he is of the wholly good."*
*She said, "O my Sustainer! How can I have a son when no man has touched me?"*
*He said, "Just like that Allah creates what He wills!*
*When He wills something, He but says to it: 'Be!'—and it is."*
[Quran, *Surah al-'Imran* 3:45–47]

The Annunciation to Mary calls us to recognize that the creative action of God is limitless. The Gospel account of Luke also affirms this: "For with God nothing is impossible."[3] The first,

---

[1] Allah, "God," is the Name of God used by Arabic speaking Christians as well as Muslims. The Name, "Allah," points to the One Creator, Source of All Sustenance, far beyond anything by which we may try to describe, beyond gender or description, the Ultimate Reality from which all beneficence flows.
[2] "Lit., 'whose name shall be "the Anointed" (*al-masih*)'. The designation *al-masih* is the Arabicized form of the Aramaic *meshiha* which, in turn, is derived from the Hebrew *mahsiah*, 'the anointed'—a term frequently applied in the Bible to the Hebrew kings, whose accession to power used to be consecrated by a touch with holy oil taken from the Temple. . . . Its application to Jesus may have been due to the widespread conviction among his contemporaries (references to which are found in several places in the Synoptic Gospels) that he was descended in direct . . . line from the royal House of David. . . . In the Greek version of the Gospels—which is undoubtedly based on a now-lost Aramaic original—this designation is correctly translated as *Christos* (a noun derived from the Greek verb *chriein*, 'to anoint')." See Muhammad Asad, *The Message of the Qur'an*, note to *Surah al-'Imran* 3:45.
[3] Bible, Gospel of Luke 1:37.

joyful mystery of the Marian Rosary prayers is the remembrance of the Annunciation of the Angel Gabriel to Mary.

In the sixth month the angel Gabriel[4] was sent from God
unto a city of Galilee, named Nazareth,
to a virgin betrothed[5] to a man whose name was Joseph,
of the house of David; and the virgin's name was Mary.
And the angel came in to her, and said:
"Hail, you who are highly favored,
the Lord is with you: blessed are you among women."
And when she saw him, she was troubled at his saying,
and cast in her mind what manner of salutation this might be.
And the angel said unto her: "Fear not, Mary:
for you have found favor with God.
And, behold, you shall conceive in your womb, and bring forth a son,
and shall call his name Jesus.
He shall be great, and shall be called the Son of the Highest,
and the Lord God will give to him the throne of his father David.
And he shall reign over the house of Jacob forever;
and of his kingdom there shall be no end.
Then Mary asked the angel, "But how shall this be,
seeing I know not a man?"
The angel answered and said to her,
"The Holy Spirit shall come upon you,
and the power of the Most High will overshadow you."
[Bible, Gospel of Luke 1:26–35]

The Quran parallels this narrative of the Annunciation, again, in *Surah Maryam* itself:

*Then We sent to her Our Spirit*[6]
*which appeared to her in the shape of a well-proportioned man.*

---

[4] The name "Gabriel" means "God's strength."

[5] At that time, there were two traditional parts to marriage in the Jewish tradition: mutual agreement or betrothal, and then, after varying lengths of time, the young woman being taken into the home of her husband.

[6] In Arabic the term for "Spirit" is *Ruh*—by most commentators *Ruh* in this verse is understood as indicating the Angel Gabriel conveying Spirit as God's messenger.

*She said, "I take refuge in the Most Compassionate from you;*
*if you are of those who are conscious of Him!"*
*He said, "Truly, I am a messenger from your Lord: for you, the gift of a pure son."*
*She said, "How can I have a son,*
*when I have not been touched by any man and I am not unchaste?"*
*He said, "Just like that! Your Lord says, 'It is easy for Me.*
*And We will make him a Sign for people and a Compassion from Us.'*
*And it is a matter that has already been decreed."*
[Quran, *Surah Maryam* 19:17–21]

Alone, in the sanctuary, Mary must have greatly wondered at the Grace of her Lord! Here she was, a young woman, content to be immersed in prayer, in recognition of the Source of her being—and yet this strange news comes to her.[7] An angel, suddenly, appears and tells her: "Now, you are with child." How could such a marvelous thing be, when she was not yet married nor had yet been known by any man? Yet, deeply, she trusted in the magnificent ability of God. Hadn't her life already been graced with such blessing? With awe at the ways of her Lord, perhaps she remembered how her own mother had received the gift of her conception and how she had then been promised in service to her Sustainer, even before she was born. It had not mattered that she was not born a boy to be devoted to the Temple ways; here she had been abiding, for so many years, sustained even in winter by the fruits of ripening.

The Protoevangelium mentions her trembling at the sudden presence of the angel and the Message of God conveyed, reminding us of the verse in Isaiah:

These are the ones I look on with favor:
those who are humble and contrite in spirit, and who tremble at My word.
[Bible (NIV), Isaiah 66:2]

---

[7] Though many Christian paintings depict Mary within an inner room, a "sanctuary," when Gabriel appears to her, as is the intimation of the Quran, the Bible is silent as to where exactly she was, though Luke indicates that she was already living in the house of Joseph in Nazareth. Maximus tells another version—relating that she had been fasting and had gone to a fountain, to draw water (Protoevangelium of James 11:1), when Gabriel suddenly appeared, saying: "Rejoice! Favored one, the Lord is with you"—indicating the fountain of Spirit she, herself, was becoming.

In the Quran, this trembling of those attentive to God's Presence is also recognized:

*The faithful are those*
*whose hearts tremble with awe whenever God is mentioned,*
*and whose faith is strengthened*
*whenever His signs are conveyed to them,*
*and who place their trust in their Sustainer—*
*those who are constant in prayer*
*and spend on others out of what We provide for them as sustenance:*
*In truth, these are the faithful!*
*They shall have stations of dignity with their Sustainer,*
*and forgiveness, and a most generous provision.*
[Quran, *Surah al-Anfal* 8:2–4]

Now Maryam must wait and see the glory of her Lord become manifest through her own body. Would this communication be realized in true fullness? How could she doubt it—she who knew so well the stories of the prophets, the visitations of angels, even to her own parents, and all the miracles of faith? Were not Joseph,[8] Moses, and Miriam her good companions? Was she not a daughter of the line of Aaron? Did not the power of God move the seas, and restore the earth when it had been barren, even bringing manna from Heaven in the midst of the dry desert? Surely this thing could be accomplished through the power of the Almighty, as the angel had spoken; even so, it must be easy! Moment by moment she would trust in her Lord's commandment, and not be afraid—of the consequences in the community, or for her family's name. Truly, God knows best, and all her life she had already relied upon His Word. Now she was called to trust from the depths of her soul, relying on that Word growing within her, to be birthed as a gift for all humankind, blessed eternally—she offered her prayers.

Whereas Zachariah had sought to know, to understand with his mind the news of the coming gift of an heir ("How will I know this is so?"),

---

[8] Her betrothed, Joseph, carried the name of the Prophet Joseph, the most beautiful among men, so deeply devoted to his Lord. Mary would have known well his story, his patience in adversity, the gracious blessings of His Lord to him, and the abundance that opened through his inner knowing gifted by God.

Mary, after her initial guardedness with the suddenness of Gabriel's stunning arrival, is courageously present in response to his words, an accepting handmaiden of the Lord, attentive in wonder, without fear of the immensity of the consequences.

And Mary said: "Behold the handmaid of the Lord;
be it unto me according to your word."
And the angel departed from her.
[Bible, Gospel of Luke 1:38]

She remained deeply conscious of God and the mysterious workings of Spirit, within the temple of her own body, within the "temple" of her heart—the Most Ancient Temple:

*And anyone who honors the symbols set up by God—*
*truly, these derive their value*
*from the God-consciousness within the heart.*
*In that God-consciousness you shall find benefits*
*until a determined time is fulfilled,*
*and its goal and end is the Most Ancient Temple.*[9]
*And always bear in mind your God is the One and Only God:*
*and so, surrender yourselves to Hu.*[10]

---

[9] "The Most Ancient Temple" signifies in specificity, the Kaaba, but in subtlety, the precious heart of the human being, created for worship before the Divine Reality, opened in recognition of the Source of All Being, a gateway to Unconditional and Infinite Love.

[10] All words in Arabic have a gender grammatically assigned to them as they do in French and Spanish, etc. Although Allah is referred to with the third person masculine pronoun *Hu* (*Huwa*), it is universally understood that Allah's Essence is beyond gender or indeed any qualification. In the translation of the Quran in this text occasionally "He/She" is used and sometimes *Hu* in an attempt to avoid the mistake of attributing human gender to That which is beyond all our attempts at definition, for *Truly, Our Sustainer is beyond anything by which we may seek to define Him/Her* (Quran, *Surah as-Saffat* 37:180), limitless in subtle glory.

The Quran is one of the few holy books with which we are familiar that speaks directly to both "men who have faith" and "women who have faith" in numerous passages. In fact when one counts the number of times that "men" and "women" are mentioned, the number is equal. In God's sight, men and women are equal; what matters is not gender, wealth, or power, but that we bring to our Sustainer *a sound heart* (Quran, *Surah ash-Shu'ara* 26:89) when we return to our Source. It is

*And give the glad tiding of God's acceptance to all who are humble—*
*all those whose hearts tremble with awe whenever God is mentioned,*
*and all who patiently bear whatever ill befalls them,*
*and all who are constant in prayer*
*and spend on others out of the sustenance We have provided for them.*
[Quran, *Surah al-Hajj* 22:32–35]

Surely, she then sought to even increase her prayer, to deepen even further her continual connection with her Sustainer. As it reminds us, also, in the Quran:

*And keep your connection [rabitah], and remain conscious of God,*
*that you may attain felicity.*
[Quran, *Surah al-'Imran* 3:200]

Completely she surrendered, in full trust, to the unfolding of what was to come, which she alone would bear. This surrender of the self is, essentially, what *Islam* means—surrender to what Is, knowing we could not design a better portion than the One who created us and seeks the best for us, even more than we are seeking Him—the Source of All Subsistence. We have been given will to accompany the unfolding with the best effort, eyes to discern the best way to proceed, hearts to know by longing, and ears to hear the Words of guidance that have been given through all manner of beings—the angels, the bees, the intimations of roses and wild flowers, the roar of the lion and the song of the nightingales of God, calling us to let go of the baggage weighing us down—the encumbrances of the wayward, resistant ego. So many have shown us that it is this surrender into the arms of the Beloved that opens the door for *Salaam* (the Peace of God) to pour through, that we might be recreated by Love.

*Witness—the only religion with God is self-surrender to Him.*
*['Innad dina 'indallahil islam]*
[Quran, *Surah al-'Imran* 3:19]

---

these who shall find themselves abiding in the Garden, now and eternally . . . *a Garden underneath which rivers flow* (Quran, *Surah al-Bayyinah* 98:8), and where everywhere one is met with the greeting, "*Peace*" (Quran, *Surah Ya Sin* 36:58).

The early Hebrew prophecy of Isaiah in the Old Testament is often understood as foretelling this virgin birth of Jesus:

> Therefore the Lord Himself shall give you a sign;
> behold, a virgin shall conceive, and bear a son,
> and shall call his name "Immanuel."
> [Bible, Isaiah 7:14][11]

Further on in Isaiah, Immanuel is referred to as the future savior of his people. "Immanuel" has the meaning of "God with us," which is indicative of the Holy Breath of God received by Mary in her utmost purity, this breath of Spirit that engendered the holy infant Jesus, who was such an inspirer of faith. Through his radiant being, he continually reminded those around him that "God is always with us," that no matter in what state we may find ourselves, the Beloved is near, even as we are also reminded through the Quran:

> *And He/She is with you wherever you may be.*
> [Quran, *Surah al-Hadid* 57:4]

It is that awareness of the Presence of God—of the Beneficent Divine Reality—holding us that can "save us," rejuvenating us with Love. Mary relied so much upon the Word of God that the Annunciation message from her Lord was quickly welcomed with courage and deep faith, even in the midst of her trembling. She did not question further, but accepted and surrendered in devotion, as the servant of God. Even as her name indicated, she was one who loved God devotedly and treasured that Companionship.

The Quran does not speak directly of Joseph, Mary's betrothed, but Islamic scholars of the early centuries refer to him, just as he is mentioned in the Christian traditions in the Bible, indicating that Joseph, a carpenter in service to the Temple, was related to Mary, and having encountered her in the Temple, was aware of her deep devotion and purity. When she had matured and was of marriageable age, the priests gathered elder widowers from among the community to be considered as possibilities for becoming the husband of this precious virgin who had been dedicated to God, to be her continued protector now that she was a mature young woman, and

---

[11] Most of the books of the Old Testament were originally written in Hebrew and were incorporated from the Jewish tradition into the Christian Bible.

it was no longer appropriate for her to remain in the Temple, that she might continue her devotions undisturbed. Once again, it was through the branch of a tree that the choice was to be determined. Each widower was asked to bring his staff, and to place that rod within the Temple. It is related that not only did the staff of Joseph flower, even as had the rod of Aaron,[12] but a dove flew forth from the top of it and perched upon his head. Marveling again, at this sign, the priests arranged that Mary should be betrothed to Joseph and given under his care.

We are not told either in the Quran or in the Bible when it was that Joseph became aware that Mary was with child. According to the Jewish law, as it was in many other cultures, severe punishment would be the portion of a woman betrothed who became with child before full relations with her husband. Surely Joseph recognized the beautiful Light within Mary, her determined devotion and love of God, and remembered that she had spent her childhood in the Temple. And could she not have in a moment conveyed to him what was in her heart? He must have pondered deeply. Though surely the shocking news must have been overwhelming, even for an elder of deep faith, was he not "a man who was just"?[13] Could he doubt her purity?

But while he considered these things,<br>
an angel of the Lord appeared to him in a dream, saying,<br>
"Joseph, son of David, don't be afraid to take Mary for your wife.

---

[12] See Chapter I, p. 4, n. 3 continuation.

[13] Bible, Gospel of Matthew 1:19.

What has been conceived in her is of Holy Spirit.
She will have a son, and you will call his name Jesus,
because he is the one who will save the people from their own errors.
[Bible, Gospel of Matthew 1:20–21]

The child is to be named not after his earthly father and protector, but rather the angel tells Joseph the child is to be called "Jesus," the Greek form of "Joshua," which means "the Lord saves." This was a confirmation of the message Mary had already received from Gabriel, even as both Joachim and Hannah were given messages by angels of the gift of the child that was Mary. In the Quranic story, also, it is Gabriel who conveys the name of her child to Mary. Some hearts are able to receive messages from the angels[14] while asleep and merged within deeper realms; others have the strength of heart to witness angels while fully awake, all senses attentive and attuned to the numinous realms. Beloved Mary was infinitely blessed with this subtle perception.

For He has been mindful of the humble state of His servant.
From now on all generations will call me blessed.
[Bible (NIV), Gospel of Luke 1:48]

We remember that only one *surah* ("chapter") in the whole Quran is named after a woman, *Surah Maryam*, and she is the only woman mentioned in the Quran with honor by name. Each *surah* of the Quran (except one) begins with the phrase *Bismillah ar Rahman ar Rahim* (*In the Name of God, the Infinitely Compassionate and Infinitely Merciful*). These two qualities of the Divine that are offered foremost, *Ar-Rahman* and *Ar-Rahim*, both, emerge from the meaning of the Arabic triliteral root word for "womb" (*rahm*). Even as the whole of the Quran is thus embraced and held within the awareness of the Infinite Generosity, Beneficence, and Nurturance of the Divine Reality, the personage of Mary, brought to remembrance within its pages numerous times, exemplifies this capacity for so generously and most graciously birthing pure Spirit into this world, the pre-eminent Mother. Rumi speaks to us of this transformative process:

The Universal Soul met a separate soul
and placed a pearl upon her breast.

---

[14] The English term "angel" is derived from the Greek word for "messenger."

Through that touch the soul, like Mary,
became pregnant with a heart-entrancing Messiah.
Not the Messiah of land and sea,
but the Messiah beyond all measured space.
So when the soul has been made pregnant by the Soul of souls,
by such a soul, the world, itself, is impregnated.
Then the world gives birth to another world,
and reveals to the congregated people
a place of enlivened congregation.
Though I should speak of this until the Resurrection,
I lack the power to describe such a Resurrection.
These words of mine, really are an "O Lord,"
a prayer, a call for the breath of a sweet-lipped One.
How should one who seeks an answer fail to pray?
How can he or she be silent,
when "Here am I" always comes in response to our "O Lord!"
It is a "Here am I" you cannot hear,
but can wholly taste from head to foot, rejoicing.
[*Mathnawi* II: 1183–91]

"O Mary, indeed Allah has chosen you and purified you and chosen you above the women of the worlds."[15] According to the Quran, Mary was chosen twice by the Lord: firstly, in the gift of her birth in response to the prayer of her mother, Hannah, and her dedication to God, and secondly with her being chosen to bear Jesus, the Messiah. In one of the sayings of the Prophet Muhammad, it is recorded he mentioned that neither Jesus nor Mary was "pricked by Satan" at birth—not touched by the usual arising of egoistic desires as happens with most human beings.[16] In another *hadith*, he names Mary as "one of the four spiritually perfected women of the world," who will "lead the soul of blessed women to the Garden" (Paradise—*Jannah*). These sayings are indications of the Way, even as Rumi reminds us:

I've called that Unlimited Beneficence a garden,
because it's the source of all abundance

---

[15] Quran, *Surah al-'Imran* 3:42
[16] *Sahih Muslim*, Book 30, *hadith* 5837.

and the gathering of all gardens;
and yet, it's "something no eye has seen":[17]
how could one ever call it a "garden"?
Yet God called the Light of the Unseen "a lamp."
Parables are offered so that one who is bewildered
might catch the fragrance of that which is Real.
[*Mathnawi* III: 3405–07]

The Real is continually calling to us, sending messages, beckoning to Truth. One Quranic commentator, Fakhr al-Din al-Razi, takes the verse regarding the Annunciation that is mentioned with honor still a third time in the Quran, in *Surah at-Tahrim*, as an indication that Mary had faith in all prior revelations, in all the "Books" of Divine communication:

*The daughter of Imran, who preserved her chastity—*
*then We breathed therein Our Spirit,*
*and she confirmed the Words of her Lord and His Books;*
*and she was among the wholeheartedly devout.*
[Quran, *Surah at-Tahrim* 66:12]

This verse also affirms the virgin birth, accepted within Islam as it is in Christianity, as a miracle of Infinite Grace. Her virginity is not only of the body, but a purity of intention of the mind and will, and of the steadfastness in devotion of her heart. It is an angel, Gabriel, who greets her, who brings her the message, a messenger suddenly appearing from the Unseen, coming through in human form with "shining face," calling out to her, "Hail Mary, full of grace," lauding the innate purity of this precious soul in relation to her Creator, Educator, Cherisher, Sustainer!

The contemporary Christian mystic, Thomas Merton, speaks of seeking in contemplative prayer a "point vierge" at the center of his being, "a point untouched by illusion, a point of pure truth . . . which belongs entirely to God, which is inaccessible to the fantasies of our own mind or the brutalities of our own will. This little point . . . of absolute poverty," he wrote, "is the pure glory of God in us."[18] It seems that Thomas Merton,

---

[17] This is referring to a *Hadith Qudsi*: The Prophet said, "God says, 'I have readied for My righteous servants what no eye has ever seen, and no ear has ever heard, and no heart of man has ever conceived.'"

[18] Thomas Merton, *Conjectures of a Guilty Bystander* (New York: IMAGE, 2014),

who in his later years was much influenced by Sufism, also understood something of what the Prophet Muhammad meant when he said, "My poverty is my pride". If Muhammad had any "pride" it was in the Glory of God, the sanctification of God's Presence, which the empty and receptive soul can receive, the Glory of which Jesus speaks of being bestowed, the inflowing of Spirit. Rumi encourages us:

Dig a well in the earth of this body,
or even before the well is dug,
let God draw the water up.
Be always at work scraping the dirt from the well.
To everyone who suffers,
perseverance brings good fortune.
The Prophet has said that each prostration of prayer
is a knock on heaven's door.
When anyone continues to knock,
felicity shows its smiling face.
[*Mathnawi* V: 2044–49]

Truly, for the Prophet Muhammad, the example of Mary, Maryam, must have been a great support of heart. He must have felt her as a companion of Spirit, an inspiration, in her devotion to God, her surrender, her compassionate Love. For Muhammad that love and devotion were also mirrored in his own wife, Khadijah, who lent her support for his time of retreat in the hills, who brought him food that he might immerse more in meditation, who was the gracious mother of his children. While in retreat there in the Cave of Hira, it is told that it was Gabriel, also, who brought the "Word" of God to Prophet Muhammad, overpowering him with an embrace that cracked open the ripened seed of his heart to "birth" the Holy Quran, beginning that night of Ramadan.

*In the Name of God, the Infinitely Compassionate and Most Merciful:*
*We have indeed revealed this during the Night of Power.*
*And what will explain to you what the Night of Power is?*

---

pp.153–56. Thomas Merton (1915–1968), a Trappist monk, also known as "Father Louis," a strong proponent of interfaith understanding, was a member of the Abbey of Our Lady of Gethsemani, near Bardstown, Kentucky.

*The Night of Power is better than a thousand months.*
*Within it the angels descend bearing divine inspiration*
*by God's permission upon every mission:*
*Peace! . . . This until the rise of dawn!*
[Quran, *Surah al-Qadr*, "The Night of Power," 97:1–5, complete]

*Say: "The Spirit of Holiness [Ruh al-Qudus]*[19]
*has brought it down from your Sustainer by stages,*
*setting forth the truth,*
*so that it might give firmness unto those who have attained to faith,*
*and provide guidance and a glad tiding*
*unto all who have surrendered themselves to God."*
[Quran, *an-Nahl*, "The Bee," 16:102]

To receive this "Holy Inspiration," a soul must be "virgin," clear, untarnished by the world. In a sense, the Prophet, too, is referred to as "virgin"—*ummi*, "unlettered, illiterate," empty of already written words, another indication of the Way, even as Rumi describes:

Does anyone write something on a place
that has already been written over,
or plant a sapling where one already grows?
No; he seeks a blank piece of paper
and sows the seed where none has yet been sown.
Brother, sister, be bare earth; be a clean piece of paper
untouched by writing, that you may be ennobled by *the pen of revelation*,[20]
so that the Gracious One may sow seed within you.
[*Mathnawi* V: 1961–64]

Some say that the opening words of the Bible, which most often are translated as "In the beginning was the Word,"[21] might be better

[19] The expression *Ruh al-Qudus* occurs also in *ayats* 2:87, 2:253, and 5:110. Literally it means "Spirit of Holiness," referring, as many understand it, to the Angel Gabriel, who is the conveyor of revelation to the prophets. Muhammad Asad mentions in his note to this verse that it can also be understood as "holy inspiration," a Quranic synonym for "divine revelation."
[20] Quran, *Surah al-Qalam*, "The Pen," 68:1: *Nun wa'l Qalam* (*By the Pen*) are the opening words of this *surah*.
[21] See the Bible, Genesis 1:1, and also Gospel of John 1:1.

translated as "Through Wisdom, was the Word." Era by era, Truth becomes manifest and we are enlivened by the "Word" of God, when our hearts crack open to hear.

*God has revealed the most beautiful message in the form of a Book*
*consistent within itself,*
*repeating its teaching in various guises—*
*the skins of those who stand in awe of their Lord tremble with it;*
*then their skins and their hearts soften*
*with the remembrance of God.*
*Such is God's guidance:*
*with it He guides the one who wills to be guided.*
[Quran, *Surah az-Zumar* 39:23]

We witness in the example of Mary one who opened with purest humility to the cherishing Power of Spirit and that enlivening growing within her, radiating through her with Grace. May we, also, drink deeply, in humility, of that Infinite, All-Powerful Love and re-birth Spirit, moment by moment.

## *Breathing Love*[1]

Every particle of our being
is a mouth to drink Your Love.
Through that Love
even the bitter becomes sweet.
What is sweetness in Reality
but a taste that resonates
within the heart as Love—
we recognize You with every breath we take,
for it is You who are the Giver,
our Mother, our Father,
our Source—
cherishing us in every moment,
from before the beginning
and long after our return,
purifying our hearts
that we might be able to hear
Your Word.
O You who are
The First, The Last,
Infinitely Compassionate,
Most Holy Pure,
O Infinitely Loving One!
*Ya Awwal, Ya Akhir,*
*Ya Rahman, Ya Quddus,*
*Ya Wadud!*[2]

---

[1] Excerpt from *Exaltations*, "Songs of the Soul" series, Camille Hamilton Adams Helminski (forthcoming from Sweet Lady Press).

[2] *Ya Awwal* ("The First"), *Ya Akhir* ("The Last"), *Ya Rahman* ("The Infinitely Compassionate"), *Ya Quddus* ("The Most Holy and Pure"), *Ya Wadud* ("The Infinitely Loving One").

## IV. FOURTH STAR OF BLESSING

# *Magnificat: Mary's Song of Praise*

# *Magnificat: Mary's Song of Praise*

*Limitless is He in His glory,*
*and sublimely, immeasurably exalted*
*above anything people may say.*
*The seven heavens extol His limitless glory,*
*and the earth, and all that they contain;*
*and there is nothing that does not celebrate*
*His immeasurable glory and praise—*
*but you fail to grasp the manner of their glorifying Him,*
*but He is Infinitely Tender, Forgiving.*
[Quran, *Surah al-Isra'*, "The Night Journey," 17:44]

Both Mary and Elizabeth glorified God with the whole of their being—their bodies, their hearts, and their words. When we attune to their meeting, we partake in the joy arising as they share the holy news each had received. Elizabeth was already six months pregnant when Mary arrived at her home.

And behold, your relative[1] Elizabeth in her old age
has also conceived a son,
and this is the sixth month with her who was called barren.
For nothing will be impossible with God."
[Bible (ESV), Gospel of Luke 1:36–37]

---

[1] Though many English translations of this verse use the term "cousin" for Elizabeth, the Greek word is not *anepsios* ("cousin") but *suggenes* ("kinswoman"), which is non-specific as to whether an aunt or a cousin or simply relative of the same lineage. In most Christian and Islamic texts, Elizabeth is recognized as Mary's aunt (in a few she is spoken of as the daughter of her mother's sister, Sobe; such sources indicate Mary's mother Anna had two sisters—the second sister also named Mary). In either case, she was of the closest of women to Beloved Mary.

Upon receiving the news from Gabriel that Elizabeth was also with child, Mary straight away went to greet her, to be of help to this closest of kinswomen, and to share her own miraculous news. In the scriptures, by the time of that unfolding, we have heard nothing further of Mary's parents, so many take it to mean that both of her parents had passed on by the time she was betrothed to Joseph. So, following the moment of Annunciation, to rush to the side of her closest kinswoman, her mother's sister, would have been the most natural thing to do. Of course, as soon as she heard, she would want to share in Elizabeth's joy, this sister of her mother who, like Mary's mother, had also gone through the challenges of barrenness and now was blessed with child.

And Mary arose in those days, and went into the hill country with haste, into a city of Juda.

[Bible, Gospel of Luke 1:39]

It is told that as she journeyed to visit Elizabeth, wherever Mary alighted and her foot touched the earth, a flower sprang up—*aquilegia vulgaris*, columbine, "Our Lady's Shoes." This sweet flower with spurred sepals reminds some of a cluster of doves' wings and has come to symbolize the Holy Spirit. It is especially included in chapel altar bouquets at the time

*Columbine*

of Pentecost,[2] in remembrance of the descent of the Holy Spirit, and the blessings of Beloved Mary and the receptivity of the soul to God.

*And remember when the angels said, "O Mary [Maryam]!*
*Truly Allah has chosen you and purified you—*
*chosen you above all the women of all the worlds."*
[Quran, *Surah al-'Imran*, 3:42–43]

The Quran mentions her in numerous passages with reverence, and her beloved son, Jesus (Isa), whom Gabriel tells her will be instructed by God:

*And He will teach him the Book and wisdom and the Torah and the Gospel.*
[Quran, *Surah al-'Imran*, 3:48]

The child Beloved Mary is to bear is to weave together the wisdom of all three Abrahamic faiths.

A shoot will spring from the stem of Jesse;
from his roots a branch will bear fruit.
[Bible, Isaiah 11:1][3]

Jesse was the ancestor of the Prophet David, and Christians point to this verse from the Old Testament Prophet Isaiah (one of the most revered of the Hebrew prophets) as foretelling the coming of Beloved Mary, herself, as the flowering branch of renewal, bearing such precious fruit, the Messiah, who from childhood will lead the community through righteousness into the Peace of God.

And being sent before him, was Yahya, John, to encourage the community in purity of heart, in receptivity to the Word of God. Elizabeth and Zachariah and their "righteous offspring," Yahya (the "alive one"), are all remembered together with honor in the Quran:

---

[2] Pentecost is the Christian celebration of the moment, fifty days after Easter, when the Holy Spirit descended among the apostles of Jesus.

[3] See Bible, Isaiah 11:1–9 in Extended Context Notes in Appendix, Star IV, 1. This Scripture quotation taken from the (NASB®) New American Standard Bible®, Copyright © 1960, 1971, 1977, 1995, 2020 by The Lockman Foundation. Used by permission. All rights reserved. www.lockman.org.

*And [thus did We deliver] Zachariah*[4] *when he cried out to his Sustainer:*
*"O my Sustainer! Leave me not childless!*
*But [I know that] You are the Best of Inheritors!"*[5]
*So We responded to him; and We bestowed upon him the gift of Yahya [John]—*
*We made his wife whole for him.*
*Truly, these three would vie with each other to do good works;*
*they used to call upon Us with longing and reverence,*
*and they were always humble before Us.*
[Quran, *Surah al-Anbiya* 21:89–90]

Altogether they were to be a family of love, generous of heart and spirit, preparing the Way for the "Word" of Jesus to be spoken. In preparation, Zachariah was immersed in silence.

The secrets of the Divine Majesty
are drunk by the ear
of one who like the lily
has a hundred tongues
and is speechless.
The grace of God bestows
a throat on the earth,
so that it might drink water
and make a hundred plants grow green.
[Mevlana Jalaluddin Rumi, *Mathnawi* III: 21–22]

As Beloved Mary greets Elizabeth, she is the first to bear witness to Beloved Mary's miraculous pregnancy:

And [Mary] entered the house of Zechariah and greeted Elizabeth.
And when Elizabeth heard the greeting of Mary,
the baby leaped in her womb.

---

[4] "There was in the days of Herod, the king of Judaea, a certain priest named Zacharias, of the course of Abia: and his wife was of the daughters of Aaron, and her name was Elisabeth" (Bible, Gospel of Luke 1:5). The name "Elizabeth" has the meaning in Hebrew of "worshipper of God."

[5] I.e.: "You will remain when all else has ceased to be." *Al-Warith*, "The Inheritor of All," is one of the Ninety-Nine Attributes, or Names, of God in the Islamic tradition, as conveyed in the Quran.

*Detail from* Visitation of Beloved Mary to Elizabeth
*by Fra Angelico.*

And Elizabeth was filled with the Holy Spirit,
and she exclaimed with a loud cry,
"Blessed are you among women,
and blessed is the fruit of your womb!"
[Bible (ESV), Gospel of Luke 1:40–42]

Elizabeth wondered at this joy bursting forth from within herself and exclaimed to Mary,

"As soon as the sound of your greeting reached my ears,
the baby in my womb leaped for joy.
Blessed is she who has believed

that the Lord would fulfill his promises to her!"
[Bible (NIV), Gospel of Luke 1:44–45]

Beloved Mary, "Our Lady," with her intrinsic humility, then pours her heart out with joy, proclaiming the greatness of God, in the *Magnificat*, known by the Latin wording of the first phrase of her response: "*Magnificat anima mea Dominum.*" The *Magnificat*, which also came to be known as the "Canticle of Mary," is said to be the first hymn that was sung within the Christian communities and remains part of the Liturgy of the Hours often recited by Christian priests in remembrance. Numerous composers have set it to music, Palestrina, Bach, and Mozart, among others, yet one can, also, simply recite it by heart, offering it, as did Beloved Mary, in gratitude to God.

And Mary said:
"My soul magnifies the Lord
and my spirit rejoices in God my Saviour.
Because He has regarded the humility of His handmaiden;
for behold from henceforth all generations shall call me blessed.
Because He that is mighty, has done great things to me;
and holy is His Name.
And His mercy is from generation unto generations,
to them that [abide in awe of] Him.
He has shown might in his arm:
he has scattered the proud in the conceit of their heart.
He has put down the mighty from their seat,
and has exalted the humble.
He has filled the hungry with good things;
and the rich He has sent empty away.
He has received Israel His servant, being mindful of His mercy:
As he spoke to our fathers, to Abraham and to his seed, forever."
[Bible, Gospel of Luke 1:46–55]

The indwelling of Spirit radiates through her Presence, filling Elizabeth with joy. "Full of Grace," she who is known as perfect in wisdom had arrived at her door, this young woman newly pregnant in her first trimester, to assist her aunt, now in her third trimester, as she prepared to give birth. "The Lord is with her," and so she is immersed in all the qualities of the

Divine, and exemplary of all virtues: steadfast here, yet reflective of the seven heavens, a blessed companion.

There are some within Islamic circles who debate how this meeting occurred, thinking that Beloved Mary had remained near the outskirts of Nazareth. Rumi reminds us of the futility of such debate, but to rather seek the kernel of meaning:

Suppose a mother cries to her nursing infant,
"Come, I am your mother: know this, my child!"—
will the infant say, "O mother, bring the proof,
so that I may take comfort in your milk!"
When within the heart of any community
there is spiritual savor from God,
the face and voice of the prophet are an evidentiary miracle.
When the prophet utters a call from without,
the soul of the community falls to worship within,
because never in the world will the soul's ear
have heard from anyone a cry like his.
That soul stranger, by immediate perception of the wondrous voice,
has heard from God's tongue, "Truly, I am near!"[6]

*How Yahya, on whom be peace, in his mother's womb bowed before the Messiah, on whom be peace.*

The mother of Yahya, while pregnant, said in secret to Mary,
"I see with certainty, within you is a king
who is possessed of firm purpose
and is a Messenger endowed with holy knowledge.
When I happened to meet you,
the child I am carrying at once bowed in worship.
This embryo bowed in worship to that embryo,
so that pain arose in my body from its bowing."
Mary said, "I also felt within me my baby bowing in my womb."

---

6 *And if My servants ask you about Me—witness, I am near;*
*I respond to the call of the one who calls, whenever he [or she] calls Me:*
*let them, then, respond to Me, and have faith in Me,*
*so that they may follow the right way.*
[Quran, *Surah al-Baqarah* 2:186]

*On raising a difficulty as to this story.*

The foolish say, "Disregard this tale; it is false and erroneous.
Mary in her pregnancy did not encounter anyone;
she didn't return from the outskirts of town.
Until that woman of sweet address was delivered beyond the town,
she indeed did not come into it.
When she had given birth to her infant,
she then took him up in her arms and carried him to her kinsfolk.
Where did the mother of Yahya see her
to speak these words to her about what had happened?"

*The answer to the difficulty:*

Let the skeptic know:
all that is absent in the world
is present to one who receives ideas from God.
To Mary, the mother of Yahya would appear,
even though she might be far from her sight.
One may see a friend even with eyes shut,
when one has made the skin a window
to let in spiritual ideas.
And even if she saw her neither from without nor from within,
still, take the essential meaning of the story, O imbecile!
Not like someone who has heard some fables,
and like "*sh*" stuck to the literal *sh*ape of them,[7]
so that he would say, "How should Kalila, having no language,
hear words from Dimna who had no power of speech?[8]
And even if they knew each other's accents,

---

[7] Mevlana makes an example of someone who is stuck to the outer form of things; he uses a simile in Persian, "like *shin* stuck the *naqsh* of them." Similarly to the beginning *sh* of "shape," *shin* is the final letter of the word *naqsh*, which has the meaning of "model" or "picture."

[8] *Kalila and Dimna* is a collection of fables that originated in India, most probably based on the Sanskrit text of the Panchatantra from around the second century BCE. It was translated into Pahlavi Persian in the sixth century. The later Arabic translation of the eighth century was the basis for further translations throughout Medieval Europe. The main heroes are animals, with, among others, a lion in the role of a king; Shetrebah is his servant ox. Kalila and Dimna are two jackals, brothers who are doorkeepers for the lion king.

how should man understand their talk,
since it was without any articulation?
How did Dimna become a messenger between the lion and the ox,
and cajole them both with his palaver?
How did the noble ox become the vizier of the lion?
How was the elephant terrified by the reflection of the moon?
This *Kalila and Dimna* is entirely fiction,
or else how has the stork a quarrel with the crow?"
O brother, the story is like a measuring cup:
the real meaning in it is like the grain.
The person of intelligence will take the grain of meaning:
he will not pay any regard to the measure,
even if it is completely removed.
Listen to what passes between the rose and the nightingale,
even though no audible speech is heard by the ear.
[Rumi, *Mathnawi* II: 3596–3624]

As Beloved Mary was just at the beginning of her pregnancy, this bowing of her infant might have been the first large movement she felt, a new miracle. As a mother, one is so sensitive to the presence of precious being developing in one's womb, awaiting with wonder the miracle of first movement. For Elizabeth, in her third trimester, the movement she experienced would have been stronger. Mothers know well how the infant in the womb can sense the sound of a voice, the presence of a beloved touch. Something in the resonance of Beloved Mary's voice in greeting, and the nearness of the energy of her presence and that of her child awakened the bow of John in Elizabeth's womb. This son of Elizabeth and Zachariah would grow to also become a prophet of God, calling people from the wilderness of the world into God's presence. In the Quran he is remembered:

*"O John! Hold fast to the Book with all strength!"—*
*for We granted him wisdom while he was yet a little boy,*
*as well as, by Our grace, compassion[9] and purity;*
*and he was always conscious of Us*
*and full of piety towards his parents; and never was he haughty or rebellious.*

---

[9] Lit., "compassion from Us"—i.e., as a special divine gift.

*And so peace was upon him on the day when he was born,*
*and on the day of his death,*
*and will be on the day when he shall be raised to life again.*
[Quran, *Surah Maryam* 19:12–15]

In Beloved Mary's *Magnificat*, one finds great resonance with earlier Jewish traditions of the prophets. There are many resonances with the Psalms of David, and it echoes the "Song of Hannah," a quintessential Jewish prayer, still recited at the beginning of Rosh Hashanah (the Jewish New Year, or "Birthday of Creation"), that poured forth in ancient days from the heart of one of the same name as the dear mother of Beloved Mary, Hannah. Hannah's song, known as the "Canticle of Anna" among Christians, continues to be sung in Catholic services, and recited in Protestant churches as part of the calendar lesson call and response. The story of this earlier Hannah is recounted in the Bible in Samuel, the book of her prophet son, with whom she is gifted by God. Like the renowned Hebrew matriarchs Sarah and Rachel, and Beloved Mary's own mother, Hannah, she had long been yearning for a child. Distraught, she sought refuge in the sanctuary of the Temple where only men were wont to go. She poured out her heart before her Lord. Discovered there by the elder, Eli, she is questioned. What is she doing in the sanctuary? It is the wrong time and the wrong place—she is the wrong gender—yet she is here, praying from the depths of her heart, not a prescribed prayer. Eli thinks perhaps she is drunk, that she should act so wantonly, but in response she declares,

"No, my lord, I am a woman of a sorrowful spirit:
I have drunk neither wine nor strong drink,
but I poured out my soul before the Lord."
[Bible, I Samuel 1:15]

Witnessing her heartfelt sincerity, Eli's heart softens and he responds:

"Go in peace,
and the God of Israel grant you the petition you have asked of Him."
[Bible, I Samuel 1:17]

Hannah becomes pregnant and bears a son, Samuel, whom she sends, after he is weaned, as promised, to work with Eli. Every year she visits him and brings him the gift of a new coat, every year a little larger. Joyfully she witnesses him become a strong leader, a prophet. And at home, she is not left bereft. The birth of Samuel opened the gate of motherhood for her. She then has other children; her heart and her body were healed with his arrival. Her hold on life had been fragile; she had almost lost the will to live, continually weeping, unable to eat, overwhelmed by sadness, unable to enjoy the blessings that she had. Yet Hannah shows us that even the deepest sense of worthlessness and despair may be overcome through prayer and hope; her example encourages us to trust, to hope, to offer our prayers, reminding us again that we are not alone: *I am with you wherever you may be.*[10]

### *Hannah's Song*

And Hannah prayed and said:
"My heart rejoices in the Lord;
My horn[11] is exalted in the Lord.
I smile at my enemies,
Because I rejoice in Your salvation.
No one is holy like the Lord,
For there is none besides You,
Nor is there any rock like our God.
Talk no more so very proudly;
Let no arrogance come from your mouth,
For the Lord is the God of knowledge;
And by Him actions are weighed.
The bows of the mighty men are broken,
And those who stumbled are girded with strength.
Those who were full have hired themselves out for bread,
And the hungry have ceased to hunger.
Even the barren has borne seven,
And she who has many children has become feeble.

---

[10] Quran, *Surah al-Hadid* 57:4.

[11] Lit., "horn," which implies "strength." (This I Samuel passage of scripture taken from the New King James Version®. Copyright © 1982 by Thomas Nelson. Used by permission. All rights reserved.)

This is a reference to the strength of the ox or ram which manifests in its horn. In Judaism, a ram's horn, the *shofar*, is blown on the high holidays in Judaism to call the people to inwardly reflect and reconnect with God. Here Hannah reflects upon how her strength is uplifted by God.

The Lord kills and makes alive;
He brings down to the grave and brings up.
The Lord makes poor and makes rich;
He brings low and lifts up.
He raises the poor from the dust
And lifts the beggar from the ash heap,
To set them among princes
And make them inherit the throne of glory.
For the pillars of the earth are the Lord's,
And He has set the world upon them.
He will guard the feet of His saints,
But the wicked shall be silent in darkness.
For by strength no man shall prevail.
The adversaries of the Lord shall be broken in pieces;
From heaven He will thunder against them.
The Lord will judge the ends of the earth.
He will give strength to His king,
And exalt the horn of His anointed."
[Bible, 1 Samuel 2:1–10]

So the story of the fertile blessing of Beloved Mary's conception of Jesus is held within these stories of barrenness of her mother and her mother's sister to whom beautiful fruitfulness was later granted, with resonance to the ancient traditions of such hearts as this earlier Hannah's yearning for fulfillment and a response arriving from their Sustainer. Without even such a need on Beloved Mary's behalf, her deep purity and receptivity drew such precious fruitfulness to her. And yet it was not without difficulties, without immense challenges to her heart. Her steadfastness in the face of everything inspires us, likewise, to know that surely, with every difficulty comes ease.[12] Not "in spite of" difficulty, but "with difficulty" which stretches our muscles of faith and forbearance, patience, and love. And as a dear friend pointed out recently, in the Arabic of this sustaining verse from *Surah al-Inshirah* ("The Opening Up of the Heart"), the grammatical article before the word for "ease" implies boundlessness for the ease, in the face of only measured difficulty, as though waves of the

[12] Quran, *Surah al-Inshirah* 94:6. *'Inna ma'al 'usri yusraa.*

Infinite Sea of God's Grace can easily overwhelm the dryness of constriction or barrenness.

It is said that Beloved Mary stayed with Elizabeth for three months; side by side these two dear ones went about the simple tasks of the house and garden, supporting each other in preparing their souls to receive these precious children into their arms, as they continued their worship, in wonder and awe at all the unfoldings of Grace. Beloved Mary was but a teenager, newly awakening to the blossoming of her body, though mature in the ways of the Lord; Elizabeth was already elderly, though physically more challenged, her quickening would bring blessing for her from the community, while Beloved Mary's might bring their calumny. Each supported the other in her travail.

And Mary abode with her about three months,
and returned to her own house.
[Bible, Gospel of Luke 1:56]

After the nine-month completion of Elizabeth's journey of pregnancy, Beloved Mary returned home to prepare for the birth of her own child. Someone else was being sent first, a son of Elizabeth and Zachariah, to prepare the way. Witnessing that joyous miracle, of a child in Elizabeth's old age, perhaps Beloved Mary thought, with God's help her people might understand the gift of her child, too. Surely, the knowledge of his presence coming into being within her was so perfectly immense, how could she hope that others would be able to comprehend, except through the inspiration from her Sustainer's voice in their hearts:

All this took place to fulfill what the Lord had said through the prophet:
"The virgin will conceive and give birth to a son,
and they will call him Immanuel" [which means "God with us"].
[Bible (NIV), Gospel of Matthew 1: 22–23]

The line of the *Magnificat* that praises God for filling "the hungry with good things" resonates with later words of the Gospel of Matthew: "Blessed are they who hunger and thirst after righteousness for they will be filled."[13] (Matthew 5:6). St Ambrose, reflecting on the *Magnificat*, said, "May the soul of Mary be in each one of us to glorify the Lord. May the

[13] See Bible, Gospel of Matthew 5:6.

spirit of Mary be in each one of us to rejoice in God."[14] Her practice encourages us to "stay hungry" for God's Presence. Is not glorification the practice of all the prophets, as was the practice of the Prophet Muhammad, the turning continually to acknowledge and offer praise to the Source of all Subsistence? In praising Beloved Mary, or praising the Prophet Muhammad, or other prophets and messengers of God, we are praising that Infinite Source held within them with awe, to which they are an open door; into that Presence of sustaining Love. It is not we who are self-sufficient, but the Divine Reality that is nourishing us moment by moment.

*Limitless in His/Her glory is your Sustainer, the Lord of Almightiness—*
*beyond anything by which they may try to define Him/Her!*
*And peace be with all His/Her messengers!*
*And all praise belongs to God alone, the Sustainer of all the Worlds!*
[Quran, *Surah as-Saffat*, "Those Ranged in Ranks," 37:180–82]

More and more aware of the Grace she carried within her womb, and with which she was continually nourished, Mary must have immersed ever more in glorification of her Lord, wondering at the increasing Light

---

[14] St. Ambrose, *Exposition of the Christian Faith*, as quoted by St. Louis de Montfort in his *True Devotion to Mary* (258). This section is often quoted, including by Pope John Paul II in his letter to the Montfort religious family, December 8, 2003. As St. Louis de Montfort encourages in this section of his True Devotion to the Blessed Virgin Mary: "We must do everything through Mary, that is, we must obey her always and be led in all things by her spirit, which is the Holy Spirit of God. . . . I have said that the spirit of Mary is the Spirit of God because she was never led by her own spirit, but always by the Spirit of God, who made himself master of her to such an extent that he became her very spirit. That is why St. Ambrose says, 'May the soul of Mary be in each one of us to glorify the Lord. May the spirit of Mary be in each one of us to rejoice in God.'"

"When we praise her, love her, honour her or give anything to her, it is God who is praised, God who is loved, God who is glorified, and it is to God that we give, through Mary and in Mary."

*Treatise on True Devotion to the Blessed Virgin*, n. 225. See http://www.catholictreasury.info/books/true_devotion/index.php, Part II, Chap. 7, 2 (258) and Chap. 6, 7 (225), accessed Aug 7, 2021. Also available through TAN books. Translated from the original French by Reverend Frederick William Faber, D.D., 1863.

she felt within and all around her. Rumi reminds us to feed on this radiant Light, immersing within the Presence of that One Who Is Light, *Ya Nur* ("O You Who Are Light")!

Feed on the Light, be like the eye,
be in harmony with the angels, O best of humankind.
Like the angel, make glorification of God your sustenance.
[Rumi, *Mathnawi* V: 295–98]

May we, also, make glorification of God our food that we might discover our own true meaning within the Magnificence of the Infinite Divine Reality and become ourselves that nourishing Light, *Nur ala Nur* ("Light upon Light")!

# *Blessed Maryam*[1]

A young woman,
betrothed to be married,
yet devoted,
still,
within the inner sanctuary
of the temple,
saw what seemed to be a man, suddenly,
within her chamber.
Quickly,
she sought refuge
with her Lord
from this apparent
intruder.
What was he doing here,
where no man should enter
except her cousin Zachariah,[2]
who attended her
so dearly?
Radiant with beauty, unearthly
handsomeness,
he, quickly,
sought to dispel
her fears;
and smiling he told her,

---

[1] Excerpt from *Exaltations*, "Songs of the Soul" series, by Camille Hamilton Adams Helminski, forthcoming from Sweet Lady Press.

[2] Zachariah was both Beloved Mary's maternal uncle and her cousin in the lineage of Aaron, as he was descended from the Chief Priest Abijah (descended from Aaron's son Eleazar), the head of the eighth of the twenty-four orders of the priesthood as designated by King David. See Bible, Chronicles 24:10.

"Blessed are you among women";[3]
*"I am but the servant*
*of your Lord.*
*I bring you good news—*
*of a son."*[4]
Startled,
she questioned,
"How can I have a son,
when no man has touched me
and I am not unchaste?"[5]
"Even so,
*for your Lord it is easy.*
Your Sustainer says:
*He shall be a symbol*
*for humankind*
*and an act of Grace*
*from Us.*"[6]
And surely,
a child
quickened
in her womb;
a son most pure
came to her bosom,
in nine months time
growing within her,
as with all mothers
birthed with travail,
and far deeper,
wringing her heart.
Yet, stars around her head, hovering,
covered her shoulders;
a stream emerged

---

[3] Bible, Gospel of Luke 1:28; Quran, *Surah al-'Imran*, "The House of 'Imran," 3:42.
[4] Bible, Gospel of Luke 1:29–31; Quran, *Surah Maryam* 19:17.
[5] Bible, Gospel of Luke 1:34; Quran, *Surah Maryam* 19:20; *Surah al-'Imran* 3:47.
[6] Quran, *Surah Maryam* 19:17–21.

from beneath a palm,
and dates cascaded
to feed her.[7]
All of nature
rose up
in support—
birds sang
and shepherds
played their flutes,
guiding flocks
to witness
a new arrival,
a Word of Spirit
made flesh.[8]
Far distant
stars journeyed
on camels,
the Wise arrived
bearing gifts.[9]
And to a doubtful
community
an infant spoke,
from deepest heart:
"I am the servant
of my Lord."
*And blessed is he*
*the day he is born*
*and the day he returns*[10]—
Everlasting
to Everlasting—
and never is the Word
of God

---

[7] Quran, *Surah Maryam* 19:23–26.
[8] Bible, Gospel of John 1:14; Quran, *Surah al-'Imran* 3:45.
[9] Bible, Gospel of Matthew 2:1, 2:9–11.
[10] Quran, *Surah Maryam,* 19:30–33.

lost or changed[11]—
intrinsic in purity—
That One Alone
knows our Name
and assists us all
in finding
our meaning
alive
with Him/Her,
The Creator of All Being,
Sustainer of All Worlds.[12]

---

[11] Quran, *Surah al-Kahf*, "The Cave," 18:27.
[12] *Rabb al-Alameen* : Quran, *Surah Yunus*, "Jonah," 10:10.

# V. FIFTH STAR OF BLESSING

## *Birthing Jesus*

# *Birthing Jesus*

*And so she conceived him, and she withdrew with him to a remote place.*
*And when the pains of childbirth drove her to the trunk of a palm tree,*
*she called out, "Oh would that I had died before this,*
*and that I were forgotten, utterly forgotten!"*
*Then a call came to her from below her saying,*
*"Do not grieve, your Lord has made for you a stream flowing out from beneath you.*
*And shake the trunk of the palm tree towards you,*
*and it will drop fresh, ripe dates upon you—*
*so eat and drink and cool your eye."*
[Quran, *Surah Maryam* 19:22–26]

The Quranic and Biblical accounts of the birth of Jesus differ in their details, but both recount the event with honor and sensitivity as resplendent with God's Grace and attendance by angels. In the Quran, Beloved Mary is alone during the throes of labor, and reaches out to a palm tree for support; this gentle woman is tested to the edge of endurance, both physically and emotionally as, unsure of what is to come, she struggles, alone, and yet supported by the emerging strength of the palm. As it is storied in the Bible, together with Joseph she finds refuge within the welcoming warmth of a stable, the abode of animals of service, creatures of sustenance. Whether she was alone or in the company of her betrothed, she was reliant upon her Lord, even in the midst of difficulty, trusting in the Breath of knowingness through which she had matured, now witnessing the fulfillment of the Word.

By the sun of July, old winter's chill transforms to heat;
by Mary's burning sighs a dry branch becomes a fruitful palm tree.
[Mevlana Jalaluddin Rumi, *Mathnawi* VI: 1290]

Within the Islamic tradition, it is understood that it was an angel who calls to her to look down and see the spring that has surfaced beneath her, to drink of it "and cool your eye." The date palm freshens and flourishes, all in a moment, and drops fresh ripe dates upon her. Once again she is provided for through the bestowal of Unseen Grace.

Rashid ud-Din Maybudi[1] emphasizes that it is her burning sighs that engender God's tender response, sustaining with beneficence both Mary, this dear mother in utter humility in the midst of the pain of birthing, and the palm tree, which it is said had dried and become apparently lifeless, but is now restored and made fruitful, even in the midst of winter, by the touch of Mary's hand in need of support:

> Maryam rose up in her weakness and seized the dry tree. When her hand touched the dry tree, it turned green, moist and fresh, bearing fruit, and in its freshness bent towards her. A Divine voice came saying, "We had the power so that even without your touching the tree it would have become green and bent towards you, but We wanted by your shaking it to bring forth two miracles; first was that in childbirth, weakness, and illness, We gave you power to shake the tree, which was to verify the miracle for you. The other was that We wanted the blessing of your hand to reach the tree so that it would bear fruit. Then the people of the world would understand that whoever is sad and grieved for Us, their hand is a remedy for pains."[2]

And "winter" again becomes "spring." Whosoever puts his (or her) trust in God, He will suffice him (or her).[3]

*Hold fast to the rope of God.*
[Quran, *Surah al-'Imran* 3:103]

---

[1] Rashid ud-Din Maybudi, an Iranian mystic of the twelfth century CE, is known especially for his extensive *tafsir* (exegesis) of the Quran: *The Unveiling of the Mysteries and the Provision of the Pious* (*Kashf al-asrar wa 'uddat al-abrar*). He spoke of ten fields of learning one must master before offering commentary on the Quran, the tenth and most important being knowledge not from study or acquisition, but from "divine bestowal and lordly inspiration" (*mawhibat-i ilahi wa ilham-i rabbani*).

[2] Al-Maybudi, *Kashf al-asrar wa 'uddat al-abrar*, ed. 'A. A. Hikmat, Tehran: Amir Kabir, 1982–3, vol 6, p. 42, as cited by Kristin Zahra Sands, *Sufi Commentaries on the Qur'an in Classical Islam*, op. cit., p. 105.

[3] Quran, *Surah at-Talaq* 65:3. *Tawakkaltu 'al Allah!* (*I trust in God!*) is a *zhikr* (chant of remembrance) that is of support in times of need.

*[One who] has faith in God has grasped the most trustworthy handhold*
*which shall never give way.*
*And God is All-Hearing, All-Knowing.*
[Quran, *Surah al-Baqarah* 2:256]

In the Biblical version of the story of the nativity, Mary gives birth in a stable, a simple wooden shelter, or in some versions, a cave (a quiet, safer place of retreat than the bustling caravanserai or inn), where she is welcomed by the animals to share their warmth and refuge. It had been necessary for Joseph and Mary to return to Bethlehem in the winter, because it was the year of the census that occurred every fourteen years under Roman rule; it had to be completed by the end of that December. Since Joseph was from the House of David, they must return to the home of the family lineage, to Bethlehem. From Nazareth to Bethlehem would have been about a week's journey in those days, so they would have had to set off by mid-December in order to arrive in time.

In those days a decree went out from Caesar Augustus
that all the world should be registered [for a census].
This was the first registration when Quirinius was governor of Syria.
And all went to be registered, each to his own [ancestral] town.
And Joseph also went up from Galilee, from the town of Nazareth,
to Judea, to the city of David, which is called Bethlehem,
because he was of the house and lineage of David,[4]

---

[4] Post-biblical tradition also recognizes Mary as a descendant of David, including Tertullian, Ambrose, Jerome, Hesichius of Jerusalem, and Pope Leo the Great. This is coincident with the Jewish tradition that a bridegroom (Joseph) would choose his bride from his own tribe, and intimates the arising of a noble one like David who would also be a savior of his people. In the "Litany of Loreto" composed in the Middle Ages in honor of Mary, she is referred to as the "Tower of David"—a tower of old Jerusalem mentioned in the Song of Songs to describe the beauty of the bride. Chapter four of the Song begins:

Behold, you are beautiful, my love, behold, you are beautiful!
Your eyes are doves behind your veil. . . .
Your lips are like a scarlet [ribbon], and your mouth is lovely.
Your cheeks are like halves of a pomegranate behind your veil.
Your neck is like the tower of David, built in rows of stone . . .
Until the day breathes and the shadows flee,
I will go away to the mountain of myrrh and the hill of frankincense.

to be registered with Mary, his betrothed, who was with child.
And while they were there, the time came for her to give birth.
And she gave birth to her firstborn son
and wrapped him in swaddling cloths and laid him in a manger,
because there was no place for them in the inn.
And in the same region there were shepherds out in the field,
keeping watch over their flock by night.
And an angel of the Lord appeared to them,
and the glory of the Lord shone around them,
and they were filled with great fear.
And the angel said to them, "Fear not, for behold,
I bring you good news of great joy that will be for all the people.
For unto you is born this day in the city of David a Savior,
who is Christ the Lord.
And this will be a sign for you:
you will find a baby wrapped in swaddling cloths and lying in a manger."
And suddenly there was with the angel a multitude of the heavenly host
praising God and saying, "Glory to God in the highest,
and on earth peace among those with whom he is pleased!"
[Bible (ESV), Gospel of Luke 2:1–14]

In the Biblical version, also, the angelic and natural world rise up in support. The mystery of the majesty of the womb of Mary is celebrated with the third joyful rosary remembrance of the birth of Jesus.

A *hadith* relates several moments in the Prophet Muhammad's Night Journey (*'Isra*) to Jerusalem and Ascension (*Miraj*) when he is told by Angel Gabriel to stop and offer a prayer, and Gabriel asks him if he recognizes the locations. One of these places Muhammad, peace and blessings upon him, indicates as being "Bethlehem, the place where Isa was born."[5] In honor of the birthplace of Jesus, the companion of the Prophet Muhammad, Abdullah ibn 'Amr ibn al-'As, used to send lamp oil to the churches in Bethlehem (Bayt Lahm), located about six miles south of Jerusalem.[6]

---

You are altogether beautiful, my love; there is no flaw in you.
[Bible (ESV), Song of Solomon 4:1–7]

[5] Nasa'i, Sunan, 222, *Kitab as-Salat*; Suyuti, *Ihtaf*, II, 16. as cited by Aliah Schleifer in *Mary The Blessed Virgin of Islam*, op. cit., p. 34.

[6] Al-Suyuti, Muhammad ibn Shihab al-Din. *Ihtaf al-Akhissa bi Fada'il al-Masjid*

In both the Quran and in the Bible the account of Jesus's birth, whether in a stable, in a cave, or in the desert under a palm tree, is related to have taken place in a lowly, simple place, with nature awake and aware, the stars witnessing with their light, or the fertile grace of the palm with water bubbling up from beneath her to quench Beloved Mary's thirst. In the Christian tradition, also, there is a beautiful story of the emergence of a spring for her, on the road to Bethlehem. Though much of the Christian tradition describes the birth as occurring with ease, there is acknowledgment of the difficulty of the journey to Bethlehem while Beloved Mary was so heavily pregnant with child; just a few miles from there it is said they paused, and Joseph lifted her down from the donkey that she might rest upon a large rock for a while. Another sign of sustaining Love emerged in a spring of clear water there, as she rested, beside the road from Jerusalem. The legendary church of Kathisma was later built at this place of miraculous generosity.

The ruins of the original Kathisma, which had long been a place of pilgrimage in remembrance of Mary before it was developed in the fifth to sixth centuries CE into the renowned Byzantine church, were only recently rediscovered near Mar Elias Monastery, just to the side of the ancient road from Jerusalem to Bethlehem. Nearby is the revered tomb of beloved Rachel who died there giving birth to Prophet Joseph's younger brother, Benjamin, also while journeying—Mary would have been quite familiar with this story and aware of the honored presence of beloved Rachel, so loved by her husband Jacob (who became known as Israel).[7]

"Kathisma" in Greek means "seat" or "place of rest." It was noted in the Protoevangelium Gospel of James that Mary and Joseph, while on their way from Nazareth, stopped here to rest when nearing Bethlehem, but the exact location had been lost in recent centuries. During road expansion work in 1992, its foundational ruins were rediscovered under the soil of an adjacent olive grove, and some years later, identified as the

---

*al-Aqsa*, ed. Ahmad Ramadan Ahmad, Cairo: Matabi al-Hay'at al-Misriyyat al-'Amma li'l-Kitab, 1982–84, II, 16. Ibid.

[7] Rachel's tomb continues to be the third most holy site of Judaism, after the Temple Mount and the Wailing Wall (and the Machpelah Cave of the Patriarchs and Matriarchs in Hebron), held in even greater reverential respect than Mt. Sinai where Moses received the Ten Commandments, the fourth most holy site. This gracious lady continues to welcome pilgrims of Jewish, Christian, and Muslim faith who pause with her in prayer and love of God.

lost Kathisma.[8] Locals said that a beautiful, ancient tree still remained there until the seventeenth century, one that recognized the travail of this beloved mother-to-be and lowered its branches to shield the pregnant Mary from the sun's heat, near the spring of fresh water that had opened for her; some Christians say the original tree was a palm tree. Some say the church of Kathisma, the "seat" of Mary, was the first church in the world dedicated entirely to the Virgin Mary, or at least in the Holy Land, for Santa Maria Maggiore,[9] an earlier church built in Rome, also claims such an honor, as does Basilica di Santa Maria in Trastevere.[10] Perhaps on the return trip the holy family rested there, and beloved Mary drank again from the spring that had burst from a nearby rock to quench her thirst.

The octagonal Kathisma church was built over that blessed rock, in honor of Mary's resting there, in the mid fifth century CE,[11] by a wealthy widow, Iqilia, who was devoted to her. It seems that the Caliph 'Abd al-Malik may have been inspired by this well-beloved church when he

---

[8] See: https://www.jpost.com/Travel/Around-Israel/Kathisma-A-place-of-rest-on-the-way-to-Bethlehem.

[9] The church on the site of Santa Maria Maggiore has had several names, known as "Santa Maria Liberiana," and also "Our Lady of the Snow"—Pope Liberius oversaw its building according to Mary's instructions which he received in a vision of her, matching the floor to the shape of a miraculous snow that fell there in the fourth century CE. It was also called "Saint Mary of the Nativity" due to a precious relic that was brought there, said to be a portion of the wooden manger in which Jesus rested after his birth. As the largest of twenty-six churches in Rome named for Mary, it became known as "Santa Maria Maggiore."

[10] The Church of Our Lady in Trastevere is one of the very oldest churches of Rome. The first sanctuary was built in 221 CE, and the basic structure of the church dates to the mid fourth century, long a place of worship under Mary's blessing. In the twelfth century, the facade was reconstructed with a mosaic frieze high up over the doorways; Beloved Mary is depicted enthroned in the center, nursing her infant Jesus, attended by ten maidens, five to each side, carrying lamps. Below her are fruiting palms, bearing abundant dates. The adjacent *campanile* (bell tower) was then also graced with an alcoved mosaic of Beloved Mary holding her blessed infant, that every burst of the bell might resonate through her heart, spreading her compassion throughout the city.

[11] *The Life of Theodosius*, written in the sixth century by hagiographer Cyril of Scythopolis, mentions the building of the church in 456 CE, not long after the Council of Ephesus.

had the architecture of the Dome of the Rock in Jerusalem designed in the late seventh century, the third most holy site for Muslims after the Kaaba in Mecca and the Prophet's Mosque in Medina. It was also built as an octagonal structure sheltering a blessed rock—the place where Prophet Muhammad stood on his Night Journey[12] before ascending through the heavens into the Presence of God, up to two bow lengths or nearer, where his eye did not swerve[13] as he came face to Face with the Divine Reality.

Archaeological evidence indicates that the Kathisma was frequented both as a church and as a mosque by pilgrims on the road, still in the eighth century housing both an altar to the east and a *mihrab* facing south, serving both Christians and Muslims. Both walked upon her gracious mosaic floors covered with palm tree and flower patterns, under the welcoming auspices of Mary, and drank from the spring that continued to provide refreshing water.

There is an account from a visit by a Christian pilgrim in 570 CE from the city of Piacenza who marveled at the water freely pouring forth: "There, in the middle of the road, I saw standing water coming out of a

---

[12] See *Surah al-'Isra*:

*Limitless in His Glory is He who transported His servant by night*
*from the Sacred Mosque [Al-Masjid al-Haram in Mecca]*
*to the Farthest Mosque [Al-Aqsa in Jerusalem], whose environs We have blessed—*
*in order that We might show [Muhammad] some of Our signs—*
*for truly, He [God] is the One who is All-Hearing and All-Seeing."*
[Quran, *Surah al-'Isra*, "The Night Journey," 17:1]

After this *'Isra*, Prophet Muhammad ascended through the heavens into the Presence of God (the *Miraj*). The Dome of the Rock (Qubbat as-Sakhra) was built over the rock that bears his footprint, the place from which he rose into the heavens.

[13] See *Surah an-Najm*:

*Then he approached and came close, until he was but two bow-lengths apart or nearer.*
*And so God revealed to His servant that which He considered right to convey.*
*In no way did the heart deny that which he saw . . .*
*For indeed he saw him a second time near the Lote-tree beyond which none may pass,*
*near which is the garden of promise.*
*Behold, the Lote-tree was veiled in a veil of nameless splendor;*
*his eye never wavered nor did it stray! For truly did he see the finest signs of his Sustainer!*
[Quran, *Surah an-Najm*, "The Star," 53:8–18]

rock, to be taken at one's discretion up to seven pints; everyone takes their fill and it never diminishes nor becomes more full. It is of an indescribable sweetness to drink."[14] The Arabic name—Bir Qadismu—of a reservoir of water that is still nearby, has preserved the "Kathisma" designation.

The story of these springs reminds us, also, of Abraham and the story of Hagar and Ishmael in the desert. There is an echo of the moment when Hagar (the Egyptian handmaiden of his first wife, Sarah, whom she gifted to Abraham when she could not conceive a child) was running across the hills of Safa and Marwah, distraught, when she had been left by Abraham in the desert to rely only upon God; she was desperately searching and praying to God for water for her infant, Ishmael, whom she feared might die of thirst. It is told that on the seventh journey between the hills, she suddenly witnessed how Ishmael, while crying, had dug his heel into the sand, and water had begun bubbling up from a hidden spring. She cried, "Stop, stop!" ("*Zam, zam!*"), that the water might remain. The city of Mecca grew up around this spring of Hagar and Ishmael, and, even after several thousand years, the Zamzam spring continues to pour forth fresh sweet water in the midst of the brackish region, supplying pure water to all those who come for the Hajj pilgrimage and re-enact her search as part of their ritual. The Prophet Muhammad is descended from Ishmael, son of Abraham. Everyone who makes the pilgrimage to Mecca pauses for an offering of prayer at the "Station of Abraham," where it is said this grandfather of Jews, Christians, and Muslims placed his foot as he lifted the stone to begin the building of the Kaaba with Ishmael.

Some say Prophet Abraham was, also, born in a simple cave, due to the persecution of another tyrant feeling threatened by the prophecy of the approaching birth of one who would put an end to idolatry, which might include the tyrant's own egoistic reign. Abraham's mother gave birth and hid him in the cave where it is said he was tended in obscurity for years until it was safe for her to bring him forth. In the midst of difficulty, there is grace; when he was grown and stood for Truth, the tyrant Nimrod attempted to catapult him into a raging fire, but through God's blessing

---

[14] *The Piacenza Pilgrim* 28, translation by Andrew Jacobs, from the critical edition of P. Geyer in *Itineraria et alia geographica*, Corpus Christianorum series Latina volume 175 (Turnhout: Brepols, 1965), pp. 129–53. See http://andrewjacobs.org/translations/piacenzapilgrim.html.

it became cool,[15] even a garden of roses or, as some say, the flames of the fire turned to water and the burning logs became golden fish. It is said the progeny of those fish now swim in a pool nearby the Halil ur-Rahman Mosque,[16] built there long ago in Şanlıurfa, also in present-day Turkey. Continually Abraham trusted in God; he was of those who say: "God is sufficient for me, He is the Best Arranger of my affairs."[17]

Mary would have known the traditions of Abraham well, and might also in pilgrimage have visited the tombs of the Patriarchs and Matriarchs at Machpelah,[18] aware of how we move from dust to dust on this human

---

15 *We said: "O fire! Be thou cool, and [a source of] inner peace for Abraham!"* See Quran, *Surah al-Anbiya* 21:69.

16 *Halil ur-Rahman:* "Beloved Friend of the Infinitely Compassionate." Abraham is referred to as the "Friend of God" both in the Bible (e.g.: James 2:23, Isaiah 41:8,) and in the Quran:

> *And who could be of better faith than he who surrenders his whole being unto God*
> *and is a doer of good withal, and follows the creed of Abraham,*
> *who turned away from all that is false—*
> *seeing that God exalted him to be His beloved friend?*
> *For, unto God belongs all that is in the heavens and all that is on earth;*
> *and, indeed, God encompasses everything.*
> [Quran, *Surah an-Nisa* 4:125–26]

> *Abraham was neither a "Jew" nor a "Christian,"*
> *but was one who turned away from all that is false,*
> *having surrendered himself unto God*
> [Quran, *Surah al-'Imran* 3:67]

> . . . *the place whereon Abraham once stood—whoever enters it finds inner peace*
> [Quran, *Surah al-'Imran* 3:97]

17 Quran, *Surah al-'Imran* 3:173.

18 The Cave of Machpelah shelters the tombs of Sarah and Abraham, Rebeccah and Isaac (son of Sarah and Abraham), and Rebeccah and Isaac's son Jacob and his first wife, Leah. Ishmael and Isaac came together there to bury their father, Abraham; it was Abraham who had first arranged Sarah's burial in the cave he had purchased. Ishmael and his mother Hagar rest beside the Kaaba, within the Hijr Isma'il, the adjacent half-moon circle. The Kaaba is believed by Muslims to be the first Temple to the Oneness of God (see Quran, *Surah al-Hajj*, "The Pilgrimage," 22:32–35, pp. 40–41 of this text), built by Abraham with Ishmael's help, about a thousand years before the building of the Temple of Solomon, and signifies the intimate and yet infinite expanse of the human heart, where we are closest to God.

journey,[19] yet are always held in grace within the cave of the heart where we are closest to our Sustainer.

*And put your trust in God,*
*for God is sufficient as your Guardian.*
[Quran, *Surah al-Ahzab* 33:3]

[And] Mary kept all these things and pondered them in her heart.
[Bible, Gospel of Luke 2:19]

*For the one who remains conscious of God;*
*He always prepares a way of emergence*
*and He provides for him/her in ways he/she could never imagine.*
*And if anyone puts his/her trust in God, sufficient is God for him/her.*
*For God will surely accomplish His purpose:*
*truly, for all things has God appointed an appropriate measure.*
[Quran, *Surah at-Talaq* 65:2–3]

In the early days of Christianity, there were many ways of understanding the being of Jesus and Mary and how divinity and humanity intermingled.[20] Some, like Hippolytus of Rome say that in the moment of Christ's

---

[19] See Abraham's counsel to his people in Quran, *Surah al-Ankabut* 29:17: *Seek, then, all sustenance from God, and worship Him and be grateful to Him: unto Him you shall all be brought back!*

[20] Ancient texts continue to be discovered that affect how we understand the early faith communities. With further Biblical study, current scholarship now dates the Gospel of Mark to about 57–65 CE, written some decades after the passing of Jesus, the Gospel of Matthew to 75–90 CE, Luke to 60–70 CE, and John to 90 CE or close to 150 CE (perhaps written by a student of his), though some passages it is considered may be earlier, perhaps 135 CE. See Extended Context Notes in Appendix, Star V, 1.

There are also many apocryphal writings from the first two centuries after the birth of Jesus (estimated now to have been about 4 BCE, before the passing of King Herod), some portions of which remain or have been newly rediscovered in recent decades. Among these are the Protoevangelium of James (the original most likely dates from the second century CE; among other aspects, it exalts the perpetual virginity of Mary and mentions her stepchildren from Joseph's previous marriage), the Infancy Gospel of Thomas (which relates stories of the early life of Jesus), the Gospel of Pseudo Matthew, the Arabic Gospel of the Infancy, The Nativity of Mary, The Passing of Mary (*Transitus Mariae*), the Gospel of Peter,

birth, "God was made man and man was made God." This is a fundamental belief of many Christians, and yet how it has been understood has varied over the centuries, by sect and by personal faith. For instance, some Protestant Christian denominations emphasize the humanity of Christ in service over his divinity. A woman in the late eighteenth century in Colonial America, Hannah Adams, compiled *A Dictionary of All Religions and Religious Denominations*, a fascinating tome (and the first of its kind) in which she describes hundreds of Christian sects and communities, with varied beliefs, which sometimes developed for political or societal reasons, as well as Judaism, mystical Islam—Sufism—and further eastern faiths.[21] Mary was at first referred to as *Christotokos*, "Bearer of Christ," which would be more synchronous with the Islamic view; it was not until after the Council of Ephesus, in 432 CE, when in a further effort to regularize faith and to counter the Nestorian perspective of Jesus, as more profoundly human, that Mary was more often referred to as *Theotokos*, "Bearer of God."

---

etc., all of which added stories where the official canon was silent.

Judea was under Roman rule from 4 BCE until 324 CE. In 325 CE, Emperor Constantine legalized Christianity, began the era of Byzantine rule and to regularize the tenets of faith called together church leaders; many of them wanted to refute Christian Arianism—which held that Jesus was created by God and not co-eternal with Him, a finite created being with some divine attributes. Though Constantine felt the determination of such beliefs was best left to the individual heart, nevertheless, this "Council of Nicea" was held, near Iznik in what is now Turkey, and the Nicene Creed, establishing the tenet of the Holy Trinity, was formulated, thereafter predominating the Christian view.

Texts like the Dead Sea Scrolls (dated from the second century BCE to the second century CE)—the first ones discovered in 1947 in desert caves by a young Bedouin shepherd—enlighten us as to various earlier Jewish sects including the Essenes, pure mystics of the desert, who are said to have influenced John the Baptist and possibly Jesus, himself. With Hebrew language like that of the Psalms, these manuscripts are a thousand years older than any previously discovered Old Testament texts (most of which have been dated to the tenth or eleventh century CE), and include non-canonical Jewish texts like "Jubilees" and "I Enoch"; among the scrolls are text fragments also written in Aramaic, Greek, Latin, and Arabic (see *Dead Sea Scrolls Bible* by Martin Abegg, Peter Flint, and Eugene Ulrich and https://www.deadseascrolls.org.il/ for reference).

[21] Hannah Adams (1755–1831), was a pioneer in the field of comparative religion, attempting in her work to present to her readers each religion as a practitioner might speak of it, rather than from a biased premise, sharing the amazing diversity. See Extended Context Notes in Appendix, Star V, 2.

Rumi's mentor, Shams of Tabriz, reflects on a saying of the Prophet Muhammad that can be of help for Muslims in understanding something of the Christian perspective on the being of Jesus, for whom most Muslims have the utmost respect and reverence and yet do not generally view him as "Divine," but as an incomparably pure prophet and servant of God, the "Messiah," born of the purest of virgins. Christians and Muslims actually have so much in common in their honoring of Jesus and his miraculous birth. Shams says:

> Thousands of useless words have been spoken about, "When poverty is complete, he is God" [a *hadith*, a traditional saying of Prophet Muhammad]. But if there is no blasphemy in the words, then it means that "when poverty [*fakr*] is completed, God appears; you find Him and see Him." If the meaning isn't that, then what difference can there be between you and a Christian? For Jesus was subtler than Mansur al-Hallaj, Bayazid,[22] and others. Why blame a Christian because he says that Jesus is God or he is God's son, when you are saying something similar. The meaning of the words, "When poverty is completed, God appears" is like the meaning in the words, "Whoever's *nafs* [commanding, egoistic self] dies, his 'Satan' also dies; having been cleared of harmful traits, he reaches God." But this attainment is not, God forbid, reaching the Self [*Dhat*] of God, but rather to enter upon His way. The servant understands that he has not attained God, but that he has only entered upon the way of God. . . . The one who can't distinguish the difference between the Light of the way of God and the Light of the Self of God, continues in darkness and is blind.
>
> God Most High has seven hundred veils of light or seven hundred thousand coverings; when it is said that if one of these veils were opened it would burn both the world and those who are in it, then the question arises, "Which veil is it that when it is gradually removed, one can reach the Divine Light of the Self, one can reach the Light that shines from the Essence?"
>
> "Ablution upon ablution is light upon light" means light upon light pours down upon one who is birthed into a state of ablution who

[22] Mansur al-Hallaj and Bayazid al-Bastami were two of the greatest mystics of Islam, who immersed in the Divine Presence.

> cleanses his inner self. It doesn't mean you should make the ablutions[23] twice. . . .
>
> God has a fragrance that comes to one's nose like the fragrance of musk and ambergris, but how could it ever really be like ambergris and musk? When God wants to manifest Himself to His servant, that fragrance can be sensed—it makes one drunk to the point of fainting. These words never come to an end.[24]

A little further in his discourses Shams continues:

> Those who call Jesus the "Son of God," don't say that he broke off from God by means of copulation. Perhaps it is like several other examples of "birth." Let's say that "this word" has been "born" from such and such a person. This does not mean "it was born" in the usual sense.[25]
>
> All the prophets confirm each other. Jesus says: "O Jews, you don't know Moses well; come and be with me so that you may also know Moses." Muhammad (may God's peace be upon him) used to say: "O Christians and Jews, you don't know Moses and Jesus very well. Come and be with me so that you may also know them better. All prophets accept and confirm each other. And their words are always words that explain and complete each other." If you had seen Moses, you would also find him in Muhammad.[26]

All the prophets have relied upon the Infinite blessings of Divine Reality and through those blessings supported their communities. Even as they considered the poor among them and were blessed, when we align with these "poor ones," the noble *faqirs* of God, we, too, are blessed with such abundance of Spirit. The prophets recognized that it is God who is *Al-Ghani, Al-Mughni* ("The One Who Is Truly Rich, the Enricher of Hearts")!

Blessed is the one who considers the poor!
In the day of trouble the Lord delivers him;

---

[23] "Ablutions" are the pattern of ritual washing and purification of the body that precedes the offering of prayer in the Islamic tradition.
[24] *Rumi's Sun,* translated by Algan and Helminski (Threshold Books), pp. 157–58.
[25] Ibid., pp. 164–65.
[26] Ibid., p. 10.

the Lord protects him and keeps him alive;
he is called blessed in the land;
you do not give him up to the will of his enemies.
[Bible (ESV), Psalms 41:1–2]

In the biography of Beloved Mary by Maximus, it is related that the birth happened, like the conception, in a miraculous way, without pain; that Mary even remained a Virgin throughout that moment and the remainder of her life; that Elizabeth was with her to assist in the birth, confirming again her sanctity. Yet even in the Biblical story, it is acknowledged that Mary carried her child for nine months,[27] and like every natural mother endured the challenges of pregnancy. Mevlana Rumi reminds us that the universe and every human being is created by this gradual process; that every creation is a journey, and that the pain of birth has its purpose:

Wasn't God able to create heaven in one moment by the word "*Be*"?[28]
Without a doubt He was.
Why, then, O you who seek to be taught,
did He extend the time to six days—
every day as long as a thousand years?
Why is the creation of a child completed in nine months?
Because gradualness is a characteristic of the action of that Sovereign.
[Rumi, *Mathnawi* VI: 1213–15]

The human being has a guide at hand for every endeavor. Nothing can be undertaken until a pain—a yearning and love for a thing—is awakened inside him or her. Without pain one's endeavor will not be easy, no matter whether it be this-worldly, other-worldly, commercial, regal, scholarly, astrological or anything else. Mary did not go to the blessed tree until she experienced birthpangs: *and the pains of childbirth came upon her near the trunk of a palm tree* [*Surah Maryam* 19:23]. Pain brought her to the tree, and the dry tree bore fruit. Our body is like Mary, and each of us bears a Jesus. If we experience birth pains, our

---

[27] The number nine in the Sufi tradition is indicative of completion.
[28] Qur'an: *Surah Ya Sin*, "O Thou Human Being," 36:81–82: *He alone is the All-Knowing Creator: His Being alone is such that when He wills a thing to be, He but says to it, "Be!" and it is.*

> Jesus will be born; but if there is no pain, our Jesus will return to his origin by that hidden road whence he came, and we will remain deprived.[29]

In other words, as a dear friend in Turkey often encourages, in resonance with the reflections of Rumi: "Let the Mary of your body give birth to the Jesus[30] of your spirit." So strive in this precious striving—be willing to endure the pain that brings the blessing of birthing the beauty and true meaning of one's innermost spirit. Another beloved saying of the Prophet Muhammad is "Paradise is at the feet of mothers." One might consider this both from the point of view of the children, whether actual or spiritual—sitting at the feet of their teacher who is to them like a most devoted mother—and from the point of view of the mother, giving birth to her child, experiencing the joy of nurturing her children; may we each give birth to that pure Essence that is within us, that we might enter and abide in the Garden beneath which rivers flow.[31]

---

[29] Mevlana Jalaluddin Rumi, *Fihi ma Fihi*, excerpt from Discourse 5 of *Signs of the Unseen*, op. cit., pp. 22–23 (adapted by the author).

[30] "Jesus," is the Greek form of the Hebrew name "Joshua"—the stalwart companion of Moses who succeeded him as leader of the Israelites and brought them into the Promised Land. The name "Joshua" and so, also, "Jesus," has the meaning of "YAHWEH is salvation" (*Yehoshu'a*)—from the ancient Hebrew, from the books of Ezra and Nehemiah in the Hebrew Bible—or in other words, "he shall save." In the time of Jesus, his name would have more likely been pronounced "Yeshua," and conveyed the blessing of God's Presence: "For in him, all the fullness of God was pleased to dwell" (Bible, Colossians 1:19). In birthing "Jesus," we would be birthing the purest of qualities with which we are endowed through the Breath and Presence of God within us, bringing forth God's "Word," that we might be welcomed into the Garden of Truth (*Haqq*). As Shams of Tabriz says, "Every human being is a 'Word of God'—which 'word' are you?"

[31] The word for Paradise in the Quran is *Jannah* which means "Garden," reminding us of the blessing of fertility and fruitfulness, the greenness and beauty that is healing to the eye, the blessing of fragrance, the gift of streaming water, and the play of Light, engendered and supported by Love.

*Those who have faith and do righteous deeds—it is they who are the best of creatures.*
*Their recompense is with God: gardens of perpetual felicity beneath which rivers flow—*
*they will dwell there forever; God well-pleased with them and they with Him:*
*all this for those who stand in awe of their Sustainer.*
[Quran *Surah al-Bayyinah* 98:7–8]

In the midst of the desert, the grace of gardens in the Middle East has been continually enhanced by palm trees. The palm tree in the Islamic tradition is much revered; for people of the Middle East who so much have relied upon its bounty it is seen as "the Tree of Life." According to a *hadith*, it was originally created from the earth remaining in God's hands after the creation of Adam, giving sustenance to human beings for the moments in which we pass through this world. The Prophet Muhammad once said, "I am a stranger in this world, just a traveler pausing for a few moments under a palm tree."

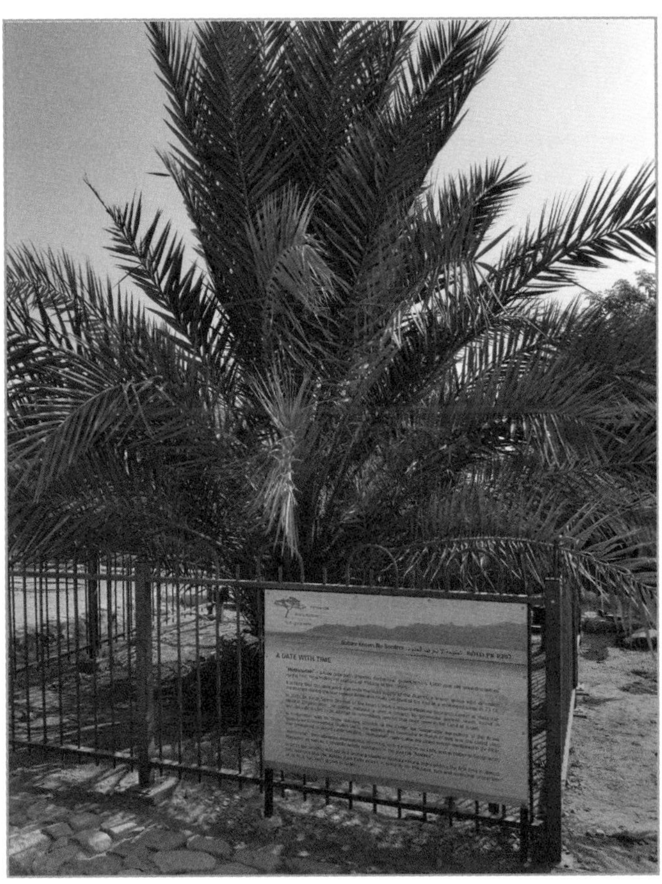


*Methusaleh Date Palm*
*(Sprouted from a 2,000-year-old seed)*

The palm, truly one of the most ancient of trees, is such a stalwart source of life; the life-force of their seeds can even last two thousand years. While exploring an archeological archive, a scientist recently discovered some ancient palm seeds in a clay pot from Jerusalem at the time of Jesus. She at last received permission to attempt to plant a couple, and miraculously, after two thousand years of dormancy, one sprouted and resurrected into a magnificent tree.[32] An infant palm returns, of ancient seed preserved, from among the community of Jesus—named "Methusaleh"! Miracles never cease; why would we think so?

The fruit of the righteous is a tree of life.
[Bible, Proverbs 11:30]

Both in the Bible and in the Quran, a "good word" is likened to a tree, bearing good fruit.

Gentle words are a tree of life.
[Bible, Proverbs 15:4][33]

*Those who have faith and do righteous deeds*
*will be brought into gardens beneath which running waters flow,*
*there to dwell by their Sustainer's consent,*

---

[32] See "'Methuselah' Palm Grown From 2,000-Year-Old Seed Is a Father." Ten years after sprouting from an ancient seed, the date palm is "a big boy now," a scientist says—"and, yeah, he can make dates." By John Roach, *National Geographic*, March 24, 2015: https://www.nationalgeographic.com/science/article/150324-ancient-methuselah-date-palm-sprout-science.

In the years following, several more seeds were located from other archaelogical sites including Qumran (where the Dead Sea Scrolls had been found); of these several more date palms were sprouted and one, then named Hannah as it was a female, was cross-pollinated with Methusaleh, and in August 2020 Hannah bore good fruit after two thousand years! The renowned Judaen dates from the time of Jesus have resurrected (and came to fruition within the Kibbutz of Keturah).

Truly, this was a moment when one might offer the *Shehcheyanu*, a blessing recorded in the Talmud giving thanks to *HaShem*: "*Baruch atah, Adonai Eloheinu, Melech haolam, shehecheyanu, v'kiy'manu, v'higiyanu laz'man hazeh.*" ("Blessed are You, Adonai our God, Sovereign of all, who has kept us alive, sustained us, and brought us to this season.")

[33] *Holy Bible*, New Living Translation, copyright © 1996, 2004, 2015 by Tyndale House Foundation. Used by permission of Tyndale House Publishers, Inc., Carol Stream, Illinois 60188. All rights reserved.

*and will be welcomed with the greeting, "Peace!"*
*Are you not aware how God offers the parable of a good word?*
*It is like a good tree, firmly rooted,*
*reaching its branches towards the sky,*
*always yielding fruit, by consent of its Sustainer.*
*This is how God offers parables to human beings,*
*so that they might consider the truth.*
[Quran, *Surah Ibrahim* 14:23–25]

Many are the gifts of trees and the earth. It is said that some of the most beneficial were brought to honor Jesus's arrival by the wise ones, "kings" of the East. Some say these were magi, of the priestly class of the Parthian Empire, who it is said had journeyed following an unusually bright star they understood to foretell the birth of a being of Light, a "king" among the Jews.[34]

Now when Jesus was born in Bethlehem of Judaea
in the days of Herod the king,
behold, there came wise men from the east to Jerusalem, . . .
and behold, the star which they had seen in the East went before them,
till it came and stood over where the young child was.
When they saw the star they were filled with great joy.
[Bible, Gospel of Matthew 2:1, 9–10]

Al-Tabari (d. 923 CE), an Islamic historian, also mentions these envoys being sent by the King of Persia with gifts for the "Messiah."

---

[34] We are reminded of the prophecy in Psalms 72:4–12:

He shall judge the poor of the people, he shall save the children of the needy,
and shall break in pieces the oppressor.
They shall [be in awe of thee] as long as the sun and moon endure,
throughout all generations.
He shall come down like rain upon the mown grass:
as showers that water the earth.
In his days shall the righteous flourish;
and abundance of peace so long as the moon endures. . . .
The kings of Tarshish and of the isles shall bring presents:
the kings of Sheba and Seba shall offer gifts. . . .
For he shall deliver the needy when he cries;
the poor also, and him that has no helper.

*Frankincense*

Only three birth gifts are specifically mentioned in the Bible, brought by these wise ones: gold, frankincense, and myrrh, all with profound healing capacities. Gold, the purest of metals, immutable, the standard for truth, is anti-inflammatory and antibacterial; myrrh, a tree resin, also, is anti-inflammatory, antiseptic, antibacterial, and was precious for purification and for embalming the dead; frankincense (boswellia), another resin, is also anti-inflammatory and contributes to bone and joint health; it helps to strengthen respiration, essential breath, and is prized as incense for sanctifying spaces with its beautiful purifying fragrance. Frankincense, this precious substance from Southern Arabia (now Yemen) was traded by the sons of Abraham (he who had been enlightened by Melchizedek),[35] by his third wife, Keturah, and the generations beyond him. Frankincense and myrrh are helpful for strengthening gums and protecting teeth—a root of the health of our brains. All three substances are anti-carcinogenic as they protect the cells of the body against harmful growth that would usurp the healthy cells' functioning, protecting the body from inner structural tyranny. All three support clarity of body, mind, and heart, gifts of our Sustainer that move us towards rebirth in Truth. These three gifts are an indication of who this child would be, honoring this new being who would bring healing among humankind. Maximus reminds us that we might take this as a model for what we might offer as gifts to humanity: "offer a good and holy character as gold. . . comprehension and spiritual insight as frankincense, and mortification of the passions [purification of desires and egoistic cravings] . . . as myrrh,"[36] in order that we might receive the kingdom of Heaven. In Ecclesiasticus we are reminded of all the blessings and beauty of healing gardens where Holy Wisdom is exalted in fertile abundance:

I [Holy Wisdom] was exalted like a cedar in Lebanon,
and as a cypress tree upon the mountains of Hermon.
I was exalted like a palm tree in En-Gaddi, and as a rose plant in Jericho,
as a fair olive tree in a pleasant field,
and grew up as a plane tree by the water.
I gave a sweet smell like cinnamon and aspalathus,
and I yielded a pleasant scent like the best myrrh,
as galbanum, and onyx, and sweet storax,
and as the fume of frankincense in the tabernacle.
As the turpentine tree I stretched out my branches,
and my branches are the branches of honor and grace.
As the vine brought I forth pleasant savor,
and my flowers are fruit of honor and riches.
I am the mother of fair love, and awe, and knowledge, and holy hope:

---

[35] Melchizedek the "king" (*melek*) of "righteousness" (*zedek* or *sedek*, or, in Arabic, *siddiq*). Some scholars understand his name as "My King is Righteousness" or "My Lord is Righteousness" referring to his pure alignment with righteousness and trustworthiness. See Extended Context Notes, Star V, 3.

[36] Maximus, *The Life of the Virgin*, op. cit., p. 69.

*Myrrh*

I therefore, being eternal, am given to all my children
which are named of him [the Creator, Most High].
Come unto me, all you that are desirous of me,
and fill yourselves with my fruits.
[Ecclesiasticus (Sirach) 24:13–19][37]

[37] Ecclesiasticus, or "Book of Wisdom" of Sirach is included in the Septuagint ("The Translation of the Seventy")—the first translation into Greek of the Torah (Pentateuch or first five books of the Hebrew Bible) with accompanying Old Testament apocrypha—ordered by Ptolemy II Philadelphus (285–247 BCE), and completed by seventy scholars, six from each of the twelve tribes of Israel. It used to be included between the Old and New Testaments of the Bible but in recent centuries has been omitted. Manuscript copies of Ecclesiasticus were found among the Dead Sea Scrolls of Qumran. In the midst of a harsh wilderness, En-Gaddi (in line 3) is an oasis, watered by four springs, a place of fertile palms and flowing waters.

We are reminded of the three holy names of God among the well-loved Ninety-Nine Names of God in the Islamic tradition that express the movement of the creative process: *Al-Khaliq*, *Al-Bari*, *Al-Musawwir*: the Creator, the Patterner or Evolver, the Fashioner of Form—comprehending the One who fashions the brightness of the brightest star in the night shining, and the smallest seed of being in the depths of the earth, and the tiniest microbe in the deep darkness of the oceans, and the beauties of holiness from the womb of the morning.[38] And we are moved to cry out in awe, "All that palpates with being in any moment is Yours, of Your Making, Your Breath and Your Love, O God!"

Therefore God, your God, has anointed you
with the oil of gladness beyond your companions;
your robes are all fragrant with myrrh and aloes and cassia.[39]
[Bible (ESV), Psalms 45:7–8]

"Messiah" (from the Hebrew), and "Christ" (from the Greek), means "the Anointed One."[40] Precious olive oil, from another tree of life-giving grace, was offered as a sanctifying anointing of people beginning service to God and those newly chosen for kingship. It would have been the oil of the olive tree that was used for consecration to recognize the Messiah, even as Samuel, son of the earlier Hannah, anointed David to designate his chosen kingship.

The LORD has sworn and will not change his mind,
"You[41] are a priest forever after the order of Melchizedek."
[Bible (ESV), Psalms 110:3–4]

Luminous olive oil, also used for lamps to lighten the darkness, brought the meaning of "Presence of the Holy Spirit" near.

---

[38] Psalms 110:3.

[39] Myrrh and cassia were two of the spices used to enhance the holy oil used for annointing. See Bible, Exodus 30:22–31. Beloved Mary is also sometimes referred to as the "flask of inexhaustible myrrh."

[40] *Al-Masih* is the Arabic form of the Aramaic *Meshiha*, derived from the Hebrew *Mahsiah* (Messiah, "the Annointed"); *Christos* (Christ) is derived from the Greek verb *chriein*, "to anoint."

[41] This Psalm of David is understood by Christians to be also referring to Jesus.

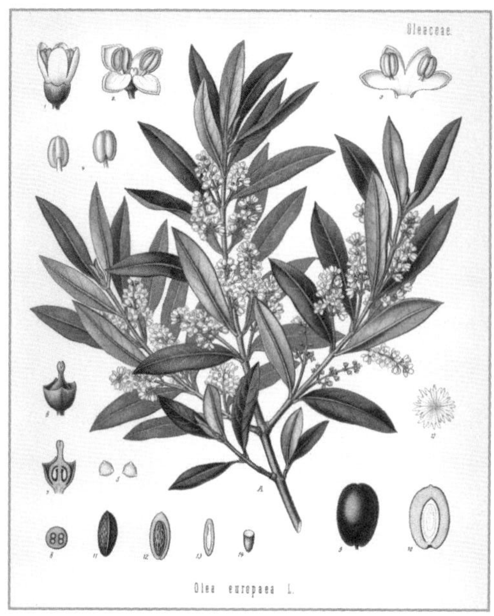


*Olive (Olea europaea)*

*Ancient Olive, Renowned as Oldest of this World*
*(3,500 years old, dated to circa 1500 bce)*

*God is the Light of the heavens and the earth.*
*The parable of His light is,*
*as it were, that of a niche containing a lamp;*
*the lamp is enclosed in glass, the glass like a radiant star;*
*lit from a blessed tree—an olive-tree*
*that is neither of the east nor of the west*[42]*—*
*the oil of which would almost give light*
*even though fire had not touched it: light upon light!*
*God guides to His light the one who wills to be guided;*
*and God offers parables to human beings,*
*since God has full knowledge of all things.*
[Quran, *Surah an-Nur,* "The Light," 24:35]

And the wise men came, acknowledging the Truth of new Light arising, and the simple shepherds, with their sheep, witnessing that brilliant star, followed it, also, and saw that Light shining before them within the stable where this newly birthed being radiated blessing.

There are many versions and understandings of the nativity story, even among Christians, and many ways of honoring this birthing still today. The nativity play celebration that many in the Western world, especially children, have come to know and love began in the thirteenth century with the inspiration of St. Francis of Assisi, after he had journeyed through the Holy Land and spent time among Muslims. He wanted everyone, whether literate landowners or uneducated peasant folk to share in the joys of the simplicity of Christ's birth, and so he took the service out of the ritual church through the forest to a cave. He brought an ox and an ass and all the village folk came with the brethren, and in the open air they celebrated under the stars, that all might be nourished with the Grace of remembrance of such a birth.

In the Quranic birth scene, God miraculously provides food and water to Mary (as had been bestowed upon her when she was in the sanctuary of the Temple) just after she expresses a desire for her own death. For many mystics, whether Catholic or Muslim, Mary is an example of how we must die to our limited self, empty out our own egoistic desires or inclinations, that we might be filled with God's abundant, beautiful sustenance,

---

42 I.e., of the Placeless Place of the Divine Reality.

with the breath of God, much like the reed flute described by Mevlana Jalaluddin Rumi. Rumi reflects on this metaphor in a poem about the blessed month of Ramadan, during which the Quran was first revealed, the month of fasting and turning in utmost devotion to God:

The lips of the Master are parched
from calling the Beloved.
The sound of your call resounds
through the horn of your empty belly.
Let nothing be inside of you.
Be empty: give your lips to the lips of the reed.[43]
When like a reed you fill with His breath,
then you'll taste sweetness.
Sweetness is hidden in the Breath
that fills the reed.
Be like Mary—by that sweet breath
a child grew within her.[44]

The major miracle of Christianity is the birth of Jesus; the major miracle of Islam is the birthing of the Quran. Continually over twenty-three years Muhammad was birthing this Beauty, as it is said in the Quran, it was *revealed in stages, little by little, in order to strengthen your heart.*[45] Every word of the Quran had to pass through the purified being of Muhammad; through his heart it was received, the "Word" of God in another form, another language, another gift and guidance for humanity from the Divine Reality. The intensity of the transmission is related in a *hadith*:

> [When] revelation came down to him—he underwent the agony that used to seize him (on such occasions) with sweat emerging like

---

[43] The reed flute is a metaphor for the human being who might offer "music" inspired by the Divine Reality, when pressed to the lips of God. Even so, the "horn of the empty belly" is reminiscent of the "horn of strength" of the earlier Hannah's song of praise, arising from the yearning within the human soul, in exaltation of the attentive nurturance of Reality.

[44] "Ramadan," Mevlana Jalaluddin Rumi, translated by Nevit Ergin with Camille Helminski, *The Pocket Rumi* (Boulder, CO: Shambhala Publications, 2001), pp.65–66.

[45] See Quran, *Surah al-Furqan* 25:32.

> pearls from him, even though it was a winter's day, because of the heavy burden of the revelation that came down upon him."[46]

As though emerging from the throes of birthing, the Prophet Muhammad conveyed the pure milk of the Quran to nourish souls awaiting like thirsty children.

*For all those who listen to God and the Messenger*
*are among those on whom God has bestowed His blessings:*
*the prophets, and those who never deviated from the truth,*
*and those who with their lives bore witness to the truth,*
*and the righteous ones; and what a beautiful friendship this is.*
*Such is the abundance of God—*
*and it suffices that God is All-Knowing.*
[Quran, *Surah an-Nisa* 4:69–70]

In the apocryphal Gospel of Bartholomew, Mary is lauded as the powerful carrier of the knowledge of great mysteries:

> "You who are highly favored, tabernacle of the Most High, unblemished, we, all the apostles ask you . . . Tell us how you conceived the incomprehensible, or how you carried him who cannot be carried, or how you bore so much greatness."
>
> But Mary answered, "Do not ask me concerning this mystery. If I begin to tell you, fire will come out of my mouth and consume the whole earth. . . ."[47]

The great Christian mystic theologian, Thomas Aquinas, speaking of Beloved Mary said, "The Virgin Mary . . . surpasses the angels in her fullness of grace."[48] Overflowing with Grace, illuminated by wisdom, her

---

[46] Ibn Kathir, Imam Abu'l-Fida' Isma'il, *The Life of the Prophet Muhammad* (*Al-Sira al-Nabawiyya*), Vols. I and II, translated by Prof. Trevor Le Gassick (Reading, United Kingdom: Garnet Publishing Ltd, 2000), Vol. I, p. 306.

[47] Gospel of Bartholomew, 2:4–5. See Edgar Hennecke, *New Testament Apocrypha*, 2 Vols. (Philadelphia: Westminster Press, 1963–1966) I, p. 492.

[48] Thomas Aquinas, "The Hail Mary", or the "Angelic Salutations," trans. Fr. Laurence Shapcote, "*Three Greatest Prayers*," pp.165–68, as cited by Rachel Fulton Brown in *Mary and the Art of Prayer, the Hours of the Virgin in Medieval Christian Life and Thought* (New York: Columbia University Press, 2018), p. 83.

body filled with the "Word of God", which she had carried devotedly for nine months, now, having birthed that "Word" into this world, she would nurse her child, Jesus (Isa), nurturing him with the pure milk flowing from her breasts, graced by the love pouring from her heart. With every breath she was passing the nourishment of her dear spirit, all the virtues flowing through her to strengthen her child: faith, hope, charity, justice, obedience, worship, repentance for any moment not in awe of the Beloved, prudence, enduring fortitude, patient perseverance, temperance, chastity, sobriety, modesty, and implicit trust in God, all enveloped with love. Whether they were together in a cave, or in the desert under the stars, surely the Light shone brightly as the babe rested in her arms.

*Consider the sky and the night-visitor.*
*And what will explain to you what the night-visitor is?*
*It is the star of piercing brightness.*
*There is no soul that does not have a protector over it.*
[Quran, *Surah at-Tariq* 86:1–4]

## *From Hand to hand*

The eye is drawn to movement;
if you want to be unnoticed,
be still,
rapt in silence.
Yet, there, too,
we are found by God,
with most intimate provision.
Mary knew such depth
profoundly;
still,
she was caught by Your Love,
filled with it;
for this she had been waiting,
prepared from before her birth,
in her purity;
even she found
herself crying,
*"Would that I*
*had been a thing forgotten!"*
in her pain of birth,
and, yet, what glory
this handmaiden brought
upon this earth,
and still brings, radiant Queen
of earth and heaven.
Dawn is caught
in a window pane,
the brightness of Your sun
bounces from There to here,
and this small eye
that can hold Your world.

From Your trees, too,
we catch Your Light,
leaping from their branches,
even as Mary caught
the dates You poured—
Your Holy-ready bestowal!
Continually we are passing
Radiance
from hand to hand,
yet, he/she did not throw
when they threw,[1]
it was You.
Hand over hand,[2]
through that light,
such beauties You awaken!
The songbirds[3] know—
they are coming out to play
this game of Your existence,
unfolded every day anew,
with such grand subsistence,
from sunrise to sunset,
and all through the night,
sprinkled with Your stars.

---

[1] Quran, *Surah al-Anfal* 8:17.
[2] Quran, *Surah al-Fath* 48:10: *The Hand of God is over their hands.*
[3] The saints of God.

## VI. SIXTH STAR OF BLESSING

# *Presentation of the Infant Jesus in the Temple: Forty Days of Love*

# *Presentation of the Infant Jesus in the Temple: Forty Days of Love*

*"And if you should see any human being, convey this to them:*
*'Behold, abstinence from speech*[1] *have I vowed unto the Most Compassionate,*
*so, I may not speak today to any human being.'"*
*And in time, she returned to her people, carrying him:*
*They said, "O Mary, you have come to us with something amazing!*
*O descendant*[2] *of the prophet Aaron,*
*your father was not an evil man nor was your mother unchaste."*
*So she pointed to him.*
*They said, "How can we talk to one who is yet an infant in the cradle?"*
[Quran, *Surah Maryam* 19:26–29]

So many moments of intensity Beloved Mary had already witnessed: after her solitary life dedicated to worship in the Temple, to become betrothed and yet receiving the mystery of The Annunciation—of conception before marriage while yet a virgin—bearing that in prayer; visiting her kinswoman Elizabeth, who also had miraculously conceived; the journey to Bethlehem with Joseph while she was heavily pregnant; the birth of her precious child; and now after forty days of holding close her beloved son, returning to the Temple and her people. Traditionally a new mother would wait for forty days after giving birth, remaining close with her infant to bond with her child and allowing healing of her body before coming into contact with crowds of others. Then purified of all bleeding, renewed in strength, the mother would with pride introduce her

---

[1] *Sawm* ("abstinence" or "self-denial") is synonymous here with *samt* ("abstinence from speech").

[2] Sometimes translated as "sister"; they were clearly reminding her of her ancestral connection with the great patriarchs of Judaism, of the priestly line of Aaron, and her responsibility in carrying the lineage.

new child to the Temple for blessing. However, Beloved Mary must now endure gossiping neighbors greeting her with accusations, questioning her; she remains silent before their taunts. And according to the Quranic version, she simply points to her son, who, though yet a tiny infant, speaks forth in her defense:[3]

*He said, "Behold, I am a servant of God.*
*He has given me the Book and made me a prophet,*
*and made me blessed wherever I may be,*
*and He has enjoined upon me prayer and charity as long as I live,*
*and has made me kind toward my mother.*
*And He has made me neither arrogant nor bereft of grace.*
*And so peace is upon me the day I was born,*
*and the day I shall die,*
*and the day upon which I will be resurrected to life once again."*
*That is Isa [Jesus], the son of Mary.*
[Quran, *Surah Maryam* 19:30–34]

The speaking of Jesus "from the cradle," as an infant in arms, is mentioned in three places in the Quran, in this passage of *Surah Maryam*, in *Surah al-'Imran* (3:46)—which relates the stories of the family of Beloved Mary and that of Moses and the lineage of the prophets—as well as in *Surah al-Maida*,[4] the *surah* of the "feast" (*maida*) pouring from Heaven in response to a prayer from Jesus when with his disciples, in his maturity. This moment of speaking when still an infant is one of six miracles attributed to Jesus in the Quran. Though not as fully described in the traditional canonical Gospels of the Bible, this miraculous moment is recorded in the Syriac Infancy Gospel,[5] from the

---

[3] The complete devotion and self-sacrifice of Mary would not let her defend herself, but trusting completely in her Lord she brought her beloved infant, Jesus, to the Temple, and a miracle occurred as his voice opened in revelation of Truth.

[4] See *Surah al-Maida* 5:110: *Behold! God will say: "O Jesus, son of Mary! Remember the blessings which I bestowed upon you and your mother—how I strengthened you with holy inspiration, so that you could speak to people in your cradle . . ."*

[5] The Syriac Infancy Gospel, which current scholarship indicates was composed in the early sixth century CE, includes stories of the birth of Jesus, miracles that occurred on the journey into Egypt, and miracles during his boyhood which are based on stories from the Infancy Gospel of Thomas text from the second

sixth century CE—compiled just a few decades before the opening of the Prophethood of Muhammad.

Even at this tender age, the voice of Jesus' heart is opened and he speaks for justice, in defense of his beloved mother from the accusation of illegitimate birth; his gentleness toward her is affirmed, and his essential nature of compassion is early revealed. Even at this tender age, he is given the capacity to voice Truth and to rectify. From this first moment, his path of Truth and Compassion opens. Here he is the "true blue"[6] shielding the rose of Mary . . . together they envelop heaven and earth, masculine and feminine, as one being, one voice. His ministry began as an infant, even though he did not manifest another miracle or teach publicly until after his maturity.

Muslims are taught to honor Jesus, peace and blessings be upon him, as one of God's mighty messengers, most pure, and to recognize his powerful clarity, and to have faith in all his miracles mentioned in the Quran, including his miraculous virgin birth. Several times in the Quran it is remembered that God created Jesus, the Word of God, without an earthly father (such as *Surah an-Nisa* 4:171) through the blessed purity of the Virgin Mary (Maryam). Within the Quran, Jesus is mentioned by name twenty-five times (Muhammad is mentioned only five times by name[7]), and numerous other times Jesus is referred to, spoken of with honor, often as the "son of Mary." No other prophet is mentioned in such a way, with the beloved name of his mother.

Beloved Mary had endured such difficulties to bring him forth; one can only imagine the duress she must have felt. Even the expression of her wish for death, to be as one forgotten, conveyed in the Quran just before the birth, is understood by many of the traditional Islamic commentators as a cry expressing the completion of that struggle and her complete victory over the ego—in her full remembrance and reliance upon God to be completely forgetful of "the world" and to be

---

century, and the Protoevangelium of James. The two extant manuscripts of the Syriac Infancy Gospel are both in Arabic.

[6] "True blue" has the meaning of unwaveringly loyal, steadfastly true as the blue of the heavens, or of the colorfast dye of the "dying vat of *Hu*," of *Al Haqq*, "The Real," *Al Quddus*, "The Infinitely Pure" (see pp. 211–12 of this text).

[7] "Muhammad" is mentioned four times: *Surah al-'Imran* 3:144; *Surah al-Ahzab* 33:40; *Surah Muhammad* 47:2; and *Surah al-Fath* 48:29; also, the alternate name of Prophet Muhammad, "Ahmad," is mentioned once, in *Surah al-Saff* 61:6.

forgotten by it, while immersing in the Divine Presence. This valiant bringing of her child to the Temple demonstrated the depth of her trust in God. When God allows Jesus to speak, he manifests her spiritual power as well as his own. It was through Mary's profound fortitude and trust in God that the voice of Jesus opened, in support of them both, to uphold Truth.

*Those who are patient in adversity, and true to their word, and truly devout,*
*and who spend in God's way,*
*and pray for forgiveness from their innermost hearts before dawn.*
*God offers signs—and so do the angels and all who are endowed with knowledge—*
*that there is no god except God, the Upholder of Justice:*
*there is no deity but Hu, the Almighty, the Truly Wise.*
*Witness—the religion with God is self-surrender to Him/Her.*
[Quran, *Surah al-'Imran*, 3:17–19]

With the speech of this holy infant, came the arrival of justice through Mary's surrender and love, God's Love. Rumi reminds us of that unfolding of Love since the first moments of creation through the conveyance of the Word:

Only God, whose attributes are perfect,
possessed speech without being taught.
And Adam whom God taught directly,
without a mother or nurse in between,
or the Messiah who was taught by Love
and came into the world with the Word,
so that he could defend himself
from accusations of an illegitimate birth.
[Rumi, *Mathnawi* IV: 3041–44]

Mystics—Christian, Muslim, or Jewish—recognize a pattern of forty days needed for transformative change. The presentation of this beloved child to the Temple, to the community, after forty days is the fourth joyful mystery of the Christian rosary. Later, in his maturity, after baptism by John in the waters of blessing,[8] Jesus retreats and fasts in the wilderness for

---

[8] As Jesus was praying by the water after his baptism, the Holy Breath (Holy Spirit) alighted upon him in the form of a dove, and a voice was heard from

forty days and nights, and, after being tested there three times,[9] returns to the people. Supported by a new strength of Spirit opening, he begins his public ministry. The number forty is of ancient significance in the Torah. The Talmud honors the process of development of an embryo in its mother's womb; the first forty days are especially significant. Within this first forty days, the fertilized egg attaches to the uterus; some cells form into the encompassing placenta while others form into the embryo.[10] It is during the fifth week (forty days) that the heart begins beating. Likewise, it is recognized that in spiritual processes it takes forty days for a shift to occur in levels of being.

The number forty occurs with great significance throughout the journeys of the prophets. We are reminded of the Prophet Noah and how it rained for forty days and nights while he was on the ark; the waters

---

heaven: "You are my son, my beloved son, in you I am delighted" (Bible, Gospel of Luke 3:21–22). Chapter 3 of the Gospel of Luke then completes with the extended lineage of Joseph (his adoptive father), through David, son of Jesse (whose lineage many say Beloved Mary also shares), and on through Jacob and Isaac and Abraham, Methusaleh and Enoch, back to "Adam, son of God." This acknowledges the whole prophetic lineage, tying Jesus's arrival as a refreshment of Love, back to the arrival of Adam as the "offspring" of God.

[9] See Bible, Gospel of Matthew 1:4–11, Extended Context Notes in Appendix, Star VI, 1.

[10] The whole beginning of conception is so miraculous, from these first moments of connection! See Extended Context Notes in Appendix, Star VI, 2.

The first *surah* of the Quran that was revealed, *Surah al-'Alaq*, "the Connecting Cell," calls to heart this first moment of connection of the human being within the womb of Divine Love, reminding us that it is through this intimate connection that our nourishment arrives, through the Pen of Creation, the Revelation of the Word:

*In the Name of God, the Infinitely Compassionate and Infinitely Merciful:*
*Recite! In the name of your Sustainer who created,*
*created the human being out of a connecting cell:*
*Recite! And your Sustainer is the Most Generous,*
*the One who taught by the pen,*
*taught humankind what it did not know.*
*No, but humankind goes beyond all bounds*
*when it considers itself self-sufficient.*
*In truth, to their Sustainer all will return.*

[Quran, *Surah al-'Alaq* 96:1–8]

cleansed the world for forty days that a transformation of spirit might occur. It usually takes forty weeks for a baby to fully develop and be birthed, from the water of the mother's womb. For forty weeks Beloved Mary had held the precious Messiah within her being, nurturing him by blood and by Spirit, and then for forty days embraced him in her arms, nourishing him by heart, before bringing him to the Temple. In the Talmud, it is said that a person doesn't come to fully comprehend the knowledge of his teacher until he has immersed in forty years of study; and in the Quran, full maturity is recognized as forty years of age.[11] Moses went up Mt. Sinai for forty days, into the Presence of God. Some would say that a day in the heights is like a year below, so in a sense Moses was taught by God for forty years, so that he might understand.

Then Moses went up on the mountain,
and the cloud covered the mountain.
The glory of the Lord dwelt on Mount Sinai . . .
Moses entered the cloud and went up on the mountain.
And Moses was on the mountain forty days and forty nights.
[Bible (ESV), Exodus 24:15–16,18]

And he was there with the Lord forty days and forty nights;
he did neither eat bread, nor drink water.
And he wrote upon the tablets the words of the covenant,
the ten commandments.[12]
[Bible, Exodus 34:28]

There is, likewise, in Islamic mysticism a long tradition of forty day personal retreats, as well as forty day periods of study or intention, with the recognition that it takes forty days for new understandings to be embedded, and new openings to flourish.

Kabbalah, the Jewish mystic tradition that fully developed in Spain in the twelfth century CE, was much influenced by Islamic mysticism. It teaches that all of reality can be apportioned into four worlds: *Atzilut* (Emanation), *Beriah* (Creation), *Yetzirah* (Formation), and *Asiyah* (Action).

---

[11] See Quran, *Surah al-Ahqaf* 46:15.

[12] The Ark of the Covenant was then constructed to carry these tablets, the "Covenant" of humankind with God.

These four worlds pour forth from their foundation in the four letters of the Essential Holy name of G-d as indicated by the mystical teaching: *Havayah* (*H, V, Y, H*). It is recognized among many traditions, as it is within Judaism, that all of creation is composed of four essential elements: earth, air, fire, and water. In Torah study, God's creative attributes are referred to as "ten *sefirot*." Forty is the result of these four elements enabled by the tenfold creative process of the Divine Reality, so forty indicates the completion of a creative process, the arisal of new being.

Rumi's mentor, Shams of Tabriz reflects on a saying of the Prophet Muhammad in this regard:

> The blessed Prophet said, "From the heart of those who sincerely worship God Most Great for forty days, springs of wisdom flow"—wisdom pours out from their tongues. These forty mornings are the key to the opening of the heart of one who is sincerely faithful, otherwise even a hundred thousand mornings won't be of use to him.[13]

Shams reminds us further that this must only be undertaken for God's sake (not our own), as was Mary's journey with Jesus:

> The blessed Prophet (may the greetings and peace of God be upon him) said, "For forty mornings, if a person completely devotes himself to God with all his/her soul and heart, springs of wisdom begin to flow from his heart to his tongue."
>
> While our Prophet was explaining these words to his Companions, one of the friends went and occupied himself with prayers for forty days. Then he complained to the Prophet, "O Messenger of God!" he said, "Such a state has come to such and such friend that his eye, word, and hue have changed. And while you were declaring this state of his, you said, 'For forty mornings . . . .' I went and made as great an effort as I could for forty days. As it has been said in the Qur'an: God offers a burden in proportion to one's capacity [2:286]. There can't be any lies, God forbid, in your words."
>
> The Prophet responded, "I said, 'If he serves[14] with all his soul and heart.' The condition for 'serving with all one's heart and soul,' is

[13] "Forty Mornings," excerpt from *Rumi's Sun*, op. cit., p. 169.

[14] The words "service" and "worship" are derived from the same root word in Arabic: *abd*.

> to do it only for God. Otherwise, it's not real service or worship if it's for the sake of other wishes or desires. You wanted those wonderful words that you heard from that companion to appear in you, too. That's what you were seeking."[15]

Shams, following Muhammad, encourages us to turn to God, trusting as purely as an infant, free of any ego, knowing only reliance upon our Beloved Sustainer, the Mother/Father/Source. When Hamdun, one of the mystics of Islam, was asked about trust in God, he answered:

> This is a degree I have not reached yet, and how can one who has not completed the state of faith speak about trust in God? It is said, "The one who trusts in God is like an infant. He knows of nothing in which he can seek shelter except his mother's breast. Like that is the one who trusts in God. He is guided only to his Lord Most High."[16]

Mary and Jesus, together, exemplify such trust. Mevlana Rumi, reflecting on this moment of the speaking of the infant Jesus, reminds us that when we bring our need truly to our Friend, our Beloved, response arrives:

Whatever God Most High bestowed and created—
the Heavens and the earths and the substances, and the unfoldings—
He created all at the demand of need;
one must render one's self in need of a thing,
so that He may bestow it.
For who but *He answers the sorely distressed*
*when he or she calls unto Him* [27:62]?[17]

---

[15] *Rumi's Sun*, op. cit, p. 317.

[16] Al-Qushayri, *Principles of Sufism*, translated by B. R. Von Schlegell (Oneonta, NY: Mizan Press, 1990), p. 121.

[17] See Quran, verses from *Surah al-Baqarah*, *Surah al-An'am*, and *Surah Hud* (and Psalm 91, p. 427 in Extended Context Notes):

*And if My servants ask you about Me—witness, I am near;*
*I respond to the call of the one who calls, whenever he or she calls Me:*
*let them, then, respond to Me, and have faith in Me,*
*so that they may follow the right way.*
[Quran, *Surah al-Baqarah* 2:186]

*Say: "Who is it that saves you from the dark dangers of land and sea*
*when you call unto Him/Her humbly, and in the secrecy of your hearts,*

Deep distress is the evidence of worthiness to receive the Divine Bounty.
It was Mary's painful need that made the infant Jesus
begin to speak from the cradle.
Part of her spoke on her behalf without her—
every part of you has a secret speech. . . .
Whatever grew has grown for the sake of those in need,
so that a seeker might find the thing he or she sought.
If God most High has created the heavens,
He has created them for the purpose of satisfying needs.
Wherever a pain is, that's where the cure goes;
wherever poverty is, that's where provision goes.
Wherever a difficult question is,
that's where the answer goes;
wherever a ship is, water goes to it.
Don't seek the water; increase your thirst,
so water may gush forth from above and below.
Until the tender-throated babe is born,
how should the milk for it
flow from the mother's breast?
Go, run across these hills and dales,
so that you may become thirsty and hunted by heat;
then, from the thundering cloud,
you will hear the voice of the water of the stream,[18] O sovereign.
Your need is not less than that of dry plants:
you gather water and draw it towards them;
you take the water by the ear
and pull it towards the dry crops that they might be refreshed.
For the spiritual crops, whose essences are hidden,

---

*'If He/She will but save us from this,*
*we shall most certainly be among the grateful'?"*
*Say: "God alone can save you from this and from every distress."*
[Quran, *Surah al-An'am* 6:63–64]

*For, truly, my Sustainer is ever-near, responding.*
[Quran, *Surah Hud* 11:61]

[18] This is a reflection of the experience of Hagar (mother of Ishmael) running across the hills of Safa and Marwah and the opening of the Zamzam spring (see p. 79 of this text).

the cloud of Divine mercy is full of the water of Kawthar.[19]
In order that the words "their Lord gave them to drink"[20]
may be spoken to you,
be thirsty! And God best knows the right course.
[Rumi, *Mathnawi* III: 3204–05; 3208–19]

When we make all our cares into a single care, focus all our attention, and bring our need, the generous Source of all Creation pours forth in response. As this *Hadith Qudsi*[21] expresses, the Divine Reality, Itself, is thirsty to be known: "I was a Hidden Treasure and I so loved to be known, that I created the two worlds, seen and Unseen, in order that My Treasure of Generosity and Loving-kindness might be known." Springs of wisdom rise through the hearts of human beings when connected to that Infinite Source; the infant Jesus is a pure sign of such a possibility:

> The Prophet Jesus, during the first days that he sucked milk, spoke just once and then did not speak again, because his first words were not by his own will.[22] Like an arrow shot without an archer.
>
> He then embraced his mother's breast, because he had tasted that milk first. As it says, "*We caused him to refuse other nurses . . . and thus restored [Moses] to his mother.*"[23]

Beloved Jochebed nursed her son, Moses, with her sincerity and her love, even as Beloved Maryam nourished the infant Jesus with the sweet purity of her dear heart.

Give him milk, mother of Moses,
then cast him into the water.
Don't be afraid of putting him to the test.
Whoever drank that milk in pre-eternity

---

[19] Kawthar: the endless overflowing spring of spiritual nourishment with the fresh cooling water of Paradise.

[20] See Quran, *al-Insan* 76:21: *And in the Garden, their Sustainer will give them to drink of a drink most pure.*

[21] *Hadith Qudsi*: a saying of God conveyed through Muhammad, outside the revelation of the Quran.

[22] See *Surah Maryam* 19:30–33.

[23] *Rumi's Sun*, op. cit, p. 327. See *Surah al-Qasas* 28:3–13 in Extended Context Notes in Appendix, Introduction, 1.

distinguishes the true milk here,
just as Moses knew his own mother's milk.
[Rumi, *Mathnawi* II: 2969–70]

How beautiful that an infant is held to the mother's heart when nursing:

A disposition that passes from the milk to the baby
comes through the body from the soul.[24]

From Mary's clear heart, wisdom graced with great blessing passed to her son—through her great love—while both were held tenderly in the embrace of God.

When Adam became the theater of Divine inspiration and love,
his rational soul revealed to him the knowledge of the Names.[25]
His tongue, reading from the page of his heart,
recited the name of everything that is.
Through his inward vision his tongue
divulged the qualities of each;
for each it bestowed an appropriate name.
Nine hundred years Noah walked in the straight way,
and every day he preached a new sermon.
His ruby lip drew its eloquence from the precious jewel
that is within the hearts of prophets . . .
He had not learned to preach from pouring over commentaries;
no, he learned from the fountain of revelations and the spirit—
from the wine that is so potent that when it is quaffed
the water of speech gushes from the mouth of the dumb,
and the newborn child becomes an eloquent divine
and, like the Messiah, recites words of ripened wisdom.
[Rumi, *Mathnawi* VI: 2648–56]

The fertility, the mysterious power of generation from the heart, by love, is manifested in so many stories in relation to Mary. It is this overflowing love that gives both Mary and Jesus the strength to endure what has already come and will yet come to them.

---

[24] Shams of Tabriz, *Rumi's Sun*, op. cit., p. 328.
[25] Quran, *Surah al-Baqarah*, "The Cow," 2:29.

*God is the Protector of those who have faith:*
*leading them out of the depths of darkness into the Light.*
[Quran, *Surah al-Baqarah* 2:257]

Mary, accompanied by noble and steadfast Joseph in the Biblical account, continued to bring Jesus forward, to make the purification offering and to present him as their firstborn in the Temple, as was the practice of the Jewish tradition. In the Biblical account, Jesus is recognized there in his holiness by Simeon, who is not a priest or Levite, but a simple, God-devoted man.

And when the days of her purification
according to the law of Moses were accomplished,[26]
they brought him to Jerusalem, to present him to the Lord . . .
and to offer a sacrifice
according to that which is said in the law of the Lord,
a pair of turtledoves, or two young pigeons.
And, behold, there was a man in Jerusalem, whose name was Simeon;
and the same man was just and devout,
looking for the consolation of Israel,
and the Holy Spirit was upon him.
And it had been revealed to him by the Holy Spirit
that he would not see death before he saw the anointed of the Lord.
And by the Spirit he came to the Temple,

---

[26] After the birth of a son, a Jewish mother would wait forty days, that her body might be renewed, before introducing her child to the Temple for blessing. In the Sufi tradition, these first forty days are also recognized as such a special time of bonding of child and mother, as the newly arrived soul is held and drinks at his or her mother's breast, and through her atmosphere is embraced within this world, while being still shielded by her powerful presence. Likewise, forty is the number of days after a person's death, for Muslims, that a soul is held closely in remembrance by near family embracing that dear one with deep prayer, while the soul wings its way through unseen realms to return Home in union with its Source. Forty days is traditionally a significant period of time for spiritual endeavors across traditions. We remember, also, that it took forty years of journeying for Moses and Aaron and Miriam to bring their people to the Promised Land, and then a transition occurred—the leadership shifted, after the passing of these three precious siblings, to Joshua (Yehoshua) who then led the people forward into a new moment, into Canaan, the "land of milk and honey."

and when the parents brought in the child Jesus,
to do for him after the custom of the law,
he took him up in his arms, and blessed God,
and said: "Lord, let Your servant now depart in peace,
according to Your word, for mine eyes have seen Your salvation . . .
a light to lighten the Gentiles, and the glory of Your people Israel."
And Joseph and his mother marveled at those things
that were spoken of him.
And Simeon blessed them, and said unto Mary, his mother:
"Behold, this child is set for the fall and rising again of many in Israel;
and for a sign which shall be spoken against;
Yea, a sword shall pierce through your own soul also,
that the thoughts of many hearts may be revealed."
[Bible, Gospel of Luke 2:22–35]

Simeon shares a blessing with them all, but it is to Mary that he speaks directly. He presages that the journey of love would not be easy. And yet,

*To everyone who is conscious of God, God always prepares a way of emergence,*
*and provides for him/her in ways he/she could never imagine;*
*and for everyone who places trust in God, God is sufficient.*
*For God will surely accomplish His purpose:*
*truly, for all things has God appointed an appropriate measure.*
[Quran, *Surah at-Talaq* 65:2–3]

Hearts would be revealed. A Light was beginning to shine forth.

Who is the "protector"? One who sets you free,
who removes the chains of bondage from your feet.
Since prophethood is the guide to freedom,
by way of the prophets freedom comes to the faithful.
Rejoice, O community of the faithful:
show yourselves to be "free,"
pure and noble as the cypress and lily!
But do you, also, like the gay-colored garden,
at every moment give unspoken thanks to the Water!
The cypresses and green orchard silently return thanks to the water
and demonstrate their gratitude for the justice of Spring—
clad in fresh robes and trailing their skirts,

drunken and dancing and jubilant, scattering fragrance,
every part of them impregnated by royal Spring,
their bodies as jewel caskets filled with pearly fruit,
like Marys, having no husband, yet big with a Messiah,
silent ones, wordlessly saying,
"Our Moon has shone brightly upon us;
from our beauty every tongue has derived its speech."
Even so, the speech of Jesus is derived from the spiritual beauty of Mary;
the speech of Adam is a ray of the Divine Breath.
This thanksgiving of the orchard is a lesson to you,
in order that from your thanksgiving, O trustful ones,
increase of spiritual glory may blossom with you,
and that still other gracious plants
might spring up from amid the green herbs.
[Rumi, *Mathnawi* VI: 4540–51]

A second confirmation of this Light emerging quickly followed, this time from a woman, another Anna.

There was also a prophet, Anna,[27]
the daughter of Penuel, of the tribe of Asher.
She was very old;
she had lived with her husband seven years after her marriage,
and then was a widow until she was eighty-four.
[Bible (NIV), Gospel of Luke 2:36–37]

Having been a widow so long, this Anna is identified in relation to her "father," Penuel (Phanuel).[28] She had probably married her husband just

---

[27] This Anna (Hannah) of the Holy Temple is one of the few women of the Bible who are recognized with the title "prophetess" (female prophet). See also Miriam (Exodus 15:20) and Deborah (Judges (NIV) 4:4):

Now Deborah, a prophet, the wife of Lappidoth, was leading Israel at that time.
She held court under the Palm of Deborah
between Ramah and Bethel in the hill country of Ephraim,
and the Israelites went up to her to have their disputes decided.

See also the Hebrew prophetess Huldah (II Chronicles 34:22), and the wife of Isaiah (Isaiah 8:3), and all four virgin daughters of the early Christian Philip (Acts 21:9).

[28] The name "Phanuel" means "face of God". *Wherever you turn there is the Face of*

after puberty, in her early teens, and had lived with her husband only seven years before his death. Rather than seeking to remarry or serve in her father's household, she then chose to serve God and devote herself to prayer for what must have been over sixty years. Anna may have been given living quarters at the Temple in recognition of her role as a female prophet, her capacity to "see," even as had been the practice with Huldah, the Hebrew prophetess from the time of Josiah, King of Judah.[29]

[Anna] never left the temple
but served God with fasting and prayers night and day.
[Bible (NIV), Gospel of Luke 2:37]

Perhaps she and Beloved Mary had become friends when Mary, herself, had been so devotedly in prayer in the Temple.

Just as Simeon is holding Jesus in his arms, praising God, Anna comes up to them also, full of joy, exalting God for this blessing:

Coming up to them at that very moment,
she gave thanks to God and spoke about the child
to all who were looking forward to the redemption of Jerusalem.
[Bible (NIV), Gospel of Luke 2:38]

Immediately Anna recognizes, "sees" that which many had been seeking, the Light shining from within the being of this tiny child, presaged in the Torah. Here was a living Torah.

The Torah, itself, is spoken of in the Quran as a guide and a Light.[30] Rabbis teach that the Torah (the "showing") is the Tree of Life, revealing the Hidden, pouring Wisdom forth, even as:

A river went forth from Eden.
[Bible, Genesis 2:10]

It is understood that all who are fed below, in this world, are fed from this place of Abundance, as it is said in the Psalms of David:

---

*God* (Quran, *Surah al-Baqarah* 2:11).

[29] See II Chronicles 34:22.

[30] See Quran, *Surah al-'Imran* 3:3–4 and *Surah al-Maida*, 5:44: *Truly, it is We who bestowed from on high the Torah, wherein there was guidance and light.*

The eyes of all wait on You,
and You give them their meat in due season.
You open Your hand and satisfy the desire of every living thing.
The Lord is righteous in all His ways, and Holy in all His works.
The Lord is near unto all those who call upon Him,
to all that call upon Him in Truth.
[Bible, Psalms 145:15–18][31]

For with You is the fountain of life,
in Your light we shall see light.
[Bible, Psalms 36:9]

Here in the Temple, both a man and a woman (masculine and feminine, both cherishing), acknowledge this beautiful Light, embracing Jesus with their love and blessing, and then, it is said, Mary and Jesus rested.

Within the Temple Mount, near the entrance to Solomon's stables, there is a little chamber with a window toward the east, known as the "Chamber of Virgin Mary"; tradition relates that it was here where she immersed in prayer, where Zachariah visited her in the sanctuary (*mihrab*), where Gabriel came to her, and The Annunciation occurred. According to tradition the recess in the stone floor adjacent, "a nest-like polished shining stone," was where Beloved Mary placed Jesus to rest just after the presentation in the Temple, retreating to this holy place she knew so well. The chamber is also known as the "Dome of Jesus' Cradle," long honored by both Christians and Muslims who come here to pray.[32]

---

[31] This passage of Psalm 145 is preceded by another lovely passage in which David witnesses to the overwhelming Beneficence of the Divine Reality:

The Lord is gracious and full of compassion: slow to anger, and of great mercy.
The Lord is good to all: and His tender mercies are over all His works.
All Your works shall praise You, O Lord; and Your saints shall bless You.
They shall speak of the glory of Your kingdom, and talk of Your power—
to make known to the sons of men His mighty acts,
and the glorious majesty of His kingdom.
Your kingdom is an everlasting kingdom,
and Your dominion endures throughout all generations.
The Lord upholds all that fall, and raises up all those that be bowed down.
[Bible, Psalms 145: 8–14]

[32] It is said that the marble pillars that now adorn the stone alcove were placed

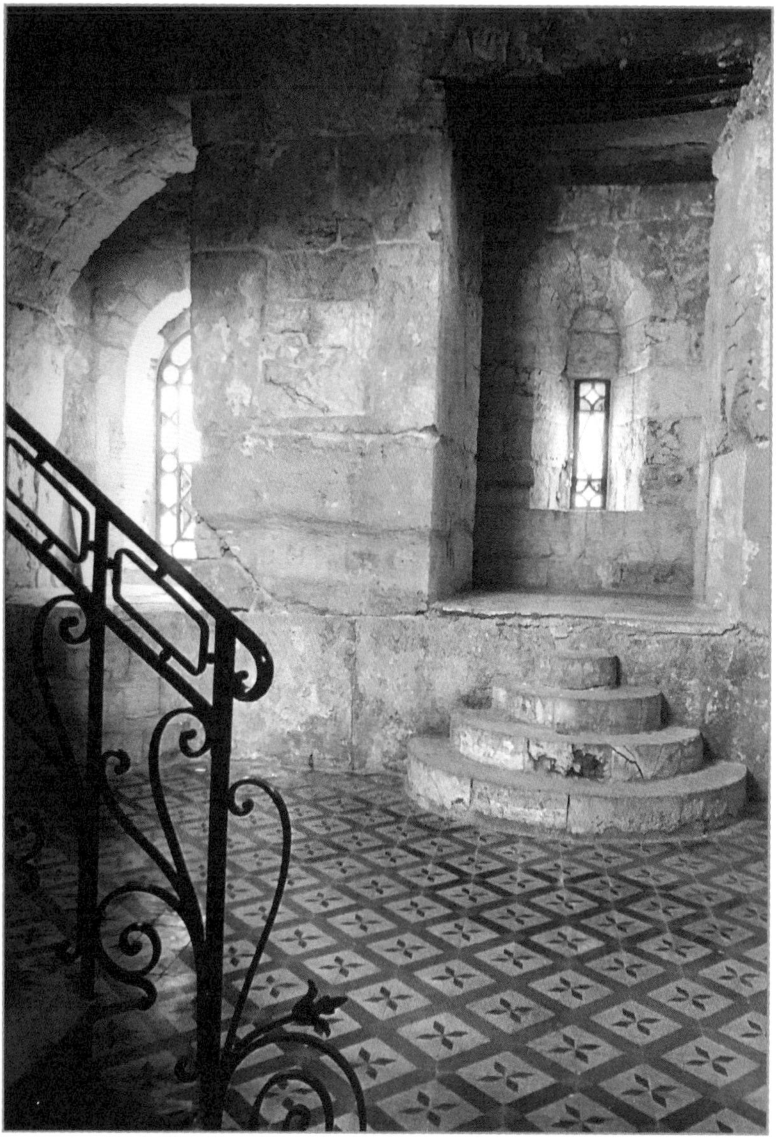

*"Chamber of Virgin Mary"*
*Beloved Mary's Sanctuary (Mihrab)*

---

there with care by Muslims during the reign of Sultan Suleyman the Magnificent in the sixteenth century CE.

*"Jesus' Cradle" (Mahd Sidna 'Isa)*
*(Adjacent, to the right of Beloved Mary's "Mihrab")*

The poor and the wise had come to greet Jesus, to honor him as a being of Light, even as the poor and enslaved, and especially women, were among the first to recognize the truth of Prophet Muhammad's message conveyed through the words of the Quran. Muhammad had long been known in his community as "the most trustworthy" (*al-Amin*), and when the revelation of the Quran began to open through his heart, it was Waraqah, the Christian cousin of his beloved wife Khadijah, who first confirmed the holiness of the Message as similar to that of the earlier prophets of the Abrahamic tradition.

Even as the infant Jesus rose in defense of his mother from his earliest days, the Prophet Muhammad, also, continually stood up for the honoring of the feminine and the natural world. Slaves and women, in recognition of Truth and the rebalancing of justice that was opening through the Quran, often turned for nourishment and support to the "Word of God" that came to them through Muhammad. During the *Jahiliyyah* ("Time of Ignorance"), before the spreading of the faith elucidated by Muhammad, the pagans of the Arab tribes would often kill their female children to avoid having to provide for them, favoring male offspring. Through Muhammad's heart several verses of the Quran were revealed to rectify this abominable practice.[33] Muhammad's own children, whom

---

[33] See, among others, Quran, *Surah at-Takwir*:

*When the souls are sorted out,*
*and when the girl-child that was buried alive is made to ask*

he helped to raise, were only girls,[34] whom he deeply loved—especially his youngest daughter, born when he was approaching forty, Fatimah, who was known for her devotion to God and her pure radiance, reminding many of Beloved Mary.

> When the Prophet saw [Fatimah] approaching, he would welcome her, stand up and kiss her, take her by the hand and sit her down in the place where he was sitting. She would do the same when the Prophet came to her. She would stand up and welcome him with joy and kiss him.[35]
>
> [Fatimah] inherited from Muhammad a persuasive eloquence that was rooted in wisdom. When she spoke, people would often be moved to tears. She had the ability and the sincerity to stir the emotions, move people to tears and fill their hearts with praise and gratitude to God for His grace and His inestimable bounties.[36]

What a grace that human hearts can recognize another heart turned in devotion to God, immersed in that Light, whether that person be young or old, and yearn to immerse with them, to rest within Truth. Truth (*Haqq*), Pure Holiness and Sincerity (*Quddus*)[37] become manifest to us when the eyes of our hearts are unveiled through the grace of God.

> An authentic tradition states that the Prophet Muhammad (peace and blessings be upon him) related, on the authority of Gabriel (peace be upon him), who related about God (may He be exalted) that God said:

---

*for what crime she had been slain.*
[Quran, *Surah at-Takwir* 81:7–9]

[34] Muhammad's sons each died in infancy. He helped to raise four daughters from his marriage with his beloved wife, Khadijah: Zaynab, Ruqayyah, Umm Kulthum, and Fatimah. Fatimah was about five years old when the Prophethood of Muhammad opened (610 CE); she was the only child to survive him (for only a few months); and it is only through her that a living stream of descendants have arrived.

[35] See "Fatimah bint Muhammad" in Alim 6.0 (educational software).

[36] Ibid.

[37] *Ya Haqq, Ya Quddus*, beautiful Names of God—that One who illuminates us with Pure Truth and Holy Sincerity—are among the many beautiful Names of God that can be of holy heart companionship for us.

"Sincerity is a secret taken from My secret.
I have placed it as a trust in the hearts of servants I love."[38]

Surely such sincerity radiated from the heart of dear Joseph, sheltering Beloved Mary within his loving trust in her and in this miraculous birth. So after the completion of the celebration of this forty-day passage, according to the Bible, steadfast Joseph—who had stood with his betrothed, this unwed mother, by his presence, also, defending her before his peers, with his clear sincerity—now brings her and the infant Jesus home to Nazareth:

So when they had performed all things according to the law of the Lord,
they returned into Galilee, to their own city Nazareth.
And the child grew and waxed strong in spirit,
filled with wisdom, and the grace of God was upon him.
[Bible, Gospel of Luke 2:39–40]

We give thanks to God (*shukrulillah*) for the rebalancing, the rectification, for the Water bubbling up from hidden springs of Truth in the midst of our dire thirst, wherever we may be, and the opening of Light.

---

[38] Al-Qushayri, *Principles of Sufism*, op. cit., p. 187.

## *The Farthest Mosque*

Good morning, Dear One!
Once again You bless us
with light.
The sky, blue
as a robin's egg,
kisses the stars,
though now
we can't see them.
Your hidden darknesses
are illumined;
friends
on the other side
know
and witness those realms.
Flying high,
we can mount
beyond the clouds,
yet, still,
Your further sky
is beyond our reach.
The farthest mosque[1]
is intimate with You,
and only rarely
do we see it—
glimpsing Your Majesty.
Up and down,
Jacob traveled
with the angels,

---

[1] See Extended Context Notes in Appendix, Star VI, 3.

near,[2]
and Solomon
blew the winds
away[3]
to rest
in Your arms.
Jesus
brought You
here,
manifesting
Your Purity
and Your Solace.
Mary,
dear Mary,
what Beauty
was rapt
in her presence,
that she heard
Your Voice

---

[2] Jacob dreamed of a ladder to heaven with angels dancing up and down, moving into and from God's Presence with Grace, bringing great blessings (see Bible, Genesis 28:10–22).

When Jacob awoke from his sleep,
he thought, "Surely the Lord is in this place, and I was not aware of it."
He was afraid and said, "How awesome is this place!
This is none other than the house of God; this is the gate of heaven."
[Bible (NIV), Genesis 28:16–17]

[3] The Prophet Solomon was known to have power over the winds—winds both of the outer world, and the winds of desire that blow the self off-course—so that he might keep rectifying his kingdom in harmony with the Divine guidance.

*So We subjected the wind to him.*
*It blew softly at his bidding wherever he wanted it to blow.*
[Quran, *Surah Sad* 38:3]

*And We had subdued to Solomon the strongly blowing wind*
*which sped at his bidding*
*to the land wherein We had placed Our blessings,*
*for it is We who have knowledge of everything.*
[Quran, *Surah al-Anbiya* 21:81]

and was still—
handmaiden
to Your Will,
and, yet, her own
strength—
with which
You gifted her—
helped her
to stand strong
before the people,
to affirm
Your Holiness
she carried
in her arms.
Her robe
encompasses
the stars,
and kissed
by heaven
she guards
all that is secret,
all that is Love,
and smiles,
gently coaxing us, also,
to come, rest,
in Your Arms,
and be
the Radiance
of Your Eternal Sun:
*Bow in worship*
*and draw near.*[4]

[4] *Bow in worship and draw near* (Quran, *Surah al-'Alaq* 96:19). And we remember the mirrored verse within *Surah Maryam* 19:96: *Truly those who have faith and do the deeds of wholeness and reconciliation, the Infinitely Compassionate will endow with Love.*

# VII. SEVENTH STAR OF BLESSING

## *Journey to Egypt*

# *Journey to Egypt*

*And we made the son of Mary and his mother a sign*
*and we made them abide in an elevated place,*
*full of quiet, and watered by clear springs.*
[Quran, *Surah al-Mu'minun*, "The Faithful,"[1] 23:50]

Though the story of the flight of the holy family of Blessed Mary and Joseph and the infant Jesus, from the persecution of Herod into Egypt, is not specifically described in the Quran, some scholars within the Islamic tradition feel that this passage from the Quran may allude to it. Narratives about it similar to those found in the Bible were related among Muslims, and stories of the life of Jesus are included in the traditional Islamic *Qisas al-Anbiya* ("Stories of the Prophets"). Some versions of the stories of the youth of Jesus tell of the holy family fleeing to Egypt and remaining there for quite some time, at least until the passing of Herod, or in some stories of the Islamic tradition until Jesus was almost twelve.

In the Bible, this chapter of their life begins when King Herod, fearful of the rumors of the birth of a new king, commanded that all children two and under be killed,[2] and Joseph is warned by an angel in a dream to take Mary and Jesus into Egypt for safety, as likewise the wise visitors from the East had also been warned:

And being warned of God in a dream
that they [the magi] should not return to Herod,

---

[1] "[In this *surah*] stress is laid on the fact of unceasing divine guidance manifested in a long succession of God-inspired prophets; and since all of them propounded one and the same truth, all who [have faith] in God are reminded—as in *Surah al-Anbiya*, 21:92–93—that "this community of yours is one single community" (verse 52) [and that it is man's "egotism, greed, and striving after power (verses 53 ff.)" that tear asunder this unity]. See, Muhammad Asad, *The Message of the Qur'an* (Introduction to *Surah al-Mu'minun*).

[2] Bible, Gospel of Matthew 2:16.

they departed into their own country another way.
And when they were departed,
behold, the angel of the Lord appeared to Joseph in a dream,
saying, "Arise, and take the young child and his mother,
and flee into Egypt, and stay there until I bring you word,
for Herod will seek the young child to destroy him."
When he arose, he took the young child and his mother by night,
and departed into Egypt.
[Bible, Gospel of Matthew 2:12–14]

In many spiritual traditions, dreams bring guidance from the well of Being, hidden from usual waking consciousness.[3] It is another dream that brings guidance to Joseph, from the realms of the Unseen, the realms of Nearness. Joseph's sensitivity and reliance upon these dreams demonstrates his own receptivity to Spirit and the Divine Provision. The message of protection is gifted to him.

It is interesting to note that members of the early Muslim community in Mecca, also, fled towards Egypt seeking refuge. They emigrated further, into Abyssinia (Ethiopia),[4] fleeing from persecution by Mecca's ruling elites. In the early days of Islam, the Quraysh—Muhammad's own tribe—and others among the powerful polytheist tribes of Mecca persecuted the Muslims, limiting their freedom of worship and movement for livelihood. After some time, the Prophet gave his permission to Jafar ibn Abi Talib, cousin of the Prophet and brother of Ali, for some of the Muslims to emigrate with Jafar to seek refuge with the Christians of Abyssinia.[5] Jafar and his beloved wife, Asma bint Umays, were among the first Meccans to accept Islam and were deeply devoted in faith. The Negus, the just Christian ruler of Abyssinia, welcomed this band of refugees, and at last these devout Muslims were able to live and worship undisturbed.

---

[3] The Prophet Muhammad, in recognition of this, used to offer a special prayer for dream guidance. See Extended Context Notes in Appendix, Star VII, 1.

[4] The former name of Ethiopia is Abyssinia (Habessinia), derived from the Arabic word *habesch* which means "mixture," referring to the mixture of races present among the people; the name was Latinized to *Abassia.* The "Abyssinians" now refer to themselves as "Itiopyavan" and use the name of "Itiopia" (Ethiopia) for their country.

[5] Muhammad would also offer a prayer when entering a town or region, asking: "O God, give me the blessing of it, and save me from its harm."

It wasn't long, however, before the Quraysh learned of the peaceful asylum they had found and sent two emissaries with sumptuous gifts to seek their extradition. The Quraysh sought the agreement of the bishops and the Negus himself.

The Negus said, "No. By God, I won't surrender them to anyone until I, myself, ask them about what they have been accused."

He questioned them. In his melodious voice, Jafar recited from the Quran *Surah Maryam*, which relates the story of Mary and the birth of Jesus. The Negus was moved to tears.

When questioned further, Jafar told him of how the Prophet had guided the new Muslims into being better, more moral human beings, with greater compassion for each other, and of what the Prophet and the Quran said of Jesus: "Our Prophet says that Jesus is the servant of God, and His Prophet; he is His Spirit and His Word which He breathed into Mary, the blessed Virgin."

The Negus drew a line across the sand and said, "The difference between your faith and ours is no more than that." He returned the gifts to the Quraysh emissaries and declared he would give the Muslims continued refuge and protection.

A recognition of the shared roots among Muslims and Christians, through the story of Beloved Mary, stands in *Surah al-Anbiya*, the *surah* of "The Prophets":

*And [remember] she who guarded her chastity,*
*whereupon We breathed into her of Our spirit*
*and caused her, together with her son,*
*to become a sign [of Our grace] unto all people.*
*Truly, this community of yours is one single community,*
*since I am the Sustainer of you all: worship, then, Me [alone].*[6]
[Quran, *Surah al-Anbiya*, "The Prophets," 21:91–92]

It was, also, to Abyssinia that it is said the Ark of the Covenant had long before been taken by the son of Solomon and Sheba, Menelik. His Holiness

---

[6] "After calling to mind, in verses 48–91 of this surah, some of the earlier prophets, all of whom stressed the oneness and uniqueness of God, the discourse returns to that principle of oneness as it ought to be reflected in the unity of all who have faith in Him." See Muhammad Asad, *The Message of the Qur'an.*

Abuna Paulos, the patriarch of the Ethiopian Orthodox Church (which has forty million adherents) continues to convey a long tradition that the Ark has remained there all these many centuries, under the constant protection of a dedicated priest, generation after generation. Each one commits his life to being solely there at the chapel in which it is housed, in constant guardianship of it. Even the kings of Ethiopia are not allowed to see it:

> It's no claim, it's the truth. . . . Queen Sheba visited King Solomon in Jerusalem three thousand years ago, and the son she bore him, Menelik, at age twenty visited [his father, Solomon, in] Jerusalem, from where he brought back the Ark of the Covenant to Aksum. It's been in Ethiopia ever since.[7]

No one but the guardian priest is ever allowed to see it, and so it has been for centuries.[8] Once anointed the virgin priest is forbidden to leave the chapel grounds. Each lives there in continual prayer until the end of his life, when a new virgin priest takes his place within the Church of Our Lady Mary Zion that was built there by the first Christian ruler of Ethiopia around 400 CE. The Negus would have been well aware of the presence of the Ark there, and Mary's special role as the "New Ark of the Covenant," the bearer of the Messiah. This ancient Covenant of Moses and Abraham, "the Rope of God," he recognized as also held by Muslims, brothers and sisters in faith.

*O you who have faith!*
*Be conscious of God with all the consciousness that is due Him,*
*and do not allow death to overtake you*
*before you have surrendered yourselves to Him.*
*And hold fast, all together, to the rope of God,*
*and do not draw apart from one another.*

---

7 His Holiness Abuna Paulos, patriarch of the Ethiopian Orthodox church, quoted in *Smithsonian Magazine*, December 2007, p. 40.

8 According to some traditions, around 400 BC there was an intervening period of some hundreds of years until possibly 400 CE when the Ark was temporarily hidden on a nearby island of Lake Tana (the source of the Blue Nile river) for safekeeping when the country was threatened by invaders, until it was safe to bring it back to Axum. It would have been returned again to Axum by the time of Jafar's arrival in 615 CE.

*And remember with gratitude the blessings*
*which God has bestowed on you:*
*how, when you were adversaries, He brought your hearts together,*
*so that through His blessings you became as though of one family;*
*and how when you were on the brink of a fiery abyss,*
*He saved you from it.*
*In this way, God makes clear His signs to you,*
*so that you might be guided,*
*and that there might grow out of you a community*
*who invite to all that is good, and encourage the doing of what is right*
*and forbid the doing of what is wrong:*
*and it is they who shall attain happiness!*
[Quran, *Surah al-'Imran* 3:102–04]

The "Golden Rule," expressed in so many religious texts, was active in this moment. It is a fundamental principle in the Torah: "You shall love your neighbor as yourself."[9]

When a foreigner resides among you in your land, do not mistreat them.
The foreigner residing among you must be treated as your native-born.
Love them as yourself, for you were foreigners in Egypt.
I am [*HaShem*] the Lord your God.
[Bible (NIV), Leviticus 19:33–34]

The Negus recognized the beauty of spirit among the Muslims and their disciplined devotion in faith.[10] He recognized a shared experience

---

[9] Bible, (Torah) Leviticus 19:18.

[10] The Prophet Muhammad also deeply recognized the devoted faith of the Negus. When some years later Prophet Muhammad received word of the passing of the Negus, returning to his Lord, Muhammad made arrangements in Mecca to have a Muslim funeral prayer offered for his soul. Some people in the community questioned this, saying, "But he was not a Muslim." Muhammad responded, "Yes, he was." He recognized that the Negus was "surrendered" in soul to his Lord. It is this deep surrender that is the meaning of "muslim." In the Quran, many of the Abrahamic prophets are remembered as "muslim" (surrendered to God). It was not until some years following the opening of the Quran that the community of faithful around Muhammad and after him became designated as "Muslims." There are those who take this title as referring to a particular community of the faithful, "followers of Muhammad," and there are those who still remember its original

among the peoples of faith; he understood that these "muslims" were refugees of spirit, even as had been Moses and the people of Israel when they were fleeing from Egypt, and as had been Beloved Mary and Jesus and stalwart Joseph when they had fled to Egypt. All these hearts were held first by the supreme commandment:

And Jesus said to him,
"You shall love the Lord your God with all your heart
and with all your soul and with all your mind.
This is the first and great commandment.
And a second is like it: You shall love your neighbor as yourself.
[Bible, Gospel of Matthew 22: 37–39]

"You shall love your neighbor as yourself," not just similarly to yourself, but as your very self. Under the protection of the Divine Reality we recognize our common bonds as of one human family; all three Abrahamic faiths teach that we must learn to care for and nurture each other as we would hope to be cared for:

So in everything, do to others what you would have them do to you,
for this sums up the Law and the Prophets.
[Bible (NIV), Gospel of Matthew 7:12]

Do to others as you would have them do to you.
[Bible (NIV), Gospel of Luke 6:31]

A renowned Jewish wise man (*tzadik*), Rabbi Hillel, was once asked to give a summary of the Torah, and to ensure it would be focused and succinct, to do so while standing on one foot. He replied: "That which is harmful to you, do not do to your fellow. This is the whole Torah. The rest is commentary. Go and learn."[11]

Sometimes we may need to be creative, as we listen for the need of a friend, or even a stranger, seeking to offer in the best way possible what might be most pleasing and of benefit to the other, what he or she might prefer, rather than what we might assume, seeking to know his or her heart's

---

meaning (with a lower case *m*, "muslim") "one who is surrendered to God," without specificity as to the particular ritual tradition one may observe.

[11] Talmud, *Shabbat* 31a.

true need, even as we, ourselves, would appreciate. With the grace of the Light of Reality we may be enabled to see what the gift of the moment might need to be, that we might respond as the Divine Reality would have us respond, with compassion and mercy, even preferring another to oneself.

One of the mystics of Islam, Abul-Husayn al-Bushanji, said:

> One of the principles of *Futuwwah* [Sufi chivalry] is to beautify one's essence with God: to love and want for one's friends the things that one loves and wants for oneself; in fact, to prefer one's friends to oneself, because Allah Most High says: *But those who, before them, had homes and had adopted the faith, show their affection to those who came to them for refuge, and do not entertain in their hearts desire for things given to them, but give them preference over themselves, even though poverty was their own lot.* [Quran, *Surah al-Hashr* 59:9]. And the Prophet (peace and blessings be upon him) said, "Your faith is not complete until you love for your brother that which you love for yourself."[12]

Just as the holy family of Mary, Jesus, and Joseph had to flee, and some of the early Muslims fled to Abyssinia and were welcomed there, some years later, after enduring thirteen years of continued persecutions and boycotts, the whole early Muslim community was forced to flee from Mecca to Medina. This was the second *Hegira*, in 622 CE (1 AH), when they were welcomed by the Jewish tribes of Medina, who shared their sustenance and homes with them. The Prophet Muhammad, and his close friend and companion, Abu Bakr, waited for the very last of the faithful to depart from Mecca, to ensure their safety, and then together they left in the night and, shielded by the darkness, hid within a cave enroute. Once the Meccans discovered they had left, they rushed in pursuit. Coming upon the cave they started to enter it in search, but then they noticed a dove had made a nest beside the opening and a spider had woven her web across a portion of it. Surely, they thought, no one had entered here any time recently, and so they left, and the Prophet and Abu Bakr were able to then safely journey on to Medina.

---

[12] *Hadith* of Prophet Muhammad: An-Nawawi's Forty Hadith: 13 (p. 56); Tarikh Dimashq 42964, as cited in Muhammad ibn al-Husayn al-Sulami, *The Book of Sufi Chivalry*, translated by Sheikh Tosun Bayrak al-Jerrahi al-Halverti (New York: Inner Traditions International, 1983), pp. 67–68.

All three Abrahamic faiths are joined in the experience of persecution and the need for the seeking of refuge. And again and again, we witness the natural world rising up in support of those seeking to align with the Eternal Source of Beneficence—even as when the Red Sea parted for Moses, then manna arrived from heaven, and water flowed from Miriam's well to quench their thirst. There is a tradition among Christians in Sicily relating how a humble juniper bush saved the lives of Beloved Mary and Jesus and Joseph when they were fleeing Herod's soldiers. As they were fleeing through fields and thickets, a large juniper bush opened up its thick branches to embrace them, enclosing them in its deep shadows until the soldiers had passed. It is said that within the core of the bush the branches bent in softness to give them rest while the outer branches wielded their customary prickliness so that no one might even think to enter.

Juniper, especially its mature female cones, has been healing human beings for thousands of years. There are many varieties, and while some have berries that can be somewhat toxic, many have berries that are pleasant tasting, anti-inflammatory, and used as a diuretic or antibiotic. The Greeks used them for purification ceremonies and for increase of stamina; Romans used them as healing herbs and as a spice substitute for black pepper; Egyptians have long used them as a medicinal herb and to assist with embalming the dead. Extracts have been used to treat many ailments, ranging from snake bites to bacterial infections, including those that compromise the breath, like pneumonia. The berries have been found to have over 87 natural antioxidant compounds. Juniper was included as one of the healing plants in *De Materia Medica*,[13] one of the first European

---

[13] "This book exemplifies the transfer of knowledge across the centuries [and cultures]. During the first century, the Greek doctor and apothecary Dioscorides, who is considered the father of pharmacology, wrote a very important five-volume text on botany and pharmaceuticals. In the 10th century, during the times of 'Abd al-Rahman III (891–961), caliph of Cordova, the work was translated into Arabic. In 1518 at the Escuela de Traductores de Toledo (the School of Translators of Toledo), Antonio de Nebrija made the first translation of the work in Spain into Latin." See World Digital Library: https://www.wdl.org/en/item/10632/ (accessed August 25, 2020).

A Spanish translation was soon thereafter produced that includes 600 beautiful botanical illustrations by an unknown engraver. *De Material Medica* remained the main pharmacological text in the western world for centuries and people of all faiths and languages made use of it.

herbal medicine texts composed in the first century CE by Dioscorides, a Greek physician. Healing and help come in the moment of need by the hand of nature, by the hand of the saints, the prophets, the lovers of God, seeking alignment with the Divine Reality; there is a response.

Woven in remembrance, again within the blessings of Mary and Jesus, is St. Catherine's Monastery[14]—on Mt. Sinai, the sacred mountain in the journey of Moses—protected, also, by the hand of Muhammad. In the monastery's library there is the "*Ashtiname* (Book of Peace) of Muhammad." This is a document with the hand seal of Prophet Muhammad that grants protection to the monastery and tax exemption to the Christian monks there, as well as exemption from military service while under Islamic rule.

St. Catherine (c. 287–305 CE) for whom the monastery is named was a virgin martyr of Roman Alexandria, Egypt. When she first witnessed to her faith, she was christened with the name Aikaterina (from the Greek *Αικατερίνα* meaning "ever clean"), signifying her deep purity. Among many Christians, St. Catherina Alexandrina is regarded as the most devoted of virgins, even next in holiness to the Virgin Mary. A princess and already a renowned scholar, she became a Christian when she was about fourteen. Her faithful devotion and wisdom encouraged many to accept the Way of Christianity, and so she was martyred in 305 CE by the Roman Emperor Maxentius, when she was only eighteen. It was a vision she experienced of the Virgin Mary with Jesus that had brought deep faith to her heart.

The "Hand of Blessing" is a shared tradition among Christians, Jews, and Muslims. For Christians, it is remembered as the "Hand of Mary"; for Jews, it is the "Hand of Miriam"; for Muslims, it is honored as the "Hand of Fatimah". Sometimes a necklace with a pendant in the shape of a hand may be worn for protection, or hung from a door frame, painted on a ceramic tile or upon a wall, or embroidered or woven into cloth. One remembers another saying among friends in Turkey that if one brings the fingers of the hand together, holding them upright, it is an expression of, "Beautiful!" Even so, when we recognize our common origins as one people of heart, joined in service, it is beautiful.

---

14 See Extended Context Notes in Appendix, Star VII, 2.

"Ashtiname *(Book of Peace) of Muhammad*"
*Sealed with his handprint, in it he declares that this is "a covenant given to the followers of Jesus the Nazarene in the East and West, the far and near, the Arabs and foreigners, the known and the unknown . . . [they] are under my protection and the testament of my safety."*[15]

---

[15] For a full translation of this text and others, and regarding the Covenants Initiative see John Andrew Morrow, *The Covenants of the Prophet Muhammad with the*

Despite differences in theological or historical detail or belief, many sites related to the life of Beloved Mary gather Muslims and Christians together within prayer and remembrance, whether to petition in moments of suffering or offering gratitude in times of joy. So often, springs of clear nourishment have emerged nearby. Tradition relates that, on their way further through the desert into Egypt, a new spring of fresh water—the "Spring of Mary"—opened for the holy family near Wadi al-Natrun.[16] In remembrance, over the centuries, it became a place of deep meditation and prayer. We are reminded again of the spiritual purity associated with the concept of Paradise, the gardens through which running waters flow, and the flow of knowledge from the heart through Grace. The ancient Egyptian Mother Goddess, Isis, who was gifted with the power to heal and to bring the dead to life, was often depicted nursing her child, Horus, whom she protected by hiding him among the marshes of the Nile.[17] When artists began to depict Beloved Mary, she was often represented in a similar moment of nurturance, with the infant Jesus embraced on her lap. Some of the earliest such representations are from among the Coptic Christian community of Wadi al-Natrun (whose Coptic name, "Scetis" Valley, from the Coptic *shi-het*, has the meaning of "measure of hearts"), where hundreds of monasteries arose and many "Desert Fathers" and "Desert Mothers" (Christian ascetics) lived immersed in prayer. The early Muslims may well have passed through Wadi al-Natrun on their way to Abyssinia and have seen such representations of Mary there, as holy icons, similar to the one that was in the Kaaba in the time of Muhammad, which he protected.

Muslims as well as Christians honor the visit of the holy family at Matariyyah, where it is told that Beloved Mary rested with her infant and steadfast Joseph on their continued journey south, away from the persecution of Herod. They were refugees in danger, and yet rest and consolation

---

*Christians of the World* (Angelico Press, 2013).

[16] Wadi al-Natrun (Arabic for "Valley of Natrun") was an area rich with natrun—a salt used for purification and for the embalming of the dead by the ancient Egyptians. It was early used as a mouthwash to protect teeth, as an antiseptic, and a preservative. Some believed it supported spiritual wellbeing for both the dead and the living.

[17] We notice how the ancient Egyptian traditions also evoke the story of Moses, how the theme threads of the tapestry of human history and comprehension of Divine Reality are interwoven, over and over.

*Balsam Tree of Beloved Maryam in Matariyya*
*(New branches have sprouted from the ancient trunk)*

was granted to them within the embrace of the natural world. In Matariyya, near Ayn-Shams (now Cairo), a sycamore tree bent to offer Mary shade where they paused in their journey, and another new spring opened for the holy family, where Mary bathed her precious child and washed his clothing, engaged in the simple caring tasks of motherhood. When she wrung out the cloth, some drops of the water fell upon the ground; there, a balsam plant grew of delicate fragrance. The tree was known for centuries as the "Tree of the Holy Virgin." The original tree has died, but another grew up in its place and still carries that honor. Healing balsam continues to grow there, lending its oil for healing and for prayer. The area is known as "Matariyya," in remembrance of "The Mother" (*Mater*).

*We granted unto Jesus, the son of Mary, clear Signs,*
*and strengthened him with the Holy Spirit [Ruh al-Quddus].*
[Quran, *Surah al-Baqarah* 2:87]

Salman reported that God's Messenger (peace and blessings be upon him) said: "Truly, on the same day that God created the heavens and the earth, He created a hundred parts of loving Mercy (*Rahma*). Every single part of loving mercy is as vast as the space between heaven and earth; and out of all this mercy He sent but a part into the world—it is from this that a mother shows affection to her child."[18]

Just over the place where Moses was found in the Nile, while his mother stood careful watch, stands the oldest synagogue in Cairo, some say, the oldest in the world: the Ben Ezra Synagogue; apparently the Nile still floods the basement. Though originally founded there, it is said, in the sixth century BCE by the Prophet Ezra, the land and current building now converted into the synagogue was purchased by the local Jewish community from the Coptic Christian community in the ninth century CE.[19] At the time of the infancy of Jesus, Egypt was under Roman rule, but the ancient Jewish and Egyptian history and communities were still vibrant. It was the Greek-speaking Jewish community of Alexandria (known for its vast ancient library) who translated the Old Testament from Hebrew into Greek (the Septuagint), upon which Christian translations for the Bible were later based.

So many interweaving strands! The fertile Nile, the holy mountains, journeys of refuge; a bond of love through the wisdom of ancient traditions. And another angel appears within the dream realms to guide Joseph:

But when Herod was dead, behold,
an angel of the Lord appeared in a dream to Joseph in Egypt,

---

[18] *Sahih Muslim* XVII, 69. Kitab al-Tawba. And thus, ninety-nine more "vast portions" of Mercy remain with God, to be bestowed continually, directly upon us, through God's Grace.

[19] Within the synagogue, near the roof, was a secret room—a *genizah*, a sacred storeroom—containing a mysterious treasure—thousands of worn religious texts, and documents, and letters which contained the name of G-d but were no longer needed. According to Rabbinic law, such outmoded documents couldn't just be thrown away; out of respect they were either buried or deposited in such a storeroom. A similar practice occurs within Islam regarding holy texts. Here for generations such documents of the Jewish community of Old Cairo (Fustat) had accumulated, and due to the cool, dry climate were preserved intact, spanning a thousand years.

In 1896 CE, a scholar from Cambridge had heard about this and came to examine the contents. He was told he could take what he liked. Thrilled, he removed 193,000 documents to Cambridge where a thousand years of history could then be more easily studied. The Cambridge University Library's "Taylor-Schechter Cairo Genizah Collection" is the largest collection of medieval Jewish manuscripts in the world.

Saying, "Arise, and take the young child and his mother,
and go into the land of Israel:
for they are dead which sought the young child's life."
And he arose, and took the young child and his mother,
and came into the land of Israel.
But when he heard that Archelaus did reign in Judaea
in the room of his father Herod, he was afraid to go there:
but even so, being warned of God in a dream,
he turned aside into the parts of Galilee:
And he came and dwelled in a city called Nazareth:
that it might be fulfilled which was spoken by the prophets,
he shall be called a Nazarene.
[Bible, Gospel of Matthew 2:19–23]

And so the refugees return again home, guided again by a dream from the Unseen, from the Mercy of the All-Compassionate. Within the Islamic tradition, it is understood that Compassion and Mercy (*Rahma*) from the womb of Reality are always greater than the trials we may experience—*My Mercy overwhelms My stringency*[20]—that the trials of the journey are even enfolded within that Ultimate Compassion, teaching us in every moment, even as the womb of the mother is always nourishing the growing child, and that God is Sufficient as a Guardian for our Affairs:

*Your Sustainer has willed upon Himself/Herself*
*the Law of Compassion.*
[Quran, *Surah al-An'am* 6:54]

*"God is enough for us; and how excellent a Guardian is He/She!"*[21]*—*
*and they returned with God's blessings and bounty,*
*without having been touched by harm:*

---

[20] *God answered: "With My stringency I try whom I will—but My Mercy encompasses everything"* (Quran, *Surah al-A'raf* 7:156).

[21] *HasbunaAllahu, Waniaama al Wakil!* (*God is enough for us; and how excellent a Guardian is He/She!*) This first line of the *ayat* ("verse", "sign") some find very helpful to hold as a chanted remembrance during the challenging journeys of life. The chant of simply "*Hasbiyallah*" ("God is enough for me") can be a beautiful haven, as we take refuge in the Presence of our Sustainer.

*for they had been striving after God's goodly acceptance—*
*and God is limitless in His/Her great bounty and grace.*
[Quran, *Surah al-'Imran* 3:173–74]

*Juniper with Mary-blue Berries*

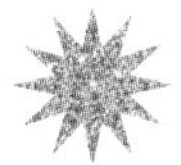

# *O Friend and Protector!*[1]
## *Ya Wali! Ya Haqq!*

O Beloved Protector, Friend, O Truth!
I, a mother, come to You
    kneeling,
    softly calling
        You
to come quickly to me
    with Your blessing
    and protect my children[2]
    from any harm
    that might truly harm them.
That they might sometimes be battered
    by the storms of life,
    I understand,
but keep them from permanent harm,
    let them move with Your Radiance,
    let them sense Your Will,
        Your Plan,
    and dance and work to fulfill it;
let them sow Your seeds.
Let them plant vineyards and orchards,

---

[1] Poem reflection excerpted and adpated from Camille Hamilton Adams Helminski, *Words from the East* (Louisville, KY: Sweet Lady Press, 2016), of the "Songs of the Soul" series.
[2] See Quran, *Surah al-'Imran* 3:173–174:

*"God is enough for us; and how excellent a Guardian is He/She!"*
*and they returned with God's blessings and bounty,*
*without having been touched by harm:*
*for they had been striving after God's goodly acceptance—*
*and God is limitless in His/Her great bounty and grace.*

let them grow many flowers . . .
for generations . . .
and also, O You Who are All-Knowing,
feed them Your Knowledge,
that they may bring new benefit
to this old world,
innovating new solutions
to difficulties here.
Let them shine among men and women
that others may be lit by their fire;
always two logs burn better than one,
keeping each other aflame.
Oh may mothers everywhere
teach their children of Your Love,
Your Generosity
and Your Care,
that each new generation
may spread Your Light farther
and deeper,
and higher.
"I asked for one kiss,
You gave me six"[3] . . .

---

[3] See *Kulliyat-i Shams-i Tabrizi,* Quatrain 1993 of Mevlana Jalaluddin Rumi. Referring to all the six directions of existence, Mevlana also says:

The mind says, "The six directions limit us; there's no way out."
Love says, "There is a way—I've journeyed through thousands of times."

The whole world of six directions is filled with His bounty:
wheresoever you look, it is making Him known.
[Rumi, *Mathnawi* III: 3108]

The Prophet said, "God doesn't pay attention to your outer form:
so in your improvising, seek the owner of the Heart."
God says, "I regard you through the owner of the Heart,
not because of prostrations in prayer
nor the giving of wealth in charity."
The owner of the Heart becomes a six-faced mirror:
through him or her God looks out upon all the six directions.
[Rumi, *Mathnawi* V: 869–70; 874]

may the worlds be filled with You,
apparently.
May You flow more and more into our existence,
and may we and our children
flow more and more from and into You.
*Ya Wakil, Ya Hakim,*
*Ya Karim, Ya Alim,*
*Ya Wali, Ya Haqq,*
*Ya Nur, Ya Wadud!*[4]

[4] *Ya Wakil* ("O Trustee, Guardian of All Our Affairs"), *Ya Hakim* ("O Most Wise, Healer of All Our Ills"), *Ya Karim* ("O Most Generous"), *Ya Alim* ("O Knower of All"), *Ya Wali* ("O Friend and Protector"), *Ya Haqq* ("O Truth"), *Ya Nur* ("O Light"), *Ya Wadud* ("O Infinitely Loving One")!

# VIII. EIGHTH STAR OF BLESSING

## *Losing and Finding Jesus: Calling the Beloved*

# *Losing and Finding Jesus: Calling the Beloved*

*We do raise by degrees whom We will.*
*Truly, your Sustainer is Wise, All-Knowing.*
*And We bestowed upon [Abraham,] Isaac and Jacob,*
*and We guided each of them as We had guided Noah earlier.*
*And among his offspring, [We bestowed prophethood upon] David, and Solomon,*
*and Job, and Joseph, and Moses, and Aaron:*
*for even so do We reward the doers of good;*
*and [upon] Zachariah, and John, and Jesus, and Elijah:*
*every one of them was of the righteous;*
*and [upon] Ishmael, and Elisha, and Jonah, and Lot.*
*And to every one of them did We grant abundant favor for the sake of the worlds,*
*and some of their forefathers and their offspring and their brethren:*
*We chose them [all],*
*and guided them onto a straight way.*
*Such is God's guidance:*
*He/She guides therewith whomever He/She wills of His/Her servants.*
[Quran, *Surah al-An'am* 6:83–88]

After the return from Egypt, it is said that Mary and Jesus and Joseph settled again in Nazareth. Throughout those years, as a young boy, Jesus would have been helping Joseph, learning his trade, and whether traveling or at home, he would have been beside Mary, learning scripture. It would have been a simple life—Mary would have been raising him with his days interwoven with prayer while he assisted Joseph with his carpentry and, perhaps later, the raising of walls of mud-brick dwellings for their neighbors. Joseph would have taken Jesus to the local synagogue three times a week, and together with both his parents he would have been carefully following Jewish practice and prayer (so interwoven with every day and night of life), learning the Ways of Abraham and the wisdom of the prophets.

After they returned from Egypt, each year, they would take Jesus to the Temple in Jerusalem to celebrate the rites of Passover.[1] It is noted that in his twelfth year, when he was just a little younger than Beloved Mary when the Angel Gabriel had visited her in the Temple announcing his arrival, they again went up to Jerusalem for the celebration of the Passover.

Now his parents went to Jerusalem every year at the feast of the Passover.
And when he was twelve years old, they went up to Jerusalem
after the custom of the feast.
And when they had fulfilled the days,
as they returned, the child Jesus tarried behind in Jerusalem;
and Joseph and his mother knew not.
[Bible, Gospel of Luke 2:41–43]

For safety and companionship in that era, many people traveled in caravans. There would have been many people on the roads returning to their homes after the celebration of Passover at the Temple. As they moved along, they might visit with friends as they walked or rode, and the children might play among themselves along the way, running back and forth, or clustering in groups beside a parent. It would have been spring, March or April, following the lunar calendar, the 15th of Nisan for the major rites (by the Jewish calendar), which might have been April 8th that year, a lovely time to travel, not too hot yet, and past the cold of winter. At twelve years of age, Jesus was already almost an adult by the standards of that era, so Mary and Joseph would not have been concerned for him, until a day had passed without seeing him. Perhaps it was at the time of sunset that they noticed his absence for the prayer.

---

[1] The Passover week-long celebration commemorates in thanksgiving the freeing of the enslaved Israelites from bondage, at the time of Moses and the Exodus: the Pharaoh had continued to persecute them, and in response, ten plagues came to Egypt, including the killing of the first-born children, but with God's guidance to the Israelites, the avenging angel "passed over" their homes; they were saved from such heartbreak and were aided on their journey into freedom.

But they, supposing him to have been in the company,
went a day's journey;
and they sought him among their kinsfolk and acquaintance.
And when they found him not,
they turned back again to Jerusalem, seeking him.
[Bible, Gospel of Luke 2:44–45]

Surely, after all Beloved Mary had been through and the warnings and challenges they had experienced in his early years, she was now concerned for Jesus, and yet, also, trusting in the ways of her Lord, surely, calling upon His/Her aid by heart in prayer, that the One Finder (*Al-Wajid*)[2] might assist them in finding her beloved son whom she, and Joseph, had always tended with such care. Perhaps they searched near where they had stayed, inquiring of people among whom they had been if they had seen him. It took three days to find him—three—again a resonance with the processes of Reality,[3] and a harbinger of experiences to come.

And it came to pass, that after three days they found him in the Temple,
sitting in the midst of the scholars,
both hearing them, and asking them questions.

---

[2] Among the "Ninety-Nine Names of God" in the Islamic tradition is "The Finder" (*Al-Wajid*).

[3] Within many faith traditions three is a significant number, the first true number according to the Pythagorians; it is seen as the symbol of harmony, describing the frequently experienced natural process of Reality unfolding with affirmation/denial/reconciliation. "Wherever two or more are gathered, I am there" (Bible, Gospel of Matthew 18:20) describes the possibility of the presence of a Third Force containing and rebalancing, enhancing Spirit. In Christian dogma one recognizes the Trinity of Father, Son, and Holy Spirit. Within Islam, the constant phrase of remembrance is *Bismillah ar-Rahman ar-Rahim* ("In the Name of God, the Infinitely Compassionate, the Infinitely Merciful"). Within many faiths, including Hinduism, three aspects of Divinity are united in One Encompassing Reality, indicating a fluidity, a cycling of Spirit. The symbol of three can also be recognized as an indicator of the weaving together of all aspects of the human being—body, mind, and heart.

As a beginning of immersion in prayer in the Islamic Sufi tradition, one might take a three-day retreat, before attempting a retreat of forty days, as within three days it is still possible to settle into a deeper awareness, removed from the world. Perhaps this three days is such an indication of retreat for Jesus, and a fractal of the unfolding from Good Friday to Easter.

And all that heard him were astonished at his understanding and answers.
And when they saw him, they were amazed . . .
[Bible, Gospel of Luke 2:46–48]

For centuries, Jewish people have had a special love for study of the Torah, and young men, especially, are trained for that. Jesus was drawn back to the Temple[4] as though by a magnetic force (even as Muslims are drawn to be at the Kaaba, or anyone inspired by Spirit is drawn to spend time with the holy). Surely his nature prompted him to inquire more about the qualities of Spirit, to understand more deeply the Ways of the prophets, to engage in the meanings of the scriptures with these men who were so well-versed in the holy writings, and to share what was in his own heart, elucidated by all the teachings of his dear mother and Joseph and his own deep heart connection to "the Father."

And his mother said unto him: "Son, why have you thus dealt with us?
behold, your father and I have sought you sorrowing."
And he said unto them: "How is it that you sought me?
Wouldn't you know that I must be about my Father's business?"
And they understood not the saying which he spoke to them.
And he went down with them, and came to Nazareth,
and was obedient to them,
but his mother kept all these sayings in her heart.
[Bible, Gospel of Luke 2:48–51]

The Quran relates a beautiful story of the sensitivity of Jacob, of his catching the scent of the shirt of his beloved son Joseph, as soon as the caravan had set out from Egypt towards him, and Jacob's sight then being

---

[4] Though there were local small synagogues for worship, there was only one Temple, the Temple of Solomon in Jerusalem where the Ark of the Covenant had originally been sheltered (and Beloved Mary in her youth). Following the example of Abraham, the Jews differed from others of the ancient peoples of the region in their belief in One God, as was upheld by all the Hebrew prophets, One Divine Reality, as later was, also, affirmed by the Quran. Like many other temples of the ancient world, the sanctuary of the Temple had two rooms, but here, the inner sanctuary was empty—there was no idol representing God.

restored to him in his joy.[5] Knowing his beloved mother Mary's sensitivity, Jesus would surely have thought she would know and recognize where he must be, not only because he had been raised deeply immersed in the scriptures and that yearning had grown in him to understand and convey Truth, but also because he and his mother had such a close bond since the first moments of his life, so that he might have been surprised she did not realize where he had returned and why. And yet a veiling occurred, perhaps to allow him the beginning of moments of independence as a young man[6] coming into his own deep knowing, and also as a portent of what was to come.

*Invite to the way of your Lord with wisdom and beautiful urging;*
*and discuss with them in the best and most gracious manner.*
[Quran, *an-Nahl*, "The Bee," 16:125]

Stories are told, among Muslim scholars like Al-Masudi, of Jesus, in his youth, teaching wisdom to the rabbis. Jesus may have in those moments inquired of the elders of the Temple—the wise rabbis and scholars—regarding the heritage of the Abrahamic prophets, and then shared the meanings that he, himself, had come to understand, giving some new comprehension that amazed them. He would have known well the story of Abraham, as himself a young man, turning aside from the idols of his father's culture and coming to recognize the vastness of the Divine Reality, beyond all earthly forms or human conceptions or idols of our making.

The Quran describes beautifully Abraham's retreat into the desert, to reflect and meditate, watching and witnessing the heavenly bodies, and his mystical experience unfolding:

---

[5] See Quran, *Surah Yusuf* (especially 12:94–96), and the Bible, Genesis, Chapters 37–50—another story of a spiritually devoted parent, of the Jewish tradition, honored as a prophet by Christians and Muslims, losing and finding a beloved child.

[6] Religious manhood would have been recognized around this age of physical maturity, when a young man would have begun to take on full responsibility in the religious community; since the medieval era this ritual passage has been honored in the Bar Mitzvah celebration, when a young man's study and grasp of scripture would be tested and acknowledged.

*And We gave Abraham [his first] insight*
*into [God's] mighty dominion over the heavens and the earth—*
*and to the end that he might become one of those who are inwardly sure.*[7]
*Then, when the night overshadowed him with its darkness,*
*he beheld a star; he exclaimed, "This is my Sustainer!"—*
*but when it went down, he said, "I love not the things that set."*
*Then, when he beheld the moon rising, he said, "This is my Sustainer!"—*
*but when it went down, he said, "Indeed, if my Sustainer guide me not,*
*I will most certainly become one of the people who go astray!"*
*Then, when he beheld the sun rising, he said, "This is my Sustainer!*
*This one is the greatest!"—but when it, too, went down,*
*he exclaimed: "O my people! Behold, far be it from me to ascribe divinity,*
*as you do, to anything beside God!*
*Behold, unto Him who brought into being the heavens and the earth*
*have I turned my face, having turned away from all that is false;*
*and I am not of those who ascribe divinity to anything beside Him."*
[Quran, *Surah al-An'am* 6:75–79]

The Truth dawned upon Abraham, of the All-Embracing Reality of the Divine, beyond adoration of idols or celestial bodies, in a full realization of the vast, transcendental existence of Divinity, the Source of all Creation. Throughout Abraham's life he then sought to be aligned with that Reality. In the time of Muhammad, there were those in his community who were seeking to, also, follow Abraham in his uprightness and alignment with Truth. While a young man, before the opening of his prophethood, Muhammad was among these *hanif*;[8] they supported each other in standing for Truth and upright character.

---

[7] *Yaqin*: "certain", "sure." *Yaqin* also has the meaning of "nearness," indicating that it is in drawing near to God that we are gifted with certainty, of the Vast, Powerful, and Beneficent Reality of the Divine.

[8] *Hanif*: true "monotheists"; see Quran, *Surah al-Baqarah* 2:130. The *hanif* might have referred to themselves even as the current scholar of the Abrahamic religions, Karen Armstrong, does—as "freelance monotheists"—recognizing a belief in the essential Oneness of God that is prior to any religious designation, as Abraham, himself, was not a "Jew" nor a "Christian" nor a "Muslim" (see Quran, *Surah al-'Imran* 3:67), but simply one purely devoted to alignment with the Divine Reality, the Oneness of Reality. It is said that the *hanif* endeavored to be trustworthy and hold themselves to a high standard of moral conduct.

*All that We relate to you of the stories of the messengers,*
*with it We strengthen your heart:*
*for through these Truth comes to you*
*as well as counsel*
*and a message of remembrance to those who have faith.*
[Quran, *Surah Hud* 11:120]

Within Islamic practice, every cycle of the ritual prayer completes with the remembrance of and greeting to Abraham and the asking for similar blessings as those with which he was blessed.[9]

*Truly, Abraham was a man who combined within himself all virtues,*
*devoutly obedient to God, and true in faith,*
*and he did not attribute divinity to anything beside God;*
*he was always grateful for the blessings of God*
*Who chose him and guided him onto a straight way.*
*And so We gave him good in this world*
*and truly in the Hereafter he will find himself in the ranks of the righteous.*
*And then We have inspired you:*
*"Follow the ways of Abraham, who turned away from all that is false,*
*and who did not join other gods with God."*
[Quran, *Surah an-Nahl* 16:120–23]

---

[9] *Allahumma Salli 'ala Muhammadin wa 'ala aali Muhammadin, kama sallaita 'ala Ibrahima wa 'ala aali Ibrahima innaka Hamidum-Majeed. Allahumma barik 'ala Muhammadin wa 'ala aali Muhammadin kama barakta 'ala Ibrahima wa 'ala aali Ibrahima innaka Hameedum-Majeed.* ("O Allah, send your grace, honor and mercy upon Muhammad and upon the family of Muhammad, as You sent Your grace, honor and mercy upon Ibrahim and upon the family of Ibrahim, You are indeed Praiseworthy, Most Glorious. O Allah, send Your blessings upon Muhammad and the family of Muhammad, as You sent Your blessings upon Ibrahim and upon the family of Ibrahim, You are indeed Praiseworthy, Most Glorious.")

Twenty-four of the Biblical prophets are remembered throughout the Quran; Abraham is mentioned more than sixty times. This ancestor, also, of Prophet Muhammad is referred to as *Khalil Allah* (the "Friend of God").

*In matters of faith, He has laid down for you the same commandment that He gave Noah,*
*which We have revealed to you and which We enjoined on Abraham and Moses and Jesus:*
*"Uphold the faith and do not divide into factions within it."*
[Quran, *Surah ash-Shura* 42:13]

*And remember Our servants Abraham, Isaac, and Jacob,*
*endowed with inner strength and vision.*
*Truly, We purified them*
*by means of the remembrance of the Life to Come.*
*They were in Our sight, truly, among the Elect*[10] *and the Good.*
*And remember Ishmail, Elisha, and Zul-Kifl:*
*each of them was among the companions of the Good.*
*This is a reminder:*
*and truly, awaiting the God-conscious is a beautiful place of return.*
[Quran, *Surah Sad*, 38:45–49]

Again, Luke recounts that Mary holds all that transpires with her precious child within her heart. Some say that it was Mary, herself, who recounted to Luke all that had taken place, from which he then wrote his "Gospel"[11]—that his account came through her heart.

A similar story of losing and finding a dear child is told of Prophet Muhammad's youth. His mother, Aminah,[12] had given him into the care of a Bedouin nurse-mother, Halima. It was the custom in those days for children of Mecca to be taken under the wing of a Bedouin foster-mother and family when possible, brought into the desert, where the air was fresher, to be raised in their early nursing years. After he had been weaned, Halima journeyed back to Mecca to restore him to his mother and grandfather, Abdul Mutallib,[13] because she had witnessed angels attending to Muhammad and was concerned for her capacity to protect

---

[10] *Mustafiyun*, "the chosen ones"; Prophet Muhammad is also known as *Mustafa* ('the Chosen').

[11] The word "Gospel" is derived from "good" plus "spel" ("story" or "message"). A later translation into Latin became *bona adnuntiatio*, itself a translation of the Greek *euangelion* ("reward for bringing good news") hence "evangelist"—"the bringer of good news." Later the meaning shifted from "good" to "God" story, as in "the glad tidings of Jesus": the Gospel Truth.

[12] Aminah ("trustworthy, faithful") carried the name by which Muhammad would also later be known, "the most trustworthy." When beloved Aminah was pregnant with Muhammad it is told that she experienced many dreams indicating the holy preciousness of her child, and that when he was born she witnessed a light emerging from her womb so great that she was overcome with its radiance.

[13] Muhammad's father had earlier passed away, before he was born, and so he was under the protection of his grandfather.

such a precious being. Halima, with great care, went to the Kaaba to meet Abdul Mutallib in a secure place to convey his dear grandson to him and his mother.[14] Suddenly, Halima heard a voice calling out to her. Rumi relates the story in great detail in his *Mathnawi*:

I will tell you the story of Halima's mystic experience,
that her tale may clear away your trouble.
When she parted Mustafa[15] from her milk,
she took him up on the palm of her hand
as tenderly as sweet basil and roses,
that she might commit that spiritual emperor to the care of his grandsire.
Since she was bringing the precious trust in fear for its safety,
she went to the Kaaba and came into the Hatim.[16]
From the air she heard a cry—"O Hatim,
an exceedingly mighty Sun has shone upon you!" . . .
Halima was bewildered by that voice:
neither in front nor behind was there anyone.
All the six directions were empty of any visible form,
and this cry was continuous—may the soul be a ransom for that cry!
She put Mustafa upon the earth,
that she might search after the sweet sound.
Then she cast her eye to-and-fro, saying,
"Where is that king that tells of mysteries?"
[Rumi, *Mathnawi* IV: 915–27]

Bewildered, Halima looked for who was speaking, without result, and then, when she turned back towards Muhammad, she discovered he had disappeared. Distraught, she cried out: "Who has carried off my unique pearl?" An old man nearby heard her and came to her aid. She told him of her plight. He brought her to 'Uzza (one of the pagan idols of the Kaaba of

---

[14] His mother Aminah, also, died a few years later, when Muhammad was six, leaving the orphan in the full care of his grandfather. Abdul Mutallib then also died a couple of years after that, leaving Muhammad under the wing of his uncle, Abu Talib.

[15] *Mustafa*: "the chosen." Another name for Muhammad (see previous page note).

[16] The *Hatim* is the semicircular place of prayer adjacent to the Kaaba where Hajar and Ishmael rest (see p. 79 and p. 80, n. 18 of this text).

that pre-Islamic era).[17] The old man told her: "This idol is greatly prized for information concerning the Unseen." He encouraged her to have patience, for even as Rumi often reminds us in his *Mathnawi*, "If you are wholly perplexed and in straits, have patience, for patience is the key to joy."[18] And the old man then turned towards the idol to ask for help:

"An infant child of hers is lost:
the name of that child is Muhammad."
As soon as he said "Muhammad,"[19]
all the idols there immediately fell down prostrate. . . .
The old man turned to her, "O Halima, rejoice;
bow down in thanksgiving and do not rend your face.
Do not grieve: he will not become lost to you;
nay, but the whole world will become lost in him. . . .
This is a marvelous epoch on the face of the earth:
I have grown old, and I have never seen anything like this!"
[Rumi, *Mathnawi* IV: 954–76]

---

[17] Before the opening of the prophethood of Muhammad and the restoration of the Way of Abraham, the Kaaba in Mecca, which was at the center of many caravan routes, had become filled with idols of all the numerous tribes who passed through to conduct trade there. Among them, 'Uzza was one of the most popular. It is said 360 idols had accumulated within the Kaaba before Muhammad cleared it, leaving only an icon of Mary with Jesus, which he protected, within the space of the sanctuary which at that time was open.

[18] Rumi, *Mathnawi* I: 2908.

[19] "Muhammad" has the meaning "praised, praiseworthy." Muslims look to Deuteronomy in the Torah and the Gospel of John as presaging the arrival of Prophet Muhammad. Moses says: "The Lord your God will raise up unto you a Prophet from the midst of you, of your brethren, like unto me" (Bible [Torah], Deuteronomy 18:15). The Prophet who brought a Law (*Shari'ah*) like that of Moses was Muhammad al-Mustafa; he was descended from the house of Isma'il, the brother of Isaac, the father of Israel (Jacob), both of whom are revered as prophets by Jews, Christians, and Muslims.

In John 14:16 of the Bible, Christ promised another "Comforter." Yusuf Ali, translator and commentator on the Quran, points out that the Greek word *Paraclete* ("Comforter"), which Christians interpret as referring there to the Holy Spirit, is by Muslim scholars taken to be *Periclyte*, (the Greek form of *Ahmad*—another variant of "Muhammad," meaning "one who has abundant praiseworthy traits, to whom praise belongs for radiantly good character").

It was another moment of the idols of religion, our limited concepts, falling before the immensity of Divine Love, an affirmation of the Way of Abraham.

This episode at the Kaaba holds within it resonances of the meeting of Simeon and Anna at the Temple when they recognized the true light of the infant Jesus, and the experience of Beloved Mary of the restoration of her precious child after losing him—the return of a child to a loving parent with the highlighted recognition of that child's righteousness and wisdom—and, also, echoes of the moment of Abraham knocking over the idols of his father's making. The fifth joyful mystery of the rosary is the remembrance of Beloved Mary finding Jesus again in the Temple. Here we have again the story of finding, of rediscovering the shining, pure-hearted one, in proximity with the holy, sacred space of prayer.

Abdul Mutallib heard news of Halima's search and quickly went towards the Kaaba, calling out to God, "Where shall I find him?" And from within the Kaaba[20] he heard a response, telling him that he could find "that righteous child" guarded by the angels: beside a nearby stream, sheltered by a gracious tree.

Rumi reminds us not to discount the lowly appearance of humble earth (or that of a child), for the Divine is a Revealer of Hidden Mysteries and the Luminous will shine forth.

We[21] have great affections towards this earth,
because it lies prostrate in humility.
In one moment We bring forth from it a spiritual sovereign;
in another We make it frenzied with love
in the presence of that majesty:
Because of him hundreds of thousands of lovers and loved ones
cry out with longing, and increase their seeking.
This is Our work,
that renders one confused and bewildered.
We confer this eminence on the earth
for the same reason We place a portion of food before the needy—
because the earth has the external form of dust,

---

[20] We remember that the Kaaba is also a metaphor for the human heart.
[21] It is the Divine "We," the voice of Divine Reality, speaking in this poem.

though inwardly it shines with all the qualities of radiance.
Its outside is at war with its inner reality:
inwardly it glows like a jewel
while outwardly it seems a common stone.
Its exterior says, 'We are this, and no more';
inwardly it says, 'Look well before and behind!'
Its outside denies it and says the inside is nothing;
its inside says, 'We will show you the truth: wait and see!'
Its outside and inside are struggling:
Divine aid rewards this patient endurance.
We make the forms of existence from this sour-faced earth;
We make manifest its hidden laughter,
for though outwardly the earth is all sorrow and tears,
within it there are hundreds of thousands of laughters.
We are the Revealer of the mystery, and Our work is just this,
that We bring forth hidden things from concealment.
[Rumi, *Mathnawi* IV: 1002–14]

Who can know Your guidance, unless You give them Wisdom,
and send Your Holy Spirit from on high?
Thus were the paths of those on earth made straight,
and people learned what pleases You, and were saved by Wisdom.
[Book of Wisdom[22] 9:17–18]

This search for the Beloved is ongoing and at the core of our human experience.

"Hear O Lord when I cry aloud, be gracious to me and answer me!
You have said, 'Seek My Face.'

---

[22] The "Book of Wisdom" (or "Wisdom of Solomon") was written around 50 BCE, before the birth of Christ. The author, probably of the Jewish community of Alexandria, wrote in Greek, but as though it were King Solomon himself speaking. It is one of the seven books of Wisdom of the Septuagint Old Testament—along with Job, Psalms, Proverbs, Ecclesiastes, Song of Songs (of Solomon) and Ecclesiasticus (Sirach). Written to be a support in times of suffering, within it the author elucidated the themes of the Exodus, the splendor of Wisdom, and the Mercy and Justice of God. Mary, Joseph, and Jesus would have been quite familiar with it; resonances can be heard in the teachings of Jesus included in the Gospels.

My heart says to You, 'Your Face, Lord, do I seek.'
Hide not Your Face from me."
[Bible, Psalms 27:7–9]

Behold, You delight in truth in the inward being,
and You teach me wisdom in the secret heart.
[Bible, Psalms 51:6]

*True piety does not consist in turning your faces towards the east or the west*[23]*—*
*but truly pious is the one who has faith in God, and the Last Day,*
*and the angels, and revelation, and the prophets;*
*and spends his/her substance—however much he or she may cherish it—*
*upon his or her near of kin, and the orphans, and the needy, and the wayfarer,*
*and the beggars, and for the freeing of human beings from bondage;*[24]
*and is constant in prayer, and renders the purifying dues;*
*and [truly pious are] they who keep their promises whenever they promise,*
*and are patient in misfortune and hardship and in time of peril:*
*it is they that have proved themselves true,*
*and it is they, they who are conscious of God.*
[Quran, *Surah al-Baqarah* 2:177]

Jesus was found in attendance at his "Father's house", the center of remembrance and holiness for those of his Jewish faith. Over those three days and nights, in addition to speaking and reflecting with the mind, surely he would have also been immersed with the prayers, attending to the word within his heart, deeply listening.

---

[23] The Quran indicates that it is not the outward forms that fulfill the acts of faith, but the inner intention, the centering of prayer within the heart. This verse was revealed at a moment when the *qiblah* (the direction of orientation towards which one would turn one's face in prayer) had shifted in outer direction for the Muslim community from Jerusalem to Mecca and the Kaaba.

[24] At the time of the revelation of the Quran, slavery was a widely established practice throughout the world. The abolition of slavery became one of the main social objectives of Islam. The Prophet encouraged the unconditional freeing of a human being from bondage as among the most praiseworthy acts that a Muslim could perform. In addition to the freeing of slaves from societal abuse, it is also understood that the prophets and saints through Revelation and their example assist us in freeing our hearts from egoistic domination, into the freedom of abundance within the Divine Presence, the vast realm of Reality.

St. Teresa of Ávila, a later follower of the way of Beloved Mary and Jesus, shares a beautiful reflection of such an experience:

> Turn your eyes towards the center, which is the room or royal chamber where the King stays, and think of how a palmetto has many leaves surrounding and covering the tasty part that can be eaten. So here, surrounding this center room are many other rooms; and the same holds true for those above. The things of the soul must always be considered as plentiful, spacious, large; to do so is not an exaggeration. The soul is capable of much more than we imagine, and the sun that is in this royal chamber shines in all parts. It is very important for any soul that practices prayer, whether little or much, not to hold itself back and stay in one corner. Let it walk through these dwelling places which are above, down below, and to the sides, since God has given it such dignity.[25]

It was here, centered within the heart, that he was "found" by the One Finder (*Al-Wajid*), the One within whose Hand is such abundance of support, who restores us and opens our hearts with gratitude.[26] For as Rumi reminds us, gratitude is also a key to joy, emerging through our difficulties:

> How should thankfulness grow from possessions and riches?
> Thankfulness grows from tribulation and illness.
> [Rumi, *Mathnawi* III:3013]

> . . . thankfulness and gratitude is the way of the prophet.
> [Rumi, *Mathnawi* VI:1829]

---

[25] Excerpt from Tessa Bielecki, *Teresa of Avila, Mystical Writings* (New York: The Crossroad Publishing Co., 1997), p. 41.

St. Teresa of Ávila, a Spanish Christian mystic of the sixteenth century was much influenced by the Desert Mothers and Fathers and worked to purify and simplify the rule of her order, establishing a new branch: The Order of the Discalced Carmelites of the Blessed Virgin Mary of Mount Carmel. "Discalced" means "without shoes"; St. Teresa and her friend and mentee, St. John of the Cross, emphasized poverty, charity, and immersion in contemplative prayer.

[26] *Ya Wali, Ya Wajid, Ya Shakur!* ("O Friend and Protector, O Finder—You Who Find Us When We are Lost, O Gifter of Gratitude!") may become a *zhikr* (chant of remembrance) in companionship through such moments of difficulty and distancing, realigning us with our Source with renewed blessing.

How deeply grateful and joyful Beloved Mary must have been to have her dear son restored to her, offering abundant thanks in return to the Giver of all Gifts who Overcomes all Obstacles (*Al-Wahhab*), the One who responds to Prayer (*Al-Mujib*)!

Abundance is seeking the beggars and the poor,
just as beauty seeks a mirror.
Beggars, then, are the mirrors of God's bounty,
and they that are with God
are united with Absolute Abundance.
[Rumi, *Mathnawi* I, 2745, 2750]

Giving thanks for abundance
is sweeter than the abundance itself:
Should one who is absorbed with the Generous One
be distracted by the gift?
Thankfulness is the soul of beneficence;
abundance is but the husk,
for thankfulness brings you
to the place where the Beloved lives.
[Rumi, *Mathnawi* III, 2895–96]

Rumi's mentor and beloved friend, Shams of Tabriz, encourages us to keep turning towards the heart to find that One who finds us—even as beloved Mary must have done in that moment—and in that process be willing to undergo the trials that expand the heart to be able to encompass more and more fully that Presence:

> Seek the heart, not instincts! Where is the place of the heart? The heart is hidden. . . . The moment the bright light of the Truth reflects upon the heart, the heart becomes joyful. Then in a moment, that light disappears, but many times it happens like this so that the heart might become a heart. It burns, and many times the heart gets broken, until it melts and only God remains.
>
> He indicated this to the Prophet David. David asked God, "Where will I look for you?" He said, "My heavens and My earth cannot encompass me, only the heart of My faithful servant can encompass Me." He also said, "I am with those whose hearts have been broken on My way." When you say, "a person of heart," say "those whose

hearts have been broken," because brokenness of heart is necessary. When you reach the Truth, you will see the divine light of His Exaltedness from within the divine light of the Truth Itself, because "No one knows them but I."[27]

Through all the tribulations of our lives we keep learning, through nights of difficulty and days of renewal:

> *God alternates the night and the day* [Quran, *Surah an-Nur* 24:44]. Again and again the light of day is drowned in the sea of darkness, and over and over again the sea of darkness is burned away within the rays of light. *Do people think that they will be saved by saying, "We have faith," and be left to themselves without being tested?* [Quran, *Surah al-Ankabut* 29:2]. What is there in the world that is accepted without passing through a test, or rejected without being tested? But if God wills, the work is corrected in the end, and you go along the right way, and then you understand who you are!"[28]

Beloved Mary's discipline, divinely inspired, her complete devotion, would have been such an example for her son, of love, of justice, of the principles of rectification and atonement—the focal completion of the ritual of the New Year.[29] Surely she would have taught him all the rituals of life observed in their Jewish traditions that may assist in the deepening of awareness of our inmost soul and of our Sustainer. "Mary kept all

---

[27] *Hadith Qudsi*: "My saints are under My dome—no one knows them but I." Excerpted from *Rumi's Sun*, op. cit., p. 402. To fully see such beloved servants, one would need to see through the eye of God. Then one might witness a unity in Truth, even as we are called to do through the Quran:

*Say: "We have faith in God, and the revelation given to us,*
*and the revelation given to Abraham, Ishmael, Isaac, Jacob and the Tribes,*
*and that given to Moses and Jesus, and that given to [all] the prophets from their Lord:*
*We make no distinction between one and another of them,*
*and to Him/Her we surrender ourselves."*
[Quran, *Surah al-Baqarah* 2:136]

[28] *Rumi's Sun*, op. cit., pp. 402–03.

[29] Observing the rituals of the New Year (from Rosh Hashanah through Yom Kippur) has long been a pre-eminent part of the Jewish tradition of renewal of Spirit and the cleansing and re-dedication of life from the depths of one's soul. See Extended Context Notes in Appendix, Star VIII, 1.

these words, pondering them in her heart" (Gospel of Luke 2:19)—she continued to hold close the revelation of God, watching "the Word" grow before her eyes—tending the garden of her son with great care.

And Jesus increased in wisdom and stature and grace,
with God and men.
[Bible, Gospel of Luke 2:52]

*For, indeed, We gave unto Moses the Book*
*and caused messenger after messenger to follow him;*
*and We gave unto Jesus, the son of Mary, clear signs,*
*and strengthened him with the Holy Spirit.*[30]
[Quran, *Surah al-Baqarah* 2:87]

The quintessential call to God of the Jewish faith, which Jesus would have recited morning and evening since his earliest childhood, is the *Shemah Yisrael* declaration of faith from the Pentateuch. It includes the last words of Moses to his people and begins:

"Hear O Israel, the Lord your God is One God.
You shall love the Lord your God with your whole heart,
and with all your soul, and with your whole strength."
[Bible, Deuteronomy 6:4]

Beloved Mary and Jesus and Joseph would have recited it upon arising and with the sunset prayers, as well as before lying down to sleep at night. They would have stood, facing the Temple in Jerusalem, calling out to God:

Hear, O Israel,[31] the L-rd is our G-d, the L-rd is One.

---

[30] "This rendering of *ruh al-qudus* (lit., 'the spirit of holiness') is based on the recurring use in the Qur'an of the term *ruh* in the sense of 'divine inspiration.' It is also recorded that the Prophet invoked the blessing of the *ruh al-qudus* on his Companion, the poet Hassan ibn Thabit (see Bukhari, Muslim, Abu Da'ud and Tirmidhi): just as the Qur'an (*Surah al-Mujadalah* 58:22) speaks of all [the faithful] as being 'strengthened by inspiration (*ruh*) from Him.'" See Muhammad Asad, *The Message of the Qur'an*.

[31] We remember that the meaning of "Israel," the name gifted to Jacob after he was wrestling with the Divine Power and the angels, is "he who wrestles with God" (see the Bible, Genesis 32:28). We could understand this passage as counsel

[Rabbis have added an extra phrase of blessing here, voiced softly: "Blessed be the name of the glory of His kingdom forever and ever."][32]

You shall love the L-rd your G-d with all your heart, with all your soul, and with all your might. And these words which I command you today shall be upon your heart. You shall teach them thoroughly to your children, and you shall speak of them when you sit in your house and when you walk on the road, when you lie down and when you rise. You shall bind them as a sign upon your hand, and they shall be as a symbol upon your forehead. And you shall write them upon the doorposts of your house and upon your gates, so that your days and the days of your children may be prolonged on the land which the L-rd swore to your fathers to give them for as long as the heavens are above the earth. [Bible (Torah), Deuteronomy (Davarim) 6:4–9]

And it will be, if you will diligently obey My commandments which I enjoin upon you this day—to love the L-rd your G-d and to serve Him with all your heart and with all your soul—I will give rain for your land at the proper time, the early rain and the late rain, and you will gather in your grain, your wine and your oil. And I will give grass in your fields for your cattle, and you will eat and be sated. Take care lest your heart be lured away, and you turn astray and worship alien gods and bow down to them. For then the L-rd's wrath will flare

---

for all of us struggling to know and comprehend the Divinity, to "hear" that we are not separate, that Reality is One. Or as it is reflected in the Quran: *Remember Me, I remember you* (*Surah al-Baqarah* 2:152). It is thus encouraged that in the wholehearted loving remembrance of our Divine Source, we are re-membered, restored, found.

[32] In the Bible the Hebrew word for God is made up of four vowels, and according to tradition it was only pronounced on Yom Kippur by the High Priest within the sanctuary. Voicing God's name aloud is considered a very serious and powerful thing; one of the Ten Commandments given to Moses prohibits the saying of God's name in vain. When a Jewish person reads the Torah, they often substitute *Adonai* (or *HaShem*, "The Name"; or *Hakadosh baruch Hu*, "The Holy One, Blessed be He") for the four letter name of God (*YHWY*) that by tradition one does not readily pronounce. So this first witnessing statement of the *Shema Yisrael* would be spoken as: "*Shema Yisrael, Adonai Eloheinu, Adonai Echad.*"

*Echad* means "One." In Arabic it is *Ahad*, recognized also in Islam as an Essential quality, or "Name," of the Divine Reality.

up against you, and He will close the heavens so that there will be no rain and the earth will not yield its produce, and you will swiftly perish from the good land which the L-rd gives you. Therefore, place these words of Mine upon your heart and upon your soul, and bind them for a sign on your hand, and they shall be for a reminder between your eyes. You shall teach them to your children, to speak of them when you sit in your house and when you walk on the road, when you lie down and when you rise. And you shall inscribe them on the doorposts of your house and on your gates—so that your days and the days of your children may be prolonged on the land which the L-rd swore to your fathers to give to them for as long as the heavens are above the earth. [Bible (Torah), Deuteronomy (Davarim) 11:13–21]

The L-rd spoke to Moses, saying: Speak to the children of Israel and tell them to make for themselves fringes on the corners of their garments throughout their generations, and to attach a thread of blue on the fringe of each corner. They shall be to you as tzizit,[33] and you shall look upon them and remember all the commandments of the L-rd and fulfill them, and you will not follow after your heart and after your eyes by which you go astray—so that you may remember and fulfill all My commandments and be holy to your G-d. I am the L-rd your G-d who brought you out of the land of Egypt to be your G-d; I, the L-rd, am your G-d. True. [Bible (Torah), Numbers 15:37–41]

This is the most essential Jewish prayer, even as is the Lord's Prayer in Christianity and the *Fatiha* in Islam.[34] The first passage is echoed again

---

[33] *Tzitzit* means "tassels." "The verse teaches that those who observe the mitzvah of tzitzit, it is as if they have greeted the face of the divine presence (*Shekhinah*), for Tekhelet [the purple-blue hued dye used for the tzitzit threads, derived from the murex trunculus sea snail] is the color of the sea, and the sea is like the sky, and the sky is like the divine Throne." Noted in *Sifrei,* Numbers 115.

[34] See p. xxi of this text.

Traditionally before beginning the recitation of the *Shema Yisrael,* one would cover one's eyes with one's right hand, bringing one's focus even further into hearing.

The Jewish day traditionally begins at sundown of the previous day; *ma'ariv* (the Jewish evening prayer which includes the *Shema Yisrael*) would be offered at sundown, even as in Islamic practice the *maghrib* prayer is offered, each cycle beginning with the *Fatiha.* For both faith communities, a new month begins with the sighting of the new moon at the time of the setting of the sun.

later by Jesus, as recorded in the Gospel of Mark 12:28–34.

> One of the teachers of the law came and heard them debating.
> Noticing that Jesus had given them a good answer, he asked him,
> "Of all the commandments, which is the most important?"
> "The most important one," answered Jesus, "is this:
> 'Hear, O Israel: The Lord our God, the Lord is one.
> Love the Lord your God with all your heart and with all your soul
> and with all your mind and with all your strength.'
> The second is this: 'Love your neighbor as yourself.'
> There is no commandment greater than these."
> [Bible, Gospel of Mark 12:28–29]

Surely this call to God reverberated through Beloved Mary's heart; surely she "loved the Lord her God, with all her heart, with all her soul."

> "Hail, Virgin, whose shout was pious love for Us,
> which was heard from the mountain when the Word was made flesh."[35]

In one of the beautiful *Ave Maria*[36] songs of praise of Beloved Mary, the singer cries out: "I have cried to the Lord with my voice and He heard me from His holy mountain." Beloved Mary is viewed as the holy mountain, from whom God carved the form of Christ without hand, because she is:

> . . . (lofty in her life and manners and excellent in her merits.)[37] Her shout (*clamor*) of love (*amor*) which the Lord heard (*exauditur*) from His

---

The *Shema Yisrael* is, also, central to the final prayer of Yom Kippur (the Day of Atonement, the most important Jewish holy day which culminates the ten days of Awe—a time of reflection and repentance—that follow Rosh Hashanah, the Jewish New Year. The *Shema Yisrael* is traditionally the last words offered by a Jewish person when he or she is dying, completing with "True" (in Arabic, *Haqq*—another Name of the Divine Reality often used in the Quran).

35 *Mary and the Art of Prayer*, op. cit., p. 88. See the Bible, Gospel of John 1:14.

36 *Ave Maria* ("Hail Mary"), is from the beginning of Luke 1:28: "Greetings, O highly favored one, the Lord is with you."

These greetings and invocations of Mary's presence and blessing form the basis for the rosary prayers. *Aves* is, also, the Latin plural word for "birds," reminding us that our prayers wing their way through the spirit offering of our hearts.

37 Conrad, Speculum, XII, 3, ed. Martinez 193–94; trans Sr. Mary Emmanuel, 136. As cited in *Mary and the Art of Prayer*, op. cit., p. 88.

> mountain was the consent she gave to the angel's words: "Let it be to me according to your Word." (Luke 1:38) at which the Word became flesh (*unitur*) in her womb. Likewise the *Ave* suggests, she is a mountain for others from which they may lift their voices to God.[38]

Even as in the tradition of King David, "music invoked the Presence":[39]

> Shout joyfully before the Lord, the King.
> Let the sea resound, and everything in it,
> the world, and all who live in it.
> Let the rivers clap their hands,
> let the mountains sing together for joy.
> [Bible, Psalms 98:6–8]

> *And We bestowed Our grace upon David:*
> *"O you Mountains! Sing with him the praises of God!*
> *And you birds!"*
> [Quran, *Surah Saba* 34:10]

The *Ave* in remembrance of Beloved Mary continues with the psalmist praying:

> Lord, let the light of Your Face set its mark upon us;
> You gave me gladness in my heart.

and then the *Ave* reflects in response:

> Hail, the one whose mind the splendor of the Father made to reflect:
> Let your servants be marked with the splendor of Your Countenance![40]

For as it is also remembered in the Quran, those who move about this life in the remembrance of their Sustainer, and bestow upon others of what has been given to them,

---

38 *Mary and the Art of Prayer*, p. 88.

39 Margaret Barker, *Temple Themes in Christian Worship* (London: Bloosmbury Publishing, 2008), p. 142. Margaret Barker, a British Methodist minister and biblical scholar, demonstrates in this book how Christian worship has been modeled on Temple worship.

40 *Mary and the Art of Prayer*, op. cit., pp. 88–89.

*only out of a longing for the countenance of his or her Sustainer, the All-Highest:*
*such, indeed, shall in time be well-pleased.*
[Quran, *Surah al-Layl* 92:20–21]

Those who call upon their Lord with all their heart, their soul, and their strength, open the possibility of merging in union with the One who is called. Shams of Tabriz reflected:

May you not be separated from the One whose name you call.
Then your calling becomes the remembrance of the heart;
remembrance with only the tongue is not enough.[41]

As we were likewise reminded by Shams, the way to heaven, into God's Presence, is not the way of limited mind or distracted senses, but the open Way of the receptive and focused heart, when we turn with the simplicity of a pure child yearning, made whole in loving humility before God. Love takes precedence.

*O you who have attained to faith,*
*remain conscious of God [with all your heart and soul and strength],*
*and seek to come closer to Him/Her,*
*and strive hard in His/Her cause [of love and justice],*
*so that you might attain felicity.*
[Quran, *Surah al-Maida* 5:35]

In all our movement through the caravans of this world, we may sometimes become lost in the wanderings of the mind, but then we are suddenly found by the One Finder (*Al-Wajid*), by Love (*Al-Wadud*) and our hearts and souls are strengthened in remembrance of that One. And so the Water of Life flows.

Our speech and action is the exterior journey:
the interior journey is above the sky.
The physical sense saw dryness,
because it was born of dry dust:
the Jesus of the spirit set foot on the sea.
The journey of the dry body befell on dry land,

---

41 *Rumi's Sun*, op. cit., pp.126–27.

but the journey of the spirit strode into the heart of the Sea.
Since your life has passed in traveling on land,
now mountain, now river, now desert,
Whence will you gain the Water of Life?
Where will you cleave the waves of the Sea?
The waves of earth are our imagination and understanding and thought;
the waves of water are mystical self-effacement
and intoxication and annihilation [*fana*].
While you are in this intoxication of the senses,
you are far from that mystical intoxication;
while you are drunk with this, you are blind to that cup.
Outer speech and talk is as dust:
for a time make a habit of silence. Pay attention!
[Rumi, *Mathnawi* I: 570–77]

The eye of the Sea is one thing, the foam another;
leave the foam and look with the eye of the Sea!
Day and night there is movement of foam on the Sea.
You see the foam, but not the Sea. Amazing!
We are dashing against each other like boats:
our eyes are darkened though we are in clear water.
O you who have gone to sleep in the body's boat,
you've seen the water,
but look at the Water of the water.
The water has a Water that is driving it;
the spirit has a Spirit that is calling it.
[Rumi, *Mathnawi* III: 1271–74]

*The Messenger, and the faithful with him,*
*have faith in what has been revealed to him by his Sustainer;*
*they all have faith in God, and His angels, and His revelations, and His messengers,*
*making no distinction between any of His messengers;*
*and they say; "We have heard and we pay heed.*
*Grant us Your forgiveness, O our Sustainer,*
*for with You is all journey's end!"*
[Quran, *Surah al-Baqarah* 2:285]

## *It Is Spring!*[1]

And today it is spring.
Aaron's rod is flowering.
Joseph's branch blossoms,
and doves take flight
to nest in our nearby window
in the room held for guests.
Are we not all guests here,
held by Your Love?
A momentary passage
"beneath a palm tree"[2]
or an oak or willow . . .
bending with Your breeze,
we can hear the river singing;
the Ocean is not far.
Realms of stars sprinkle our nights
with patterns of Light.
And Your whispers

---

[1] Excerpt from *A New World*, "Songs of the Soul" series, Camille Hamilton Adams Helminski (forthcoming from Sweet Lady Press).

[2] The Prophet Muhammad once said: "In this life we are just a stranger, pausing for a moment under a palm tree."

[Ibn Kathir comments] that when first built, the mosque of the Prophet (peace and blessings be upon him) had no *minbar* [elevated pulpit] from which to address the congregation. He would speak while leaning against a palm tree trunk in the wall next to the *qibla* near where he prayed. Eventually he began to use a *minbar*. . . . As he moved over towards it to make his address from it and passed by that tree trunk, it moaned like a love-lorne camel because it had always heard his speeches delivered near itself. And so the Prophet (peace and blessings be upon him) returned to it and hugged it until it settled down, just like a baby, and became quiet.

See Ibn Kathir, *The Life of the Prophet Muhammad*, Vol. II, op. cit., p. 205.

reach us,
even in the dark—
when sometimes we can hear more clearly,
when less distractions mar our minds and hearts,
even though we may miss the sun's brightness;
ever You are with us[3]—
let us remember.
Let us pray,
until there is no "other" less,
and more, in need—
are we not all equal
in our longing,
in our birthright?
Aspirations differ;
some would forget,
amid the world's paltry pleasures,
lulled by the siren's song,[4]
distanced from home,
and yet,
we cannot be lost, for You are the Finder,
Most Glorious,
the One and Only
Giver of all that has been
known or will be
needed
or will be returned[5]

---

3 *I am with you wherever you are.*
*Witness! Your Sustainer inspired the angels*
*to convey His message to the faithful: "I am with you!"*
[Quran, *Surah al-Anfal* 8:9–12]

4 The sirens of Homer's *Odyssey*: with their alluring songs they distracted sailors from their destinations.

5 See Quran, *Surah al-Hadid*:

*God knows all that enters within the earth and all that comes forth out of it,*
*as well as all that descends from heaven and all that ascends to it.*
*And God is with you wherever you may be and sees well all that you do.*
*To God belongs the dominion of the heavens and the earth. And all things return to God*

into the folds of Your Being,
Expansive,
vast—
wave upon wave of resonance
holds us fast
in Your Love,
in Your Compassion,
in Your Mercy!
*Ya Rahman,*
*Ya Rahim,*
*Ya Ahad,*
*Ya Karim,*
*Ya Wajid,*
*Ya Wasi,*
*Ya Wadud!*[6]

---

*who merges night into day and merges day into night*
*and knows completely the secrets of hearts.*
[Quran, *Surah al-Hadid* 57:4–6]

[6] *Ya Rahman* ("O Infinitely Compassionate"), *Ya Rahim* ("O Infinitely Merciful"), *Ya Ahad* ("O the One"), *Ya Karim* ("O Infinitely Generous"), *Ya Wajid* ("O Finder"), *Ya Wasi* ("O All-Encompassing One"), *Ya Wadud* ("O Infinitely Loving One")!

# IX. NINTH STAR OF BLESSING

## *Miracles of Nourishment and New Life*

# *Miracles of Nourishment and New Life*

*And [remember the time] when I inspired the white-garbed ones:*
*"Have faith in Me and in My Messenger!"*
*They answered: "We have faith;*
*and bear witness that we have surrendered our selves."*
*Behold, the white-garbed ones said:*
*"O Jesus, son of Mary! Could your Sustainer send down to us a repast from heaven?"*
*[Jesus] answered: "Be conscious of God, if you are of the faithful!"*
*Said they: "We desire to partake of it, so that our hearts might be set fully at rest,*
*and that we might know that you have spoken the truth to us,*
*and that we might be of those who bear witness to it!"*
*Said Jesus, the son of Mary: "O God, our Sustainer!*
*Send down upon us a repast from heaven: it shall be an ever-recurring feast for us*
*for the first and the last of us—and a sign from You.*
*And provide us our sustenance, for You are the Best of Providers!"*
*God answered: "Truly, I am always sending it down to you."*
[Quran, *Surah al-Maida* 5:111–15]

After the moments of the three days of Jesus' immersion in the Temple, the Bible is silent as to the outer events of his life until his teaching begins when he is thirty. Some scholars reflect that as he was maturing he was spending time with the Desert Fathers and Mothers, most probably with the Essenes, who dressed in white as an indication of their aim for utmost purity.[1] The Gospels recount that in his

---

[1] *Al-hawariyyun* ("the white-garbed ones"; singular: *hawari*) is the designation applied in the Quran to the disciples of Jesus. (See p. 212 of this text; n. 60.) In Muhammad Asad's commentary on verse 3:52 of the Quran which also mentions the *hawariyyun*, he explains:

> Many interpretations of this term (derived from *hawar*, "whiteness") are given by the commentators, ranging from "one who whitens clothes by washing them" (because this was [it is told] the occupation of some of Jesus' disciples)

maturity, after his baptism and his retreat into the desert, Jesus had begun preaching around the shore of the sea in Galilee and calling to those who could hear to become "fishers of men."

In the Bible it was just after this that the first miracle of his maturity occurred. The feast from heaven mentioned in the above Quranic passage from *Surah al-Maida* ("The Feast")—that takes its name from this passage—evokes resonances with the first miracle of Jesus at Cana, as well as the later stories of the abundant loaves and fishes with which he miraculously fed the multitudes,[2] as well as the intimate "Last Supper." It is in the Gospel of John that this first miracle is mentioned—a wedding, a time of feasting, when suddenly there was a lack of wine to continue the celebration. Beloved Mary noticed. She was paying attention to the need of the moment. And she knew her son's inherent capacity. So it unfolded that Jesus' first public miracle in his maturity manifested through Mary's encouragement:

On the third day a wedding took place at Cana in Galilee.
Jesus' mother was there,
and Jesus and his disciples had also been invited to the wedding.
When the wine was gone, Jesus' mother said to him,
"They have no more wine."
"Madam, why do you involve me?" Jesus replied.
"My time hasn't yet come."
His mother said to the servants, "Do whatever he tells you."
[Bible, Gospel of John 2:1–5]

---

to "one who wears white garments," or "one whose heart is white," i.e., pure (cf. Tabari, Razi, Ibn Kathir). It is, however, most probable—and the evidence provided by the recently discovered [1948–1956 CE] Dead Sea Scrolls strongly supports this view—that the term *hawari* was popularly used to denote a member of the Essene Brotherhood, a Jewish religious group which existed in Palestine at the time of Jesus, and to which, possibly, he himself belonged. The Essenes were distinguished by their strong insistence on moral purity and unselfish conduct, and always wore white garments as the outward mark of their convictions. . . . The fact that the Prophet [Muhammad] once said, "Every prophet has his *hawari*" (Bukhari and Muslim) does not conflict with the above view, since he obviously used this term figuratively, recalling thereby Jesus' "helpers in God's cause."

[2] See the Bible, Gospel of Matthew 14 and 15, Mark 6 and 8, Luke 9, and John 6.

Jesus at first expresses that he is not ready. Mary doesn't discuss the matter; she doesn't take "no" for an answer. Beloved Mary indeed had been the teacher of Jesus in many ways, for years; in a way, one might see this as his spiritual graduation celebration in this earthly realm. She simply says, "Do as he tells you," affirming that it was indeed the moment to fulfill a need, to assist in celebration, the moment to acknowledge the capacity now fully awakened in Jesus, as though to say to him, "With God's ever abundant grace, you can do this; you are ready; this is the moment of blessing!" And Jesus listened; obedient to her word, he moved into action, following in the ways of his Creator, of abundance and transformation.

O truthful seeker, keep your heart happy!
For the One who makes hearts happy is busy working
to complete your work,
for *Every day He is about some new endeavor.*[3]

Cana was eight miles north of Nazareth, a long journey in that era, not a nearby neighborhood; for Mary and Jesus to be invited along with a number of his disciples it must have been the wedding celebration of a relative or close friend. Some scholars indicate there were six of them attending; and it is noted in the Gospel that it was also six jars that were filled. It seems the company had been drinking a while before the miracle took place, and that it must have been a large party in a spacious home for there to have been such servants and a storage space for six large stone jars.

Nearby stood six stone water jars,
the kind used by the Jews for ceremonial washing,
each holding from twenty to thirty gallons.
Jesus said to the servants, "Fill the jars with water";
so they filled them to the brim.
Then he told them,
"Now draw some out and take it to the master of the banquet."
They did so, and the master of the banquet tasted
the water that had been turned into wine.

---

[3] Shams of Tabriz, excerpt from *Rumi's Sun*, op. cit., p. 37. The quotation from the Quran is from *Surah ar-Rahman* 55:39.

He did not realize where it had come from,
though the servants who had drawn the water knew.
Then he called the bridegroom[4] aside and said,
"Everyone brings out the choice wine first and then the cheaper wine
after the guests have had too much to drink;
but you have saved the best till now."
This, the first of his [miraculous] signs, Jesus performed in Cana of Galilee.
He thus revealed his glory, and his disciples believed in him.
[Bible (NIV), Gospel of John 2:6–12]

After having been in the wilderness and returning to Jerusalem and Galilee to gather people to deeper awareness of the Divine Presence, the ministry of Jesus opens more fully with this witnessing in Cana—a wedding, a celebration of the abundant flowing of Spirit. A beloved passage of the Quran celebrates this potent Beauty of the Creative Power, a verse within which many of the "Names of God" are gathered.

*God is He/She other than whom there is no god,*
*Who knows what is hidden in the Unseen and what can be witnessed, manifest;*
*Hu, the Infinitely Compassionate, the Infinitely Merciful.*
*God is He/She other than whom there is no god,*

---

[4] There are some who speculate that the "bridegroom" was Jesus himself; he is described by John the Baptist with that epithet in the subsequent chapter of the Gospel of John 3:28–29:

Ye yourselves bear me witness, that I said, I am not the Christ,
but that I am sent before him.
He that hath the bride is the bridegroom: but the friend of the bridegroom,
which stands and hears him, rejoices greatly because of the bridegroom's voice:
this my joy therefore is fulfilled.

Similarly in the Gospel of Matthew 9:14–15 (and in Mark 2:18–19 and Luke 5:33–4) Jesus refers to himself as "the bridegroom" when speaking with the disciples of John, carrying the theme of celebration of Spirit, the "bride" of *Shekhinah*:

Then came to him the disciples of John, saying,
"Why do we and the Pharisees fast oft, but thy disciples fast not?
And Jesus said to them, "Can the children of the bridechamber mourn,
as long as the bridegroom is with them?"

*the Sovereign, the Holy One, the Source of Peace,*
*the Inspirer of Faith, the Preserver of Security,*
*the Exalted in Might, the Compelling, the Supreme:*
*Glory belongs to God*
*who is above partners they attribute to Him/Her—*
*He/She is God, the Creator, the Evolver, the Bestower of Form.*
*To Hu belong the Most Beautiful Names:*
*whatever is in the heavens and on earth*
*declares His/Her Praises and Glory,*
*and He/She is the Exalted in Might, the All-Wise.*
[Quran, *Surah al-Hashr*, "The Gathering," 59:22–24][5]

And the first public miracle, since his speaking in her defense as an infant in arms, occurred here, in the context of a wedding, highlighting Jesus' true purpose of facilitating transformation through love. In a sense, this gift was also flowing through Mary's heart, and one might catch in this resonance of the water becoming even more full of nourishment as the wine of love a reminder once again of the moment when Zachariah came to her in the sanctuary to bring her food—how he found she was already provided for, and when he asked how this arrived, she responded, *"See how our Lord provides for whom He wills, beyond all reckoning"* (3:37), in this instance also, re-opening awareness of that all-embracing, abundant Love:

*Truly, they who attain to faith and do righteous deeds shall have gardens*
*through which running waters flow—that triumph most great!*[6]

---

[5] For the remembrance of *Hu*, the Divine Presence see p. 40, n. 10 of this text. These *ayats* of *Surah al-Hashr* are a much-beloved passage, often recited in prayer by Muslims, a "gathering" in remembrance of many of the beautiful and nourishing qualities of the Divine Reality, Knower of the Unseen, continually creating, and inspiring faith:

*Huwallahullazhi laa ilaha illa Huu;*
*Alim ul ghaybi wash-shahadati, Huwar Rahman ur Raheem.*
*Huwallahullazhi laa ilaha illa Huu;*
*Al Malik ul Quddus us Salaam ul Mumin ul Muhaymin ul Aziz*
*ul Jabbar ul Mutakabbir. Subhanallahi amma yushrikuun.*
*Huwallahul Khaliq ul Bari ul Musawwiru lahul asmaa ul husnaa.*
*Yusabbihu lahu ma fissamawati wal ardi wa Huwal Aziz ul Hakeem.*

[6] This is the earliest reference in the unfolding of the Quranic verses to "gardens

*Truly, your Sustainer's grasp is exceedingly strong!*
*Behold, it is He/She who creates [the human being] in the first instance,*
*and He/She will bring him/her forth anew.*
*And He/She alone is Truly-Forgiving, All-Embracing in His/Her Love,*
*in Sublime Almightiness enthroned,*[7] *Sovereign Doer of whatever He/She wills.*
[Quran, *Surah al-Buruj*, "The Great Constellations," 85:11–16]

Beloved Mary's reliance upon that encompassing Love was infinitely strong; she carried such a deep comprehension of the power of Love that can transform, even as Rumi reflects:

Love makes the wine of realization bubble:
He is the cupbearer to the *siddiq*[8] in secret.
When you seek the Reality with good help from God,
the essential water of the spirit is the wine, and the body is the flagon.
[Rumi, *Mathnawi* III: 4742–43][9]

---

through which running waters flow" as an allegory of the supreme felicity that opens for the righteous, embraced by the Love of God.

[7] Lit., "He/She of the sublime Throne of Almightiness" (*al-'arsh al-majid*), that encompasses all that is—see also the "The Throne Verse," a much-beloved passage recited often in prayer (and often together with the preceding verses from *Surah al-Hashr* 59:22–24):

*God—there is no deity but Hu, the Ever-Living, the Self-Subsisting Source of All Being.*
*No slumber can seize Him/Her nor sleep.*
*All things in heaven and on earth belong to Him/Her.*
*Who could intercede in His/Her Presence without His/Her permission?*
*He/She knows all that lies open before human beings and all that is hidden from them,*
*nor can they encompass any knowledge of Him/Her except what He/She wills.*
*His/Her Throne extends over the heavens and the earth,*
*and He/She feels no fatigue in guarding and preserving them,*
*for He/She is the Highest and Most Exalted.*
[Quran, *Surah al-Baqarah* 2:255]

[8] *Siddiq*: "the true, sincere, and faithful one."

[9] The metaphor of wine drinking occurs frequently in Sufi poetry and literature. It is understood that the "wine" is the metaphorical "wine" of "love of the Beloved (God)". In the early days of Islam, many people still drank wine, especially as a fermented drink was often healthier than water that might be tainted or simply unavailable. Later as the community was developing, amid the arising awareness of the difficulties caused by intoxication, a verse of the Quran was revealed cautioning against it. And further cautions as to caring for water, and not wasting,

In this moment of the wedding, there is a restoration of Eden, a return to the Garden, when man and woman are joined in harmony. Together, Beloved Mary and Jesus assist in fulfilling the continued celebration of the marriage, honoring this moment of union, allowing the pouring of the subtlest Love. The mystical works of the Torah contain many references to "husband" and "wife" being two halves of one whole, made whole in Spirit,[10] in Love; likewise in the Quran:

*It is He who created you from a single soul and likewise his mate of like nature,*
*in order that he might dwell with her [in love].*
[Quran, *Surah al-A'raf* 7:189][11]

Genesis, the first book of the Bible, verse 2:24, says that when a man is married he becomes one flesh with his wife, implying a return to the state prior to separation, when the soul is in the Garden, within

---

were also revealed in recognition of the sacred essentialness of water for life:

And everything was created from water.
By means of water, We give life to everything.
[Quran, *Surah al-Anbiya* 21:30]

The metaphor of drunkenness became indicative of the "intoxication" with God's love, and annihilation in God—when the wine, the cup (or the flagon), and the Cupbearer become one.

Listen, don't be deceived, O heart, by every intoxication:
Jesus is intoxicated with God, the ass is intoxicated with barley.
[Rumi, *Mathnawi* IV: 2691]

Shams of Tabriz in his *Maqalat* speaks of the limitations of mere intoxication, explaining that the greater attainment is the "sobriety" that can contain intoxication, when we are steadfast in the all-encompassing awareness of God's Love (see *Rumi's Sun*, op. cit., pp. 80–81).

[10] See Extended Context Note in Appendix, Star IX, 1.

[11] It may be pointed out that grammatically, as here the word *nafs* (translated as "soul" or "self") is feminine, the verse actually says, *created from a single soul and likewise* her *mate*. For a further discussion of the feminine gender of the *nafs*, see Sachiko Murata in *Women of Sufism, A Hidden Treasure*, edited by Camille Helminski (Boston: Shambhala Publications, Inc., 2003), pp.177–85.

See Quran 39:6 and 31:28. See also Quran 4:1 as quoted here:

*O humankind! Be conscious of your Sustainer, who has created you out of one living entity,*
*and out of it created its mate,*
*and out of the two spread abroad a multitude of men and women.*

the encompassing Presence of God. It is said that, "When a man and a woman marry they represent the fullness of God." In the Quran, the first couple of consciousness, Prophet Adam and Eve, are pointed to as exemplary of the original harmonious "one-to-one" relationship intended for us as human beings:

> *O Adam, dwell thou and thy wife, in the Garden . . .*
> [Quran, *Surah al-Baqarah* 2:35]

*Angels Bow before Adam and Eve in Paradise*
*Detail from the* Falnama *ascribed to Jafar as-Sadiq,*
*Iran (Tabriz or Qazwin) circa 1550 CE*

*And among His Signs is this:*
*that He created for you [O human beings] mates from among yourselves*
*that you may dwell in tranquility with them,*
*and He engenders love and compassion between you;*
*truly in that are signs for those who reflect.*
[Quran, *Surah ar-Rum* 30:20]

One of the most beautiful passages in Mevlana Jalaluddin Rumi's writings is a moment of blessing he offered for the wedding of his son, Sultan Weled, and dear Fatimah (named after the daughter of the Prophet Muhammad), whom he himself had taught and helped to raise in spiritual awareness from an early age, the daughter of his dear friend Salahuddin Zarqubi. Over the subsequent seven centuries this burst of joy has been shared in multitudes of moments, at wedding celebrations around the world, in recognition of the felicity pouring through a blessed marriage:

May these vows and this marriage be blessed.
May it be sweet milk,
this marriage, like wine and halvah.
May this marriage offer fruit and shade
like the date palm.
May this marriage be full of laughter,
our every day a day in paradise.
May this marriage be a sign of compassion,
a seal of happiness here and hereafter.
May this marriage have a fair face and a good name,
an omen as welcome
as the moon in a clear blue sky.
I am out of words to describe
how spirit mingles in this marriage.[12]

And so, within these two beings, together, heaven and earth are rejoined, engendering new life:

*A Sign for them is the earth that is dead;*
*We give it life and produce grain from it of which you eat.*

---

[12] Mevlana Jalaluddin Rumi, *Pocket Rumi*, op. cit., p. 43. Translation included with the kind courtesy of my beloved husband, Kabir.

*And We produce there orchards with date-palms and vines*
*and We cause springs to gush forth from within it,*
*that they may enjoy the fruits thereof.*
*It was not their hands that made this;*
*will they not then give thanks?*
*Limitless in His/Her glory is God Who created in pairs*
*all things that the earth produces*
*as well as their own humankind*
*as well as things of which as yet they have no knowledge.*
[Quran, *Surah Ya Sin* 36:33–36]

Here it is the mirrored number verse 36:36 that abides in the middle of *Surah Ya Sin* ("O Thou, Human Being", regarded as one of the most essential *surahs* of the Quran) that speaks of pairs, reflective of the dichotomous leaves at the beginning of the gestation of a plant, that grow into a full tree of life, even as from "Adam" and "Eve" it is said the human family has opened. Even so, Genesis 2:24 also implies that monogamy—and through it the return to wholeness—was God's intention from the beginning. Here on earth, a couple engaged in a sacred marriage commitment to each other alone are reflective in this realm of the major tenet of Islam, *La illaha il Allah*, "no other god but God,"[13] keeping alignment in the Oneness true, both outwardly and inwardly, vibrantly living together within that Unitive Grace. In the Gospel of Thomas, Thomas indicates that "salvation" consists of self-knowledge, and "baptism" of the Spirit opens the restoration of our primordial state—the unity of the male and female principle within one being, pointing to the "inner marriage."

Yeshua (Jesus) says:
"I choose you, one from a thousand,

---

[13] Halima of Damascus, a descendant of the Prophet Muhammad, who lived and taught in Syria would remind people not to let themselves be distracted but to focus with the blessing of a single partner as reflective of the pure undivided devotion to God: "Have you not heard the interpretation of the Quranic verse *But for one who comes towards God with pure heart* . . . ? [Quran, *Surah ash-Shuara* 26:88-89] . . . Its meaning is that you should attend to God, the Exalted, and not have anything other than Him in your heart!" Recorded in the *Nafahat al-ons* of Jami, excerpted from *Sufi Women* by Dr. Javad Nurbaksh (New York: Khaniqahi Nimatullahi Publications, 1980), p. 120, included in *Women of Sufism*, op. cit, p. 35.

two from ten thousand,
and you will stand to your own feet having become single and whole."
[Gospel of Thomas: Logian 23][14]

*O children of Adam!*
*Indeed, We have given you garments to cover your nakedness,*
*and as a thing of beauty;*
*but the garment of God-consciousness is the best of all.*
*This is one of God's messages—*
*that human beings might take it to heart.*
[Quran, *Surah al-Ar'af* 7:26]

Endeavour to gain refreshment from God's cup of Love—
then you will become selfless and have no will but God's.
[Rumi, *Mathnawi* V: 3105]

As we reflect on all these unfoldings, we might consider these moments to be actual recorded history, or we might also reflect upon them as symbols, as metaphors, as archetypes for the stages of the journey of the soul. This marriage, this "Wedding of Cana," is a pivot point, through which the fulfillment of the mission of Jesus, the Christ, opens, through the unification of aspects of the soul's inner feminine and masculine, the committed sanctification of life in alignment with God's Will through Love. Since her youngest years Beloved Mary had exhibited such unity, as being the temple herself, the "house built by wisdom" (Bible, Proverbs 9:1); the heart of the Virgin, Beloved Mary, could be witnessed as the "Tabernacle," radiating grace, illuminating the Way:

Know, child, that everything in the universe
is a pitcher brimming with wisdom and beauty.
The universe is a drop of the Tigris of His/Her Beauty,
this Beauty not contained by any skin.
His/Her Beauty was a Hidden Treasure[15] so full

[14] Lynn C. Bauman, Ward J. Bauman, and Cynthia Bourgeault, *The Luminous Gospels, Thomas, Mary Magdalene, and Philip* (Telephone, TX: Praxis Publishing, 2008), p. 17.
[15] See p. 319 of this text.

it burst open and made the earth
more radiant than the heavens.
[Rumi, *Mathnawi* I: 2860–62]

Considering this overflowing of Beauty and priceless abundance, it is quite meaningful that it is six jars of water that are transformed into wine at the wedding. In Hebrew, the letter that represents "six" is the *vav* which is shaped like a hook (ו); it is understood as signifying something that catches on and holds things together, a "connection." This evokes likewise the "alaq" of the Quran, the first moment of revelation opening through the "connection" from which we are created.[16] In the Hebrew Torah, the first *vav* that occurs in the text is the first letter of the sixth word, "and": "In the beginning, G-d created the heavens and (*vav*) the earth" (Bible, Genesis 1:1). And so "six" is the indicator of a pivotal connecting power between heaven and earth.

This connecting power of "six" is also indicated in Isaiah's vision of God and the angels of the Throne who connected heaven and earth with their six-winged presence:

In the year that King Uzziah died
I saw also the Lord sitting upon a Throne,
high and lifted up, and His train filled the temple.
Above it stood the seraphims: each one had six wings;
with two he covered his face, and with two he covered his feet,
and with two he did fly.
And one cried unto another, and said,
"Holy, holy, holy, is HaShem [Lord] of hosts:
the whole earth is full of His glory."
[Bible, *Yeshayahu* (Isaiah) 6:1–3]

The concept of the number six flows from the six directions of earthly existence, preparing us for the recognition of the seventh point—the central point of "witness," the Abode of the Holy within the heart. As Mevlana Rumi says, "I asked for one kiss and you gave me six."[17] The connecting

---

[16] See page p. 106, n. 10. of this text.

[17] *Kolliyaat-e Shams-e Tabrizi*, edited by B. Forouzanfar, quatrain 1993.

The Light Prayer of Prophet Muhammad also comes to heart; it was recited every day by Mevlana Rumi as part of his morning prayer. Opening to the Light

point in the center is the seventh, reflective of the beginning octave and the original note of "Be!" where the Essential, purified self, *nafs as-safiyah*, stands as witness, rooted in the heart. When we stand in this place of witnessing, we can recognize the possibility that every human being is holy and

*Men and women are awliya [saints and protectors] for each other.*
[ Quran, *Surah at-Tawba* 9:71]

O You who without a cup gave to the soul
an ecstasy better than eternal drunkenness,
come, if only for a moment.
Give us the blessing of that moment,
so empty of everything
including emptiness.
How long must we wait for that one moment?
Open the lock of the heart,
walk toward the treasure.
With this treasure, you'll have the answers
to all the questions in both worlds.[18]

---

in all six directions, and bringing it within the body, within the heart, within the self, through God's Grace, one's inmost being becomes infused with Light and radiates that Light back out into the world.

O God! Grant me Light in my heart, Light in my grave,
Light in front of me, Light behind me,
Light to my right, Light to my left,
Light above me, Light below me,
Light in my ears, Light in my eyes,
Light on my skin, Light in my hair,
Light within my flesh, Light in my blood, Light in my bones.
O God! Increase my Light everywhere.
O God! Grant me Light in my heart,
Light on my tongue, Light in my eyes, Light in my ears,
Light to my right, Light to my left,
Light above me, Light below me,
Light in front of me, Light behind me,
and Light within my self; increase my Light.

[18] Excerpt of ghazal from Mevlana Jalaluddin Rumi, *Divan-i Shams-i Tabrizi*, translated by Nevit Ergin and Camille Hamilton Adams Helminski.

Through a non-dimensional point within the heart, where we are closest to our Infinite Sustainer, we receive that overflowing Love that can pour through each of us. Mevlana Jalaluddin Rumi opened further for anyone to see the great treasure of heart revealed through Prophet Muhammad, and the unfoldings of the earlier Abrahamic prophets through him—he had brought a message of integration of spirit and matter, of essence and everyday life within justice and an all-encompassing Love. Through Rumi's words we recognize a Love that encourages us to remove our coats—the veils of our hearts which burden us—through the power of that Love shining like the bright radiance of the sun, rather than admonitions bursting from the blustering winds of the ego, which only cause people to enshroud themselves further. This new voice of the Abrahamic tradition attempted to re-establish the recognition of the Unity of Being. It is understood by some that Moses established the foundation of the Law and balance for the mind through Holy Wisdom, that Jesus brought rebalancing with the heart through Love and healing Compassion, and Muhammad brought a renewed message of the re-integration of both. The words of the Quran, and Muhammad as their guardian, came forward to address the imbalances that had arisen over the centuries, advising respect and honor for the feminine as well as for the graciousness and harmony of nature, and recognition of all the grace that flows to and through us when we turn in orientation towards the Divine Reality, listening by heart, to see beyond appearances into the Infinite. As Rumi indicates:

If the world appears to you vast and bottomless,
know that to Omnipotence it is not so much as an atom.
This world, indeed, is the prison of your souls:
oh, go in yonder direction, for there lies your open country.
This world is finite, and truly that other is Infinite:
image and form are a barrier to that Reality.
The myriads of Pharaoh's lances were shattered
by the hand of Moses with a single staff.
Myriads were the healing arts of Galen,
but facing Jesus and his enlivening breath they were an embarrassment.
Myriads were the books of pre-Islamic poets,
but all were humbled
when the word of an unlettered prophet poured forth.
[Rumi, *Mathnawi* I: 524–29]

In the continuing tradition of Moses, Shabbat, the Jewish Sabbath, is celebrated as a bond of love between human beings and G-d, honoring the primordial connection and the Source of our nourishment; a bond that is eternally fresh, even as the braided *challah* loaves woven in wholeness of six strands for the Sabbath. To welcome the opening of Shabbat (*Erev Shabbat*), with the Friday evening sunset candles are lit, prayers are offered, and songs are sung. One favorite Shabbat "hymn" still shared from heart to heart among dear friends is the lovely welcome of the Sabbath bride, "*L'chah Dodi*" ("Come, My Beloved") composed by Rabbi Shlomo Halevi Alkabetz, a Safed Kabbalist, in Edirne, in the then Ottoman (Muslim) Empire of the sixteenth century.[19] Another beloved, sixteenth-century mystic who developed the teaching of Kabbalah, Rabbi Isaac Luria (Ha'ARI Hakadosh, "The Holy Lion") of Ottoman Syria, in his well-beloved poem celebrates the arrival of the *Shekhinah*.[20]

I sing in hymns
to enter the gates,
of the Field
of holy apples.

A new table we prepare for Her.
A lovely candelabrum
gives its light to us.

Between right and left
the Sabbath Bride approaches,
in holy jewels
and festive garments.

---

[19] See Appendix, "Songs of Love," p. 419.

[20] Both Rabbis were teachers of Kabbalah based in the *Zohar* ("Radiance"), a text written in Aramaic (the spoken language of the Jewish people of Israel from sixth century BC to 70 CE) of mystical teachings gathered in Spain toward the end of the thirteenth century through the efforts of Moses de León. See Daniel C. Matt, *Zohar, Annotated and Explained* (Woodstock, VT: Skylight Paths Publishing, 2002). In the Bible, the word *Zohar* (conveying the presence of radiant light), is mentioned in Ezekiel's vision (Ezekiel 8:2) and in the book of Daniel 12:3: "Those who are wise will shine like the brightness of the heavens."

Let torment and trouble be ended,
let there be joyous faces
and spirits and souls.

All the worlds are engraved
and concealed within Her,
but all shine forth
from the Ancient of Days.

May it be your will
to dwell among your people.
Now let us welcome Shabbat,
Israel's day of light and happiness.[21]

Jewish weddings are not usually performed on the Sabbath as Shabbat itself is considered to be as a wedding. "Remember Shabbat and keep it holy" (Torah/Old Testament, Exodus 20:8) is the fourth of the Ten Commandments conveyed to Moses. The Hebrew word for "keep it holy" also conveys the meaning of "marriage." "Shabbat" has the meaning of "rest"; on the "seventh day" after God had completed Creation, He/She rested. The blessing of being able to rest is an indication of royalty (*malchut*), one of the attributes of God of which we may all partake by our birthright from Spirit. *Malchut* is also known as the "*Shekhinah*," the feminine aspect of G-d, emanating as Holy Wisdom.[22]

The wedding of Cana is the second "Luminous Mystery" of the Christian rosary, remembering this changing of the water into wine, and

[21] We remember that within "Israel" we comprehend "Jacob" (see p. 162, n. 31 of this text) and all those "who wrestle with God," welcoming the Light, resting there within the blessing of Shabbat. When a congregation sings this hymn in the Temple celebration of the Shabbat, with the singing of the last verse all rise and turn in unison towards the opened door to greet the "Shabbat Queen" as She arrives with the blessing of Holy Presence. It is taught that after six days of work, on the seventh we rest in that Presence, in glorification and thanksgiving, in witnessing: "The heavens will be glad and the earth will rejoice, the sea and its fullness will roar; the field and everything in it will exult, then all the trees of the forest will sing with joy" (Bible, Psalms 96:11–12).

(Included with gratitude to Shakira Debra Shatoff for bringing this lovely hymn into our awareness.)

[22] See p. 26, and n. 21 on that page of this text.

the hearts of the disciples further opening to faith, to the "Wine of Love."[23] A wedding is witnessed as a transformative moment—the transformation of earth and heaven to a complete Paradise, through Love, commitment, and devotion. Mary saw the need; Jesus fulfilled it, together in unified will and blessing, for the continued unfolding, passing from generation to generation.

In the same *Surah al-Maida*, verse 75, Mary is spoken of as "truthful" (*siddiqa*) which places her in the company of the Quranic prophets, who are known by that epithet. She is also the one who testifies again and again to the truth of Jesus' prophethood and message, even as it was Khadijah, the beloved first wife of Prophet Muhammad who first testified to the truth of his prophethood—soon affirmed by her cousin Waraqah, who was familiar with the prophetic traditions of Christianity and recognized the "taste" of prophecy. This wedding of Cana is a promise of continued life, through Love; we are reminded of the rivers of Paradise and the description of Paradise frequently repeated as a refrain in the Quran: *Gardens beneath which running waters flow*. These "running waters" might also be understood as wisdom, scripture, grace that helps to nourish and ripen the fruits of Love.

*A Commentary on the Tradition:*
*"Truly, God Most High has a wine that He has prepared for His friends:*
*when they drink it they become intoxicated,*
*and when they become intoxicated they are purified,"*
*to the end of the Tradition:*

"The wine is bubbling in the jars of the mysteries
in order that anyone who is empty of self may drink of that wine."
God most High has said, *"Lo, the righteous shall drink."*[24]

---

[23] The story of the Wedding at Cana is only told in the Gospel of John, understood by many to be the most mystical of the Gospels.

[24] *Behold, the truly virtuous shall drink from a cup*
*flavoured with the calyx of sweet-smelling flowers—*
*a source of bliss whereof God's servants shall drink, seeing it flow in a flow abundant—*
*they who fulfill their vows, and stand in awe . . .*
*who give food—however great be their own want of it—*
*unto the needy, and the orphan, and the captive,*
*[saying, in their hearts,] "We feed you for the sake of God alone."*
[Quran, *Surah al-Insan* 76:5–9]

Endeavour through dying to self to become really existent  
and to be intoxicated with God's wine.  
[Rumi, *Mathnawi* VI: Section heading to verse 643]

The earlier Hannah, whom Eli mistook as being drunk,[25] comes to heart, she who then became even more intoxicated with God's wisdom, conceived, and raised a stalwart and wise son, Samuel, who became a prophet. Her passionate song to God has long been considered by Jews to be a pre-eminent model of how to pray. That "overflowing cup" is also echoed in the Twenty-third Psalm of David in the Bible, with another "table" of abundance:

The Lord is my shepherd: I shall not want.  
He makes me to lie down in green pastures;  
He leads me beside the still waters.  
He restores my soul:  
He leads me in the paths of righteousness for His name's sake.  
Yea, though I walk through the valley of the shadow of death,  
I will fear no evil:  
for You are with me, Your rod and staff, they comfort me.  
You prepare a table before me in the presence of my [challengers]:  
You anoint my head with oil; my cup runneth over.  
Surely goodness and mercy shall follow me all the days of my life:  
and I will dwell in the house of the Lord forever.  
[Bible, Psalms 23, complete][26]

---

This is an allusion to "the sweet, extremely delicate fragrance of the symbolic 'drink' of divine knowledge. . . . It is to be noted that in this context the concept of 'giving food' ['however much they themselves may cherish (i.e., "need" it)'] comprises every kind of help and care, both material and moral. . . . The term *asir* denotes anyone who is a 'captive' either literally (e.g., a prisoner) or figuratively, i.e., a captive of circumstances which render him [or her] helpless; thus, the Prophet said, 'Thy debtor is thy captive; be, therefore, truly kind to thy captive' (Zamakhshari, Razi, et al.)—the injunction of kindness towards all who are in need of help—and therefore 'captive' in one sense or another. . ." See Muhammad Asad, *The Message of the Qur'an* (notes to verses 5–9 of *Surah* 76).

[25] See p. 61 of this text.

[26] A practice of repetition of this passage has long brought great blessing among Jews and Christians (as well as many Muslims who accept the Psalms as a Holy Book of David), reorienting the mind and heart with thanksgiving for all the

In sharing together the nourishment that is given, we ourselves ripen; under the Sun of Divine Beneficence, it is said in the Sufi tradition, "Grapes ripen, smiling at each other."[27] Another verse of *Surah al-Maida*, "The Feast," "The Table Spread," reminds us that Jesus and Beloved Mary both ate food, as human beings taking in nourishment; just before that portion of the verse, is the passage that mentions *And his mother was truthful* (5:75). They were both nourished by the Truth, filled with God's abundant blessing through the Word.

An ancient table for Torah reading, for holding the sacred book—of such sustenance to so many for centuries—one of the oldest and most beautiful examples ever discovered, was just recently found in 2009. Archaeologists were reviewing a site planned for a guest house for pilgrims, when, suddenly, they were excited to unearth ruins of an ancient synagogue, one of only eight so far recognized in Israel as dating from the first century CE, the time of Christ. This synagogue was in Magdala, the town associated with Mary Magdalene, and within it, at the center of the structure, they found a stone table, with stone arches depicted upon it and a seven-branched *menorah*, as though representing the temple in Jerusalem.[28] The top surface of the Magdala stone table is particularly lovely—at its center is a six-petaled flower of life motif, surrounded by two clusters of three hearts, six hearts in all.[29]

---

blessings pouring. As Ralph Waldo Emerson said, "A man is what he thinks about all day long", reminding us of the verse from Proverbs: "For as he thinketh in his heart, so is he" (Bible, Proverbs 23:7). Or as Rumi says, "If your thought is a rose, you are a rose garden" (*Mathnawi* II: 278).

[27] See Rumi's *Mathnawi* II:3723:

The immature grapes capable of ripening,
are at last made one in heart
by the breath of the masters of heart [the saints].

[28] See https://www.biblicalarchaeology.org/daily/biblical-sites-places/biblical-archaeology-sites/discoveries-in-mary-magdalenes-hometown/ (accessed March 31, 2019) and "The Magdala Stone: The Jerusalem Temple Embodied" by Jennifer Ristine: https://www.biblicalarchaeology.org/daily/ancient-cultures/ancient-israel/the-magdala-stone/ (accessed September 30, 2020).

[29] The "Flower of Life" is an ancient symbol in the shape of a wheel of life with a six-petaled flower at the center, radiating its petals into the circular surrounding realm. The oldest example so far discovered is from a portion of the floor of the palace of Assyrian King Ashurbanipal in northern Iraq, dating

*Magdala Stone*

---

to 645 BCE, that is now in the Louvre; it is decorated with an interlocking pattern of multiple flowers. Some Jewish archaeologists reflect that the petals and segmented circumference of the single flower on the Magdala stone could also be depicting loaves of bread of the *shewtable*, and that the hearts, as well,

Some Jewish historians feel that the six-petaled rosette symbolizes the veil before the Holy of Holies of the Sanctuary, which was described by the ancient historian Josephus as being decorated with flowers. It is the bees who sip from the flowers to create healing liquid for our bodies and who build six-sided houses for the golden honey, another metaphor for the process of the receiving and sharing of Divine knowledge and blessing.[30]

As the Quran in *Surah al-Maida* witnesses to Mary and Jesus both eating food—being of us, among humanity—in so doing, it acknowledges again the blessing of this holy and continual sustenance granted to his mother in the sanctuary when she was a young girl, and to him in his maturity:

---

could be similarly formed from loaves of bread—two loaves each aligned at one end—echoing the number of handmade loaves on a *shewtable*. A *shewtable* was placed within the Tabernacle sanctuary to receive on the Sabbath an offering of twelve loaves of fresh bread, indicative of the twelve tribes of Israel and the nourishment that flowed through them. It was called "the bread of the Presence." At the end of each week, this offering bread was eaten by the priests and replenished. The rites of the "Last Supper" of Christ are reminiscent of this ritual, reminding participants of our dependence upon the Divine Reality for our food both physical and spiritual, as it is reflected in the Quran: *In Heaven is your sustenance and all that which you are promised* (51:22). Even as Jesus is recorded in the Bible as saying, "I am the living bread which came down from heaven; if any man eat of this bread, he shall live forever" (Gospel of John 6:51–53). Jesus further clarified in that moment for his somewhat bewildered disciples, "It is the spirit that quickens; the flesh profits nothing: the words that I speak to you, they are spirit, and they are life" (Gospel of John 6:63). I.e., the Word is the true bread. Jesus said, "The word which you hear is not Mine, but the Father's which sent Me" (Gospel of John 14:24). It is understood that, even so, as we listen open-heartedly to the Word of God, we receive eternally enlivening nourishment. "People shall not live by bread alone, but by every word that proceeds out of the mouth of God" (Gospel of Matthew 4:4; Deuteronomy 8:3).

30 See also Quran *Surah an-Nahl*, "The Bee," 16: 68–69:

*And your Sustainer inspired the bee, "Build your [six-sided] cells*
*in hills, on trees, and in dwelling places,*
*and eat of all that the earth produces,*
*and skillfully follow the spacious paths of your Lord."*
*There issues from within their bodies a drink of varied hues*
*containing healing for human beings.*
*Truly, in this is a sign for those who reflect.*

*Continually I am sending it down* (5:115). Al-Tha'labi connects it also with the sustenance received by Moses and Miriam and their people enroute to the Promised Land:

> Qatadah said that when the Table descended from Heaven bearing fruit from among those of the Garden, it would come down to them in the morning and in the evening, since it was like the manna and quail for the Children of Israel.[31]

And even so, the loaves and fish kept multiplying, feeding thousands. Such abundant sustenance comes to us through the prophets and saints who partake of God's Fragrant Beauty and, like the bees, share the golden words of healing, awakening in our own hearts the capacity to receive directly from the Divine Source. When we open to receive it, trusting in the arrival, even as Mary trusted the capacity of Jesus to turn the water into wine, richer and richer in enlivening capacity, a miracle of Love transpires. As Shams of Tabriz reflects:

> There is nothing more enjoyable
> than the remembrance of food eaten in certainty
> at the table of Divine satisfaction.[32]

Or as Mevlana reflects, in a moment, the cup, the wine, and the one who pours, all three become One, transformed in Beauty through the remembrance of the heart:

> The beauty of the heart is the lasting beauty:
> its lips give to drink of the water of life.
> Truly it is the water, that which pours,
> and the one who drinks—
> all three become one when your talisman is shattered.
> That Oneness you can't know by reasoning.
> [Rumi, *Mathnawi* II, 716–18]

The aim is to manifest that dynamic Oneness, becoming the chalice,

---

[31] Al-Tha'labi, *Lives of the Prophets*, p. 665.

[32] See *Rumi and His Friends, Stories of the Lovers of God, Excerpts from the Manaqib al-'Arifin of Alfaki*, translated by Camille Adams Helminski and Susan Blaylock (Louisville, KY: Fons Vitae, 2013), "Never Tiring of the Friend," #526, II, p. 279.

receptive of the Wine of God, and offering it back through Grace, in glorification, engendering new life.

According to Maximus, after the wedding at Cana, "Wherever he went, [his mother, Beloved Mary] went with him, and she was considered the life and the light of his eyes and soul, going with him and listening to his words."[33] When Jesus healed the mother-in-law of Peter (Gospel of Matthew 8:14–15), Beloved Mary was there. Peter's mother-in-law and his dear wife then accompanied Beloved Mary in service.[34] Maximus relates that Beloved Mary and Christ and their followers then returned to Nazareth, because Joseph had completed his earthly life of one hundred and ten years; so they returned to offer a blessing for his journey to eternal life. The Protoevangelium of James (verse 9:2) recounts that the sons of Joseph—James and Jude—became disciples of Christ, accompanying him on his journeys, and Joseph's two daughters became disciples of Beloved Mary.

There were also many women there who followed Jesus from Galilee and provided for him.
[Bible, Gospel of Matthew 27:55]

As they journeyed on, and many more healings and miracles occurred, "the holy and glorious mother [of Jesus] was the leader of them all, their source of support."[35]

> During Christ's ministry, Beloved Mary remains constantly at her son's side and is portrayed as having a uniquely authoritative knowledge of his teachings. She is identified as the leader of those women who followed Christ and occasionally they are named as being Mary's rather than Christ's disciples.[36]

---

[33] Maximus, *The Life of the Virgin*, op. cit., p. 96.
[34] Some say that Peter's wife was the granddaughter of Herod who had ordered the killing of the Hebrew infants—it was he from whom Joseph and Beloved Mary had fled. Peter's wife's grandmother (Herod's second wife) was a Jewish princess, Mariamne (of the Hasmonean or "Maccabean" dynasty). And now this woman with Herod's blood in her veins, through Peter, was offering her devoted service to Jesus and Mary. Another weaving, through marriage and the workings of Spirit, of a healing into moments of Oneness.
[35] Maximus, *The Life of the Virgin*, op. cit., p. 97.
[36] Ibid., Introduction by Stephen Shoemaker, p. 22.

At pivotal moments, continually, Beloved Mary was with Jesus; they all immersed in prayer, men and women together:

> They all joined together constantly in prayer,
> along with the women and Mary, the mother of Jesus,
> and with his brothers.
> [Bible (NIV), Acts of the Apostles 1:14]

About a year after the wedding at Cana, as Mary entered a crowd where Jesus was teaching, a woman in the crowd listening to Jesus was carried away with enthusiasm. She called out:

> "Blessed be the womb that bore you and the breasts that suckled you!"
> [Bible, Gospel of Luke 11:27]

This unnamed woman was the first person to publicly witness to the essential relationship between the grace flowing from Jesus and that bestowed upon him through his mother, Beloved Mary (echoing Elizabeth's declaration when Beloved Mary visited and the child, John, leapt in Elizabeth's womb). It was quite unusual at that time for a woman to speak out in public. For this woman to speak up, especially at a moment when some people in the crowd were challenging Jesus, is an indication of how much she was moved by the flowing of Spirit, and her deep recognition of the extent to which the grace of the mother is gifted to a child through the mother's nurturance and support.

Jesus responded,

> "Blessed are they who hear the word of God and keep it."
> [Bible, Gospel of Luke 11:28][37]

With this statement, stepping aside from a focus on himself, he was affirming God's *a priori* right. Rather than a discounting of the woman's words, as some might construe his response, in addition to reorienting the discourse, one could consider this to be an even deeper recognition and honoring of Beloved Mary, pointing further to her as a pre-eminent example—not only had she borne him and nursed him with her Love,

---

[37] The Quran echoes this in *Surah al-Baqarah* 2:285 speaking of the faithful: *And they say we hear and we pay heed.*

but she had heard the "Word" of God in the most deeply receptive way, and she had "kept" it deeply, and it had come to fruition within herself. She who had been so devotedly in service in the sanctuary, and with such complete receptivity had received and nurtured the "Word" within her very being and protected it, continued to support "the Word" with every breath, offering the whole of her life, as an inspiration for all of us.

*Who will loan to God a beautiful loan?*
*For God will increase it many times to his/her credit*
*and he/she will have a generous recompense.*
*One Day you will see the faithful men and the faithful women,*
*how their Light runs forward before them and to their right:*
*"Good news for you today:*
*gardens beneath which running waters flow, where you may live—*
*this, this is the highest achievement!"*
[Quran, *Surah al-Hadid* 57:11–12]

Beloved Mary's utter humility radiated light. She herself was a demonstration of that unity and harmony of body, mind, and soul; every cell embedded with grace. Reflecting on the purity of her creation, the Venerable Anne Catherine Emmerich relates a vision:

> I saw a movement like a great shining mountain, and yet also like a human figure. . . . Then I saw this shining brightness standing separate before the Face of God, turning and shaping itself—or rather being shaped, for I saw that while this brightness took human form, yet it was by the Will of God that it received a form so unspeakably beautiful.[38]

---

[38] *The Life of the Blessed Virgin Mary from the Visions of Ven. Anne Catherine Emmerich*, translated by Sir Michael Palairet, https://www.acatholic.org/wp-content/uploads/2014/05/Life-of-Blessed-Virgin-Mary.pdf (accessed August 29, 2021); available also through TAN books. See also http://annecatherineemmerich.com/ (accessed July 18, 2021). As recorded in the journals of Clemens Brentano and William Wesener: "Ven. Anne Catherine Emmerich was one of the great Catholic mystics of the last centuries. From her earliest childhood, she was a soul of exceptional kindness, devotion, and purity."

She describes a moment of her upbringing and the awareness of the miraculous even as a child, through her father's gentle instruction:

I had to go out to the country with my father and take a horse, drive the reins

It was soon after the exchange with this woman in the crowd that, in the Gospel of Luke, Jesus offers the beautiful metaphor of the Light of the body, the "temple" of God:

The light of the body is the eye:
therefore when your eye is single, your whole body also is full of light.
But when your eye is evil [unhealthy], your body also is full of darkness.
Pay attention, then, that the light within you be not darkness.
If your whole body therefore is full of light, and no part of it dark,
the whole shall be full of light
as when the bright shining of a lamp gives you light.
[Bible, Gospel of Luke 11:34–36]

In his efforts to cleanse the outer Temple and also restore the Light there, Jesus drove the money changers from the Temple in Jerusalem; then he and Beloved Mary and their disciples turned again towards Galilee. Journeying among the towns in that region, he went to Magdala where he met the young woman, another Mary, of noble birth, who was transformed by their meeting. "Mary of Magdala" became a devoted disciple and served Christ and his mother. She also, through his ministry, had been freed from the "demons" that had haunted her.[39] Freed from inner

---

and do all kinds of work. When we would turn around or stop, he would say: "How beautiful this is! Look, from here we can see the church of Koesfeld and contemplate the Blessed Sacrament and adore Our Lord and Our God. From there, He is seeing us and blessing our work". When they officiated mass, he took off his hat and prayed, saying: "Let's hear Mass now!". As he worked, he said: "Now the priest is saying the Gloria; now it reaches Sanctus; and now we must ask with him this or that and receive the blessing". Afterwards he sang or repeated some tune. When I raised the corn, he said: "People are frightened when they hear the word 'miracle', and behold, we live by pure miracle and grace of God. Look at the grain in the earth: there it is and from it comes a stem that produces a hundred for one. Is not this a great miracle?"

[39] Some understand the "seven demons" mentioned in the Biblical text regarding her (Mark 16:9, Luke 8:2) as the "seven deadly sins": lust, gluttony, greed, sloth, wrath, envy, and pride; symptoms of an unbalanced ego. However, one might also understand this moment, faced with the Presence of Jesus, as an intensified process of moving through the stages of being, of full awakening into Spirit, in which moment all of these, any "diseases of the self," would simply fall away.

Though in Reality we have never left our Source, we can see how sometimes

contradictions, purely focused in Love of God, she became "filled with every grace."

> Consider your inward contraction and expansion as a root.
> When it is an ill root, cut it off quickly,
> so that an ugly thorn may not grow in the garden.
> You have felt the contraction—seek a remedy for it,
> because all growing plants begin from a root.
> You have felt the expansion—water your expansion,
> and when the fruit appears, share it with your friends.
> [Rumi, *Mathnawi* III:360–63]

Mary of Magdala became both a disciple and a minister, a faithful companion intimately near, beside Beloved Mary. Surely Beloved Mary herself taught her much as they went about the simple tasks of daily life, journeying together, endeavoring in Truth, with love. By many accounts, even as John became well beloved among the male disciples of Jesus, it was Mary Magdalene—of Magdala, the "Tower"[40] of Spirit—who shone among the women, in nearness to Beloved Mary, mother of Christ. She earned the grace of being an apostle and went about from city to city teaching and ministering to the ill, those yearning for Truth and for God's love.[41]

---

we must journey a long way to remove the veils placed upon us by life in this world so that we might see the Truth; yet for some the awakening arrives suddenly. The Sufi Path, the mystic path of Islam, recognizes seven stages/stations of the Way—our journey passes through recognizable stages, referred to in the Sufi tradition as the seven levels of the *nafs* or "self." See Extended Context Note in Appendix, Star IX, 2.

[40] The name "Magdala" means "tower." Some say this Mary is the same person as Mary of Bethany, the sister of Lazarus and Martha of Bethany; but she is remembered as "Mary of Magdala"—where this "enlightenment" experience occurred. We could recognize that Mary "Magdalene" was a woman of towering spirit; the name by which she is remembered is an indication of her complete awakening, being reborn in the presence of Jesus, through all the seven levels of being. See Extended Context Note in Appendix, Star IX, 3.

[41] There are many stories about further unfoldings regarding Mary Magdalene. Some say she was later martyred in Rome, others, that with her siblings, Lazarus and Martha, she was set adrift by their persecutors, but that their boat was divinely guided to the coast of Provence, France, where they had also brought

He/She is always pulling our ears, saying,
*"Do not lose hope!"*[42]
Although we are in a ditch
and overwhelmed by despair,
let's go dancing along since He/She has invited us.
Let's dance along like spirited horses
galloping towards a familiar pasture.
Let's toss our feet, though no foot is there;
let's drain the cup, though no cup is there,
because all things there are spiritual:
it is reality upon reality upon reality.
Form is the shadow, Reality is the sun.
[Rumi, *Mathnawi* VI: 4742–47]

When Jesus heard that his cousin John was preaching widely, he knew the way was being opened further for his teaching; the pouring of Spirit intensified.

*And We vouchsafed unto Jesus, the son of Mary, all evidence of the Truth,*
*and strengthened him with holy inspiration.*
[Quran, *Surah al-Baqarah* 2:87]

Further miracles began to unfold as he awakened the bird of the Soul in those who listened to him. Among the six miracles of Jesus mentioned in the Quran is the story of the enlivening of a bird of clay. This moment is mentioned within *Surah al-'Imran* ("House of 'Imran"), which relates the stories of the family of Beloved Mary and of John (Yahya) the Baptist. It also speaks of Jesus' miraculous capacity for curing the blind, the lepers, and raising the dead through God's Grace:

*And He will impart to [Jesus] the Book, and Wisdom,*
*and the Torah, and the Gospel,*[43]

with them the remains of St. Anne, Mother of Beloved Mary, for safe-keeping. There are also those who say that Jesus and Mary of Magdala had married and that journeying with Mary of Magdala was their daughter (who some refer to as "the grail," the chalice of Love).

42 See Quran, *Surah az-Zumar*, "The Throngs," 39:53.

43 The "Gospel" of the Quran refers to the actual words of Jesus, which may not

*And he [Jesus] will be a Messenger to the Children of Israel, (saying):*
*"I have come to you with a Sign from your Lord.*
*I will make for you out of clay the likeness of a bird,[44] and then breathe into it,*
*and it will become a bird by the permission of God.*
*I shall heal the blind and the lepers, and give life to the dead by the permission of God,[45]*
*and I shall inform you of what you may eat and what you may store up in your houses.[46]*
*Truly in that is a sign for you, if you are sincerely of the faithful.*
*And I have come to confirm what is before me in the Torah*
*and to make lawful unto you some of the things which had been forbidden to you.*
*And I have come to you with a Sign from your Sustainer.*
*So remain conscious of Allah, and follow me.*
*Truly, Allah is my Lord and your Lord, so worship Him—*
*this is a straight path."*
[Quran, *Surah al-'Imran* 3:48–51]

Jalaluddin Rumi, ever inspired by the Quran, expands the witnessing of this moment further in his *Mathnawi*:

Water and clay, when fed on the breath of Jesus,
spread wings, became a bird and flew.
Your praise of God is a breath
from your body of water and clay.
Make it a bird of paradise

---

have been completely recorded in what we know as the Gospel books of the Bible.

[44] Muhammad Asad in his note to this passage in *The Message of the Qur'an* indicates that the word for bird (*tayr*) here also has the connotation of "destiny": "Thus, in the parabolic manner so beloved by him, Jesus intimated to the children of Israel that out of the humble clay of their lives he would fashion for them the vision of a soaring destiny, and that this vision, brought to life by his God-given inspiration, would become their real destiny by God's leave and by the strength of their faith."

[45] Muhammad Asad suggests that this may also have a metaphorical meaning: "It is probable that the 'raising of the dead' by Jesus is a metaphorical description of his giving new life to people who were spiritually dead . . . the 'healing of the blind and the leper' has a similar significance: namely, an inner regeneration of people who were spiritually diseased and blind to the truth." Ibid.

[46] I.e., "what good things you may partake of in the life of this world, and what good deeds you should lay up as a treasure for the life to come." Muhammad Asad, ibid.

by breathing into it your heart's sincerity.
[Rumi, *Mathnawi* I: 866–67]

God said, "Truly there has never been a people lacking a friend of God,"
someone with power of the spirit;
and he it is who makes the soul-birds sing
unanimously, sincerely, free of all ill-will.
They become as kind as a mother:
Muhammad said of the Muslims,
"They are like one soul."
Through the Messenger of God they became one.
[Rumi, *Mathnawi* II: 3709–12]

And in the Quran we are reminded:

*Have they, then, never beheld the birds above them,*
*spreading their wings and drawing them in?*
*None but the Most Gracious upholds them:*
*for, truly, He keeps all things in His sight.*
[Quran, *Surah al-Mulk* 67:19]

*Say: "He is the Most Gracious: we have attained to faith in Him,*
*and in Him have we placed our trust.*
[Quran, *Surah al Mulk* 67:29]

The prophets, peace and blessings be upon them all, songbirds of the soul, are gifted to humanity by our Most Gracious Sustainer and enjoined with a responsibility to convey a Way of Being in response to a need that wells up within a community. The *Din*, the Way, the primordial religion, has been repeatedly revealed in new unfoldings in response to the need of humankind.[47] These messengers come to us as human beings like ourselves, yet shining brightly with the Light of Divine inspiration,

[47] A dear friend and mentor in Damascus, Syria, Dr. Asad Ali, who loves the interplay of words across languages pointed out to us how the word transliterated as *din* or *deen* from Arabic script, which is read from right to left, if read in the opposite direction of English becomes "need"—an indication of how the *deen* (the religion, our bond with God) is an unfolding of "need" that re-emerges and is granted a response from the Infinite Wisdom of Divine Reality within the particular moment of a community or people.

as a grace and a mercy to draw us closer to the Truth. A similar story of transforming nourishment is also told of the Prophet Muhammad, related by Fuhayra, of a moment during a journey when the Prophet Muhammad and Fuhayra and their guide passed by the tent of Umm Ma'bad al-Khuza'iyya:

> "Umm Ma'bad was a good, fearless, strong woman who would sit with her legs drawn up, wrapped in her garment, at the entrance to the tent and give out food and drink. They asked her whether she had any meat or milk they could buy from her. But they obtained none from her and she told them, 'If we had anything, you would not lack for hospitality, but our people are all out of provisions and we've been suffering drought.'
>
> "The Messenger of God (peace and blessings be upon him) noticed a goat at the side of her tent and said, 'What about that goat, Umm Ma'bad?' She replied, 'She's a goat left over from the goats after the drought.' 'Does she give milk?' he asked. 'No, she's too dried up for that,' she replied. 'Would you permit me to milk her?' he asked. 'If she has any milk you can,' she replied.
>
> "The Messenger of God (peace and blessings be upon him) called to the goat and stroked it, speaking God's name, wiped her teat and again invoked God's name. Then he called for a vessel large enough to satisfy them, and the goat opened its legs and milk poured out in a copious flow until it was full. He gave [the vessel to] her to drink, and then his Companions and thereafter they all had a second drink. When they were all quenched, he drank too, saying, 'The one who pours drinks last!' He put milk in it again, left it with her, and then they departed.
>
> [Fuhayra] continued, "Soon her husband, Abu Ma'bad, came home, leading emaciated goats, staggering they were so weak, and their brains scarcely functioning. When he saw the milk, he was amazed and said, 'Where did this milk come from, Umm Ma'bad? We don't have a milch-camel and the goat has not been with a male.' 'Well, a man who was blessed came past us. . . .'"[48]

---

[48] It is Umm Ma'bad's description of this blessed man to her husband that is one of the most well-known and beloved descriptions of Muhammad (peace and blessings be upon him) that has come down to us. See Camille Helminski

Fourteen hundred years ago the Prophet Muhammad, peace and blessings be upon him, conveyed the revelation of the Quran, renewing the monotheistic religion of Abraham and bringing together the law of the Prophet Moses and the love of Jesus into the manifestation of a harmonious way of life balanced within nature and all realms of human society. Seven hundred years later, Mevlana Jalaluddin Rumi, with inspiration from the Beneficent Sustainer, brought a fresh renewal of that intrinsic faith and spoke of how it is continued, community by community, saint by saint:

*Comparison of the form of the saints and the form of the speech of the saints to the form of the rod of Moses and to the form of the incantation of Jesus, peace be upon them both!*

The human being is like the staff of Moses;
the human being is like the incantation of Jesus.
For the sake of justice and for the sake of courtesy,
the truly faithful one's heart is in the Hand of God,
between His/Her two fingers.
The staff's exterior form is a piece of wood,
but existence is but one mouthful to it when that staff opens its throat.
In the incantation of Jesus do not regard merely the letters and the sound:
pay attention to the fact that Death turned and fled from it.
In his incantation do not focus on the simple words:
consider that the dead sprang up and sat down.
And that staff—do not think about how easily it came—
pay attention to how it cleft in two the green sea. . . .
From afar you see nothing but the dust:
advance a little and see the man within the dust.
His dust makes eyes bright; his manliness uproots mountains.
When Moses arrived from the most remote nook of the desert,

---

(ed.), *The Book of Character, Writings on Character and Virtue from Islamic and Other Sources* (Watsonville and Bristol: The Book Foundation, 2004), p. 2: "He gave an impression of dignity when silent and of high intelligence when he talked. His logic was impressive, he was decisive, not trivial, not trite, his ideas like pearls moving on their string."

Excerpt from Imam Abu'l-Fida Ismail ibn Kathir, *The Life of the Prophet Muåammad*, translated by Prof. Trevor Le Gassick (Reading, UK: Garnet Publishing Limited, 1998, 2000), Vol. II, p. 172.

at his coming Mount Sinai began to dance.

*Commentary on "O you mountains,*
*sing with him the praise of God, and you birds":*[49]

The face of David shone with His glory:
the mountains sang plaintively along with him.
The mountain became his accompanist:
both minstrels were drunk in love for a King.
Came the Divine command, *O mountains, repeat [the praise of God]*:
both joined their voices and kept the tune together.
God said, "O David, you have suffered separation:
for My sake you have parted from your intimates."
O lonely stranger who has become friendless,
from whose heart the fire of longing has flamed high,
you are longing for minstrels and singers and heart companions:
the Eternal One brings the mountains to you.
He makes them minstrels and singers and pipers:
He makes the mountain blow in measure before you,
so that you may know that, since the mountain is permitted to sing,
the saint also sings songs without teeth or lips.
The melody of the particles of that pure-bodied one
is reaching his or her sensitive ear every moment.
His or her companions don't hear it, he/she hears;
oh, happy is the soul that believes in his [or her] hidden mystery.
The saint beholds a hundred discourses in himself,
while his companion has caught no scent.
Within your heart a hundred questions and a hundred answers
are arriving from the Realm of the Placeless to the place of your abode.

[Rumi, *Mathnawi* III: 4258–79]

Beloved Mary and Jesus, inheritors of David, were both immersed in the songs of these Hidden Mysteries, and the natural world also sang along with them, in Truth, in Love.

---

[49] See Quran, *Surah Sheba* 34:10:

*And We bestowed Our grace upon David:*
*"O you Mountains! Sing with him the praises of God!*
*And you birds!"*

Out of the mouth of babes and nursing infants
You have perfected praise.
[Bible, Psalms 8:2]

Our dear teacher in the Way of Mevlana Rumi, Suleyman Hayati Dede, once shared a story of his youth when he was about six years old. He told us how one day as he and his mother were walking into town to do errands, in the town square they came upon people standing clustered around, listening to a visiting imam speak; the imam was haranguing the people for their sins. Dede's mother drew him closer to the center, among some of her neighbors, as people watched and continued to gather. The imam kept speaking only of Hell and the punishments that lay in wait, vehemently emphasizing the pending "wrath" of God.

After a while, Dede could bear it no more and cried out: "This man is lying!"

As a young child, Dede's heart knew that of which others there in that moment had lost track—the Truth of God as Love, Most Forbearing, and Generous (*Al-Wadud*, *Al-Halim*, *Al-Karim*). Others there had been mesmerized, paying attention to the man's supposed authority, but with the cry of this young boy, other people suddenly woke up, as though from a deep sleep, nodded their heads in agreement, and said, "Yes, this child is right!"

They all dispersed, leaving this supposedly "religious" man to wonder perhaps and reassess his "religiosity." It seems the imam had forgotten the meaning of religion, rooted in *religare* (to be tied to), to *hold fast to the rope of God*,[50] in intimacy and nearness in God's Presence, within the nourishing vibration of Love.

Jesus continued journeying through Galilee, healing the blind and the leper, pouring Love:

Jesus went throughout Galilee, teaching in their synagogues,
proclaiming the good news of the Kingdom,
and healing every disease and sickness among the people.
News about him spread all over Syria,
and people brought to him all who were ill with various diseases,
those suffering severe pain, the demon-possessed, those having seizures,

[50] Quran *Surah al-'Imran* 3:103 (see pp. 73 and 129–130 of this text).

and the paralyzed; and he healed them.
Large crowds from Galilee, the Decapolis, Jerusalem, Judea
and the region across the Jordan followed him.
[Bible (NIV), Gospel of Matthew 4:23–25]

Similarly to the New Testament, the Quran also speaks of Jesus healing the blind and the lepers (*Surah al-'Imran* 3:49). Al-Baydawi, a Persian Islamic scholar[51] of the thirteenth century, wrote of how it had been recorded that tens of thousands of people had come to Jesus to be healed, and how Jesus had healed them through prayer alone. Al-Tha'labi, the eleventh-century Islamic scholar,[52] expounded further on how these diseases were medically incurable, but Jesus, with the power of the Spirit, was enabled to cure them—miraculous healings, clear signs of Truth for those witnessing.

> [Jesus] did as God had commanded him, and the people loved him and inclined towards him and felt comforted by him. His following increased and his fame grew. Often as many as fifty thousand sick and paralyzed people gathered around him in a single hour. Whoever of them was able to walk, came to him on foot; if anyone was unable to do so, Jesus came to him.[53]

In the Bible, three people are mentioned in particular whom Jesus enlivened from death: the dear only son of a widow at Nain, the beloved daughter of Jairus (the ruler of a synagogue), and Lazarus, dear brother of Martha and Mary.[54] The Quran also refers to the capacity of Jesus to raise the dead: *when you put life into the dead, by My leave.*[55] Al-Tha'labi relates the story of Lazarus:

---

[51] Al-Badawi's major work is *Anwar al-Tanzil wa-Asrar al-Ta'wil* (*The Lights of Revelation and the Secrets of Interpretation*).

[52] Ahmad Ibn Muhammad al-Tha'labi , *Ara'is al-madjalis fi kisas al anbiya: Lives of the Prophets,* translation by William M. Brimmer, Brill Studies in Middle Eastern Literature (Boston and Leiden: Brill Academic Publishers, 2002). Al-Tha'labi includes stories of many of the prophets; he writes of Jesus, the most worthy *(al Wajih)* and the Holy Land, the land of the Gathering (for the Day of Judgment, of Recognition) and of Resurrection. He mentions that it is here that Jesus, son of Beloved Mary, will descend, in a fertile land of many trees, rivers, and fruits.

[53] Al-Tha'labi, *Lives of the Prophets*, op. cit., p. 653.

[54] See Gospel of Luke 7:15, Mark 5:42, and John 11:44.

[55] *Surah al-Maida* 5:110; see also *Surah al-'Imran* 3:49.

Among those was Lazarus (*Al-Adhar*), a true friend of [Jesus]. His sister had sent for Jesus, saying, "Your brother Lazarus is dying, come to him." Jesus and his companions traveled for three days[56] to reach Lazarus, but found that he had been dead for that length of time. They told his sister to bring them to his tomb, so she brought them to his tomb which was underground. Then Jesus said, "God, Lord of the Seven Heavens and the Seven Worlds, You have sent me to the Children of Israel to call them to Your religion, and You have told them that I, by Your leave, shall bring the dead to life. So bring Lazarus back to life." And Lazarus arose, came out of his tomb, and survived, and children were born to him.[57]

Mevlana Jalaluddin Rumi conveys further for us this atmosphere of healing power, referring again to the "Table" of beneficence:

*How the smitten would assemble every morning at the door of the seclusion cell of Jesus, on whom be peace, craving to be healed through his prayer.*

The table of the spiritual is the seclusion cell of Jesus:
O afflicted one, beware, beware! Do not forsake this door!
From every direction people would gather—
blind and lame and palsied and clothed in rags—
at the door of the cell of Jesus each morning,
that he by his breath might deliver them from pain.
As soon as he finished his prayers,
that man of goodly religion [Jesus] would go forth in early morning,
and would see troops of afflicted feeble folk
seated at his door in hope and longing.
He would say, "O you who are smitten,
the wants of all of you here present by God have been granted.
Hark, set off and go without pain or trouble
towards the forgiveness and kindness of God."

---

[56] The Gospels of Luke and Mark and Matthew are silent in regard to Lazarus. Only John records the story and notes that four days had passed (some other accounts say it was three or eight days after Lazarus died—four days where he lay at home, and then four days in the tomb) before Jesus arrived and restored him to life, but in both Islamic historical accounts and Christian tradition, this power was with Jesus.

[57] Al-Tha'labi, *Lives of the Prophets*, op. cit., p. 657.

All, like tethered camels
whose knees you unbind with foresight,
with his prayer would begin to run well on their feet,
hastening gladly and joyously to their homes.
Even so, you have experienced many maladies within yourself,
and have gained health from these sovereign saints.
How often has your limping been transformed into a smooth gait,
how often has your soul been relieved of grief and pain!
O heedless one, tie a string to your foot,
that you may not lose track of yourself, O lazy one!
Your ingratitude and forgetfulness
lost the memory of your drinking of honey.
And so the open way to blessings became barred to you,
since the hearts of the "people of heart" were made sore by you.
Quickly catch up to them and ask pardon of God;
weep lamentably like a cloud,
so that their rose-garden may open its blossoms to you,
and that the ripe fruits may burst and reveal themselves.
[Rumi, *Mathnawi* III:298–313]

Jesus, by his grace, made the dead to be living:
I am in the hand of the Creator of Jesus.
How should I remain dead in the grasp of God?
[Rumi, *Mathnawi* IV: 1065–66]

Rather than rejoicing at this possibility of awakening to vibrant Life, it is told that the Jewish Pharisees were disturbed by the news, seeing a threat to their power and to the status quo, choosing to remain with closed hearts. Not long afterwards it is recorded that Jesus conveyed to his disciples the importance of true integrity, the unity of being (*tawhid*):

Jesus saw infants being suckled;
he said to his disciples: "These little ones being suckled
are like those who enter the kingdom."
They said to him: "Then will we enter the kingdom as little ones?"
Jesus said to them: "When you make the two into one,
and when you make the inside like the outside
and the outside like the inside and the above like the below—

that is, to make the male and the female into a single one.
[Gospel of Thomas 22:1–5][58]

Jesus was indicating how when we return to that state of coherency, of inner alignment of body, mind, and heart, in unification, we re-enter Heaven:

At that time the disciples came to Jesus and asked,
"Who, then, is the greatest in the kingdom of heaven?"
He called a little child to him, and placed the child among them.
And he said: "Truly I tell you,
unless you change and become like little children,
you will never enter the kingdom of heaven.
Therefore, whoever takes the lowly position of this child
is the greatest in the kingdom of heaven.
And whoever welcomes one such child in my name welcomes me."
[Bible (NIV), Gospel of Matthew 18:1–5]

This Biblical passage brings to heart another moment of Mevlana's reflection regarding the unitive power of Jesus:

The dyeing-vat of Jesus—
from that pure vessel a garment of a hundred colors
would become as simple and one-colored as light.
This isn't the unicolority from which boredom ensues;
no, it is like fish in clear water:
although there are thousands of colors on dry land,
fish are in combat with dryness.
Who is the fish and what is the sea in my simile,
that the Sovereign, Almighty and Glorious, should resemble them?
In the world of existence myriad seas and fish

---

[58] See https://www.biblicalarchaeology.org/daily/biblical-topics/bible-versions-and-translations/the-gospel-of-thomas-114-sayings-of-jesus/ (accessed September 22, 2020), as translated by Stephen J. Patterson and James M. Robinson and republished from The Gnostic Society Library: http://gnosis.org/naghamm/gth_pat_rob.htm (accessed also August 29, 2021). Stephen J. Patterson, James M. Robinson, and Hans-Gebhard Bethge, *The Fifth Gospel: The Gospel of Thomas Comes of Age* (Harrisburg, PA: Trinity Press International, 1998), pp. 7–32.

prostrate themselves in adoration before that Munificence and Bounty.
How many a rain of beneficence has poured,
so that the sea was by it made to scatter pearls!
How many a sun of generosity has shone,
so that cloud and sea learned to be bountiful!
The sunbeams of Wisdom struck on soil and clay,
so that the earth became receptive of the seed.
The soil is faithful to its trust, and whatever you have sown in it,
you gather in the same, without faithlessness on the part of the soil.
It has derived this faithfulness from that Divine Faithfulness,
since the Sun of Justice has shone upon it.
Until spring brings the touch of God,
the soil does not reveal her secrets.
[Rumi, *Mathnawi* I:500–11]

The Quran witnesses to the power of this unicolority—the purity of surrender and alignment with Spirit—of Jesus and Muhammad, and the earlier Hebrew Prophets, and their followers, that allowed the opening of compassion among them along the eternal Way of Truth.

*And when Isa [Jesus] perceived that they covered over the Truth,*
*he asked, "Who will be my helpers in the cause of Allah?"* [59]
*The white-garbed ones*[60] *replied, "We will be your helpers in the cause of Allah.*
*We have faith in God.*
*And you are the witness that we are self-surrendered [muslim].*
*"O our Sustainer, we have faith in what You have sent down from on high,*

---

[59] "Allah," the word for "God" used by both Muslims and Christians who speak Arabic, designates the Divine Reality witnessed in Truth, beyond sects or denominations, the primordial Creative Reality, beyond any description or naming (even as in the understanding of the Torah) from which we all emerge and to which we all return.

[60] "Al-Dahhak said that they were called *hawariyun* because of the purity of their hearts. 'Abdallah b. Mubarak said that they were called *hawariyun* because they were luminous with a sign of worship upon them with its light, whiteness, and splendor. The root *h-w-r* among the Arabs, means 'intense whiteness.'" See Al-Tha'labi, *Lives of the Prophets*, op. cit., p. 655; see also n. 1 of this chapter, p. 174.

*and we follow the Messenger,*
*make us one, then, with all those who bear witness."*
*And the deniers schemed [against Jesus];*
*but God brought their scheming to nothing:*
*for God is greater than all schemers.*
[Quran, *Surah al-'Imran* 3:52–54]

*It is He Who has sent His Messenger with guidance*
*and the Way of Truth,*
*so that it might prevail over all false ways;*
*and God is sufficient as witness.*
*Muhammad is the Messenger of God;*
*and those who are with him stand firm*
*when facing those who deny the Truth,*
*and are compassionate with each other.*
*You can see them bow and prostrate themselves in prayer,*
*seeking grace from God and His good pleasure.*
*On their faces are their marks, traced by prostration.*
*This is their parable in the Torah,*
*and their parable in the Gospel:*
*like a seed which sends forth its shoot, which grows strong,*
*so that it becomes thick, and then stands firm on its stem,*
*delighting those who sow with wonder.*
*And through them the deniers are confounded.*
*God has promised those among them who have faith*
*and do righteous deeds forgiveness and a supreme reward.*
[Quran, *Surah al-Fath* 48:28–29]

*Say: "Behold, all bounty is in the hand of God;*
*He/She grants it unto whom He/She wills:*[61]
*for God is Infinite, All-Knowing,*
*singling out for His/Her grace whom He/She wills.*
*And God is limitless in His/Her great bounty."*
[Quran, *Surah al-'Imran* 3:73–74]

---

[61] The term *fadl* ("bounty") here also carries the connotation of "bestowal of divine revelation."

*In the hearts of those who truly followed [Jesus],*
*We [the Divine Reality] engendered compassion and mercy.*
[Quran, *Surah al-Hadid* 57:27]

As we move to heal what needs to be healed, spiraling upward, touching again and again the points of pain until they are healed by the Ever-Strengthening Light of Love, we offer gratitude for the bounty, the healing grace and favor of the Divine. The verse of *Surah Maryam* with which we began again reverberates:

*Those who have faith and do the deeds of wholeness and reconciliation,*
*the Infinitely Compassionate will endow with Love.*
[Quran, *Surah Maryam* 19:96]

# *The Totality of Beingness*[1]

Beloved Mary,
words came for you in the night.
In my sleep, your gentle voice spoke
reminding me of your being, your presence,
and the softness of your voice;
yet within it, such strength lives;
such depth of feeling has no floor,
but endless as the waters,
your love flows out of you
into our hearts
to comfort and to nurture
    as we each may need—
you stretch out your hands
    and your heart
        to feed
all the people, everywhere,
    as you did your son,
with the love of God,
    and the knowledge of the One,
the Totality of Beingness
    that lives
within, without, and through
each and every one of us
    as we turn
to look at you,
    and through you
see His/Her Face . . .
    God,

---

[1] Poem reflection excerpted from Camille Hamilton Adams Helminski, *Words from the East*, op. cit., of the "Songs of the Soul" series, p. 59–60.

who truly has no gender
    but is the impulse
        and fruition
of every seed,
    no matter what the name.
*Wherever we turn,*
*there is the Face of God.*[2]

[2] Quran, *Surah al-Baqarah*, 2:115: *Wherever you turn there is the Face of God.*

# X. TENTH STAR OF BLESSING

## *The Gathering to God: Death and Resurrection*

# *The Gathering to God: Death and Resurrection*

Then Pilate said to him, "So you are a king?"
Jesus answered, "You say that I am a king.
For this purpose I was born
and for this purpose I have come into the world—
to bear witness to the Truth.
Everyone who is of the Truth listens to my voice."
Pilate said to him, "What is truth?"
After he had said this, he went back outside to the Jews and told them,
"I find no guilt in him."
[Bible (ESV), Gospel of John 18:37–38]

There are many mysteries held within the story of the Crucifixion of Jesus and the Resurrection. Here, too, the three faiths of Judaism, Islam, and Christianity differ as to their understanding of it, but each contains within its comprehension acknowledgement of the path of a soul and the role of suffering in its transformation.

For most Christians, the Crucifixion is the central passion, that intense suffering of one so innocent, a being of Truth, so full of Spirit, and the suffering of his beloved mother. Even though Pilate did not condemn him, according to the Biblical account, as noted in the above passage from the Gospel of John, there were those among the community who still determined him guilty. They pressed that the process set in motion might continue, and so, it is said, he was crucified, and among Christians it is taught that this sacrifice of Jesus and Beloved Mary continues to redeem worlds of souls who recognize it, through the power of the Divine Will:

These words Jesus spoke, and lifted up his eyes to heaven, and said,
"Father, the hour is come; glorify your son,

that your son also may glorify You:
As You have given him power over all flesh,
that he should give eternal life to as many as You have given him.
And this is life eternal, that they might know You the only true God,
and Jesus Christ, whom You have sent.
I have glorified You on the earth:
I have finished the work which You gave me to do.
And now, O Father, glorify me with Your own self
with the glory which I had with You before the world was.
I have manifested Your Name unto the persons
whom You gave me out of the world:
Yours they were, and You gave them me; and they have kept Your word.
Now they have known that all things whatsoever You have given me
are of You.
For I have given unto them the words which You gave me;
and they have received them,
and have known surely that I came out from You,
and they have believed that You did send me.
I pray for them: I pray not for the world,
but for them which You have given me; for they are Yours.
And all mine are Yours, and Yours are mine, and I am glorified in them.
And now I am no more in the world, but these are in the world,
and I come to You. Holy Father, keep through Your own Name
those whom You have given me, that they may be one, as we are."
[Bible, Gospel of John 17:1–11]

In the Quran it is stated that it only seemed as if they crucified Jesus. Some Muslims believe that Jesus was taken up to Heaven before the Crucifixion; others consider that eyes were veiled, that he only seemed to die but recovered in the sepulcher and came forth again refreshed by Spirit. Many Muslims accept the Assumption of Jesus into Heaven, even directly body and soul, brought close within the Divine Reality.[1]

[1] Some Muslims and also some Christians consider the possibility that Beloved Mary could have given birth to identical twins, and that his twin could have died instead of Jesus. Al-Tabari relates that a number of Muslim scholars consider that one of the Apostles may have become imbued by God with the presence of Jesus so that he was mistook for him by the Roman soldiers and killed in his stead,

*For, of a certainty, they did not slay him:*
*nay, God exalted him unto Himself—*
*and God is indeed Almighty, Wise.*
[Quran, *Surah an-Nisa* 4:157–158]

One might understand, from the words of Jesus in the Gospel of John 17, a depth of unity with Spirit that Jesus is acknowledging is within each of us through the action of the "Name":

Holy Father, keep through Your own Name
those whom You have given me, that they may be one, as we are.

Here is an indication as to how the lazer light of Love can burn away the edges of self allowing a coalescence, a unity with Spirit. Hearts can be harder than rock and yet even as rocks may burst forth with water, hearts can melt:

*There are rocks from which streams gush forth;*
*and, behold, there are some from which, when they are cleft, water issues;*
*and, behold, there are some that fall down for awe of God.*
*And God is not unmindful of what you do!*
[Quran, *Surah al-Baqarah* 2:74]

*Had We sent down this Quran on a mountain,*
*truly, you would have seen it humble itself and break apart out of awe of God—*
*such are the parables which We offer to human beings that they might reflect.*
[Quran, *Surah al-Hashr* 59:21]

There have been many ways of understanding the stories of the Bible (both Old and New Testament) and of the Quran. There have been a

---

while Jesus was taken up into Heaven. The Ahmadiyya Muslims believe that Jesus continued to live and journeyed on to Kashmir together with Beloved Mary, abiding a while there before his return to his Lord. See p. 256, note 85 of this text.

The Quranic view of Jesus as filled with pure spirit and yet a prophet, a human being, albeit a uniquely pure human being, is consistent with verses of the New Testament that convey the humility of Jesus before God, such as Philippians 2:6–8, and Luke 18:19:

"Why do you call me good?" Jesus asked him.
"Only God is truly good."

number of Christian sects who have differed in their perspective from the predominant Christian view held by the Roman Catholic Church, some who have emphasized the spiritual nature of Jesus, rather than his human experience, like the Cathars of the Iberian peninsula. Cathar "Perfects," men and women (*parfaits* and *parfaites*)—who were intensively devoted to the purification of the soul—practiced celibacy; both genders could preach and instruct in practices, and many were healers. Following the practice of the early followers of the Apostles, mentioned in Acts of the Apostles 2:44–47,[2] a newly initiated Cathar, when joining the community, would share all worldly goods in common. The Cathars were persecuted as heretics and were themselves martyred by other Christians for their beliefs, in the Albigensian crusade of the Middle Ages (1209–1229 CE). Cathars believed Jesus was completely Spirit, manifesting like a radiant hologram, so that it would not have been possible for him to be crucified. Protestant denominations, emergent beginning in the sixteenth century CE, of which there are now thousands of denominations, also each have their own views regarding the theology of this experience, and many have sought to simplify the role of the church in defining people's beliefs and "salvation."[3]

In the early churches of the first centuries of Christianity, the depiction of Christ, rather than as the crucified Christ, was as *Pantocrater* (All-Powerful),[4] featured in the uppermost dome of a church or cathedral. The

---

[2] And all who believed were together and had all things in common.
And they were selling their possessions and belongings
and distributing the proceeds to all, as any had need.
And day by day, attending the temple together and breaking bread in their homes,
they received their food with glad and generous hearts,
praising God and having favor with all the people.
[Bible (ESV), Acts 2:44–47]

[3] See p. 402 of this text and as one summarizing reference, *A Dictionary of All Religions and Religious Denominations* by Hannah Adams (see p. 82 and n. 21).

[4] *Pantocrater* often translated as "All-Powerful" has the meaning from the Greek of "Sustainer of the World," emphasizing the overwhelming sustenance flowing through the being of Christ. Many such images of Christ have been located in the high dome of a church or cathedral, with his encompassing Presence radiating from the heights. See *Early Christian and Byzantine Art*, by John Lowden (London: Phaidon Press, 1997), p. 66 and also http://www.touregypt.net/featurestories/catherines2-1.htm (accessed Feb 22, 2021).

earliest known of such icons resides in St. Catherine's monastery on Mt. Sinai; the icon, painted on wooden panels, is probably of Byzantine origin of the sixth century CE and likely to have been a gift to the monastery from the Emperor Justinian I. It was Justinian who had also rebuilt Hagia Sophia (the church of "Holy Wisdom")[5] at his wife, Theodora's, encouragement. Hagia Sophia was the largest church in Christendom for almost a thousand years, where *Christ Pantocrater* has long gazed down from the

*Mosaic of the Virgin Mary and Child (detail), circa ninth to tenth centuries CE, Hagia Sophia, Istanbul, Turkey*

[5] Hagia Sophia, as well as Hagia Eirene (the church of "Holy Peace") and Hagia Dynamis (the church of "Holy Power"), were all originally built in Constantinople by Constantine in the fourth century CE. Hagia Eirene still exists within the grounds of Topkapi Palace, near the vast Hagia Sophia (rebuilt by Justinian I), in Istanbul (formerly Constantinople). The inner arch of Hagia Eirene is inscribed in mosaic letters with a verse from the Old Testament: "We shall be filled with the good things of Thy house; Thy temple is holy. (Thou art) wonderful in righteousness. Harken to us, O God our Saviour; the hope of all ends of the earth, and of them afar off on the sea." This excerpt from Psalm 65, verses 4–5, is a reminder of the resplendent beauty of creation lauded in the Psalms of David, so evocative of passages of the Quran. See Pslam 65 in Extended Context Notes in Appendix, Star X, 1.

central dome and "Our Lady of Wisdom" still shines forth from golden mosaics depicting her holding Jesus in his infancy.[6]

More than any other, the imagery of Madonna and child—Beloved Mary with her infant Jesus—has permeated Christian art throughout the centuries. Many of the magnificent cathedrals of the thirteenth century focused on the imagery of the caring motherhood of Beloved Mary, "Our Lady," the Madonna; a cathedral church is known as *ecclesia mater*, indicating that it is the "mother church" of a diocese. In Poland for instance, her image is everywhere—including numerous small statues on street corners surrounded by little gardens of remembrance. For Poles, Beloved Mary, "Our Lady of Czestochowa,"[7] has long been an inspiration and a reminder of the freedom of the human spirit held within the embrace of God. It seems that it was not until the Middle Ages that the crucified Christ became more predominant in church iconography.

In the depiction of Beloved Mary as *Hodegetria*, "She Who Shows the Way," on the page following, Beloved Mary places the focus with Christ. Held within her embrace, Jesus raises two fingers in blessing, symbolizing the two integrated natures of his being—human and divine in one being, even as Christ is recorded in the Gospels as saying, "When the eye is single, the whole body is filled with Light" (Gospel of Matthew, 6:22). Through this unity of being, permeated with the Divine Reality, the Power

---

[6] Monumental yet expressed with such tenderness, this Madonna in the icon style of Our Lady of Wisdom Enthroned is a mosaic of glass and marble tesserae, radiating from on high in the ceiling of the apse of Hagia Sophia.

[7] "Our Lady of Czestochowa," the "Black Madonna of Poland," is a wooden painted icon dating back to at least the sixth to ninth century CE that was brought to Poland in the fourteenth century. She is depicted as *Hodegetria* ("The One Who Shows the Way"), in the pattern of St. Luke's original icon, which some say it is. She is among a number of representations of Beloved Mary referred to as the "Black Madonna," bringing to heart the passage from the Bible "I am black and I am beautiful . . ." (Song of Songs 1:5). Golden *fleur-de-lys* adorn her veil. It is told that her presence of blessing through this icon saved the Polish monastery of Jasna Góra ("Luminous Mountain") in Czestochowa, Poland, from the Swedish invasion in 1655. Her protection recognized by the King of Poland, Beloved Mary was declared "Queen of Poland" in 1656. Our Lady of Czestochowa Shrine continues to be a place of devoted pilgrimage, where tens of thousands gather to offer prayers especially on her remembrance day of August 26.

Our Lady of Czestochowa *(Hodegetria)*

of blessing flows. Beloved Mary indicates this possibility, held within her loving embrace. Perhaps it was an icon similar to these, or another of the *Eleusa* style of "Our Lady of Tenderness,"[8] that was within the Kaaba over which the Prophet Muhammad, peace and blessings be upon him, placed his hand in protection.[9]

For Beloved Mary to have witnessed such a persecution as the Crucifixion would have been excruciating—the sword piercing her son's beloved flesh as though it were piercing her own heart also, and every blow, a blow to her being; she would have so deeply suffered, surely every fiber of her being accompanying in resonating prayer with him, through his experience, and with prayers for all those who might not see the Truth of the Oneness she so deeply knew. Losing a child is heart-breaking for any parent; to lose such a precious being and the promise of his further life,

[8] See p. 330 with n. 75, and p. 331 of this text.
[9] See p. 136 of this text.

and to witness the denial of the Reality she understood him to represent, in such a way, would have been an unimaginable suffering for such a sensitive soul. And yet she would have comprehended their destiny in the vastness of her heart, and the promise of renewal through God's Grace; what could she do but entrust him to God, and herself to God, and their interwoven destinies, knowing and relying upon the Infinite Wisdom and Love that was continually embracing them, as she had always done with such strength!

It is not within the scope of this exploration to contain the fullness of that experience and its theological implications. Whatever our theological beliefs may be, we witness in the story of this moment a journey through intense suffering and the possibility of immense transformation. The cross, the "crucifixion" is an indication of a conjunction of horizontal and vertical realms, the abasement and constriction of the soul in this "historical" world, engendering an expansive exaltation in the subtle realms, from earth straight to Heaven, turning the tables so that which may appear as faulty or unworthy according to the status quo, becomes luminously holy, and abundant blessing is restored through healing Grace. The possibility of a human soul's victory over the power of death through complete immersion in Spirit, the joining again of earth and Heaven in spiritual nobility and humility of personhood within the palpable Presence of Reality, frees the heart and soul like a column of Light bursting into the Infinite.

*The creation of you all and the resurrection of you all is but as a single soul:*
*for, truly, God is All-Hearing, All-Seeing.*
[Quran, *Surah Luqman* 31:28]

Some Sufis teach that everything Jesus lived outwardly, we must live inwardly. It is understood that we, too, each must undergo our own "crucifixion" in the journey of purification of the soul, that we might be restored to wholeness. When the soul is ready for such a trial, an experience may arrive of intense challenge or abasement in some aspect that is most dear—even as Beloved Mary endured earlier, in a first cycling of that experience, with The Annunciation and subsequent accusations—that through such an experience, the soul might be even further purified, letting go of everything but the recognition of the Oneness with Spirit of which Jesus speaks, breathing, being breathed by Love: "Forgive them, for they know not what they do" (Bible, Gospel of Luke 23:34).

But to those of you who will listen, I say:
Love your enemies, do good to those who hate you,
bless those who curse you, pray for those who mistreat you.
[Bible, Gospel of Luke 6:27–28]

Love and Compassion and Mercy can pour through the wound, a deep opening, so that every moment might be a moment of grace radiated, of the blessing of all creation, even as so much grace poured through Beloved Mary, and through her most beloved son. The eternal Law of Oneness, of Healing Unitive Love is then restored, *My Mercy overwhelms My Stringency*: "Love your enemies," those within and without, through all the stages of the self until all that remains is God.

In his *Risala* (*Principles of Sufism*), Al-Qushayri (986–1072 CE), the beloved Sufi mystic, taught that "Inspiration [*nafas*—literally "breath," also "breathing space" or "ample room"] is the refreshment of hearts by subtleties from the Unseen," even hour by hour as we move, with God's Grace, into that Unitive Seeing. In this process we are encouraged to remember God, to be attentive to palpable Reality (*Haqq*), throughout every moment of our day, every stage of our lives, recognizing that within every breath is a resurrection.

*Extol, then, God's limitless glory when you enter upon the evening hours,*
*and when you rise at morn;*
*and unto Him is due all praise in the heavens and on earth,*
*in the afternoon as well, and when you enter upon the hour of midday.*[10]
*He it is who brings forth the living out of that which is dead,*
*and brings forth the dead out of that which is alive,*
*and gives life to the earth after it had been lifeless:*
*and even thus will you be brought forth.*
[Quran, *Surah ar-Rum* 30:17–19]

[10] "Apart from this general exhortation, the hours mentioned above circumscribe the times of the five daily prayers incumbent upon a Muslim. The 'evening hours' indicate the prayer after sunset (*maghrib*) as well as that after nightfall (*'isha*)." See Muhammad Asad, *The Message of the Qur'an*, note to verse 30:18. One might also understand from this, the "evening" of one's lifetime, drawing near in presence, and the "resurrection" with God.

*Have you not turned your vision towards your Sustainer?*
*See how He/She lengthens the shadow!*
*If He/She willed He/She could make it stand still!*
*But We have made the sun its guide,*
*and then We draw it in towards Ourselves—a contraction by easy stages.*
*And He/She it is Who makes the night as a robe for you,*
*and sleep as repose, and makes every day a resurrection.*
*And He/She it is Who sends the winds as heralds of glad tidings*
*preceding His/Her Mercy.*
*And We send down purifying water from the sky*
*that with it We may give life to a dead land*
*and assuage the thirst of beings We have created.*
[Quran, *Surah al-Furqan* 25:45–49]

As we move through such intensity, we trust that God's nurturance will be provided, support will be near. It was the devoted women, Beloved Mary and her "sister" Mary, identified in some passages as the wife of Clopas (the brother of Joseph, dear adoptive father of Jesus),[11] and Mary

---

[11] Some say this Mary is the "sister-in-law" of Beloved Mary, others say her aunt—the sister of her mother; still others say her own sister, who had been born after she had been dedicated to the Temple. Though the Bible mentions very little about Beloved Mary's family, reference is made to this "sister" in the Gospel of John:

Standing by the cross of Jesus were his mother,
and his mother's sister [*adelphe*] Mary the wife of Clopas, and Mary Magdalene.
[Bible, Gospel of John: 19:25]

In the Gospels of Matthew and Mark, another Mary is mentioned as present, the "mother of James the younger and of Joseph":

There were also women looking on from afar,
among whom were Mary Magdalene,
and Mary the mother of James the younger and of Joseph, and Salome.
[Bible, Gospel of Mark 15:40]

Some feel that these two Marys are the same person—known as the sister (or sister-in-law) of Beloved Virgin Mary, wife of Clopas (spelled variously, also "Cleopas," "Cleophus"), and the mother of St. James and Joseph. At the time of the writing of the Gospels, many in the community would have been aware of the family connections, and so further mention or clarification might not have been considered necessary.

of Magdala, who are recorded in the Bible as standing by Jesus on the cross. By many it is said that Beloved Mary herself is the source of the witnessing accounts of these final moments, especially those noted in the Gospel of Luke. According to some, it was Beloved Mary who enlisted the aid of Joseph of Arimathea, a wealthy Jewish elder of the community (who according to all four gospels was a secret disciple, and whom some say later journeyed to Marseilles, France, and on to Glastonbury in England[12]). It is said that she sent him to Pilate (who was a friend of his) to ask for the body of her son. Then Joseph of Arimathea, enlisting the help of Nicodemus, another member of the Sanhedrin (Council of elders) secretly following Jesus, brought Jesus to the new tomb Joseph had been preparing for himself. John recounts that they then anointed him with oils of myrrh and aloes and wrapped him with a linen cloth. This is the only time men are mentioned as assisting, and they are elders of the community.

The Gospels themselves differ in the record of the unfoldings of those days, yet the women are always mentioned. Those closest to Jesus came to be known as the "myrrh-bearing women"—the women who had ministered to Jesus during his lifetime, who are noted in some of the Gospel accounts as watching the crucifixion from a distance (though in the Gospel of John they are depicted as nearer) and of whom it is said that they came to the tomb that first day of the week seeking to further anoint the body of Jesus, for his burial. These "myrrh-bearing women" in the Orthodox tradition are called *eisapostolai*, "equal to the apostles", equally apostolic.[13]

Rather than through the male disciples, the story of the Resurrection is conveyed most fully in the Gospels through the women who are nearest, through the depth of their love and devotion. And it is Jesus himself and

---

[12] See Gospel of Matthew 27:57, Mark 15:43, Luke 23:50–52, and John 19:38. It is related that Joseph of Arimathea was a respected member of the Jewish Sanhedrin who stood against them in their condemnation of Jesus. He was known to be a wealthy merchant; tradition relates he was a dealer in metals, especially tin. Among the traditions, it is told that during the following persecutions this Joseph was together with a number of the closely devoted who were set adrift in a boat without sails or oars that carried them to France by the Grace of God, where they found refuge. See note 64 of this chapter and also Extended Context Notes in Appendix, Star X, 2.

[13] See Gospel of John 19:25, Matthew 27:56, Mark 15:40–41 and 47, Luke 23:55–56, and Matthew 27:61 in Extended Context Notes in Appendix, Star X, 3.

the angels who send them to bring word to the male apostles. According to Maximus, Beloved Mary, mother of Jesus, kept constant vigil and witnessed the earthquake that rolled away the stone, and his Resurrection, and was the first to testify to his life, rather than Mary Magdalene and the other myrrh-bearing women who later discovered the opened tomb as it is described in the Gospels. Surely, Beloved Mary always was present for her son, attending, supporting with her love. Yet it is Mary Magdalene, out of whom he had cast seven demons, as noted in two of the Gospels, who is first, in most accounts, to see Jesus and to bring the "good news" to the others.[14] When they encounter Mary of Magdala she recounts to them that the tomb is empty and that Jesus is Living, through Spirit. And so, Mary Magdalene was referred to by St. Ambrose of Milan (340–397 CE) as *Apostola apostolorum*, the "Apostle to the apostles,", or "Apostle of the apostles."

Now when [Jesus] was risen early the first [day] of the week,
he appeared first to Mary Magdalene,
out of whom he had cast seven demons.
And she went and told them that had been with him,
while they mourned and wept.
And they, when they had heard that he was alive
and had been with her, would not believe it.
[Bible, Gospel of Mark, 16:9–11]

Now upon the first day of the week, very early in the morning
they came unto the sepulcher bringing the spices which they had prepared
and certain others with them.
And they found the stone rolled away from the sepulcher.
And they entered in and couldn't find the body of Lord Jesus. . . .
Returning from the sepulcher they told all these things unto the eleven,
and to all the rest.
It was Mary Magdalene and Joanna and Mary the mother of James

---

[14] This fact is another indication that it was she who could in a moment "see," who could perceive Truth, and also convey it. St. Mary Magdalene is mentioned by name fourteen times in the Gospels (never as a "fallen woman"); two instances refer to her healing, and the remainder speak of her presence with Jesus as he journeyed, at the Crucifixion, and throughout the experience of his arising, when she recognizes him in the garden beside the sepulchre.

and other women that were with them,
who told these things to the apostles.
[Bible, Gospel of Luke 24:1–11][15]

Eight women are mentioned by name and known as myrrh-bearers (healers), clustered in different moments at the cross and beside the tomb of the risen Christ, as recorded by the Gospels: Mary Magdalene, Beloved Mary, Joanna, Salome,[16] Mary the wife of Cleopas (or Alpheus), Susanna,[17] Martha of Bethany, and Mary of Bethany (who some say is Mary Magdalene, mentioned with this other appellation). These "midwives of the moment" provide support and accompaniment throughout this awakening to new life. They dared to go early before dawn, to anoint his body, when the male disciples were hiding, fearing for their own lives. It was the women who first knew of his rising, they who then carried the news to the male apostles, and

---

[15] See also Gospels of Matthew and Mark:

In the end of the sabbath, as it began to dawn toward the first [day] of the week,
came Mary Magdalene and the other Mary to see the sepulchre.
[Bible, Gospel of Matthew 28:1]

And when the Sabbath was passed Mary Magdalene,
and Mary the mother of James, and Salome had bought sweet spices,
that they might come and anoint him.
And very early in the morning, the first day of the week,
they came to the sepulcher at the rising of the sun.
[Bible, Gospel of Mark 16:1–2]

[16] In medieval tradition, Salome (who is also sometimes referred to as Mary Salome) was included as one of the "Three Marys," considered to be the daughters of St. Anne, and so a younger sister of Beloved Mary, mother of Jesus. Others say she was the sister of Beloved Mary's mother, Saint Anne (see also p. 52, n. 1 and p. 227, n. 11. of this text), but invariably a close relation, who also had been moved and inspired by the teachings and being of Jesus and the Presence of Beloved Mary, accompanying them on the journey of Spirit. She is mentioned in the Bible as the wife of Zebedee and the mother of James the Greater and John the Evangelist (Gospel of Matthew 20:20; 27:56). Her name "Salome" derives from the Aramaic word for "health, well-being" and "peace," similar to "Shalom" in Hebrew and the Arabic "Salaam."

[17] In the Gospel of Luke (8:2–3), in addition to Mary Magdalene, Joanna the wife of Chuza (the manager of Herod's household), and Susanna are the women mentioned by name who were among the many women journeying with Jesus and the twelve male disciples, who provided for them out of their own means.

Mary Magdalene is mentioned over and over again as the first to bring the "good news," the *bushra* ("glad tidings").[18]

One of the foremost early proponents of the Quaker faith, Margaret Fell,[19] wrote a well-known treatise in defense of women preaching based especially on the role of Mary Magdalene and these myrrh-bearing women: *Women's Speaking Justified, Proved and Allowed of by the Scriptures, All Such as Speak by the Spirit and Power of the Lord Jesus And How Women Were the First That Preached the Tidings of the Resurrection of Jesus, and Were Sent by Christ's Own Command Before He Ascended to the Father (John 20:17)*.[20] Published in 1666 CE, while she was imprisoned in England due to her Quaker beliefs, it is recognized as a foundational document demonstrating the vision of woman as an equal partner with man, with equal intrinsic spiritual capacity to encompass the Inner Light. Quaker women as well as men were encouraged to preach as the Spirit moved, and the community would support either gender in their journeying to share their comprehension that no priest or government could stand as mediator between a heart and the Divine.[21]

The complete role Mary Magdalene played in Jesus' life and mission is still debated, however, it seems by many accounts that she was truly a very

---

[18] In the *surah* of "The Bee," such "good tidings" are remembered:

*Say, "The Holy Spirit has brought it down as truth from your Lord,*
*so that He may strengthen those who have faith,*
*and also as guidance and as good tidings for those who surrender."*
[Quran, *Surah an-Nahl* 16:102]

[19] A strong supporter of George Fox (Founder of the Quaker faith) who later became his wife after the passing of her first husband, Margaret Fell (1614–1702 CE), the "Mother of Quakerism," wrote a number of treatises as exposition of the Quaker faith, and herself preached widely in England. She supported the growing community with her possessions and her life, opening her home, Swarthmoor Hall, in the Lake District of England, as a meeting place for worship. Much of their married life she and George Fox were separated by being imprisoned due to their professed faith.

[20] See Gospel of John 20:17–18 on pp. 232–33 of this text, and pp. 236–38 (with n. 26).

[21] One of the few ancestral grandmothers of ours (on our father's mother's side) whose name was Mary also became a strong proponent of the Quaker faith—Mary Dyer (1612–1660 CE). Even after being imprisoned in Massachusetts Bay Colony and threatened with death, Mary Dyer continued to preach. She had met Margaret Fell and learned of the teachings of George Fox when she went to England in 1651. See Extended Context Notes in Appendix, Star X, 4.

close companion. Numerous sources record, both in the canonical gospels and others, that she is the only one to remain constantly near throughout the persecution, apparent crucifixion, the burial and awaiting the Resurrection, though Maximus states that Beloved Mary was, of course, also there throughout these passages, as of course a beloved mother, especially this mother, would be. Very few details of Mary Magdalene's life are related, but the Bible, itself, confirms the strong bond between her and Jesus, as when she recognizes him after the Resurrection, as it is related in the Gospel of John. In this Gospel account, it is to Mary alone that Jesus appears. Seemingly knowing that she would be drawn to grasp him, he cautions her not to hold onto him, but trusts her implicitly to convey with sincere heart his words to the other apostles:

On the first day of the week, so early it was still dark,
Mary Magdalene comes to the tomb,
and sees the stone taken away from the tomb.
So she runs and finds Simon Peter
and the other student whom Jesus was close to,
and says to them;
"They've taken the Lord out of the tomb
and we don't know where they've put him."
So Peter and the other student came out and headed for the tomb.
And they were both running,
but the other student ran faster than Peter and got to the tomb first . . .
[Bible (UG), Gospel of John 20:1–4]

They discover the discarded wrappings; seeing the tomb empty they leave and return home, but Mary, undeterred, steadfast, stays and is greeted by angels and then by Jesus, himself:

But Mary was standing outside by the tomb crying.
So as she was crying, she bent down and looked into the tomb.
And she sees two holy messengers in white sitting there,
one at the head and one at the foot
of where the body of Jesus had lain.
And they say to her: "Madam, why are you crying?"
She tells them: "They took my Lord away,
and I don't know where they put him."
So saying, she turned around,

and she sees Jesus standing there, but she didn't know it was Jesus.
Jesus says to her: "Madam, why are you crying? Who are you looking for?"
She, thinking it was the gardener, says to him:
"Sir, if you have carried him someplace, tell me where you put him
and I'll go get him."
Jesus says to her, "Mary!"
She, turning around, says to him in Hebrew:
"Rabbuni!" (which means "teacher!")
Says Jesus, "Don't cling to me, I have not yet ascended to the Father.
Go find my brothers and tell them
I am ascending to my Father and your Father,
and my God and your God."
Mary Magdalene goes and tells his students,
"I have seen the Lord!" and what he said to her.
[Bible (UG), Gospel of John 20:11–18]

Though few women, among the reportedly thousands who followed him, are named in the accounts of Jesus' life and teaching, in all of the Gospel accounts Mary Magdalene is prominently mentioned, usually first among the women; she was among those who helped and supported him out of her wealth in the days of his teaching in Galilee. In three of the Gospel accounts angels speak with her; in this passage of John, after the angels solicitously inquire about her weeping, Jesus himself appears and speaks to her outside the tomb and only to her. At first he seems to her as the gardener, one who might nurture the plants, caring for the living among the dead. Some feel it was she who had earlier anointed Jesus with a precious ointment in preparation for the time of his burial, just two days before Passover and the Passion; many icon representations of St. Mary Magdalene depict her carrying an alabaster jar such as that which held such precious perfumed ointment:

Now when Jesus was at Bethany in the house of Simon the leper,
a woman came up to him with an alabaster flask
of very expensive ointment,
and she poured it on his head as he reclined at table.
And when the disciples saw it, they were indignant,
saying, "Why this waste?
For this could have been sold for a large sum and given to the poor."

But Jesus, aware of this, said to them, "Why do you trouble the woman?
For she has done a beautiful thing to me.
For you always have the poor with you, but you will not always have me.
In pouring this ointment on my body,
she has done it to prepare me for burial.
Truly, I say to you, wherever this gospel is proclaimed in the whole world,
what she has done will also be told in memory of her."
[Bible (ESV), Gospel of Matthew 26:6–13]

The above account is almost the same as the account in the Gospel of Mark 14:3–9, where the woman also remains unnamed, humbly in anonymity. Mark specifies the ointment is nard, a costly, fragrant perfume. Nard, known also as spikenard (*nardostachys jatamansi*), native to Asia, has been growing since ancient times in the Himalayas and had long been conveyed for trade from the Ganges area of India to countries to the west, along the ancient spice routes. Known for its medicinal, antibacterial, and anti-inflammatory properties, spikenard is also valued for its fragrance, which itself is quite healing. It was highly prized by the ancient Greeks, Egyptians, and Romans. In the passage in Mark the value of the nard is mentioned as 300 drachma, an extreme expense, the equivalent of an entire year's salary for many people of that era. Both its anti-inflammatory properties and its healing fragrance also assisted with relief of neuroinflammation and pains related to muscle aches from menstruation.

*Spikenard* (Nardostachys Jatamansi)

There are several accounts of anointing in the Gospels, rather than relating the story of a single woman, a single moment, many scholars now reflect that these could be different moments and different women. In the anointing accounts related in the Gospels of Matthew, Mark, and John, the woman anointing beloved Jesus is not a "fallen woman"; that is only mentioned in Luke where she, also, is not named.[22] In his accounts, John refers to anointing twice, first to Mary, the sister of Lazarus, anointing Jesus, as "she who anointed the Lord's feet (*he aleipsasa*)":

> It was that Mary which anointed the Lord with ointment,
> and wiped his feet with her hair, whose brother Lazarus was sick.
> Therefore his sisters sent unto [Jesus], saying, Lord,
> behold, he whom thou lovest is sick.
> [Bible, Gospel of John 11:2–3]

This could have been a reference to an earlier moment. In this chapter 11 of John, relating the story of the raising of Lazarus from the dead, John also mentions how much Jesus loved Martha and Mary, as well as their brother, Lazarus. Then again John, in his next chapter, 12, more fully describes an anointing, occurring six days before Passover, and mentions that it was again "Mary," though he does not specify here which "Mary," who anointed Jesus with spikenard, and that she then wiped his feet with her hair. It might be possible that this is a different moment and that this "Mary" John mentions is Mary of Magdala, who most surely would have been with them.[23]

> So six days before Passover, Jesus came to Bethany,[24]
> where Lazarus was, whom Jesus had raised from the dead.

---

[22] Gospel of Luke 7:36–50. The anointing described in Luke takes place about two years prior to the other moments of anointing.

[23] Every time an anointing occurs, while he is alive, it is the women who are mentioned as anointing Jesus.

[24] Bethany was not far from Jerusalem, only a couple of miles. Magdala it seems was a small city on the western shore of the Sea of Galilee, approximately three miles north of Tiberias, at the foot of Mt. Arbel. In Greek it was known as "Taricheae"; in Hebrew "Migdal" ("Magdala" in Aramaic). It is there that the Magdala stone was discovered. As one of those who is mentioned in the Gospel as supporting Jesus and the disciples with her wealth as they journeyed, Mary of Magdala, who was recounted in the Gospels as being close by throughout the Crucifixion and Resurrection, would most surely have been with them, also, at this dinner just a few days prior.

So they gave a dinner for him, and Martha was serving,
and Lazarus was one of the guests with him.
So Mary, taking a pound of genuine spikenard, very expensive,
anointed the feet of Jesus and used her hair to wipe his feet.
The house was filled with the smell of the perfume.
[Bible, Gospel of John 12:1–3]

Then again, Judas Iscariot, one of his students, "the one who was going to betray him," complains:

"Why wasn't that perfume sold for three hundred drachmas
and given to the poor?"
He said that not because he cared about the poor,
but because he was a thief
and as purseholder was dipping into common funds.
[Bible (UNT), Gospel of John 12:5–6]

Then Jesus said, "Let her alone;
against the day of my burial has she kept this.
For the poor always you have with you; but me you have not always."
[Bible, Gospel of John 12:7–8]

The indication that this Mary who anointed him had kept the nard from some former time may provide a clue as to the possibility of Mary of Magdala and Mary of Bethany perhaps being the same person, though if it were Mary of Bethany in this moment, she could also have kept it from the time of Lazarus's burial. The fact that nard was so costly would indicate that the one anointing is well-to-do. Given that it is also a remedy for difficult menstruation, perhaps al-Tha'labi is not unfounded in his connection of Mary of Magdala to the woman of the story who had touched the robe of Jesus and was healed (rather than to the "fallen woman" of Luke). Al-Tha'labi's rendition of the story of Mary Magdalene brings another view:

> Now the story of Mary Magdalene (Maryam al-Majdalaniyah) was that she was a very righteous Israelite woman from a village of Antioch called Majdalan. She was a pious woman, but she used to menstruate continually without being purified. Various Israelite nobles asked her in marriage, but she refused, so they thought that she was too

proud for them. It was not a feeling of superiority, but only that she wished to conceal her illness. So when she heard of the coming of Jesus, and of how, by his hands, God cured the sick and the crippled, she came to him in hope of recovery. But when she saw Jesus, and the awesome countenance with which God had endowed him, she became shy, and retired behind him, and put her hand on his back. Jesus said, "Someone diseased has touched me with good intent; and God has given him what he hoped for, and has purified him by my purity." Then God removed from her what had been in her, and she was healed and purified.[25]

There are many mysteries within the Gospel stories, threads still being traced, and some untangled. It was in the sixth century that the conflation of Mary Magdalene with the "fallen woman" described by Luke was promulgated by the Pope, St. Gregory the Great.[26] That story continued

---

[25] Ahmad ibn Muhammad al-Tha'labi, *Arais Al Majalis Fi Qisas Al Anbiya* (*Lives of the Prophets*), p. 672. See https://archive.org/stream/AhmadIbnMuhammadThalabiAraisAlMajalisFiQisasAlAnbiyaLivesOfTheProphetsLivesOfTheProphets/AhmadIbnMuhammadThalabi-AraisAl-MajalisFiQisasAl-AnbiyaLivesoftheProphets_LivesoftheProphets_djvu.txt (accessed February 20, 2021).

There is a similar story conveyed in Luke 8:43–48 and Mark 5:25–34, though in neither account is the woman identified as Mary of Magdala. Yet perhaps this illness could have also been an aspect of the "demons" Jesus dispelled.

[26] St. Gregory the Great (540–604 CE), a monk who became pope in 590, is known as one of the four greatest Latin-speaking Fathers and Doctors of the Church. It was due to his love of liturgical music that chants were encouraged—"Gregorian chants," the beautiful plain song chants, are named in his remembrance.

Yet, not long after becoming Pope, in a sermon he offered in 591, Pope Gregory declared: "She whom Luke calls the sinful woman, whom John calls Mary [of Bethany], we believe to be the Mary from whom seven devils were ejected according to Mark." (Who knows, perhaps he was trying to counteract the rising veneration of Mary Magdalene in infant "France," where she was also known as the sister of Lazarus, and to re-establish the overriding church authority of Rome, even as he sent St. Augustine to Kent to bring Christianity again to the tribes there, the country later to be known as "England"—"Land of the Angles.") This conflation of Mary Magdalene with the "fallen woman" of Luke became church teaching for Roman Catholics, but was not adopted by Orthodox Christianity or all Protestants when each later split from Catholicism, yet it still persists in the minds of many. Little by little the reputation of Mary of Magdala is being cleared; it has taken over fourteen hundred years!

then to be repeated within the Roman Catholic Church for centuries, though "Gnostic" traditions[27] have long existed recounting otherwise, and Eastern Orthodox and some Protestant denominations did not acknowledge it. At last, in 1969, the Roman Catholic Church rescinded the determination of Mary of Magdala as the prostitute, the repentant "fallen woman" in Luke, acknowledging that it has no scriptural basis, slowly restoring her primary place as "Apostle to the apostles." The lectionary was revised by Pope Paul VI, changing the Gospel for her feast day to John 20:11–17, commemorating her meeting with Jesus in the garden beside the sepulcher when he calls to her: "Maryam" ("Mary" in Aramaic, as well as in Arabic). In 2016, her remembrance day of July 22 was elevated by Pope Francis to a fully recognized festive "Feast Day" within the calendar of the Roman Catholic Church.

In chapter 11 of the Gospel of John, it was "Mary," the sister of Lazarus, who was mentioned as having anointed Jesus, she who is remembered as being so full of yearning to learn and to immerse in the vibration of Truth she hears, to immerse in Spirit, that her sister Martha had complained to Jesus that she was not paying attention to her household duties, as it is recounted by Luke. Jesus had then affirmed that this Mary was seeking the "better part," as she sat at his feet listening to his words. There is also no exact scriptural basis for conflating Mary of Bethany with Mary Magdalene, but they do seem to be kindred spirits; it is the ancient traditions of France that especially link the two.

Now it came to pass, as they went, that he entered into a certain village:
and a certain woman named Martha received him into her house.
And she had a sister called Mary,
which also sat at Jesus' feet, and heard his word.
But Martha was cumbered about much serving,
and came to him, and said,

---

[27] Early Christian spiritual traditions emphasizing self-knowledge as a way to know God came to be known as "Gnostic," from *gnosis* ("knowledge"). There is a similar term in Sufism, *arifin* (the "knowers," as in "Knowers of God"), as in *marifat* ("knowledge" of God), the third stage of development as the soul journeys from *shariat* ("the law") to *tariqat* ("the brotherhood, sisterhood for traveling the Way") to *marifat* ("inner-knowing"), to *Haqiqat* ("Truth"). Many of the Gnostic schools that developed especially revere Mary Magdalene as exemplary apostle and most beloved companion of Jesus.

"Lord, do you not care that my sister has left me to serve alone?
Bid her therefore that she help me."
And Jesus answered and said unto her, "Martha, Martha,
you are careful and troubled about many things;
but one thing is needful:
and Mary hath chosen that good part,
which shall not be taken away from her."
[Bible, Gospel of Luke 10:38–42]

It would seem that Mary "of Magdala," she of towering spirit, is a closer match for this Mary of Bethany so filled with yearning. This Mary, also, like Mary of Magdala, was in close attendance, she also seems to have recognized that though everyone has a work to which they are drawn, the true purpose of this creation is as a welcoming tent for the communion of Spirit, for the meeting of the lover with the Beloved, even as Mevlana Rumi indicates in his discourses[28] and his *Mathnawi*:

---

[28] See Discourse 21, excerpted in *The Rumi Daybook, 365 Poems and Teachings from the Beloved Sufi Master,* translated by Kabir and Camille Helminski (Boston: Shambhala Publications, 2012), p. 108.

> The jurisprudents are clever, and a hundred per cent competent in their own profession, but between them and the other world a wall has been created to maintain their realm of *licet* and *non licet.* If that wall were not a barrier for them, they would not want to do what they do and there would be no use for their work.
>
> This is like our great master's saying that the other world is like a sea and this world is like foam. God Most Great and Glorious wanted the foam to flourish, so He put some people on the back of the sea to make it prosper. If they were not occupied with this, people would destroy each other and the foam would eventually fall into ruins.
>
> So a tent was pitched for the King, and He inclined some people to occupy themselves with constructing it. One of these says, "If I didn't make rope, how would the tent be held up?" Another says, "If I didn't make stakes, where would they tie the ropes?" Everyone knows that they are all servants of the King who will come into the tent to gaze upon his beloved.
>
> If the weaver gives up weaving and seeks to become a vizier, the whole world will go naked; so he was given joy in his craft and is content in it. That group, then, was created to keep the world of foam in order, and the world was created for the support of the saint.

The Jesus of your spirit is within you:
ask his aid,
for he is a good helper;
but do not every moment lay upon the heart of your Jesus
the unprofitable work of providing for a body full of bones . . .
Don't seek from your Jesus the comforts of the body.
Don't ask from your Moses the wish of a Pharaoh.
Don't burden your heart with thoughts of livelihood;
livelihood will not fail:
be constant in attendance at the Divine Court.
This body is a tent for the spirit, or like an ark for Noah.
[Rumi, *Mathnawi* II: 450–55]

It seems Mary Magdalene understood this. Perhaps this is the era of the Resurrection of Mary Magdalene, in recognition of her full power as witness to Truth, she who was as a mirror for the Pure Beauty and Power she had discovered through the being of Jesus:

"So all I could bring to you is a mirror
like the inner light of a pure breast,
that you might behold your beautiful face within it,
O you who, like the sun, are the candle of heaven.
I have brought you a mirror, O light of my eyes,
so that when you see your face you might think of me."
He (she) drew forth the mirror from under his (her) arm:
the fair one's business is with a mirror.
What is the mirror of Being? Non-being.
Bring non-being as your gift, if you are not a fool.
[Rumi, *Mathnawi* I: 3197–201]

Just prior to the events of the Crucifixion, at the "Last Supper," some traditions relate that Beloved Mary was taking charge of the female disciples, serving in parallel to Jesus in overseeing the male disciples during this sacred meal offering of nourishment through Spirit.[29] Then Jesus knelt and washed the feet of the disciples, bathing them with love, even as "Mary" had done for him with the precious nard just a few days

[29] See Maximus, *The Life of the Virgin*, op. cit., p. 22.

earlier. Together they merged in this shared understanding of the Way of humility: he had even disrobed, to his undergarments, wrapping a towel around himself in service; she had knelt and after anointing his feet, had wiped them with her hair.

When he had washed their feet, put his outer garment back on,
and sat down again, he said to them,
"Do you know what I have done to you?
You call me Rabbi, and it is fitting that you do so, for so I am.
If I then, the teacher, have washed your feet,
you also ought to wash one another's feet.
For I have given you an example,
that you also should do as I have done for you."
[Gospel of the Beloved Companion 35:4] [30]

This Way Jesus demonstrated—of honoring each other in service to the glory within the human being as a Creation of God—Rumi reflects, encouraging us to enliven our consciousness of the Messiah abiding within this human form:

---

[30] *The Gospel of the Beloved Companion, The Complete Gospel of Mary Magdalene*, translation and commentary by Jehanne de Quillan (Ariège, France: Éditions Athara, 2010), p. 63. The original manuscript of this Gospel of Mary Magdalene was in Greek. Some believe that in the middle of the first century CE it was brought from Alexandria to Languedoc, now southern France, and later translated into Occitan in the twelfth century. See pp. 244–45, n. 37 of this text.

This moment of Jesus washing the feet of his disciples is expressed similarly in the canonical Gospel of John:

When he had washed their feet
and put on his outer garments and resumed his place,
he said to them, "Do you understand what I have done to you?
You call me Teacher [Rabbi] and Lord, and you are right, for so I am.
If I then, your Lord and Teacher, have washed your feet,
you also ought to wash one another's feet.
For I have given you an example,
that you also should do just as I have done to you.
Truly, truly, I say to you, a servant is not greater than his master,
nor is a messenger greater than the one who sent him.
If you know these things, blessed are you if you do them.
[Bible (ESV), Gospel of John 13:12–17]

O body that has become the spirit's dwelling-place,
enough is enough:
how long can the Sea abide in a water-skin?
O you who are a thousand Gabriels
in the form of a human being,
O you who are many Messiahs inside Jesus' donkey,
O you who are a thousand Kaabas[31]
concealed in a house of prayer,
O you who cause *'ifrit*[32] and devil to fall into error,
you are the spaceless Object of worship in space:
you destroy the devil's business,
for they say, "How should I pay homage to this clay?
How should I bestow on a mere form
a title signifying obedience?"[33]
This human being is not form: rub your eye well,
so that you may behold in him (or her)
the radiance of the light of God's glory!
[Rumi, *Mathnawi* VI: 4583–88]

It would seem that among all his disciples and those accompanying him, Mary Magdalene was the one most fully able to witness the radiant glory of God's light and to meet Jesus in that awareness, of spiritual alignment through the heart. A contemporary Christian priest, influenced by contact with Sufism, Cynthia Bourgeault, in her recently published book regarding the meaning of Mary Magdalene, interprets: "Blessed are the pure in heart for they shall see God . . . everywhere." One hears here an echo of the inspiring passage from *Surah al-Baqarah* 2:11: *Wherever you turn, there is the Face of God*; and truly all around us *there are signs to see for those who reflect* (Quran, *Surah al-Jathiyah* 45:13). Cynthia Bourgeault likewise acknowledges that rather than discounting this world as illusion or "fall," we can see it as "fully inhabited by the divine energies":

[31] Kaaba: the holy shrine, at the center of the Masjid al Haram in Mecca, the *axis mundi* of Islamic life, "the Most Ancient Temple," signifying also the heart of the human being, within which abides the most precious and intimate non-dimensional point of connection with our Sustainer.
[32] *'Ifrit,* similar to djinn, are wayward fiery spirits.
[33] See Quran, *Surah al-A'raf* 7:10–13.

> This world is good, worthy, and fully inhabited by the divine energies—"the Good comes among you"—so long as it stays united with its root. The blending of incarnational and Platonic elements is a distinctive mix, which I believe is Jesus's original contribution to the metaphysics of the West. It presents itself as a profoundly incarnational, warm-hearted, and hopeful path, where the realms support and interpenetrate each other and divine fullness is accessed simply by keeping the heart in natural alignment with its invisible prototype. . . . When the heart is aligned with its eternal image, abundance cascades forth from that place of origin, infinitely more powerful than the scarcity and constriction of this world. It is not a matter of believing in flying elephants so much as of purifying the heart.[34]

This purification of the heart is foundational to "Resurrection" and arrival into the "Garden," even as the Quran counsels:

> *Consider the soul and the order and proportion given to it,*
> *and its enlightenment as to that which is wrong and right:*

---

[34] Cynthia Bourgeault, *The Meaning of Mary Magdalene, Discovering the Woman at the Heart of Christianity* (Boulder: Shambhala Publications, 2010) p. 51.

Cynthia Bourgeault, a respected colleague of Spirit, was a co-teacher as we journeyed for a number of years in the endeavor of the Spiritual Paths Foundation—an interspiritual endeavor (see www.spirtualpaths.net) convened by a dear colleague of Buddhist training, Ed Bastian. Ed had been inspired by beloved Father Thomas Keating, dear friend, former abbot of St. Joseph's monastery in Massachusetts and former superior of the Snowmass monastery, a Roman Catholic priest and Trappist monk, who was also among Cynthia's mentors. Father Thomas had recognized a need to reinvigorate the contemplative practice within the Catholic community and so was inspired to assist in developing Centering Prayer and Contemplative Outreach (www.contemplativeoutreach.org). The Snowmass Monastery—St. Benedicts Monastery—is a Cistercian (Trappist) monastery whose practice is based upon the rule of St. Benedict. Through the Snowmass Interfaith Dialogues that Father Thomas also initiated he encouraged the common recognition of the Ultimate Reality towards which all religions point, acknowledging that we may have varied ways of speaking about It, but together practitioners of multiple faiths were able to come into agreement on core principles. See https://www.scarboromissions.ca/interfaith-dialogue/principles-and-guidelines-for-interfaith-dialogue/17.

This author also served as a mentor within the Snowmass Interspiritual Dialogues for a number of years.

*truly, the one who purifies it shall reach a happy state*
*and the one who corrupts it shall truly be lost!*
[Quran, *Surah ash-Shams* 91:7–10]

It seems that Mary Magdalene was the pre-eminent disciple who had fulfilled this, and who was able to see the Truth of the mission of Jesus, the Christ, to reaffirm the purity of his anointing, in recognition of his carrying of the mantle of kingly servanthood, in the tradition of the wise kings of the east and of Melchizedek, who assisted in the enlightening of Abraham.[35] As Jesus conveys through the words of the Quran,

*"[I have come] to confirm the truth of whatever there still remains of the Torah,*
*and to make lawful unto you some of the things which [aforetime] were forbidden to you.*
*And I have come unto you with a message from your Sustainer;*
*remain, then, conscious of God, and pay heed to me.*
*"Truly, God is my Sustainer as well as your Sustainer:*
*so worship Him: this is a straight way."*
[Quran, *Surah al -'Imran* 3:50–51]

Al-Tha'labi also further affirms the close connection of Mary Magdalene and Jesus in the description of the moments of his reappearance:

> When God commanded Jesus to descend to her after seven days because of His compassion, he went down to her swiftly. When he descended, the mountain blazed with light; and Mary Magdalene assembled the Disciples for him, and he scattered them over the Earth as missionaries for God.[36]

She was his beloved companion, acknowledged by the other apostles, in the Gospel of Mary (Magdalene):[37]

---

[35] One might consider the repeated anointings by the women as a deep recognition of this, his "Christhood," confirming his mission as the "Anointed one."

[36] Al-Tha'labi, *Lives of the Prophets*, op. cit., p. 673.

[37] An ancient manuscript dating back almost 1500 years, a lost "Gospel of Mary," considered by many to be of Mary Magdalene, has come to the greater attention of scholars in recent decades, encouraged by the discovery in Egypt of two ancient Greek papyrus fragments of the same text. In 1896, the Coptic copy was found near Cairo, Egypt and taken to Berlin, a part of the "Berlin Codex." It was determined to be from approximately the fifth century CE and a copy

"Surely the Teacher knew her very well,
for he loved her more than us."
[Gospel of Mary Magdalene, text p. 18:13–14][38]

Over the centuries, some have even surmised that Mary Magdalene and Jesus were married. In the Jewish tradition, rabbis were required to be married.[39] At the Last Supper, Jesus had acknowledged that it was

---

of an earlier Greek text. The first scholarly publication of that text in German appeared in 1955. In 1917 a second, small Greek fragment of the same text was discovered, dating to the early third century: about the same time that some now consider the Gospel of John to have been written (by one of his students). (The fragment of the Gospel of Mary found in 1917 is held by the Rylands Library in Manchester, England.) Then a third Greek fragment of the Gospel of Mary, also from the early third century, was discovered near the Nile and was published in 1983; that papyrus now abides in the Ashmolean Library at Oxford. The extant texts are brief—from the Coptic text it is discernible that the original was nineteen pages long; this most complete manuscript in Berlin is missing the first six pages and five pages in the middle. Even though only fragments have so far been discovered, all the copies indicate an especially close relationship between Mary Magdalene and Jesus. A number of translations and related books are emerging. See *The Gospel of Mary of Magdala, Jesus and the First Woman Apostle* by Karen King (her translation is also included in *The Nag Hammadi Scriptures* collection); *The Gospel of Mary Magdalene*, translation from the Coptic and commentary by Jean Yves Leloup (originally published in French and now available in English translation). From a more particularly "Gnostic" perspective of a French tradition, *The Gospel of the Beloved Companion, The Complete Gospel of Mary Magdalene*, translation and commentary by Jehanne de Quillan, details a manuscript regarding Mary Magdalene that according to the author was brought to Languedoc from Alexandria in the early first century and translated from the Greek into Occitan (*langue d'oc*— the "language of 'yes'") in the twelfth century; the translation of an ancient Syriac manuscript from the sixth century has also emerged, *Joseph and Aseneth*, in *The Lost Gospel* by Simcha Jacobovici and Barrie Wilson as well as the other texts of The Nag Hammadi Scriptures collection which also shed light on the importance of the Gospel of Mary.

[38] *The Gospel of Mary Magdalene,* translation from the Coptic and commentary by Jean-Yves Leloup, English translation and notes by Joseph Rowe (Rochester, VT: Inner Traditions International, 2002), p. 39.

[39] Unlike priests of the Roman Catholic Church, rabbis are not only allowed to marry, they are obligated to do so, in accordance with the common command of Genesis 1:28:

Then God blessed them, and God said to them, "Be fruitful and multiply."

appropriate for the disciples to call him "Rabbi"; in the garden of the sepulcher, when Mary Magdalene recognizes him, it is as "Rabbouni!" ("My dear master, close to my heart") that she acknowledges him.[40] In the apocryphal Gospel of Philip, discovered among the Nag Hammadi texts,[41] their special relationship is also highlighted: "For Jesus used to walk with her and kissed her frequently upon the mouth" (Gospel of Philip 63,31).[42]

Yeshua [Jesus] said to her, "Maryam [Mary],
do not hold to me, for I am not of the flesh,
yet neither am I one with the Spirit;
but rather go to my disciples and tell them you have seen me,
so that all may know that my words are true
and that any who should choose to believe them

---

Rabbis are expected to participate in the normal struggles and pleasures of life, just as "ordinary" members of the community, as well as rabbis, are expected to sanctify all aspects of their lives every day, so that a holy society might grow. As within Islam, it is understood that no intermediary is needed between a soul and God; a rabbi or an imam may indicate the Way, but it is understood that each of us can engage in direct communion with God.

[40] See the Gospel of John 20:16 and *The Gospel of the Beloved Companion*, p. 75.

"Maryam!" She turned and, overcome with joy, said to him, "Rabbouni!"
[Gospel of Mary Magdalene 40:5]

[41] The "Nag Hammadi" texts were discovered in 1945 near Phon, Egypt; they had been preserved, hidden for centuries in a clay jar. These fourth century CE Coptic texts have been determined to be copies of Greek originals, some of which may predate the canonical gospels. The texts point a way to spiritual development through self-knowledge, rather than dogma, encouraging "inner knowing." See *The Nag Hammadi Scriptures, the Revised and Updated Translation of Sacred Gnostic Texts*, (Complete in One Volume), edited by Marvin Meyer (New York: HarperCollins, 2008). In the Gospel of Thomas, Jesus encourages us to come to know our own self as the key to the full recognition of our Source, saying: "The kingdom is inside you and it is outside you. When you know yourselves, then you will be known, and you will understand that you are children of the living Father" (*The Nag Hammadi Scriptures*, p. 139). In the "Secret Gospel of John" (2,25), it is related: "The One is a sovereign that has nothing over it. It is God and Parent, Father of the All, the invisible one that is over the All, that is incorruptible, that is pure light" (*The Nag Hammadi Scriptures*, p. 108).

[42] Gospel of Philip, as quoted in Cynthia Bourgeault, *The Meaning of Mary Magdalene*, op. cit., p. 41.

and keep to my commandments
will follow me on their last day."
[Gospel of Mary Magdalene 40:6]

It is as though there is another spiral of fulfillment of the passage of the Song of Songs 4:12–16. The beautiful enclosed garden of Beloved Mary (her dear pure being that had given birth to Jesus, the "Word" of God, and assisted in opening the fragrance of the Garden through his being, with the "word" of his teachings as well as her own) now through one she had also taught, her close companion as well as his, through Mary Magdalene cascades forth a fountain of love—the garden's fragrance is shared further, on the breeze of awakening.

Thy plants are a paradise of pomegranates with the fruits of the orchard.
Cypress with spikenard.
Spikenard and saffron, sweet cane and cinnamon,
with all the trees of Libanus,
myrrh and aloes with all the chief perfumes.
The fountain of gardens: the well of living waters,
which run with a strong stream from Libanus.
Arise, O north wind, and come, O south wind,
blow through my garden, and let the aromatical spices thereof flow out.
[Bible, Song of Solomon:13–14]

There are many mysteries, the secret of which God alone knows. Some Muslims interpret the Crucifixion and Resurrection as metaphorical events; some scholars see the Crucifixion as an impossibility—that "God's Word" is eternal—that the Spirit of God could not die. Whatever our theology, the principle of the power of transformation is evident in the conveyance of the story of this "dying" and "rising" to new life. Rumi highlights this process by describing the transmutation of matter through the power of the Soul of the soul:

A piece of bread
wrapped in a cloth remains inanimate,
but digested by a human being
it becomes enlivening spirit.
The human soul transmutes it

with the water of Salsabil.[43]
Dear reader, such is the power of the soul:
what, then, must be the power of the Soul of that soul?
. . . If the heart should open the purse of this mystery,
the enraptured soul would rush to the highest of heavens.
[Rumi, *Mathnawi* I: 1474–76; 1479]

Even so, the heart and soul of dear Mary of Magdala rushed to the heights. It is she who was able to hold the concentration, whose heart did not swerve or deny what she had seen and known. In the Gospel of Mary, the only Gospel now ascribed to a woman by scholars, it is she who is recorded as embracing and bringing solace to the other disciples:

Mary arose, then, embracing them all and began to address them
as her brothers and sisters saying:
'Do not weep and grieve nor let your hearts remain in doubt,
for his grace will be with you all, sustaining and protecting you.
Rather, we should praise his greatness
for he has prepared us
so that we might become fully human.'[44]
As Mary said these things their hearts opened towards the Good.
[Gospel of Mary Magdalene, second dialogue 9,5–24][45]

In this moment, Mary of Magdala encourages the disciples to be of steadfast heart, to fulfill the teachings within themselves, as true human beings, and so to carry the words of the Master out into the world. Energy

---

[43] Salsabil is one of the overflowing springs of Paradise. See Quran, *Surah al-Insan* 76:18.

[44] To become an *anthropos* (a completed human being), here pointing towards the meaning of becoming "a single one," *ihidaya* in Aramaic (see Cynthia Bourgeault, *The Meaning of Mary Magdalene*, op. cit., p. 54–55). *Ahad* (the One) in Arabic, is indicated by *alif*, the first letter of the Arabic alphabet, a simple vertical line, symbolic of the unity of being (*tawhid*). The whirling ceremony of the Mevlevi dervishes (*sema*) is a meditation in motion witnessing to this, to the process of becoming fully human, immersed in continual remembrance of Allah: *Those who enter it find peace* (Quran, *Surah al-'Imran* 3:97). Those who truly enter the heart become complete.

[45] See Cynthia Bourgeault, *The Meaning of Mary Magdalene*, op. cit, p. 53, and "The Gospel of Mary with the Greek Gospel of Mary," *Nag Hammadi Scriptures*, op. cit., pp. 742–43.

flows and is conveyed through her heart. As inspiration, she relates to them a moment when Yeshua (Jesus) spoke to her of a great tree, saying:

"Whosoever listens to my words and ascends to its crown
will not taste death,
but know the truth of eternal life."
[Gospel of Mary 42:2][46]

She is recorded as describing to the apostles the vision Jesus showed her of the great tree and how she understood the journey as upward through the seven branches.[47] After the sixth bough, having passed through the various purifications of the egoistic structure, she arrives with "fierce joy" into brilliant Light, through the seventh, witnessing the eighth, she experiences a dissolving into the embrace of feminine Beauty clothed in brilliant white light[48]— she knows herself as free, and resting in silence.

> "I am liberated from the chains of forgetfulness which have existed in time. From this moment onward, I go forward into the season of the Great Age, the Aeon, and there, where time rests in stillness in the Eternity of time, I will repose in silence." And having said this, Mary [Magdala] fell silent since it was to this point that the Savior had brought her.[49]

---

[46] *Gospel of the Beloved Companion*, op. cit, p. 116.

[47] This could, also, be a symbolic description of her earlier "enlightenment" experience—of the clearing of the seven "demons." It also brings to heart echoes of symbolism of the *menorah*, the seven branched holder of Light for the Temple, and the symbolism of the "Tree of Life" of the Kabbalah which culminates in the "Crown," (*Keter*) the "most hidden of the hidden," the Sublime Essence of the Divine Reality that encompasses all aspects of being as Absolute Compassion, even as it is expressed in the Quran, *My Rahmat [Compassion] encompasses everything* (7:156).

[48] Here again we have an image of the *Shekhinah*, Holy Spirit, as a bride. Similarly, Rumi refers to the Quran as a "Shy Bride" who is ever awaiting us to be purely present, that we might receive revelation of the Word, the breath of Life. As Shams of Tabriz (*Rumi's Sun*, op. cit., p. 80) also says:

The Blessed Quran is a shy bride who opens her veil
only if she sees that the land of faith is safe from war.

[49] "The Gospel of Mary" translation from *The Luminous Gospels*, as quoted by Cynthia Bourgeault, *The Meaning of Mary Magdalene*, op. cit., p. 67. This brings to

In the Gospel of Mary of the *Nag Hammadi Scriptures*, when the disciple Peter criticizes Mary after she relates this experience, the disciple Levi (Matthew) stands up for her, recognizing the fact that Jesus might well have given her secret teachings not shared with the other disciples,[50] for:

"He knew her completely and loved her steadfastly."
[The Greek Gospel of Mary, P. Ryl. 463][51]

In clear seeing (*basirah*), Levi[52] recognizes, as Cynthia Bourgeault describes it, that "the person standing before them is not simply Mary Magdalene, but Mary Magdalene and Jesus flowing together as a single whole in the unbroken beauty of the inner communion."[53] It was even as Jesus had told Mary, as conveyed in the Gospel of Mary Magdalene:

Yeshua [Jesus] says to her:
"Miryam [Mary], whom I have called the Migdalah,[54]
now you have seen the All,
and have known the Truth of your self, the Truth that is I am.
Now you have become the completion of the completion."
[Gospel of Mary Magdalene 42:13][55]

Mary of Magdala had come to comprehend that "word" spoken by God to the "rose" that causes it to bloom, encouraging our inner spirit,

---

heart a reflection of Rumi's, "Like the Speechless Lily . . ." (see page 55 of this text).

[50] See *The Nag Hammadi Scriptures*: BG 8502,1 manuscript, p. 745, and P. Ryl. 462 manuscript, p. 747, translations by Karen L. King.

[51] Ibid., p. 747.

[52] Levi is also known as Matthew, the former tax-collector who had left his stringent accounting to follow Jesus in his Path of Loving Compassion.

[53] Cynthia Bourgeault, *The Meaning of Mary Magdalene*, op cit., p. 80 (referencing P. Ryl. 463 text fragment, *The Nag Hammadi Scriptures* collection, p. 747).

[54] Migdalah, which has the meaning of "tower", also carries the meaning of "pulpit" (from which one may speak, conveying wisdom), as well as "a raised bed of flowers" (especially of pyramidal form). It derives from *gadal*, Hebrew for "grow up" or "become great." Jesus indicates again in stressing her name that she has fulfilled it, and come to elevated completion as a true human being, radiant with Truth.

[55] *The Gospel of the Beloved Companion, The Complete Gospel of Mary Magdalene*, op. cit., p. 80.

our true nature, that through the earthen darkness the fragrance of the rose might emerge:

> Whoever shall strive in tribulation for Our sake,
> Heaven will give support to his or her feet.
> Your outward form is wailing because of the darkness;
> your inward spirit is roses within roses.
> [Rumi, *Mathnawi* IV: 1023–24]

In addition to the magnificent rose, among the flower symbols for Beloved Mary, mother of Jesus the "Anointed," she who had long known her true nature, are the three-petaled blue iris, the pure white "Easter" lily of resurrection, and the water lily or lotus. In ancient Egyptian mythology the water lily or lotus was also a symbol of rebirth after death, as it arises into the light from the fertile darkness of the watery earth. Ancient Egyptians looked forward to the possibility of new life after death, anticipating the possibility of emerging into life again like the lily. There is a

*Iris*

*Madonna Lily*

*Lotus*

recognition of the interplay of dark and light, of how both are needed for the continuation of life. The water lily or lotus was for them a symbol of transformation, from the ancient hidden darkness to the manifest world filled with light, rebirthed. As often has occurred, the meaningful symbolism of one culture is subsumed into another. Even so, the beauty of the emergent pure lily shining in the sun also became a symbol of Beloved Mary, mother of Christ; she is referred to often as the "lily of divine beauty,"[56] holding within herself the promise of resurrection.

Most Christian scholars agree that the public teaching of Jesus had unfolded over a period of about three years, beginning when he was thirty, so that he would have been 33 years old when the Crucifixion occurred. The Hebrew method of counting time in that era, the noting of the lunar–solar cycle, takes 33 years to be completed—the lunar year consists of 354 days; a solar year has 365 days, so it takes 33 years for a full cycling of both to arrive again at the beginning. The number 33 has many resonances and meanings. The normal human spine, the core support of the body as a whole and of the nervous system, consists of 33 vertebrae; it is recognized that the energy of life flows up the spine.[57] It is the 33rd time that Noah's name is mentioned in the Bible that God promises not

---

[56] Maximus, *The Life of the Virgin*, op. cit., p. 37.

[57] In the spiritual traditions of the East, this is known as *kundalini* energy, arising into the bursting light of the crown chakra (see pp. 384–85, n. 6 and p. 435).

to bring another such flood, and the sign of His promise is the rainbow, a unified band of seven stunning colors reflected when both sunlight and moisture of rainclouds are present together.[58]

In Islamic practice, prayer beads are usually arranged in sets of 33; such beads may number 33 in total or consist of three groups of 33 combined for a total strand of 99, corresponding to the 99 Names of God, with a hundredth unifying larger bead of "Allah" holding all together. One might consider that 33 holds a resonance of the three-fold *Bismillah ar-Rahman ar-Rahim* multiplied by 11, the *abjad*[59] number for "Hu," signifying the

---

[58] See the Bible, Genesis 9:16–17:

> And the bow shall be in the cloud; and I will look upon it,
> that I may remember the everlasting covenant between God
> and every living creature of all flesh that *is* upon the earth.
> And God said unto Noah, "This is the token of the covenant,
> which I have established between me and all flesh that is upon the earth."

In many cultures, rainbows are a sign of blessing, of communication of Spirit; in Native American culture rainbows are considered to be a bridge between the spiritual and the human world. See also Chapter 12 of the *Zohar*, as translated in *Zohar Annotated and Explained*, p. 63:

> "Moses went inside the cloud
> and ascended the mountain." [Bible (Torah), Exodus 24:18].
> What is this cloud?
> the same one of which it is written:
> "I have placed My bow in the cloud." [Bible (Torah), Genesis 9:13]
> We have learned that the rainbow took off her garments
> and gave them to Moses.
> Wearing that garment, he went up the mountain.
> From inside it he saw what he saw,
> delighting in the All, up to that place."
> [Zohar, Chapter 12]

In traditions of the East, the colors of the rainbow are associated with the seven chakras, energy centers of the human body, which are noted (and can be seen by some sensitive souls) in the same order of colors: violet, indigo, blue, green, yellow, orange, red. In a sense, we are all walking rainbows, even though we may not be aware of it and may vary greatly in the capacity of our radiance.

[59] In both Judaism and Islam, letters carry a significance of number, and, through the combination of letters, a value for a word can be determined. Even so, one can hear someone call out, "786," and know they mean *Bismillah ar-Rahman ar-Rahim* (which has 786 as the corresponding numerical value of its letters), or

Divine Presence pouring forth compassion in its fullness, and the overwhelming beneficence of the Divine Reality so abundant in Its gifts.

*"O our Sustainer!*
*Do not let our hearts swerve from the Truth*
*after You have guided us;*
*and bestow on us the gift of Your Grace:*
*truly, You are the Giver of Gifts."*[60]
[Quran, *Surah al-'Imran* 3:8]

*Truly, those who have attained to faith in this Word,*
*as well as those who follow the Jewish faith,*
*and the Sabians,*[61] *and the Christians—*
*all who have faith in God and the Final Day and do righteous deeds—*
*no fear need they have,*
*and neither shall they grieve.*
[Quran, *Surah al-Maida* 5:69]

The Acts of the Apostles (1:9) describe how, after the Resurrection, Jesus was "lifted up, and a cloud took him out of sight." The Gospels of Mark (16:19–20) and Luke (24:50–53) also describe the moment of Christ's ascension into heaven.

"And, behold, I send the promise of my Father upon you:
but linger awhile in the city of Jerusalem,
until you are endowed with power from on high."
And he led them out as far as to Bethany,[62]
and he lifted up his hands, and blessed them.
And it came to pass, while he blessed them,

---

"66," meaning "Allah."

60 *"Rabbana la tuzigh qulubana ba'da 'izh hadaytana*
*wa hab lana mil ladunka rahmatan innaka anntal wahhab."*

61 "Sabians" are understood by many to have been the followers of John the Baptist.

62 Bethany was only about three kilometers (two miles) from Jerusalem. Magdala on the western coast of the Sea of Galilee is about eighty miles from Bethany (where Martha and Lazarus and Mary lived), and in between them is the city of Nain. A journey from the Sea of Galilee to the Dead Sea, where Bethany is, was a well-worn road, not a great distance even for those who traveled by foot in those days.

he was parted from them, and carried up into heaven.
[Bible (ESV), Luke 24:49–51]

Similarly, al-Tha'labi speaks of how Jesus was brought to Heaven, a being of light, radiant human and angelic, integrated, both earthly and heavenly, to the Throne of God.[63]

For the disciples, what followed was a time of persecution, the testing of their faith, a time of teaching, of sharing what was beloved to them of what Jesus had taught them. During this time of difficulty, some say that Mary Magdalene and Martha and Lazarus journeyed together to France;[64] some traditions relate that Jesus survived and that he and

---

[63] Among Christians, the Feast of the Ascension of Jesus is celebrated forty days after Easter (the rising from the tomb)—another forty-day passage of maturing, of ripening of Love.

[64] For centuries people have been making the journey to Saint-Maximin-la-Sainte-Baume in France in pilgrimage in honor of Mary Magdalene. Provence traditions relate that Mary Magdalene, along with Lazarus and Martha and a few others were set adrift in a small boat without sails or oars, and, miraculously, they landed on the shores of Gaul (France) in a place now called *Saintes Maries de la Mer*. These devoted included St. Mary, wife of Clopas (Cleopas), St. Salome (also called Mary Salome), St. Mary Magdalene, her sister St. Martha with their attendant Marcella, their brother Lazarus, Trophimius, Maximin, Cleon, Eutropius, Sidonius (Restitutus, "the man who had been born blind"), Martial, and Saturnius. See John W. Taylor, *The Coming of the Saints: Imaginations and Studies in Early Church History and Tradition* (New York: Dutton, 1907), p. 126. They continued to spread the "Good Word" of Jesus; Lazarus baptized many souls. Mary Magdalene retreated to a secluded mountain cave (now known as "the grotto," or La Baume of Mary Magdalene) until her passing. Christian pilgrimages to the site have been recorded since the fifth century CE, when Christianity became more predominant under the converted Frankish King Clovis.

Local tradition relates that Maximin, the first "bishop" of Aix-en-Provence, arranged her burial under his oratory. When the tomb was opened in the thirteenth century (December 10, 1279), though her body was no longer present (an ancient wooden tablet remained indicating that she had been laid to rest there; her relics had been hidden), yet a wonderful fragrance was perceived wafting into the air. A basilica dedicated to Sainte Mary Magdalene was then built in that location in 1295. It is related that the monks of the Abbey church of Sainte Marie Madeleine in Vézelay, France, had translated her relics there. There is also a relic of her left hand held with great reverence in the Simonopetra Monastery on Mount Athos in Greece. It is considered to be incorruptible and also exudes a special fragrance; numerous miracles are associated with it. When

Beloved Mary and some of the apostles journeyed to India and Pakistan. Many of the recountings of these moments are based on non-canonical texts or oral traditions held within hearts. Beautiful traditions continue to be kept in all these places as well as within the region now encompassed by Turkey, where many of the early events of Christian history unfolded.

Within our own faith traditions we may find ourselves differing with others of our faith as to the meaning of sacred texts or events that might have occurred within the tradition that we love and follow. For centuries, debates have existed among Christians as to the nature of Jesus, what portion of the Gospels were really his words, etc.[65] Throughout our human religious history sometimes serious arguments and schisms have arisen due to such differences of opinion and political ramifications. The first few centuries of Islam were no different than in Christianity in their tumultuousness, though the practice of prayer continually remains as the

---

the great fire took place in 1945 in a forest near the monastery, it is told that through her auspices, the Holy Water Service and prayers for her assistance, the monastery and forest were preserved (even as occurred at Meryem Ana Evi under the auspices of Beloved Mary; see p. 344 of this text).

[65] See, for instance, the recent work of Marcus Borg, Ray Riegert, and Mark Powelson; *The Lost Gospel Q: The Original Sayings of Jesus.*

As with many emerging faith traditions, the early years of Christianity were less defined by dogma, and more lived by inspiration according to the teachings Jesus had conveyed among the people and the oral traditions that were shared. The Council of Nicea in 325 CE had sought to regularize and define; Beloved Mary was there declared *Theotokos* ("God bearer"); whereas before she had been known as *Christotokos*, "Christ Bearer" (see p. 82 of this text). Even so, over the centuries, many schools of thought and understanding still survived and have been promulgated alongside the officially approved narrative and theology of the Roman Catholic or Orthodox Church and the powers of governments who have declared a particular approach to a faith as the accepted way to God. Even in the thirteenth century CE there were still many variations of Christian thought, and over the next centuries, numerous Protestant sects emerged who based their observance on renewed understandings of Christ's teaching and being (see Hannah Adams, *A Dictionary of All Religions and Religious Denominations*, and p. 82 and n. 21 of this text). There has been an unfolding, also, within Islam, over the centuries, of devoted practitioners who encourage a return to the root of scripture, of holy inspiration, and encourage the clearing of the heart and mind in concentrated prayer that one might reach a closer connection with God (with that Reality that is *closer than our jugular vein, Surah Qaf* 50:16), even as Beloved Mary/Maryam sought to do in her devotion in the Temple, immersed in prayer, day by day, moment by moment.

common foundation. Within the Jewish faith, sometimes, even Rabbis jest that among two Jews there may well be three opinions.

There are many ways of understanding, many different platforms of perception. It is possible that in a moment our understanding may suddenly shift, depending on the stance of our soul, the openness of our mind and heart. The process of dying to the constrictive opinions and views of the limited self and the resurrecting in Spirit that is needed, into the greater Self, into Truth, some say was modeled in metaphor by the "Crucifixion" and "Resurrection" of Jesus. Or as the Prophet Muhammad encouraged: "Die before you die!"[66] As Rumi elucidates further:

The body is a narrow house,
and the soul within is cramped.
God ruined it so that He might make a royal palace.
I am cramped like the embryo in the womb:
I've become nine-months old.
This migration is now urgent,
but unless the throes of childbirth overtake my mother,
what am I to do?
In this prison I am amidst the fire.
My mother, my bodily nature,
with its death throes is birthing Spirit,
so that the lamb may be released from the ewe,
and begin to graze in the green fields.
Come, open your womb, for this lamb has grown big.
[Rumi, *Mathnawi* III: 3555–59]

In his discourses, Rumi continues:

---

[66] "Die before you die": let the compulsive ego dissolve; *"Be!"* in Love. Every year, Muslims experience something of a process of death and resurrection in the unfolding of the fast of Ramadan, a lunar month, thirty days of fasting from before sunrise each day until after sunset, incumbent upon every Muslim, a clearing of the streambed of one's life so that pure water may flow again, enlivening the "nearby land," offering prayers to heaven. See Extended Context Notes in Appendix, Star X, 5. One might say to "Die before you die," is to "die" to the customary compulsions of the ego, to gift the "self" back to Love, our Source, that we might be completely immersed in the Divine Breath, a servant of Compassion.

Whoever labors for the glory of God is never lost, though he shuts both his eyes. *Whosoever does a particle of good shall see it* [Quran, *Surah az-Zalzalah* 99:7]. Here you are in darkness; you are "veiled" so that you cannot see how far you have progressed. In the end, however, you will perceive that "this world is the 'seedbed' of the hereafter."[67] Whatever you sow here you will reap there.

Jesus laughed a lot. John the Baptist wept a lot. John said to Jesus, "You have become mighty secure from God's subtle deceits to laugh so much."

"You," replied Jesus, "are mighty heedless of God's subtle and mysterious favor and grace to weep so much!"

One of God's saints, who was present at this exchange, asked God which of the two was the more exalted in station. God answered, "The one who thinks better of me," that is, "Wherever my servant thinks of me, I am there.[68] I have a form and image for each of My servants. Whatever each of them imagines Me to be, that I am. I am bound to images where God is; I am annoyed by any reality where God is not. O My servants, cleanse your thoughts, for they are My dwelling places. Now try, yourself, and see what is more beneficial to you—weeping, laughter, fasting, prayer, or retreat. Adopt whichever of these suits you best and causes you to advance more."[69]

Even the way of weeping can transform into springs of joyful grace:

And happy the pilgrims inspired by You
with courage to make the ascent!
As they pass through the Valley of Weeping,[70]

---

[67] The prophetic *hadith* (*al-dunya mazra'at*) is given in *FAM* 112 #338, as cited in *Signs of the Unseen*, op, cit.

[68] The *Hadith Qudsi* is given in Jalaluddin Abd al-Rahmanal-Suyuti, *al-Jami al-saghir fi ahadith al-bashir wa'l-nadhir* (Lyallpur: al-Maktaba al-Isllamiyya, 1394 AH, 1974 CE), ii, 82.

[69] *Fihi ma Fihi*, Discourse 11, *Signs of the Unseen*, op. cit., pp. 50–51 (adapted by the author).

[70] The Valley of Baca, the "Valley of Tears." The Hebrew conveys both the meaning of oozing, brackish water, and of dripping balsam trees, which "weep" what appear as tears of balsam and grow in dry, barren places. Some interpret this "Valley of Baca" to be the same as the Bacca mentioned in the Quran, modern-day Mecca. As pilgrims pass through the "vale of tears" of this life,

they make it a place of springs
clothed in blessings by early rains.
From there they make their way from height to height,
soon to be seen before God on Zion.[71]"
[Bible, Psalms 84:5–7][72]

Biblical commentators note that the Hebrew word for "rain" also has the meaning of "archer" and "teacher." For those engaged in the spiritual journey, as they pass through the wilderness, traversing rough and tortuous paths, God opens springs for them—teachers appear to convey the nourishment of Wisdom, and, while feeding the people, they also receive nourishment themselves. Blessings flow and tears of sorrow become joy, transformation occurs. When the journey of life is consecrated to God,

---

through God's grace, their faith turns it into a place of refreshing springs (even as occurred for Hagar and Ishmael; see p. 79 of this text), filled with blessings. For the faithful, *Truly with every difficulty comes ease.* (Quran, *Surah al-Inshirah* 94:5–6).

[71] Zion can refer to one of three places: the hill where the most ancient areas of Jerusalem stood; the city of Jerusalem itself, the "City of David"; or the dwelling place of God. See Psalm 2:6 where Zion is referred to as "God's Holy Mountain" and "the Place where God is enthroned" (Psalm 9:11). See also Isaiah 4:3: "Those who are left in Zion, who remain in Jerusalem, will be called holy"; and Isaiah 18:7: "Gifts will be brought to Mount Zion, the place of the Name of the Lord Almighty." Leaving behind the limited self, setting out from "home" step by step we are brought into God's Presence, our true "Home," from where a vast vista opens.

[72] Translation of Psalm 84:5–7 from "VESPERS Feast of Elizabeth Seton," as offered by the Sisters of Charity: http://www.srcharitycinti.org/about/images/jan11Vespers.pdf (accessed August 27, 2021). The Sisters of Charity have been inspired by the being and example of Saint Elizabeth Ann Seton (1774–1821 CE) who was deeply devoted to the Virgin Mary. She is the first American to have been recognized as a saint by the Roman Catholic Church. The Sisters of Charity express their aim "to choose to live simply in a complex world committed to the healing of our global home." In the same Vespers Feast call and response, they also recite in their devotion to God:

It was You who created my inmost self,
and put me together in my mother's womb;
For all these mysteries I thank You;
for the wonder of myself, for the wonder of Your works.

to alignment with Divine Reality, then even in the midst of dry, barren wilderness, and the most challenging circumstances, springs emerge; all that comes to us can be received as a teaching, and those who can be of support to us arrive.

Some might say the journey is a seven-storied mountain, an intense climb, and like the children's game of chutes and ladders, one may stumble and fall down and need to begin again, cycling upward little by little, passing through the seven valleys,[73] learning the intrinsic support of virtue—of prudence, justice, restraint and patience, courage, faith, hope, blossoming into love. It is not often a simple journey to reach the moment of rebirth, of union, and yet, it is taught that the tests along the way strengthen our capacity, and we can learn much from those who have traveled the Way before us:

*"We have heard, and we pay heed.*
*Grant us Your forgiveness, O our Sustainer, for with You is all journeys' end!*
*God does not challenge any human being*
*with more than he/she can bear:*
*in his/her favor shall be whatever good he/she does,*
*and against him/her whatever harm he/she does.*
*"O our Sustainer!*
*Do not take us to task if we forget or unknowingly do wrong!*
*O our Sustainer! Do not lay upon us a burden*
*like that which You placed on those who lived before us!*
*O our Sustainer! Do not make us bear burdens*
*which we have no strength to bear!*
*And efface our sins, and grant us forgiveness,*
*and bestow Your mercy on us!*
*You are our Supreme Lord:*
*help us when we face those who stand against truth."*
[Quran, *Surah al-Baqarah* 2:285–86]

This prayer for Divine help is of sustaining strength when we face those who stand against truth, especially when it is voices within our own

---

[73] The Sufi poet Fariduddin Attar (1145–1221 CE) wrote a magnificent allegory of this journey of the soul across mountains and valleys in his *Conference of the Birds* (*Mantiq ut-Tayr*).

hearts. One might understand it as a call for help to recognize, even as did Abraham, that the lesser lights of our ego's reflective arising are not the ultimate reality, but that there is always a reality greater than our awareness; as long as we are alive, our knowing may increase, our capacity for love may grow. Abraham continually turned from the lesser to the Greater,[74] and, acknowledging how he was supported by his Sustainer, continued to pray for increase of wisdom, for increased capacity for conveyance of Truth, and for soundness of heart, moment by moment:

*"The Sustainer and Cherisher of the Worlds,*
*who created me, it is He who guides me,*
*who gives me food and drink*
*and when I am ill it is He who restores me to health,*
*who will cause me to die and then to live,*
*and who I hope will forgive me my faults on the Day of Reckoning.*
*O my Sustainer! bestow wisdom on me and make me one with the righteous;*
*grant me the ability to convey the truth to those who will come after me;*
*place me among the inheritors of the Garden of Bliss;*
*forgive my father for being among those astray;*
*and let me not be in disgrace on the Day when we will be raised up,*
*the Day when neither wealth nor children will be of benefit,*
*but only the one who brings to God a sound heart."*
[Quran, *Surah ash-Shu'ara* (Prayer of Abraham) 26:77–89]

We arrive through Grace at a heightened state of Love and compassion, enabled through union with the Inspiring Source of Life. The principle of Resurrection is what is essential—the eternal Law of Oneness, of Healing, Unitive Love that gives life to the dead through the regenerative power of union with God. Through the grace of our most intimate Beloved, Creative and Generous Source, we are healed of false separation as we come to recognize with gratitude so many capacities with which we have been gifted—through which we may experience that enlivening Love.

---

[74] Even as Abraham turned from the worship of stars to consideration of the moon and then the sun, and then recognized God is greater than all, even so Muslims declare, "*Allahu akbar,*" in recognition that God is far greater than any of our conceptions, Infinite in Grace, Power and Beauty, Generosity and healing Love.

*Such is He/She who knows all that is beyond the reach of a created being's perception,*
*as well as all that can be witnessed by a creature's senses or mind:*
*the Almighty, Bestower of Grace,*
*who makes most excellent everything that He/She creates.*
*Thus, He/She begins the creation of the human out of clay;*
*then He/She causes him to be begotten out of the essence of a humble fluid;*
*and then He/She forms him in accordance with what he is meant to be,*
*and breathes into him of His/Her spirit:*
*and He/She endows you with hearing, and sight, and feelings as well as minds:*
*yet how seldom are you grateful!*
*For they say, "What! After we have been lost in the earth,*
*shall we indeed be restored to life in a new act of creation?"*
*Nay, but they deny the truth that they are destined to meet their Sustainer!*
*Say: "The angel of death who has been given charge of you will gather you,*
*and then unto your Sustainer you will be brought back."*
[Quran, *Surah as-Sajdah*, "Prostration," 32:6–11]

We come to understand that the Beloved is calling us, pulling us, even more than we are yearning . . .

Our desire for You arises from Your urgency—
wherever there is a wayfarer, it is God pulling.
Does the dust leap upward without a wind?
Does a ship voyage without the sea?
No one ever died in the presence of the Water of Life:
compared with Your Water the Water of Life is just dregs.
The Water of Life is the goal of those to whom life is dear:
by water the garden becomes fertile and smiles.
But those who drain the cup of death are living through His love:
they have torn their hearts away from life and the Water of Life.
When the water of Your Love reached out to us,
the Water of Life became worthless in our sight.
Every soul derives freshness from the Water of Life,
but You are the Water of the Water of Life.
You bestowed on me a spiritual death and a resurrection continually,
that I might experience the conquering power of Your Bounty.
This bodily dying became as easy to me as sleeping,
from my confidence that You, O God, would raise me from the dead.

If the Seven Seas become a mirage at every moment,
You will take the water by the ear and bring it back, O Water of the water.
Reason trembles with fear of death, but Love is valiant.
[Rumi, *Mathnawi* V: 4216–26]

He communicates to the eye that which He wills of beauty
and of perfection and of Loving Glances;
And He communicates to the ear that which He wills of music
and glad tidings and exaltations.
The world is full of remedies,
but you have no remedies until God opens a window for you.
Though you are unaware of that remedy now,
God will make it clear in the hour of need.
[Rumi, *Mathnawi* II: 680–83]

Within Jerusalem—the region that is regarded as holy and beloved by all three Abrahamic faiths—the Church of the Holy Sepulcher, the church built over the place it is believed by Christians that Jesus was interred and from which he resurrected, has been for some time under the shared custodial guardianship of Greek Orthodox Christians, Armenian Christians, Coptic Christians and Roman Catholic Christians, while Muslims have for centuries simultaneously held the responsibility of the key. The first building was constructed over the area of the tomb after it was found by Helena, the beloved mother of Constantine I, when in 327 CE she, at the age of about eighty, had gone on pilgrimage to Jerusalem, just a couple of years before she passed away. With the help of Bishop Eusebius, they discovered the tomb under what had been a Roman temple to Jupiter and Venus constructed by Hadrian, built after the demolition of Jerusalem in the Roman–Jewish wars in 70 CE.

The Church of the Holy Sepulcher on the Mount of Olives was consecrated on September 13, 335 CE on behalf of Constantine, the first of the Roman emperors to convert to Christianity. Through the Edict of Milan he officially legalized the Christian religion; persecution ebbed and churches began to be built.[75] This was the Church of the Holy Sepulcher visited

[75] The early Christians also were persecuted for their beliefs. In the catacombs they found refuge, and in caves in Cappadocia they carved multi-storied abodes of safety where they could pray undisturbed.

by gentle Egeria, whose pilgrimage journal is the oldest extant, written in the 380's.[76] The church complex has been rebuilt numerous times over the centuries; it is said that in the time of Salahuddin, in the twelfth century, two Muslim families were given guardianship of the key and the door. It is Adeeb Joudeh, whose father began training him in this responsibility when he was eight years old, who now brings the key that has been in his family for 800 years, and a member of the Nusseibeh family has the responsibility of then opening the doors for all those who wish to enter (whether of a Christian denomination or Muslim or other).[77] Some say that the interdenominational, interfaith guardianship of the Holy Sepulcher is an aspect that helps to keep the peace there, and the remembrance of the inner garden of the soul.

*Don't they look at the sky above them?*
*How We have made it and adorned it*
*and how there are no flaws in it?*
*And the earth—We have spread it wide*
*and firmly established mountains on it*
*and caused it to bring forth every kind of beautiful growth,*
*so offering an insight and a reminder*
*to every human being who willingly turns to God.*
*And We send down from the sky rain charged with blessing*
*and with it cause gardens to grow, and fields of grain,*
*and tall palm trees with their thickly clustered dates,*
*as sustenance for human beings;*
*and by all this We bring dead land to life:*
*even so will be the Resurrection.*
[Quran, *Surah Qaf* 50:6–11]

Even as we are reminded through this story of the Resurrection of Jesus, we each have the possibility of entering the cave of the heart,

---

76 Egeria, see p. 430 in Extended Context Notes.

77 During the Covid-19 health crisis of 2020 CE, the Holy Sepulcher was kept shut for a period of time. The keeper of the key, Adeeb Joudeh, said this was the first time since the time of the Black Plague in 1349 CE that his family had not conveyed the key to open the door each day. Prayer offerings were restricted to a few clerics within and those of a few hearts offering prayers outside the locked door, until eventually the Keeper of the Key and the Opener of the Door were able to resume their duties.

of coming closer to the Beloved in our inmost being, and resurrecting through Love. In Hebrew the word for the human being, "Adam" (*Ha-Adam*), shares the same root with the word for earth, the soil of the ground (*adamah*). When a seed of spirit is planted in the earth, the possibility of new life emerges. The cave is a place of initiation, of intimate education in the inner realities. Through doing this inner work, we find wholeness, healing.

> Heal yourself now while your Jesus is on earth,
> for when Jesus has risen to heaven
> your cure will have departed.[78]

As Mevlana further advises, don't make your Jesus carry your donkey; let your donkey carry Jesus.[79]

A continual refrain throughout human history has been the persecution of the holy by the worldly, those held by illusions of greed or power, tribal affiliation or country, forgetting the open plain of God's country, the vast expanse of "His/Her" Love, that immense unlimitable Power. And yet the "faithful," those attuned to the underlying Source, continue to recognize the healing power of the Creative Force of Love, always turning to "God" to connect with the Source of Sustenance, that One who is the Healer of all our ills, Opener of the Garden:

> By the august influence of Mary's hand,
> the withered bough may open with the fragrance
> of musk and freshness and fruit. . . .
> "O God, You who know the manifest and the hidden,

---

[78] Khaqani, *Divan,* quoted in *The Book of Khaqani*, translation and introduction by Paul Smith (New Humanity Books, 2014), p. 10, lines 7 and 16. These lines are quoted by Rumi in his *Fihi ma Fihi.* Khaqani, a revered Sufi poet, was born in Shirvan, Persia, in 1122 CE into the family of a carpenter. His mother, a Nestorian Christian, had been a slave-girl, but it is said was a descendant of the first Roman Emperor of Arab birth, who was tolerant towards Christianity, Marcus Julius Verus Phillipus (204–249 CE). Khaqani's Muslim father passed away when he was quite young; his uncle, a physician and court astronomer raised him. Khaqani's work influenced many court and Sufi poets; Jesus features in many of his poems. He died in 1199 (just a few years before Jalaluddin Rumi was born) and is buried in the Poet's Cemetery in Tabriz.

[79] See *Mathnawi* II: 1849–54.

to whom but You should Your servant lift his hand?
Both the prayer and the answer are from You.
You at first give the desire for prayer,
and You at last give likewise the recompense . . .
God, for the sake of His servants,
became the *kaf* of *Kafi* [All-Sufficing],
in token of the truth of the promise of *Kaf, Ha, Ya, 'Ayn, Sad.*[80]
God said, "I am All-Sufficing: I will give you all good,
with no intervening cause, without any mediator.
I am All-Sufficing: I will give you fullness without bread;
without spring I will give you narcissi and wild roses.
I will instruct you without books or teachers.
I am All-Sufficing: I will heal you without medicine,
I will make the grave and the pit open into a spacious playing field."
[Rumi, *Mathnawi* IV: 3497–3500; 3515–20]

*"Hence, peace was upon me on the day when I was born,*
*and [will be upon me] on the day of my death,*
*and on the day when I shall be raised to life [again]!"*
[Quran, *Surah Maryam* (Words of Jesus) 19:33]

As our dear friend Father Tarcy, the guardian of beloved Mary's house near Ephesus, a devoted man of heart, once said: "There are two great mysteries of our life—death and resurrection—or is it only one mystery of being reborn to a more profound life of our daily human life."[81]

---

[80] The mystical letters that open *Surah Maryam,* indicating the cracking open of revelation bringing sustenance within the heart of the human being in resonance with the Sound before sound.

*In the Name of God, the Infinitely Compassionate, the Infinitely Merciful:*
*Kaf, Ha, Ya, 'Ayn, Sad*
*An account of the grace which your Sustainer bestowed upon His servant Zachariah,*
*when he called out to his Sustainer in the secrecy of his heart,*
*he prayed: "O my Sustainer! Feeble have become my bones, and my head glistens with grey hair.*
*But never yet, O my Lord, has my prayer to You remained unanswered.*
[Quran, *Surah Maryam,* 19:1–4]

[81] Excerpt from a talk offered by Father Tarcy Mathias on 4/7/05 at the House of Maryem Ana. See pp. 343–47 of this text.

Since the heart is invisible, if you want a symbol of it,
seek it from one who has connection with the heart.
The wind is hidden from the eye, O trusty friend,
but behold it in the dust and in the movement of the leaves,
see whether it is blowing from the right or from the left:
the movement of the leaves will describe its condition to you.
If you're unfamiliar with intoxication of the heart and ask where it is,
seek its description from the intoxicated eye.
Since you are far from knowing the Essence of God,
you may recognize the description of the Essence
in the Prophet and his miracles.
Certain secret miracles and graces pouring
from the elect Elders impress a heart;
for within those Elders there are a hundred spiritual resurrections,
of which the least is this, that their neighbor becomes intoxicated;
and so that fortunate one who has devoted himself or herself
to a blessed saint
has become the companion of God.
The evidentiary miracle that produced an effect
upon something inanimate
is like the rod of Moses or the passage within the sea,
or the splitting of the moon.
If that miracle produces an immediate effect upon the soul,
it's because the soul is brought into connection
by means of a hidden connection.
The effects produced upon inanimate objects are secondary:
they are really for the sake of the fair invisible Spirit,
in order that the inmost heart
may be affected by means of that inanimate object.
How excellent is bread without the dough!
How excellent is the Messiah's table of food without ceasing!
How excellent is Mary's fruit arriving without orchard!
Miracles proceeding from the spirit of the perfected one
affect the soul of the seeker as rejuvenating life.
The miracle is the sea,
and the heedless man or woman is a land-bird who cannot swim,
but the water-bird is safe there.

The miracle bestows infirmity on any one who is uninitiated,
but it bestows power on the spirit of one who is intimately aware.
[Rumi, *Mathnawi* VI:1295–1310]

The prophets have spiritual notes within,
whence there comes life beyond price to those who seek Reality. . . .
If I tell just a bit of those saintly notes,
souls will lift up their heads from the tombs.
Put your ear close, for that melody isn't far,
but it's not permitted to convey it to you.
Pay attention! for the saints are the Israfils[82] of the time:
from them to the dead comes life and freshness.
At their voice the dead souls in the body's grave
jump up in their shrouds.
One awakened says, "This voice is distinguished
from all other voices:
to quicken the dead is the work of the voice of God.
We had died and were completely decayed:
the call of God came: we all arose."
[Rumi, *Mathnawi* I:1919; 1928–32]

*Call to your Sustainer humbly, and in the secrecy of your hearts.*
*Truly, He does not love those who go beyond the bounds of what is right.*
*And so, do not spread corruption on earth*
*after it has been so well ordered.*
*And call to Him with awe and longing:*
*truly, God's grace is very near those who do good.*
*And He/She it is who sends the winds*
*as joyous news of His/Her coming grace—*
*so that, when they have brought heavy clouds,*
*We may drive them towards dead land and cause rain to descend;*
*that by it We may cause all manner of fruitfulness to spring forth.*
*Even so shall We cause the dead to emerge—*
*perhaps you will remember.*
[Quran, *Surah al-A'raf* 7:55–57]

82 Israfil is the angel of the Resurrection, calling us to awaken.

When we are enabled through God's grace to be so enlivened, we may become a force for enlivening, for healing, even as was Beloved Mary. A small plant of the Sinai Desert and the Arabian peninsula, *anastatica hierochuntica*, has come to be known as *Kaff Maryam*, "Mary's Palm," for the blessing of the palm of her hand. It is said that while pregnant with Jesus she carried it with her, and when struggling in childbirth she clasped it in her hand. For many centuries now, women of Arabia, both Christian and Muslim, have sought its healing aid, drinking tea made from it to help ease labor pains.

Abandon the dry prayer of words,
for the tree presupposes the scattering of seeds.
Yet even if you have no seed, due to your prayer,
God will bestow upon you a palm tree
saying, "How well did he labor!"
Like Mary—she had heart-felt pain, but no seed:
an artful One made that withered palm tree green for her sake.
Because that noble Lady was loyal to God,
God fulfilled a hundred desires without desire on her part.
[Rumi, *Mathnawi* V: 1188–91]

Another tradition related about *Kaff Maryam* is that when Mary and Joseph were fleeing with Jesus away from Bethlehem and King Herod towards Egypt, they stopped along the way in the Judean desert of Jericho.[83] It is said that when Mary dismounted from her donkey to rest, this little plant that lay at her feet suddenly flowered in greeting. And so it came to also be known as the "Rose of Jericho."[84]

Wheresoever I shine forth from the lamp-niche of a breath, a Divine word,
there the difficulties of a whole world are resolved.
The darkness which the earthly sun did not remove,
through My breath that darkness becomes like bright morning.
[Rumi, *Mathnawi* I: 1941–42]

---

[83] The Judean Desert is where the Essenes and, later, many Christian monks and hermits would spend time meditating and in prayer, in the silence, under the stars.

[84] The name "Jericho" ("Yeriho" in Hebrew) is thought to be derived from the Canaanite word for "fragrant" (*reah*) or "moon" (*yareah*).

Kaff Maryam *(Resurrection Plant)*

Often found in the dry river-beds (*wadis*) of the desert, and scattered across the hills, it is blue-grey in foliage with tiny white flowers when it blooms. Once the plant has flowered, it curls up in a tight ball, protecting its precious seeds, and seems to die. It can remain somnolent like this for many years, but when moisture returns and the rains arrive, suddenly it begins to unfurl, and with a second rain the seeds come to life, and it blooms again, in full beauty. This is why it has, also, come to be known as the "Resurrection Plant."[85] On that journey from Bethlehem, the presence of Beloved Maryam, such a fountain of Blessing, awoke it from its apparent death into new life. Clusters of this little plant continue to be brought into homes as a blessing of hope, for good luck, and good health.

[85] The name "Anastatica" or "Anastasia" is derived from the Greek *anastasis,* meaning "resurrection." Another variant of the name that is often used is "Natashya."

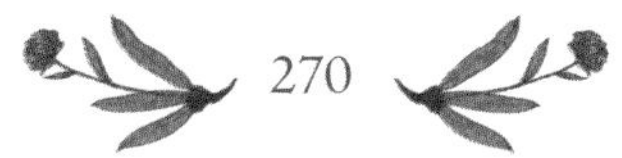

Truly nature is miraculous! Everywhere around us miracles abound every day; we only need open our eyes and hearts to see them.[86] The saints and prophets are constant witnesses to such grace. Hildegard of Bingen, a Christian mystic, healer, and abbess of the thirteenth century[87] CE speaks eloquently of the spark of Divine Radiance she witnessed as present in every aspect of creation:

> All living creatures are, so to speak, sparks from the radiation of God's brilliance, and these sparks emerge from God like rays of the sun. . . . How would God be known as life if not through the fact that the realm of the living, which glorifies and praises God also emerges from God? On this account God has established the living, burning sparks as a sign of the brilliance of the divine renown. [The fiery firmament is a footstool to the throne of God and all creatures are sparks from this fire. We sparks come from God.][88] But if God did not give off these sparks, how would the divine flame become visible? And how would God be known as the Eternal One if no brilliance emerged from God? For no creature exists that lacks a radiance—be it greenness or seed, buds or beauty. Otherwise it would not be a creature at all.[89]

---

[86] See Extended Context Notes in Appendix, Star X, 6.

[87] St. Hildegard of Bingen (1098–1179 CE), a Benedictine abbess, was gifted in many realms, of the Spirit, music, the healing arts, biology, philosophy, theology and cosmology. She refused to be defined by the established church hierarchy and continually pushed the boundaries of what was possible for a woman of her era. An inspiring, courageous leader and prodigious writer, she composed several medical texts, including *Physica* and *Causae et curae,* and a mystery play as well as theological works and music, and offered counsel through correspondence to many of the luminaries of her era, both ecclesiastical and royal. Her book, *Scivias* (shortened from *Scito vias Domini* —"Know the way of the Lord") and the later *Liber Divinorum Operum* (*Book of Divine Works*) recount some of her strong visionary experiences which she also illustrates. Her heavenly musical compositions continue to inspire generation after generation. She understood music as a communication with the Divine and surely, as we come to comprehend more about music therapy and relearn much of ancient traditions that have been lost, we will come to understand more fully the healing power of song. She saw God in both female and male aspects, both needed for wholeness, and the natural world as filled with the Grace of the Divine inflowing, enlivening everything.

[88] Bracketed portion is a commentary by Matthew Fox.

[89] Hildegard of Bingen, excerpt from *Illuminations of Hildegard of Bingen* by

*Truly, God is the One who splits the grain and the kernel apart,*
*bringing forth the living from the dead,*
*and He/She is the One who brings forth the dead out of that which is alive.*
*This then, is God: how then can you be so deluded?*
*He/She is the One who causes the dawn to break;*
*and He/She has made the night to be a source of stillness,*
*and the sun and the moon for reckoning*
*by the order of the Almighty, the All-Knowing.*
*And He/She it is who has made the stars for you*
*so that you might be guided by them*
*through the darknesses of land and sea:*
*clearly have We detailed Our signs for people of inner knowing.*
*And He/She it is who has brought you all into being out of a single soul,*
*and so designated for each of you a time-limit on earth*
*and a resting-place after death:*
*clearly have We detailed Our signs for people who can grasp the truth.*
[Quran, *Surah al-An'am* 6:95–98]

*For with God are the keys to the Unseen:*
*the treasures that none knows but He/She.*
*And He/She knows all that is on the land and in the sea;*
*and not a leaf falls but He/She knows it;*
*and neither is there a grain in the earth's deep darkness,*
*nor anything alive or dead, but is recorded in a clear record.*
*And He/She it is who causes you to be as dead at night,*
*and knows what you do during the day;*
*and each day He/She brings you back to life*
*so that a term set by Him/Her might be fulfilled.*
*In the end, to Him/Her you must return;*
*and He/She will make you understand all that you did.*
[Quran, *Surah al-An'am* 6:59–60]

Rumi encourages us not to focus on looking for the water, but to increase our thirst, that through that magnetism we might draw the water to us, for "we are Its, and It is ours."

---

Matthew Fox (Santa Fe, NM: Bear & Company, 1985), pp. 47–48.

If you really come to know this pure water,
the Word of God which is of the spirit,
all distress will vanish from your soul,
and your heart will find its way to the rose garden,
for everyone who catches a scent of the mystery of Revelation
discovers a spiritual orchard with a running brook.[90]
[Rumi, *Mathnawi* IV: 3470–72]

---

[90] Scientists who have been given to deep contemplation of the realities of nature have also expressed their realization of the miraculous—which perhaps one might note as the realm where science and faith intertwine. As Albert Einstein once said, "There are only two ways to live your life. One is as though nothing is a miracle. The other is as though everything is a miracle." And through this witnessing of the miraculous, every "thing" can become again sacred, vibrant with Spirit, numinous with Light.

## *Infinite Journeys*[1]

O Beloved One,
through so many journeys
You carry us—
over land and sea[2]—
infinite avenues
of Your Love.
Why do we not see?
That You are always with us!
Through the rapids
and sloughs,
storms and stillness
when there is no wind
and we feel adrift,
yet Your whisper begins
to enliven our hearts
from within the deepest,
darkest cave
held by this earth—
Your Love
is Ever-Present;
Your care
is always near,
so why do we fear
that we may stumble
in the darkness
of our unknowing,

---

[1] Excerpt from *On the Way Home*, "Songs of the Soul" series, Camille Hamilton Adams Helminski (forthcoming from Sweet Lady Press).

[2] See Quran, *Surah al-Isra'* 17:70: *We have honored the children of Adam; we have carried them on the land and on the sea.*

when You are the Knower,
*Ya Alim, Ya Quddus,*
*Ya Wadud!*[3]
And always
will You grant us
something
of what we may be asking,[4]
and protect us from its harm,
when we turn
to Your Light,
*Ya Nur, Ya Karim,*
*Ya Wahhab,*
*Ya Muhaymin,*
*Ya Shakur!*[5]
What You choose for us,
we choose;
may it all
illuminate our soul
and bring us again to You,
who have never left us,
but would have us know,
how much we are loved,
how much we are held
by Your Infinite Compassion,
by the Mercy of our *Rabb,*
*Ya Rahman,*
*Ya Rahim,*
*Ya Haqq,*
*Ya Mumin,*

---

[3] *Ya Alim* ("O You Who Are All-Knowing"), *Ya Quddus* ("O Most Holy and Pure"), *Ya Wadud* ("O Infinitely Loving One")!

[4] See Quran, *Surah Ibrahim* 14:34:

> *And always does He/She give you something out of what you may be asking of Him/Her; and should you try to count God's blessings, you could never compute them.*

[5] *Ya Nur* ("O You Who Are Light"), *Ya Karim* ("O Infinitely Generous One"), *Ya Wahhab* ("O Giver of All, Overcoming All Obstacles"), *Ya Muhaymin* ("O Preserver of Security"), *Ya Shakur* ("O Inspirer of Gratitude")!

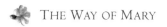

*Ya Wakil,*
*Ya Wadud!*[6]

[6] *Rabb*: "Lord and Cherisher, Nurturer, Educator of our Souls." (The word "rabbi" is similar, even as the Jewish rabbi is the spiritual instructor of souls.)

*Ya Rahman* ("O Infinitely Compassionate"), *Ya Rahim* ("O Infinitely Merciful"), *Ya Haqq* ("O Truth, Reality"), *Ya Mumin* ("O Most Faithful"), *Ya Wakil* ("O Guardian and Trustee of All Our Affairs"), *Ya Wadud* ("O Infinitely Loving One")!

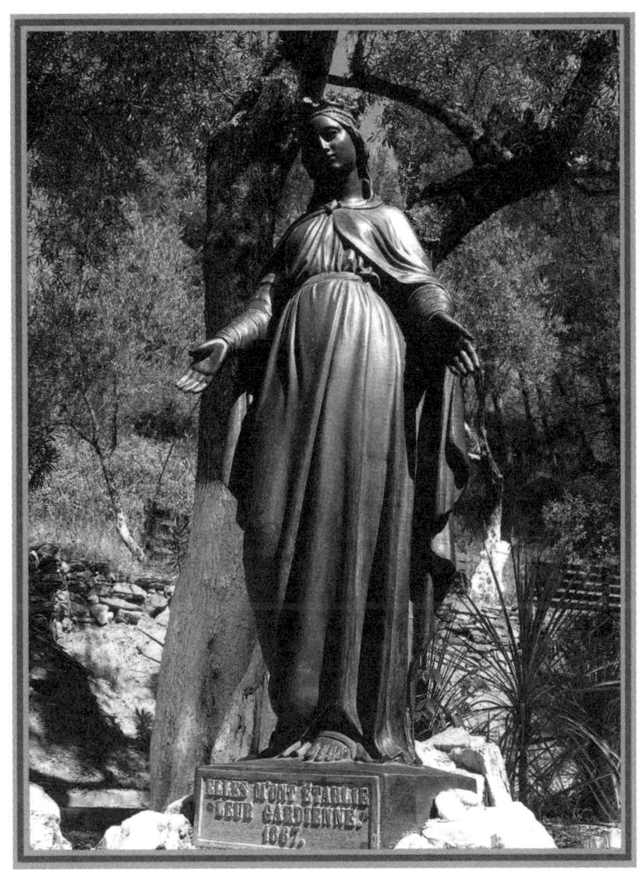


# XI. ELEVENTH STAR OF BLESSING

## *Teaching Journeys*

# *Teaching Journeys*

*"Who could give life to bones that have crumbled to dust?"*
*Say: "He who created them in the beginning*
*will give them life again,*
*for He is supremely skilled in every kind of creation!*
*He who produces for you fire out of the green tree;*
*witness, how you kindle your own fire from it!"*
*Is not He who created the heavens and the earth able to create their like?*
*Of course! For He is the Creator Supreme in skill and knowledge!*
*His Being alone is such that when He wills a thing to be,*
*He but says to it, "Be"—and it is.*
*Limitless, then, in His glory*
*is He in whose hand rests the mighty dominion over all things;*
*and to Him will you all return!*
[Quran, *Surah Ya Sin*, "O Thou Human Being," 36:78–83]

[John said,] I indeed baptize you with water unto repentance,
but he that comes after me is mightier than I,
whose shoes I am not worthy to bear:
he shall baptize you with the Holy Breath, and with fire.
[Bible, Gospel of Matthew 3:11]

The tree green with life regenerates through the fire of Love, even as John the Baptist had indicated in this verse from the Gospel of Matthew. Jesus (Isa), commanded by God to "Be," and with Holy Breath inspired within the beautiful being of Beloved Mary, was brought forth from her heart, her body, her soul, as an inspiration for this world, for all humankind; together with her, supported by her, he brought awareness of the Garden near, breath by breath, moment by moment.

This *Holy Family with Palm Tree* was painted by Raphael (named after the Archangel Raphael whose name means "God heals," the guardian

The Holy Family with Palm Tree *by Raphael*

angel of those who are ill and of travelers) in around 1506 CE, in round *tondo* form to be of inspiration in the personal space of a home. Perhaps Raphael[1] had come across the Islamic tradition of Beloved Mary giving birth while grasping a palm tree, whose nourishment rained upon her, this "Tree of Life" in Islamic culture. The "ever-green" palm tree, flowers, and springhead may have also been incorporated as elements from a Marian Litany of Hours. Here one feels her rootedness with the earth and, with the palm, spanning the realms of earth and heaven, all held in circling

[1] Raphael (Raffaello Sanzio da Urbino: Good Friday, 1483 – Good Friday, April 6, 1520) one of the three greatest masters of Renaissance art (with Leonardo da Vinci and Michelangelo), returned to his Creator at the young age of 37 in 1520, just as he was completing the masterpiece of *The Transfiguration*. See Extended Context Notes in Appendix, Star XI, 1.

wholeness. Together with the palm, Beloved Mary anchors the expanse of the painting, her feet caressed by flowering plants, while Joseph bends his knee in humble service yet strongly supportive with his staff, stalwart, and present with Love. The infant Jesus, bridging the space of masculine and feminine presence joins them both, bestowing flowers, with a spring of life-giving water emerging. The Garden is everywhere.

After the meeting with Mary Magdalene in the garden of the sepulchre, when Jesus had first appeared to the other disciples in the upper room of Cleophus' house (whose doors had been closed for safety, and yet Jesus suddenly appeared), his first words were: "Peace be with you." This "greeting of peace" continues to be extended among members of Christian church congregations before the offering and communion, as each congregant turns and exchanges the greeting of peace, heart to heart, clasping hands briefly with each person near him or her.[2] It is this same greeting of peace ("*As-salaam alaikum,*" "Peace be with you") with which Muslims honor and bless each other whenever first they meet, as well as when they depart from each other, and at the completion of every ritual prayer, voiced to their right and their left, sending greetings of peace to the angels near, the congregation, and to all of creation. We remember that among the "Ninety-Nine Names," or attributes, of God, is the treasured Name of *Salaam* ("Peace"). Already this "greeting of peace" had long been a practice among Jewish people: "*Shalom.*" In so many ways the faithful of the Abrahamic lineages are interwoven in practice and comprehension.

Jesus said to them again,
"Peace to you!
Just as the Father sent me, so I send you."

---

[2] The oldest document in the New Testament of the Bible is a letter (1 Thessalonians) of Paul which he begins by offering, "Grace and peace to you." It was written earlier even than the Gospels. The early Christians had taken over the practice of the "greeting of peace" (*eirene* in Greek, *pax* in Latin) from their Jewish ancestors. In 1 Corinthians, Paul again begins: "Grace to you and peace." In the pastoral Epistles, he adds "mercy," blending Greek and Jewish salutations. Again in Ephesians 1:2, written to the new followers in Ephesus, Paul, who had begun to minister not just to Jews but also to Greek-speaking gentiles, begins his missive with a blessing upon them, "Grace to you and peace from God." For Greeks the word "grace" carried a meaning of joy, light, and prosperity.

And so saying, he breathed upon them, saying,
"Receive the sacred breath."
[Bible (UG), Gospel of John 20:21–22]

And Christ appeared to Mary Magdalene frequently it is said, in the days between the Resurrection and his Ascension; it is clear that beside Beloved Mary she was the most attuned to his Presence. He evoked the Garden everywhere he moved, calling each soul to see it, to witness Truth—surely Mary of Magdala knew this deeply in her soul, and would also have been taught it by Beloved Mary during the days of their journeying together, just as Beloved Mary would have taught her son and also have been taught by him in return. Together they would surely have reflected by their being, male and female together, wholeness, a unity of Love.

*To the righteous soul will be said:*
*"O soul in complete rest and satisfaction!*
*Return to your Sustainer well-pleased and well-pleasing!*
*Enter then among My devoted ones!*
*Yes, enter My Garden!"*[3]
[Quran, *Surah al-Fajr* 89:27–30]

It is said that on the fortieth day (again forty days of completion), Jesus led the companions into the countryside; *spacious is God's earth* (Quran 39:10).[4] There he lifted his hands and blessed them, and from there he ascended.

While he blessed them, he was parted from them,
and carried up into heaven.

---

3 *Ya ayyatuha an-nafsul mutmainna*
*Irji'ai ila Rabbiki radiyatan mardiyya.*
*Fadkhuli fi 'aibadi.*
*Wadhkhuli jannati.*

4 *Say: "O you My servants who have come to faith!*
*Be conscious of your Sustainer:*
*good is for those who persevere in doing good in this world.*
*Spacious is God's earth!*
*Those who patiently persevere*
*will truly receive a reward beyond measure!"*
[Quran, *Surah az-Zumar* 39:10]

And they . . . returned to Jerusalem with great joy:
And were continually in the temple, praising and blessing God.
[Bible, Gospel of Luke 24: 51–53]

All these [the apostles] were persevering
with one mind in prayer with the women,
and Mary the mother of Jesus,
and with his brethren.
[Bible, Acts 1:14]

In John's Gospel he speaks of the women standing by the cross, and this time not at a distance but very close to the cross—Jesus' mother and his mother's sister, Mary, the wife of Cleophus,[5] and Mary Magdalene. He relates that they were quite close, close enough for Jesus to speak to them, because he records Jesus as saying to his mother, "Woman, behold your son," and then saying to the disciple understood to be the Apostle John, "Behold your mother," commending them to each other's care. "And from that hour the disciple took her into his home" (Gospel of John 19:25–27). This was a family of Spirit. In prayer, they immersed with the other disciples until the fiftieth (Pentecost) day, when it is said they were all filled deeply with the Holy Breath, were enabled to communicate in whatever language was needed for hearts to hear, and soon set off journeying to teach of the Ever-Living.[6]

So Beloved Mary soon set off journeying with John, now as her son, with the tenderness of mother and child, together as one, that they might support each other, and that in their journeying they might continue to convey the teachings of her son Jesus, and to heal, through the Light and Peace of God extended through their own remembrance and prayer.

The Jesus of your spirit is within you:
ask his aid, for he is a good helper.
[Rumi, *Mathnawi* II: 450]

---

[5] In the Greek and Latin texts the word "wife" is not included, only "of Cleophus," but "wife" is understood.

[6] This moment is known as the Pentecost, an experience of deep inflowing of Spirit, of inspiration, and so they set out, also, to nourish souls who were thirsting for enlivening Spirit. See Bible, Acts of the Apostles 2, and Maximus, *The Life of the Virgin*, op. cit., p. 121.

*As for those who strive hard on Our Way—*
*We shall most certainly guide them onto paths that lead to Us.*
*For behold, God is indeed with the doers of Good.*
[Quran, *Surah al-Ankabut* 29:69]

Beloved Mary would continue to care for the community, for the disciples of Jesus, for the women, for all as an illuminated mother.

*And lower the wings of your tenderness*
*toward the faithful who follow you.*
[Quran, *Surah ash-Shu'ara* 26: 215]

In both the *Protoevangelium*, and *The Life of the Virgin* by Maximus, Beloved Mary is spoken of with a more encompassing role than is related in the canonical Gospels of the Bible.

> His mother in particular is singled out as the one who directs the apostles in their ministries, offering them spiritual guidance as well as teaching them how and what they should preach. Mary's maternal bond with Jesus and her unique understanding of Christ's person and teaching endow her with an unparalleled authority according to this Marian vision of Christianity's origins.[7]

Surely among the teachings she conveyed would have been the beautiful beatitudes of the moment on the mountain:

And seeing the multitudes, [Jesus] went up into a mountain:
and when he was set, his disciples came to him:
And he opened his mouth, and taught them, saying,
"Blessed are the poor in spirit: for theirs is the kingdom of heaven.
Blessed are they that mourn: for they shall be comforted.
Blessed are the meek: for they shall inherit the earth.
Blessed are they which hunger and thirst after righteousness:
for they shall be filled.
Blessed are the merciful: for they shall obtain mercy.
Blessed are the pure in heart: for they shall see God.
Blessed are the peacemakers: for they shall be called the children of God.

---

[7] Introduction by Stephen J. Shoemaker in Maximus, *The Life of the Virgin*, op. cit., p. 23.

Blessed are they which are persecuted for righteousness' sake:
for theirs is the kingdom of heaven.
Blessed are you, when men shall revile you, and persecute you,
and shall say all manner of evil against you falsely, for my sake.
Rejoice, and be exceeding glad: for great is your reward in heaven:
for so persecuted they the prophets which were before you.
You are the salt of the earth: but if the salt have lost his savour,
wherewith shall it be salted? It is thenceforth good for nothing,
but to be cast out, and to be trodden under foot of men.
You are the light of the world. A city that is set on an hill cannot be hid.
Neither do men light a candle, and put it under a bushel,
but on a candlestick; and it gives light unto all that are in the house.
Let your light so shine before men, that they may see your good works,
and glorify your Father which is in heaven."
[Bible, Gospel of Matthew 5:1–16]

Surely these are some of the principles that Beloved Mary taught, by her very being, her light shining brightly. Aligned with the Source of Being, always with unswerving devotion, eternal kindness, never sanctimonious or superficial but from the depths of her soul, greeting each being with love, in every encounter, even with the rocks upon the earth, whose praise surely she could hear, and from which she knew springs can emerge.

In a well-known *hadith*, Prophet Muhammad spoke of how all of nature is in communication, even rocks: "I know a rock in Mecca that would greet me before I received my mission. I still know it now." In the Mevlevi tradition of Rumi, there is a practice known as *Gorushmek*, of pausing in greeting, even with each apparently "inanimate" thing, "seeing and being seen" by everything and everyone we encounter. When taking up a cup to drink, one would pause and "see with" the cup, kiss it, and then drink. And even before rising from prayer upon the rug before us, one would kiss it, and bow again, in recognition of its service. Continually seeing, being seen, by all that is, moment by moment, even as the rose smiles at the sun as its rays kiss her face. Surely this was a natural practice for Beloved Mary, whose heart was so attuned to every creature, every particle of being, of her Sustainer's Magnificence. Surely within every soul there is a longing to be recognized, to "be seen." This manner of seeing is a most foundational practice that can enliven all our days:

To see a World in a grain of sand,
And a Heaven in a wild flower,
Hold Infinity in the palm of your hand,
And Eternity in an hour.[8]

We can witness the Resurrection here, now, beholding everything alive with meaning. As recounted by John, Jesus had said: "I am the Resurrection and the Life" (Gospel of John 11:25).

When someone asked the saintly Imam Ali about the Resurrection, he replied, "You ask about the Resurrection *from* the Resurrection?" Whatever faith, all are called to resurrect in meaning by the prophets, to be in Truth, here, now.

*God gives succour to whomever He/She wills,*
*since He/She alone is Almighty, a Bestower of Grace.*
*This is God's promise. Never does God fail to fulfil His/Her promise—*
*but most people know [it] not: they know but the outer surface of this world's life,*
*while of the ultimate[9] things they are utterly unaware.*
*Have they never reflected within themselves?*
*God has not created the heavens and the earth and all that is between them*
*without an inner Truth and a determined term:*
*and yet, witness, there are many people who stubbornly turn away from the truth*
*that they are destined to meet their Sustainer!*
*Have they, then, never journeyed about the earth*
*and beheld what happened in the end to those who lived before their time?*
*Greater were they in power than they are; and they left a stronger impact on the earth,*
*and built it up even more than these [are doing];*
*and to them [too] came their Messengers with all evidence of the Truth:*
*and so, it was not God who wronged them,*
*but it was they who had wronged themselves.*
[Quran, *Surah ar-Rum* 30:5–9]

---

[8] William Blake (1757–1827 CE), excerpt from his poem, "Auguries of Innocence." See *William Blake: Collected Poems* (New York: Penguin, 1991).

As our botanical artist father, also, used to say, "There is poetry in the simplest weed." He painted so that others might see what he had seen and loved.

[9] "The term *al-akhirah* ['the End,' 'the ultimate'] circumscribes, in this context, both the inner reality of this world's life and the ultimate reality of the hereafter." See Muhammad Asad, *The Message of the Qur'an*, commentary to 30:7.

*Say: "The Truth is from your Lord."*
*As to those who have faith and do the deeds of wholeness and reconciliation,*
*truly, We shall not allow to perish*
*the recompense of anyone who does a good deed.*
[Quran, *Surah al-Kahf* 18: 29–30]

The *doing of deeds of wholeness and reconciliation* is a natural unfolding from Truth. Let us not miss the moment, the opportunity of bestowing blessing, and in so doing being blessed ourselves, as we align with the Aliveness of all Creation, participating in the flowing grace of the Infinitely Generous, the Infinitely Loving One. Continually we are invited to re-examine our intentions and to seek to be in clear connection with our Sustainer, moment by moment, in all our activities and our rest. Whether *standing, sitting, or lying down* (Quran, *Surah an-Nisa* 4:103), our remembrance and our intention may be held with the Ultimate Reality, seeing, being seen. It is said that Beloved Mary "gave neither sleep to her eyes, nor slumber to her eyelids, nor rest to her body, seeking always a place for the Lord."[10] Maximus relates that, "She was a support and comfort to the apostles and an inspiration in struggles and labors and every act of charity,"[11] a co-minister with them. Knowing well the power of intention, of devotion, she would continually set an example for those around her of one turned and attuned completely to her Sustainer, through every moment, every action, every breath of her life. Surely she kept her heart free from any ill-will, and taught, even as had her son, the value of kindness and reconciliation, of doing our best to see and quickly heal difficulties that may arise among us:

You have heard that it was said by them of old time, You shall not kill;
and whosoever shall kill shall be in danger of the judgment:
but I [Jesus] say unto you, That whosoever is angry with his brother
without a cause
shall be in danger of the judgment:
and whosoever shall say to his brother, "Raca,"
shall be in danger of the council:
but whosoever shall say, "You fool," shall be in danger of hell fire.
Therefore if you bring your gift to the altar,

---

10 See the Bible, Psalms 132:4–5.

11 Maximus, *The Life of the Virgin*, op. cit., p 123.

and there remember that your brother has ought against you;
Leave there your gift before the altar, and go your way;
first be reconciled to your brother, and then come and offer your gift.
[Bible, Gospel of Matthew 5:21–24]

A sober-minded man said to Jesus,
"What in this existence is the hardest to bear?"
"O dear soul," he replied, "the hardest is God's anger,
from which Hell is trembling as we are."
"And what is the protection against God's anger?"
Jesus answered, "To abandon your own anger at once."
[Rumi, *Mathnawi* IV: 113–15]

Would you have me tell you about actions
that are better than fasting, prayer, and charity?
Bring goodness and exalted principles between people.
[*Hadith* of Prophet Muhammad]

*Whoever purifies himself/herself*
*does so for the benefit of his or her own soul;*
*and all are journeying to God.*
[Quran, *Surah al-Fatir* 35:18]

In Islamic practice, it is said that ablution is the key to prayer, that one should strive always to be in a state of ablution, prepared for the meeting with one's Lord. There is a pattern of outer ablution that is an indication of a subtle, inner ablution. Before prayer one needs to clear one's heart and remember that this entails the cleansing of one's hands—that which one touches or crafts with one's capacities; one's mouth—the words one speaks; one's nose—that which one breathes; one's face—one's eyes and the sensitive receptors of perception; one's forearms—all one's endeavors; one's head—the energy points of the scalp; one's ears—that to which one listens; the back of one's neck and one's feet—the whole of one's supportive strength, mindful of where one walks, toward what one turns one's attention.

In the Hasidic (Jewish) tradition, it is taught to take special care to guard one's tongue, especially before the morning prayer, as a person who wakes up in the morning "is like a new creation." We must be careful, especially then, to avoid speaking unkind or trivial words, as our first moments of awaking would then be "untrue" to our creation. They say:

All of your words each day
are related to one another.
All of them are rooted
in the first words that you speak.[12]

One aims to open in attunement to the guidance of one's Sustainer.

*O humankind! there has come to you a direction from your Lord*
*and a healing for your hearts*
*and for those who have faith, guidance and grace.*
*Say: "In the abundance of God and in His grace,*
*in that let them rejoice;*
*that is better than whatever they may hoard."*
[Quran, *Surah Yunus*, "Jonah," 10:57–58]

It is taught both in Christianity and in Islam that it is not by our good deeds alone that one might gain the Garden, but through the Grace of God. Yet, we are encouraged to continually increase our striving so that the magnetism of our yearning might call forth the responsive clouds of Divine Bounty to pour forth enlivening rain. Muhammad said, "It is by your intentions that deeds are judged," and as Rumi has reflected, "Perseverance brings good fortune."

*O you who have attained to faith! Bow and prostrate yourselves,*
*and worship your Sustainer [alone], and do good,*
*so that you might attain to a happy state!*
*And strive hard in God's cause with all the striving that is due to Him/Her:*
*it is He/She who has chosen you [to carry His/Her message],*
*and has laid no hardship on you in religion,*
*[and made you follow] the creed of your forefather Abraham.*
*It is He/She who has named you—in bygone times as well as in this [divine writ]—*
*"those who have surrendered themselves to God,"*[13]

---

[12] *Your Word is Fire: the Hasidic Masters on Contemplative Prayer*, translated by Arthur Green and Barry W. Holtz, Schocken Books Inc., as cited by J. Ruth Gendler in *Changing Light, the Eternal Cycle of Night and Day* (New York: HarperCollins Publishers, 1991), p. 92.

[13] The term *muslim* signifies "one who surrenders himself to God" as was Abraham and the whole lineage of prophets; correspondingly, *islam* denotes "self-surrender to God."

*so that the Messenger might bear witness to the truth before you,*
*and that you might bear witness to it before all humankind.*
*And so, be constant in prayer, and render the purifying dues,*
*and hold fast to God.*
*He/She is your Supreme Sustainer: and how excellent is this Sustainer Supreme,*
*and how excellent this Giver of Succour!*
[Quran, *Surah al-Hajj* 22:77–78]

God manifested the earth and heavenly spheres
through the deliberation of six days—
even though He was able through "*Be, and it is,*"[14]
in a moment, to bring forth a hundred earths and heavens.
Little by little until forty years of age
that Sovereign raises the human being to completion,
even though in a single moment He could have
sent fifty flying up from non-existence.
Jesus by means of one prayer
could make the dead spring to life—
is the Creator of Jesus unable
to suddenly bring full-grown human beings
fold by fold into existence?
This deliberation is for the purpose of teaching you
that you must seek God slowly, without any break.
A little stream that moves continually
doesn't become tainted or foul.
From this deliberation are born felicity and joy:
this deliberation is the egg;
good fortune is the bird that comes forth.
[Rumi, *Mathnawi* III: 3500–08]

Through that "good fortune," the subtlety of our perception increases so that as many mystics have witnessed, everything is alive with Spirit. The beloved Christian mystic, Julian of Norwich (1342–1416 CE) noted:

> I saw that He is to us everything which is good and comforting for our help. He is our clothing, who wraps and enfolds us for love, embraces

---

[14] See Quran, *Surah Ya Sin*, "O Thou Human Being!" 36:82, on p. 278 of this text.

and shelters us, surrounds us for his love, which is so tender that he may never desert us. . . . Everything has being through the love of God.[15]

*And if you are patient in adversity and conscious of Him/Her—*
*truly, this is something upon which to set one's heart.*
[Quran, *Surah al-'Imran* 3:186]

How many victories are won
without spiritual struggle and patience?
To show patience for the sake of the cup of Divine Knowledge
is no hardship: show patience,
for patience is the key to joy.
[Rumi, *Mathnawi* III: 211–12]

Surely Beloved Mary went about her days patiently, with her intrinsic humility, yet quietly blessing all before her with her Presence, with just a glance, often in hidden ways, even as in this story Rumi relates in his discourses:

A saint went on a retreat to seek a sublime goal. A voice came to him, saying: "Such a sublime goal can't be attained by means of a retreat. Leave your retreat, so that a great man's gaze may fall upon you and cause you to reach your goal."

"Where am I to find this great man?" he asked.

"In the congregational mosque," he was told.

"How am I to recognize him among so many people?"

"Go!" said the voice. "He will recognize you and gaze upon you. And the sign of his gaze shall be this, that a ewer shall fall from your hand, and you shall fall unconscious, whence you shall know that he has gazed upon you." And so he filled a ewer with water and, going from row to row, gave drink to the assembly at the mosque. Suddenly he had a strange sensation and, uttering a loud shriek, dropped the ewer. While he was lying unconscious in a corner, the congregation departed. When he came to, he saw that he was alone. He never saw that "king" who had cast his glance upon him, but he did attain his goal.

[15] Julian of Norwich, *Showings*, edited by Edmund Colledge, O.S.A., and James Walsh, S.J. (New York, Paulist Press, 1978), 183.

> God has [persons] who never show themselves because of God's excessive jealousy of them, but they do bestow gifts and exalted goals upon those who seek them. Such great [sovereigns] are rare and precious indeed.

Shams indicates how such truly great ones may not even have a home. He relates how once Jesus was wandering in the desert when a heavy rainstorm began:

> [Jesus] took momentary shelter in a jackal's den in a cave until the rain should stop. While there he received an inspiration to this effect: leave the jackal's den for its young cannot rest with you here.
>
> "O Lord," he cried, "there is refuge for the jackal's young but none for the son of Mary!"[16]
>
> "Though the jackal's young has shelter," God replied, "it doesn't have a Beloved to drive it from its home. You do have such a motivator. If you have no home, what cause for concern is it? The grace and honor done specially to you by such a motivator to drive you on is a thousand, thousand times more valuable than the sky, the earth, this world, the next world, and the Divine Throne all together."[17]

Sometimes we do not even know when the glance of a saint may have fallen upon us and yet our hearts, our souls are uplifted. A *Hadith Qudsi* relates: "My saints are under my domes; no one knows them but I," because of the love God has for them.

> Who can see them? He is within the Glance of God.
> Those who want to see him must come into the Glance of God.
> Come into the Glance of God so that you may see him![18]

As Shams of Tabriz taught, the Way of Muhammad was continual immersion in contemplation, enveloped by the Divine Presence. He likewise encouraged the acceptance of God's invitation—to engage in the five daily prayers and the fast of Ramadan, gifted so that the whole community might experience immersion in contemplation toward which

---

[16] This is a further elucidation of verse 9:58 of the Gospel of Luke of the Bible.
[17] *Fihi ma Fihi,* Discourse 10, *Signs of the Unseen,* op. cit., pp. 42–44 (adapted by the author).
[18] Shams of Tabriz, *Rumi's Sun,* op. cit., p. 417.

they might not otherwise by personality be inclined. Through God's grace, the whole community is invited, to experience that Beauty. Even so, as they journeyed, surely Beloved Mary and John invited all they encountered to engage with them in prayer of the heart.

*Behold, We have inspired you just as We inspired Noah and all the prophets after him—*
*as We inspired Abraham, and Ishmael, and Isaac, and Jacob, and their descendants,*
*including Jesus, and Job, and Jonah, and Aaron, and Solomon;*
*and as We vouchsafed unto David a book of divine wisdom;*[19]
*and as [We inspired other] Messengers whom We have mentioned to you before this,*
*as well as Messengers whom We have not mentioned to you;*
*and as God spoke His word unto Moses:*
*[We sent all these] Messengers as heralds of glad tidings and as warners,*
*so that human beings might have no incongruity before God after these Messengers:*
*and God is indeed Almighty, Truly Wise.*
[Quran, *Surah an-Nisa* 4:163–65]

Beloved Mary and John would have known the text from Job of the Old Testament, and along their way surely she would have intrinsically known to practice his counsel:

Ask the animals, they will teach you.
Inquire of the birds, they will tell you.
Speak to the earth, she will inform you.
The fish of the sea, they will instruct you.
They all know that God is the Source.
In God's hand rests the life of all the living,
And the breath of all humankind.
[Bible, Job 12:7–10][20]

Continually they would have placed their trust in their Sustainer, the Source of all that breathes, all that is seen.

It is from placelessness that the world has received place.
Turn back from existence towards non-existence,

---

[19] I.e., the Psalms.
[20] Rabbi Rami Shapiro, *The Divine Feminine in Biblical Wisdom Literature, Selections Annotated and Explained* (Woodstock, VT: Skylight Paths, 2005), p. 101.

if you seek the Sustainer and belong to that One.
Non-existence is the place of income;
don't run away from it.
This existence of more and less
is the place where we spend.
[Rumi, *Mathnawi* II: 684–89]

*For all those who listen to God and the Messenger*
*are in the company of those upon whom is the Grace of God—*
*the prophets, the sincere [lovers of Truth],*
*those who with their lives bear witness [to the Truth],*
*and the righteous ones [who do the good]; what a beautiful friendship this is!*
*Such is the abundance of God!*
[Quran, *Surah an-Nisa* 4:69–70]

*O you who have attained to faith!*
*Seek help through steadfast patience and prayer:*
*for observe, God is with those who patiently persevere.*
[Quran, *Surah al-Baqarah* 2:153]

This journey of connection, of seeking knowledge, is spoken of also in a threefold process: *Ilm al-Yaqin*, *Ayn al-Yaqin*, *Haqq al-Yaqin*. The first stage, *Ilm al-Yaqin*, "Knowledge of Nearness," begins with hearing about it:

So then faith [comes] by hearing, and hearing by the word of God.
[Bible, Romans 10:17]

The second stage is seeing—*Ayn al-Yaqin* ("the Eye of Certainty"). *Yaqin* has both the meaning of "nearness" and "certainty," indicating the certainty that comes through nearness. We reach a comprehension, and we begin to experience it. For instance, we are drawn to know Damascus after hearing about it, so we go there, and seeing it firsthand we begin to understand it's meaning as an abode.

I love them that love me; and those that seek me early shall find me.
[Bible, Proverbs 8:17]

The third stage is *Haqq al-Yaqin* ("Truth of Certainty, of Nearness"). Immersing with singleness of heart within the reality of a place, an abode, the Presence of God, one merges with the Truth of It, becoming fully present, in Being. As Shams of Tabriz once said, "An *alif*[21] lept forth from the universe of meaning; whoever understands that *alif*, understands everything."

I have hidden Your word in my heart.
[Bible, Psalms 119:11]

"I am plunged in the Light, like the sun;
I cannot distinguish myself from the Light.
My going to prayer and to solitude
is for the purpose of teaching the people the Way."
[Rumi, *Mathnawi* III (words of Prophet King David): 2408–09]

A good man out of the good treasure of his heart
brings forth that which is good . . .
For out of the abundance of the heart the mouth speaks.
[Bible, Gospel of Luke 6: 45]

Perhaps as Beloved Mary and John were journeying, they might sit beside a fire in the evenings in a carvanserai, in the home of a sympathetic villager who might have given them refuge, or in the desert under the stars, and quietly offer songs in praise of God. We do not have many indications as to the details of their practice, but in the Acts of the Apostles (written around that time by St. Luke), Paul and Silas are described as offering songs of praise even when in prison, through the darkness of the night:

About midnight Paul and Silas were praying and singing hymns to God,
and the other prisoners were listening to them.
[Bible, Acts of the Apostles, 16:25]

Not long after, as Luke relates, an earthquake occurred, and the prison doors flew open, highlighting the power of song of the spirit.

A manner of responsive chant singing was adapted by early Christians from the roots of Hebrew worship. Practiced especially in Syria, it was introduced further into the West by St. Ambrose in the fourth century CE. The refrain, illuminating the meaning of the core psalm text was called

[21] See p. 248, n. 44 of this text.

an "antiphon." In Catholic liturgical music, this practice of antiphonal singing developed further— the melodic chanting of a portion of text before and after a verse from the Psalms, often by alternating choirs. Canticles from the Old or New Testament are sometimes sung in this way.

A dear Sufi mentor in Istanbul, Turkey, a master musician and deeply present soul, Cahit Goskan Hoja, would say, "God is always together with us. Wisdom is being able to sense His Presence." He would often encourage: "Music softens everything and makes hearts one. . . . It is through our struggles that God matures people—through disease, poverty and enemies. . . . Prayer is the same attitude in every language. Every particle chants the praises of God."

To the Prophet, this world is plunged in glorification of God,
while to us it is heedless.
To his eye this world is filled with abundant love;
to the eyes of others it is inert and lifeless.
To his eye, valley and hill are in fluid motion:
he hears subtle discourses from sod and bricks.
To the vulgar, this whole world is a dead thing in chains:
I have never seen a veil of blindness more amazing than this.
[Rumi, *Mathnawi* IV: 3532–35]

All of nature is calling to us, the birds, the trees, awaiting our response. Qawwali (from the Arabic *qawl*, "speak"), a manner of devotional singing rooted in India and Pakistan, is based upon an exuberant rhythmic rendering of Sufi Muslim poetry[22] aimed at guiding the listener into spiritual union with God, even as we are encouraged in the Quran: *Call upon Me, I will answer.*[23] In recent decades Qawwali music has become well-known and

---

[22] Amir Khusraw (1253–1325 CE), is credited with being the originator of the Qawwali style of devotional singing. His poetry often forms the basis of the songs, and the closing song of a session then honors his Sufi teacher, Nizam al-Din Awliya (1238–1325), one of the most renowned Sufis of the Chishti Order that opened through the example and being of Shaykh Abu Is'haq (d. 940 or 966 CE) who taught in the village of Chisht near Herat, Afghanistan.

[23] See Quran, *Surah al-Baqarah* 2:186:

*And if My servants ask you about Me—witness, I am near;*
*I respond to the call of the one who calls,*
*whenever he or she calls Me.*

beloved in the West through its charismatic call and response heart-felt rhythms. When the renowned Qawwali singer of recent eras, Nusrat Fateh Ali Khan, passed into the Unseen in 1997, even the Wall Street Journal joined the voices honoring him for all the beauty he had introduced to the West. "The message of Sufi mysticism, like the songs Mr. Khan wove from it, traveled well. It was the message of love for God and all his creations."[24] The poetry of Rumi, traditionally sung in the original Persian, which has an intrinsic musical rhythm, also lends itself well to this practice of sharing songs of responsive love. For centuries, people of Afghanistan have shared conversation and song by exchanging verses from his poetry. A beloved passage of his that might be sung in this call and response manner is offered as a prayer from his heart in his *Mathnawi*:

O my God, our intoxicated eyes have blurred our vision.
Our burdens have been made heavy, forgive us.

You are hidden, and yet from East to West
You have filled the world with Your radiance.[25]
Your Light is more magnificent than sunrise or sunset.

And You are the inmost ground of consciousness,
revealing the secrets we hold.
You are an explosive force causing our damned up rivers to burst forth.

You whose essence is hidden while Your gifts are manifest,
You are like water and we are like millstones.

You are like wind and we are like dust;
the wind is hidden while the dust is plainly seen.
You are the invisible spring, and we are Your lush garden.

You are the Spirit of life and we are like hand and foot.
Spirit causes the hand to close and open.

You are intelligence; we are Your voice.
Your intelligence causes this tongue to speak.

---

[24] "Clean Living," *Wall Street Journal*, August 19, 1997.
[25] See Quran, *Surah ar-Rahman* 55:17.

You are joy and we are laughter,
for we are the result of the blessing of Your joy.

All our movement is really a continual profession of faith
bearing witness to Your eternal power,
just as the powerful turning of the millstone
professes faith in the river's existence.

Dust settles upon my head and upon my metaphors,
for You are beyond anything we can ever think or say.

And yet, this servant cannot stop trying to express Your beauty;
in every moment, let my soul be Your carpet.
[Rumi, *Mathnawi* V: 3307–19][26]

*Are you not aware that it is God whose limitless glory*
*all that are in the heavens and on earth extol,*
*even the birds as they spread their wings?*
*Each knows indeed how to pray to Him/Her and to glorify Him/Her;*
*and God has full knowledge of all that they do:*
*for God's is the dominion over the heavens and the earth,*
*and with God is all journeys' end.*
[Quran, *Surah an-Nur* 24:41–42]

Along the way, the more we deeply listen, the more we can hear the intimations of our Beloved guiding us, the songs of praise of everything created, and the need of hearts around us, that we might respond with the best within us, gifted by God.

Walk in Wisdom toward the rest of the world,
making the best use of the time.
Let your speech always be gracious, seasoned with salt,
so that for each person you may know what answer to give.
[Bible, Colossians 4:5–6][27]

---

[26] "You are Joy and We Are Laughter," *The Rumi Daybook*, op. cit., p. 1. See Extended Context Notes in Appendix, Star XI, 2 for Persian transliteration.
[27] It seems Paul is referring here to Jesus's words on the mountain:

You are the salt of the earth,
but if salt has lost its taste,

Now purge your ear of forgetfulness
and listen to the forlorn yearning of the sorrowful one.
Know that when you set your ear to his or her tale,
that is the alms which you give to the sad.
You will hear the sorrows of the heart-sick—
the starvation of the noble spirit by the water and clay of the earthly body.
Even though it may be one filled with knowledge,
it is a house filled with smoke:
open a window for it by listening.
When your ear becomes a way of breathing for it,
the bitter smoke will lessen and clear from its house.
[Rumi, *Mathnawi* III: 482–86]

Apply your heart to instruction and your ear to words of knowledge.
[Bible, Proverbs 23:12]

When wisdom enters into your heart,
and knowledge is pleasant to your soul,
discretion shall preserve you, understanding shall keep you.
[Bible, Proverbs 2:10–11]

---

how shall its saltiness be restored?
[Bible (ESV), Gospel of Matthew 5:13]

It is love that gives our speech flavor, even as salt seasons food, bringing out the best of each quality. The blessing of that Loving Presence can pour through our hearts and permeate all we do and say, as Paul encourages here in Colossians. When we remember how essential salt is, we comprehend perhaps better, also, how needed is that Love. We human beings learned about salt from the animals, who instinctively locate salt licks; we followed their tracks, extending them to become our first roads and then built settlements nearby. An instinctive knowing helped human beings to recognize that salt is essential to our survival as well as to that of animals. See Extended Context Notes in Appendix, Star XI, 3.

"In both Islam and Judaism, salt seals a bargain because it is immutable. . . . Loyalty and friendship are sealed with salt because its essence does not change." See Mark Kurlansky, *Salt, a World History*, Penguin Books, Penguin Putnam Inc. NY. NY, 2002, p. 6 and 7, as quoted in *The Book of Nature, A Sourcebook of Spiritual Perspectives on Nature and the Environment,* edited by Camille Helminski (Bristol and Watsonville: The Book Foundation, 2006) p. 173.

[Wisdom's] Ways are ways of pleasantness,
and all Her Paths are peace.
She is a Tree of Life to those who lay hold of Her;
those who hold her close are happy.
[Bible, Proverbs 3:17–18][28]

Whoever knows the truth is free . . .
Truth is the Mother, knowledge is the Father. . . .
"Love builds up."[29]
Whoever is free through knowledge
is a slave because of love for those
who do not yet have freedom of knowledge.
Knowledge enables them to be free.
Love [never says] it owns something, [though] it owns everything.
Love does not say, "This is mine,"
but rather, "[All that is mine] is yours."
[Gospel of Philip 77, 15–35][30]

Surely abiding within the Truth she knew so completely, Beloved Mary then journeyed on with John, to share the teachings further, opening from her heart moments of felicitous healing, carrying that Love of which Jesus spoke so eloquently:

O righteous Father, the world has not known You:
but I have known You, and these have known that You have sent me.
And I have declared unto them Your name, and will declare it:
that the love wherewith You have loved me may be in them,
and I in them.
[Bible, John 17:25–26]

Wisdom shines without dimming.
All who love Her, see Her,
All who desire Her, embrace Her.

---

[28] *The Divine Feminine in Biblical Wisdom Literature, Selections Annotated and Explained*, op. cit. p. xxi.
[29] Bible, I Corinthians 8:1.
[30] Gospel of Philip, *The Nag Hammadi Scriptures*, op. cit., pp. 180–81.

She rushes to reveal Herself, to those
who yearn for Her;
No matter how early you arise to meet Her,
She is already waiting for you at the gate.
[Bible, Wisdom of Solomon 6:12–14][31]

That Eternal Loving Truth was also at the heart of the Message shared by Prophet Muhammad. Recognizing that our knowledge, our knowing can always be expanded, from within the depths of the heart where we are taught intimately by the Beloved, he was known to pray with the words of the Quran, *O my Sustainer! Increase my knowing* (Quran, *Surah Taha* 20: 114). As long as we are alive, our knowledge from the heart, our love, can grow. Prophet Muhammad also personally encouraged, as recorded in a well-recognized *hadith*, "Seek knowledge even unto China." At the time of Muhammad, extensive trade routes linked China with the Middle East along the ancient "silk routes" that had for centuries facilitated exchange between the lands of the Roman Empire and the Far East. As someone who had been much involved in the caravan trade, Muhammad would likely have become aware of the streams of knowledge flowing from there, and the lights of people of wisdom from the Far East, and perhaps may have absorbed some of the wisdom of Confucius (551–479 BCE) and Lao Tzu (circa sixth to fourth century BCE), shared perhaps around the evening fire in a caravanserai.

In living be close to the land,
in meditation look deep into the heart,
in working with others be gentle and kind.
[Tao te Ching of Lao Tzu]

Nestorian Christianity had also reached China along these same trade routes as did Buddhism from India. The teachings of the Way of Islam were carried to China during the first generation after Muhammad, during the Tang dynasty (618–907 CE). We sometimes presume that ours is the first era of global exchange, through extensive air travel and the modern internet, but since quite ancient times, people seeking knowledge

[31] As translated by Rabbi Rami Shapiro in *The Divine Feminine in Biblical Wisdom Literature*, op. cit., p. 65.

Chinese Madonna Scroll *by Tang Yin*

and better trading possibilities and more auspicious lands of habitation have wandered this earth and shared with each other of the knowledge that was beneficial to them. A network of spirit has long been functioning.[32]

Recently, a striking Chinese scroll painting of Beloved Mary by the renowned Chinese artist, Tang Yin,[33] of the sixteenth century was rediscovered among the archives of the Field Museum of Natural History. The scroll references the well-known Byzantine icon *Salus Populi Romani*, said to be the icon painted by St. Luke—copies of which may have been earlier brought to China by traders or missionaries. The painting also carries the resonance of renderings of the East Asian bodhisattva Guanyin;[34] often the two were blended together, especially at times of persecution, whether of Buddhism or of Christianity, veiling within the representation of one of these beloved feminine aspects, the other, merging traditions, hoping, trusting in that Love to shield them.

It has been understood by people of Spirit throughout this world, throughout the centuries, that the real object of knowledge is the

---

[32] It seems it was predominantly through Sufi traders that the Muslim faith, also, was introduced into China beginning in the eighth century CE. As much of the tradition was conveyed orally, for centuries, it was not until much later that the first Sufi written text was translated into Chinese: *The Path of God's Servant from the Origin to the Return* by Najm al-Din Razi (d. 1256 CE), a Kubrawi Sufi master. See also Sachiko Murata, *Chinese Gleams of Sufi Light* (Albany: State University of New York, 2000). With the arrival of Islam there, another beautiful cross-fertilization took place resulting in numerous Chinese Sufis with a Confucian-Muslim perspective. There are now numerous Chinese Muslims, many of whom practice a Sufi mystic approach to Islam.

[33] See scroll illustration on previous page. Tang Yin (1470–1524 CE): renowned Chinese artist and poet who on occasion combined poems within his paintings, as he did with a fan (Tang Yin, "Bamboo in a Spring Thunderstorm," Edward Elliott Family Collection, Douglas Dillon Gift, 1988, Metropolitan Museum of Art), incorporating a poem with a lovely cluster of bamboo—a plant so flexible, it bows with the storms. Its branches trail to the earth like the long tails of the mythical phoenix, and then luminous tranquility returns:

The roar of spring thunder arouses the green bamboo,
Dragon whiskers sweep across the ground, along with long phoenix tails.
Looking up from the boat awning I play the flute,
A bright moon, filling the sky, shines in the Xiao and Xiang Rivers.

[34] See illustrations on pp. 384–85 and p. 386, n. 60 cont.

knowledge of the Divine Reality, of Truth (*Haqq*), in whatever way it may be rendered in speech, or represented in art, or deeply known by heart. Continually hearts are being opened, souls arriving and departing, opportunities for knowing Spirit being revealed. That Creative One is every day about some new endeavor.[35] As Shams of Tabriz tells us:

> Since the day God created this universe, like an arrow shot from a bow, every day, every moment, He/She has been opening and closing doors. This takes place at such a limitless speed that one's mind stops.[36]

In another *hadith*, the Prophet Muhammad indicated that there had been 124,000 prophets, many unknown, awakened within the human community, each arising through God's grace, as need arose for Truth and clarity to be restored within a community.[37] This possibility is affirmed in the Quran in *Surah al-Maida*, the Feast pouring from heaven towards Jesus and his companions . . . *continually I am sending it down!* We might understand this as the nourishment of Wisdom, the springs of which have opened in many hearts, in every land—that all peoples might strive in understanding and arrive in nearness, within the Divine Reality:

---

[35] See *Surah ar-Rahman* 55:26–30:

*All that lives on earth or in the heavens is bound to pass away:*
*but forever will abide thy Sustainer's Self, full of majesty and glory.*
*Which, then, of your Sustainer's blessings will you deny?*
*On Him depend all creatures in the heavens and on earth;*
*[and] every day He/She manifests Himself/Herself in yet another [wondrous] way.*
*Which, then, of your Sustainer's blessings will you deny?*

[36] *Rumi's Sun*, op. cit., p. 177.

[37] This would allow for recognition of such beings as the Buddha and Lao Tzu in the East, and White Buffalo Calf Woman in the West, who brought the teaching of the Peace Pipe to the Lakota Sioux Native Americans and restored respect for the feminine among them. For as the Divine conveys again through the Quran:

*To every community We have appointed ways of worship,*
*which they ought to observe.*
*And so, do not let others draw you into arguing about it,*
*but invite them to your Sustainer . . .*
*Indeed, God will judge between you on the Day of Resurrection*
*concerning everything about which you would differ.*
[Quran, *Surah al-Hajj*, "The Pilgrimage," 22:67–69]

*For every one of you have We designated a law and a way of life.*
*And if God had so willed,*
*He/She could surely have made you all one single community:*
*but He/She willed it otherwise in order to test you*
*by means of what that One has bestowed on you.*
*Strive, then, with one another in doing the good!*
*Your goal is God;*
*and then, He/She will make you understand*
*the truth of everything in which you have differed.*
[Quran, *Surah al-Maida* 5:48]

> Whomever you see who has a beautiful temperament and a beautiful face, if his/her words are straight forward, if he/she is open-hearted, and if he/she prays for good things for everyone, a joy of heart comes from the speech of such a person. He/she makes you forget the anxieties and tightness of this universe; your inside opens in such a way that even if he/she swears at you, you laugh. Maybe, when he/she speaks of unity, like Sirajuddin, you weep, but you feel a hundred thousand joys and laughter within yourself. Such a person is a being of Paradise.[38]

Shams also reminds us that we are all in God's hands and assisted by His/Her beloveds as we make this journey into newly awakened life:

In the end, the spirits of the great attained ones are ready.
They recognize the living ones and help them.[39]

Mevlana encourages further:

Serve God, so by chance you may become a lover:
devoted service is a means toward Love.
The servant desires to be freed from fate,
but God's lover wishes never to be set free again.
Some servants seek benefits and robes of honor;
the lover's robe of honor is vision of the Beloved.
Not contained by speech or hearing,

---

[38] Shams of Tabriz, *Rumi's Sun*, op. cit., p. 177.
[39] Ibid., p. 223.

Love is an ocean whose depth cannot be seen.
The drops of this Sea are innumerable:
in comparison all seven seas disappear.
[Rumi, *Mathnawi* V: 2728–32]

As the lyrics of a beloved Sufi song remind us,

The Secret is an ocean hidden in a lover's tear.
Love is not an end to pain; it's said, "Thou shalt not fear."

Our bravery will be tested, and yet,

Remembrance is a quality that can't be called your own.
A dervish is a doorway; a seeker needs no throne.

A way exists in every heart to Mecca and Jerusalem.
You who've wandered far away, come find your home again.[40]

Repentance (*tawba*), a turning of heart, is very much a principle of the Path; it is the pivot of repentance for a wayward heart that allows an opening for the full blossoming of the soul. *Taqwa* ("vigilant and loving God-consciousness") then needs cultivation, so that one may arrive more fully, present. Through many faith traditions this is realized through fasting, rituals of purification, prayer, meditation (*muraqaba*), charity, pilgrimage in companionship with the holy, and yet it is through Love that one at last is welcomed Home. When there is repentance in the soul (*nafs al-lawamma*),[41] a true turning (*tawba*) in receptivity, and heartfelt *taqwa*, miracles can occur.[42] The Gospel of Luke (and only Luke) relates

---

[40] *Ilahi* (sacred song) based upon a poem of the beloved Sufi mystic Haji Bektash. English lyrics by Kabir Helminski, The Threshold Society.

[41] See seven stages of the soul, Extended Context Notes in Appendix, Star IX, 2.

[42] See Quran, *Surah an-Nasr* 110:1–3:

*In the Name of God, the Infinitely Compassionate and Infinitely Merciful:*
*When the help of God comes and the opening,*
*and you see people enter God's Way in throngs,*
*celebrate the praises of your Sustainer and pray for His/Her forgiveness:*
*for He/She is Ever Turning One Towards Repentance.*

*Bismillahir Rahmanir Rahim:*
*'Izha jaa'a nasrullahi wal fath.*
*Wa ra'aytan nasa yadkhuluna fi dinillahi 'afwajaa.*

the story of the "prodigal son," the iconic parable of the repentant sinner welcomed home with so much grace.[43] The word "sin" in the original Greek simply means one who has missed the mark, a term from archery. May our aim, our intention, our skill, through God's grace be rectified, and our love increased.

Likewise, I say unto you, there is joy in the presence of the angels of God
over one sinner who repents [who reorients again in Truth].
[Bible, Gospel of Luke 15:10]

The father said to his servants,
"Bring forth the best robe, and put it on him;
and put a ring on his hand, and shoes on his feet . . .
let us eat, and be merry:
For this my son was dead, and is alive again;
he was lost, and is found."
[Bible, Gospel of Luke 15:22–24]

Then generosity is alive with Love, and an abundant harvest is celebrated with soulful gratitude:

Farming in this world depends on four things,
and a harvest is gathered and taken into the barn
as a result of water, earth, air, and light.
God's farming also depends on four things:
faith, hope, love, and knowledge.
Faith is the earth in which we take root.
Hope is the water with which we are nourished.
Love is the air [spirit] through which we grow.
Knowledge is the light by which we ripen.
[Gospel of Philip][44]

The fruits of the spirit . . .
are love, joy, peace, patience, kindliness, goodness,

---

*Fa sabbih bihamdi Rabbika wastaghfirh.*
*'Innahu kana tawwabaa.*

[43] See the Bible, Gospel of Luke 15:10–36.

[44] Gospel of Philip, *The Nag Hammadi Scriptures*, op. cit., p. 182. See, also, the Bible, 1 Corinthians 13.

faith, gentleness, and self-control.
There is no law against things like that. . . .
If we live by spirit we also walk by spirit.
[Bible (UNT), Galatians 5:22–23]

*Celebrate the praises of God often,*
*that you may prosper.*[45]
[Quran, *Surah al-Jumu'ah* 62:10]

*"Ask forgiveness of your Sustainer*
*and turn to Him/Her:*
*for truly, my Sustainer is Infinitely Merciful and Infinitely Loving."*
[Quran, *Surah Hud* (words of Prophet Shu'ayb) 11:90]

It is also Luke who relates the story of a widow who is recognized by Jesus for her generosity of heart in the midst of her poverty, honoring her, praising her in contrast to the display of influential, wealthy men:

And looking on, [Jesus] saw the rich men cast their gifts into the treasury.
And he saw also a certain poor widow casting in two brass mites.
And he said: Truly I say to you,
that this poor widow has cast in more than they all:
for all these have of their abundance cast into the offerings of God:
but she of her want, has cast in all the living that she had.
[Bible, Gospel of Luke 21:1–4]

*With Him are the secrets of the heavens and the earth:*
*how clearly He sees; how finely He hears!*
*They have no protector other than Him.*
[Quran, *Surah al-Kahf* 18:26–27]

*And speak what has been revealed to you of the Book of your Lord:*
*nothing can change His Words*
*and you will find no refuge other than Him/Her.*
*And keep your soul content with those*
*who call on their Sustainer morning and evening seeking His/Her Face;*
*and do not let your eyes pass beyond them*

---

45 *Wazhkuruu Allaha katheeran la'allakum tuflihuun.*

*seeking the fame and glitter of this life;*
*nor obey any whose heart*
*We have permitted to neglect the remembrance of Us—*
*one who follows his or her own desires and has gone beyond all bounds.*
*Say: "The Truth is from your Lord."*
*As to those who have faith and work righteousness,*
*truly, We shall not allow to perish*
*the recompense of anyone who does a good deed.*
[Quran, *Surah al-Kahf* 18:28–30]

There are two kinds of intelligence—
one like that acquired by a child at school,
from books and teachers, new ideas and memorization.
Such intelligence may become superior to others,
but retaining all that knowledge is a heavy burden—
you who are so busy searching for knowledge
must be a preserving tablet.
But the preserved tablet[46] is the one
who has gone beyond all this,
for the other kind of intelligence is the gift of God:
its fountain is deep within the soul. . . .
Seek the fountain within yourself.
[Rumi, *Mathnawi* IV: 1960–68]

In the effort to discover this fountain within and to plumb its depths, many have gone into the desert, digging deep within the cave of the heart. There is a beautiful story of the Seven Sleepers of the Cave, beloved in Christianity (they are considered saints in both Catholic and Eastern Orthodox traditions), that is also told within the Quran, in *Surah al-Kahf*, named "The Cave" for their story within it (18:10–26). At a time of the persecution of Christians under Emperor Decius (third century CE), these *seven* young men retreated into a cave, while their steadfast dog guarded the cave at the threshold entry.

---

[46] *Lawhin mahfuz:* See Quran, *Surah al-Buruj* 85:20–22:

*All the while God encompasses them without their even being aware of it.*
*No, but this is a sublime discourse, inscribed upon an imperishable tablet [of the heart].*

*Take refuge in that cave: God will spread His grace over you,*
*and will endow you— whatever your condition—*
*with all that your souls may need!*
[Quran, *Surah al-Kahf* 18:16]

As it is said in the Quran, God turned them left and right, as they immersed in spirit, asleep to the world.[47] And so they remained for some years until when they finally emerged, "resurrected," awakened by God, it became apparent that several hundred years had passed, for when they went to the local market to purchase food, their coins were recognized as from a long bygone era. By the time they emerged, Christianity had become accepted and established as the official religion. Faithfully the dog had kept guard. Many understand the "dog" to be symbolic of the ego (sometimes referred to as "the carnal self"), here steadfast in submission at the threshold of the cave of the heart. Mevlana Rumi encourages us to not be less than a dog, to always abide close to the "doorway" of Truth:

Pace round that same door: do not be less than a dog,
if you have become a fellow-servant with the dog of the Cave.
Because even dogs admonish dogs,
saying, "Fix your heart on your first home . . .
for fidelity is the badge by which dogs are renowned."
[Rumi, *Mathnawi* III: 314–21]

*When those youths took refuge in the cave, they prayed,*
*"O our Sustainer! Bestow on us Your grace*
*and endow us, whatever our condition,*
*with consciousness of what is right!"*[48]
[Quran, *Surah al-Kahf* 18:10]

*If I am on the right path,*
*it is because of inspiration to me from my Sustainer—*

---

[47] Some relate the story as taking place near Tarsus; many others say that this occurred near Ephesus, where a church is dedicated to them, built over the cave where it is said they had slept, present with God.

[48] *"Rabbanaa atina min ladunka rahmatan*
*wa hayyi' lana min amrina rashadaa."*

*it is He/She Who Hears all things; He/She Who is always near.*"
[Quran, *Surah Saba'*, "Sheba," 34: 50]

There are many caves throughout Asia Minor, where "Desert Mothers" and "Desert Fathers," devoted early Christians, immersed in prayer and surrendered to God.

*Ancient Christian Caves of Maaloula near Damascus, Syria*[49]

To discern the Way, many centuries earlier (ninth century BCE) the Hebrew prophet Elijah had sought refuge within the cave of Mt. Horeb near Moses' holy mountain. Feeling his own unworthiness, he had withdrawn from the waywardness of his people into the wilderness. It was here that angels began to minister to him, while, as with Beloved Mary on the journey to Egypt, a juniper sheltered him.

He himself went a day's journey into the wilderness,
and came and sat down under a juniper tree:

---

[49] Maaloula is one of the few places in the world where the inhabitants continue to speak Aramaic, the every-day language Jesus would most often have spoken, along with Hebrew and Greek.

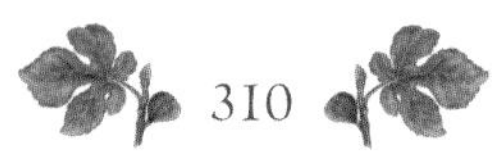

and he requested for himself that he might die;
and said, "It is enough; now O Lord, take away my life;
for I am not better than my fathers."
And as he lay and slept under a juniper tree, behold
then an angel touched him,
and said unto him, "Arise and eat."
and he looked, and behold, there was a cake baken on the coals,
and a cruse of water at his head.
And he did eat and drink,
and laid him down again.

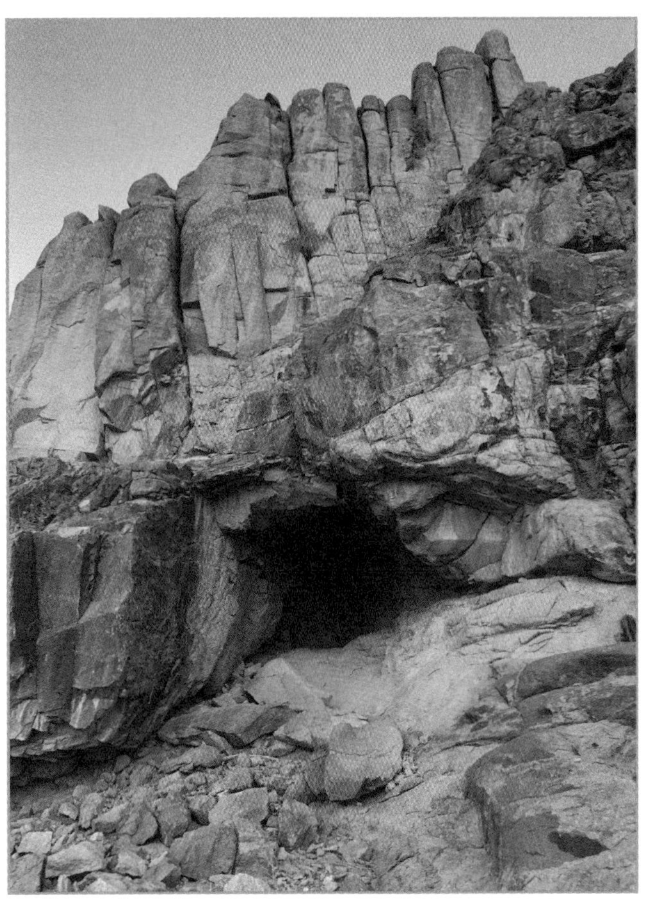

*Cave of the Hebrew Prophet Elijah on Mt. Horeb*

And the angel of the Lord came again the second time,
and touched him and said,
"Arise and eat; because the journey is too great for you."
And he arose, and did eat and drink, and went in the strength of that meat
forty days and forty nights unto Horeb, the mount of God.
[Bible, 1 Kings 19:4–8]

This is the "Mountain of God" where Moses also received the Ten Commandments. The name "Horeb" implies burning (reminiscent of the brilliance of the bush alive with God's Presence), bright with the sun; "Sinai" implies the moon, the receptive eastern face of the mountain; both names are spoken interchangeably in the Bible.

There he came to a cave and lodged in it.
And behold, the word of the Lord came to him,
and [He] said to him, "What are you doing here, Elijah?"
[Bible (ESV), I Kings 19:9]

Elijah speaks of his discouragement with his people, their forgetfulness of God, of giving up, and he is told to go forth and stand before God, upon the mountain. While Elijah is in retreat there, a violent wind arises, tearing at the mountain; the earth shakes and fire blazes, but Elijah sees, even as had Abraham, that this is not yet the full Divine Reality; he waits, steadfast. Then, alone with God, in Presence, intimate in inmost being, he hears "a still, small voice," (literally in Hebrew "the sound of silence").[50]

Rather than the fiery power of earlier moments of Divine interface with the Hebrew prophets, God was revealing Himself/Herself to Elijah within the silence, a gentle rustling of the air. From within the silence God spoke to Elijah; the silence itself was God's voice, in the pre-eternal language of God, Heart to heart.[51]

---

[50] See Bible, 1 Kings 19:12.

[51] It is only after this silent communion that he understands what he must do; he receives his instructions; he understands to whom he must convey his mantle:

And the Lord said unto him,
Go, return on your way to the wilderness of Damascus:
and when you come, anoint Hazael to be king over Syria:
and Jehu the son of Nimshi shall you anoint to be king over Israel:

It is when we are aware of this Silence enveloping, permeating the present moment of being, that true conversation is possible. As the Sufi mystic, Abul Hasan Kharaqani (963–1033 CE) taught, "Only speak if you know God is listening, only listen if you know God is speaking."[52] Cultivating an inner silence is an essential preparation for prayer, for relationship with the Divine and with each other, that we might truly hear. It was even so for Prophet Muhammad in the cave of Hira the night the Quran opened.[53]

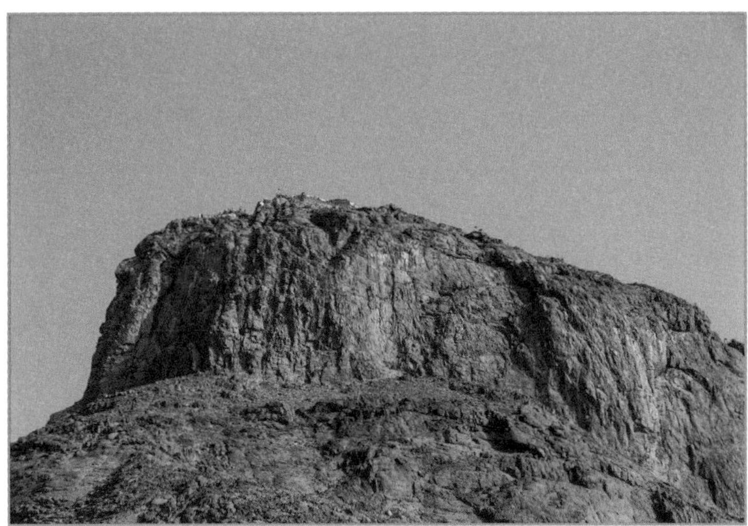

*Jabal an-Nur (Mountain of Light)*
*where Muhammad Retreated in the Cave of Hira*

---

and Elisha, the son of Shaphat of Abelmeholah
shall you anoint to be prophet in thy room. . . .
So he departed thence, and found Elisha the son of Shaphat,
who was plowing with twelve yoke of oxen before him, and he with the twelfth:
and Elijah passed by him, and cast his mantle upon him.
[Bible, 1 Kings 19: 15–19]

[52] Written above his doorway in Iran was, "Whoever enters my abode, feed them without asking about their faith—if they were favored by God Most High who saw them as worthy of the gift of life, then they are certainly worthy of being fed at the house of Abul Hasan."
[53] See p. 47 of this text.

As Rumi reminds us, through silence the beauty of the voice is restored. In that lived inner prayer, we have the possibility of reorientation, of renewed connectedness with Spirit. We enter the Mystery and return with new eyes:

> No wonder the soul doesn't remember its ancient home,
> its original dwelling and place of birth,
> since the sleep of this world covers it as clouds hide the stars.
> It has walked through so many cities,
> and the dust hasn't yet been wiped from its perception.
> It hasn't yet worked to purify its heart and behold the past,
> that its heart might peek from the aperture of mystery
> and see its beginning with open eyes.
> [Rumi, *Mathnawi* IV: 3632–36]

We do not have documentation of the actual practice of Jesus and Beloved Mary, nor of their disciples as they began the journey out into the world to spread their teachings, to serve, and to heal. One might consider that this practice of silent listening and paying attention to the breath could have been a foundational part of their moments of continual practice. And as they began to journey further into the world, they might have followed guidance similar to that of the Masters of Wisdom of Central Asia (the Khwajagan),[54] who were most careful in their speech, in their steps, in their remembrance. One focus of their practice was to accompany each step with awareness of God's Presence, every breath, as they journeyed through this life on the Way of Return. The following code of awareness and behavior as formulated by Abd al-Khaliq Ghujduvani in the twelfth century CE continues to be a strong basis of remembrance for many:

---

[54] The Khwajagan, the "Masters of Wisdom" of Central Asia, were a long lineage of Sufi masters. See *The Masters of Wisdom of Central Asia* (Rochester, VT: Inner Traditions, 2014) by Hasan Lutfi Shushud, a beloved friend of the Way, may God bless his soul. One of the most renowned of the early masters is Abd al-Khaliq Ghujduvani (d. 1179 CE), who formulated the principles of their practice that are included here. One catches within this teaching the resonance of aspects of the mindfulness practice within Buddhism. Surely there have been many cross-fertilizations happening amongst people of Spirit, throughout the centuries.

## *Laws of the Khwajagan*

*Remember every breath.* As we breathe we should place our attention on each successive breath and be aware of our own presence. Inattention is what separates us from God. The more that one is able to be conscious of one's breath, the stronger is one's inner life.

*Watch each step.* Remember where you came from and where you are going. You wish for freedom and you must never forget it. Keep your attention on the step you are taking at this moment.

*Journey toward your homeland.* You are traveling from the world of appearances to the world of Reality. Man cannot know his destiny as long as he is in the subjective dream state.

*Solitude in the crowd.* Enter into the life of the outer world without losing one's inner freedom. Remember God and do not allow yourself to be identified with anything.

*Remember your Friend.* You may discover the Friend, i.e., God, through the *being* of your guide. Let the prayer of your tongue be the prayer of your heart.

*Return to God.* No aim but to attain Reality. We must be single-minded about our goal. The possibility of transformation is a gift to be valued above all other possessions.

*Remain watchful.* Struggle with alien thoughts. Keep your attention on what you are doing, whether outwardly or inwardly. Observe what captures your attention and why.

*Be constantly aware* of *the Divine Presence.* Accustom yourself to recognize the quality of the Divine Presence within your heart. The "loss of self" allows us to participate in a greater Being.

Every step can be a prayer upon sacred earth.[55] If I am aware of God's Presence in all that exists, with every breath, how can I act in separation? How can I judge harshly? I can discriminate, as to what action or state of being may unveil God's Presence more fully, but I can do nothing to

---

[55] This is also a practice well-known among the Native American peoples. As Black Elk (1863–1950 CE), the beloved, wise elder of the Oglala Lakota used to say, "As you walk upon the sacred earth, treat each step as a prayer." See Extended Context Notes in Appendix, Star XI, 4.

alienate myself from anything that is of His creation, for ultimately, we are all of the same Being, even every stone or stony-hearted one, and will inevitably return to the same Source. To help us remember this, Mevlana tells us to consider everyone to be in their death throes. In his *Mathnawi* he says:

Everyone in the world, whether man or woman,
is dying and continually passing through the agony of death.
Regard their words as the final injunctions
which a father or mother gives his or her son or daughter.
In this way consideration and compassion may grow in your heart,
and the root of hatred and jealousy may be cut away.
Look upon your kinsperson with that intention,
that your heart may burn with pity for his or her death agony.
Everything that is coming will come:
consider it to have already arrived;
consider your friend
to already be in the throes of death, losing his or her life.
If selfish motives prevent you from this insight,
cast them from your heart;
and if you cannot cast them out, don't stand inertly in incapacity:
know that with every one who feels incapable,
there is a goodly Incapacitator.
Incapacity is a chain laid upon you:
you must open your eye to behold the One who lays the chain.
[Rumi, *Mathnawi* VI: 761–68]

In order that the chain of incapacity might be released, that any anger might be dispelled, and that the Garden might be restored, Jesus also encouraged, "Love one another!"

A new commandment I give to you, That you love one another;
as I have loved you, that you also love one another.
By this shall all men know that you are my disciples,
if you have love one to another.
[Bible, Gospel of John 13:34–35]

And again in the Gospel of John, he repeats this commandment:

Herein is my Father glorified, that you bear much fruit;
so shall you be my disciples.
As the Father has loved me, so have I loved you:
continue you in my love.
If you keep my commandments, you shall abide in my love;
even as I have kept my Father's commandments, and abide in His love.
These things have I spoken unto you, that my joy might remain in you,
and that your joy might be full.
This is my commandment, That you love one another, as I have loved you.
[Bible, Gospel of John 15:8–12][56]

Little by little we come to realize that it is Love that is behind everything, calling us:

The fig tree putteth forth her green figs,
and the vines with the tender grape give a good smell.
Arise, my love, my fair one, and come away.
O my dove, that art in the clefts of the rock,
in the secret places of the stairs,
let me see thy countenance, let me hear thy voice;

---

[56] It is in this context that the passage speaking of the Comforter who will come after Jesus opens. This is the passage Muslims look to as indicating the coming of Prophet Muhammad, peace and blessings upon them both.

See the Bible, Gospel of John 15:15; 15:26–27(also 16:7–8); and 14:26–27:

Henceforth I call you not servants;
for the servant knows not what his lord does: but I have called you friends;
for all things that I have heard of my Father I have made known unto you. . . .
But when the Comforter is come, whom I will send unto you from the Father,
even the Spirit of truth, which proceeds from the Father, he shall testify of me:
And you also shall bear witness,
because you have been with me from the beginning.
[Bible, Gospel of John 15:15; 26–27]

But the Comforter . . . he shall teach you all things,
and bring all things to your remembrance,
whatsoever I have said unto you.
Peace I leave with you, my peace I give unto you:
not as the world gives, give I unto you.
Let not your heart be troubled, neither let it be afraid.
[Bible, Gosepl of John 14: 26–27]

for sweet is thy voice, and thy countenance is comely.
[Bible, Song of Solomon 2:13–14]

And so as we traverse this Way, this Path of Return, we might pray, just as the seven sleepers of *Surah al-Kahf* ("The Cave"),

*Do not say, "I will do so and so tomorrow" without adding, "If God pleases."*
*And call your Sustainer to mind when you forget and say,*
*"I hope that my Lord will guide me ever closer even than this to the right path."*[57]
[Quran, *Surah al-Kahf* 18:23–24]

Continually in the journey, we ask to be able to see more clearly, to travel in rectitude, to be brought into the vision of Unity. As the taste of Union grows stronger, we are enabled to slough off the blinding scales from our eyes, to shed the rough skins that separate us; we simply outgrow them in this process of becoming that which we most essentially are. As the Venerable Anne C. Emmerich expressed it,

> I cannot make it clear, but it is certain that we are all members of one body. It is as if a healthy member, in consequence of a secret, intimate bond between, suffers for another that is not sound.[58]

If you and I are truly One and gain our sustenance from the same Source, how can we not act together to enhance that which sustains us all? The Prophet Muhammad, peace and blessings be upon him, likewise said, "The parable of the faithful in their affection, mercy, and compassion for each other is that of one body. When any limb is in pain, the whole body aches with sleeplessness and fever."[59] If a member is in pain, the whole body feels it and cannot rest until the pain is alleviated. That pain can

---

57 *Wala taqoolanna lishay'in 'inni faailunthalika ghada.*
*Illa an yashaa Allah.*
*Wazhkur rabbaka izha naseeta wa qul*
*'asaan yahdiyani Rabbi*
*li 'aqraba min hatha rashadaa.*

58 *The Life of Jesus Christ and Biblical Revelations: From the Visions of Venerable Anne Catherine Emmerich*, Vol. 1–4, translated by Sir Michael Palairet (Charlotte, NC: TAN Books), Vol. 2, p. 210.

59 *Hadith* reported by al-Nu'man ibn Bashir. See *Sahih al-Bukhari* 5665, *Sahih Muslim* 2586.

ultimately only be healed by Love and all Its enlivening. As the beloved Christian mystic Catherine of Siena (1347–1380) also relates of her intimations from God: "Love of [Me] and love of neighbor are one and the same thing; since love of neighbor has its source in Me, the more the soul loves Me, the more she loves her neighbor."[60] As Muhammad also said, "Truly, the faithful are like a structure, each part strengthening the other."[61] We come to comprehend that the revelation of Love is the aim of all Creation:

These creatures of the world exist
to manifest the Divine Treasure.
God said, "I was a Hidden Treasure."
Listen, don't let your substance be wasted,
become manifest!
[Rumi, *Mathnawi* IV: 3028–29]

Incomparable God has made all the six directions a theatre
for the display of His signs to the clear-seeing,
in order that, whatever animal or plant they look upon,
they may feed on the meadows of Divine Beauty.
And so He said to the company of mystics,
"*Wherever you turn, His/Her Face is there.*[62]
If in thirst you drink some water from a cup,
you are beholding God within the water."
O person of insight, one who is not a lover of God
only sees his or her own self in the water;
but since a lover's image has disappeared within the Beloved,
whom now should he or she behold in the water?
Tell me that!
[Rumi, *Mathnawi* VI: 3640–45]

The ancient text of Ecclesiasticus echoes this in its description of the glorious effulgence of the Most High, in all Its manifestations:

---

60 *The Prayers of Catherine of Siena*, edited by Suzanne Noffke, O.P. Paulist Press, 1983, as cited by Carol Lee Flinders in *The Little Book of Women Mystics* (New York: HarperCollins Publishers,1995), p. 59.

61 *Hadith* reported by Abu Musa. See *Sahih al-Bukhari* 467, *Sahih Muslim* 2585.

62 See Quran, *Surah al-Baqarah* 2:115.

The glory of the heights, the clear firmament,
the beauty of heaven, with its magnificent display,
the sun when it appears declaring at its rising a marvelous skill—
the work of the Most High!
At midday it parches the land, and who can abide its burning?
A man blowing a furnace endeavors in heat,
but the sun burns the mountains three times more;
exhaling fiery vapors and sending forth bright beams, it dims the eyes.
Great is the Lord that made it, and at His command it runs quickly.
The moon He made also to serve in her season,
to set forth time's passage, as a sign for the world.
From the moon comes the sign of feasting,
a light decreasing in her perfection;
the month is named for her, increasing wonderfully in her transformation;
an instrument of the hosts of heaven, shining in the firmament—
the beauty of heaven, the glory of the stars,
an ornament gifting light in the highest places of the Lord!
At the command of the Holy One they stand in order
and do not tire in their watchfulness.
Look upon the rainbow, and praise the One who made it;
so beautiful it is in its shining brightness.
It encompasses the heavens with a glorious circle,
bent by the hands of the Most High.
By His command He makes the snow to fall here and there,
and sends swiftly the lightning of His judgment.
Through this treasures are opened, and the clouds fly forth like birds.
By His great power He makes the clouds firm
and the hailstones broken small.
At His sight the mountains shake,
and at His will the south wind blows.
The noise of the thunder makes the earth tremble;
so does the storm from the north and the whirling wind.
He scatters the snow like birds flying,
and the falling down of it is like grasshoppers alighting.
The eye marvels at the beauty of the whiteness thereof,
and the heart is astonished at how it pours down.

[Ecclesiasticus (Sirach) 43:1–18]

The eye marvels at the beauty of the whiteness, this whitest snow of purity, pouring perfection, *Al-Quddus* ("The Infinitely Holy and Pure"), rendering the heart astonished with Its generosity, renewing the earth with *Salaam*, "peace, on earth, goodwill towards men," Love pouring in so many ways towards all human beings, towards all creation.[63]

If there had not been Love, how would there have been existence?
How would bread have attached itself to you and become assimilated?
The bread became you through your love and appetite;
for how else should bread have had any access to your living spirit?
Love makes lifeless bread into spirit:
it can make the spirit that was perishable everlasting.
[Rumi, *Mathnawi* V: 2012–14]

Surely it was their love that propelled John and Beloved Mary in their journey north, to share what they experienced of Truth, of the word of God that had flowed through Jesus, despite the persecutions by those who would not understand, to share Love. As Bernard of Clairvaux wrote in his commentary on the Song of Songs of the Bible,

> If anyone desires to grasp these writings, let him love! For anyone who does not love, it is vain to listen to this song of Love—or to read it, for a cold heart cannot catch fire from its eloquence. The one who does not know Greek cannot understand Greek, nor can one ignorant of Latin understand one speaking Latin. So, too, the language of Love will be a meaningless jangle, like the sounding brass or tinkling cymbal, to anyone who does not love.[64]

Here Bernard is also referencing I Corinthians 13:

---

[63] A late spring snow is known as "the poor farmer's fertilizer," for rather than nipping most things in the bud, it brings nitrogen to the soil and increases fertility. The swing in temperature of the soil also increases microbial activity which assists the soil in retention of moisture. Even so, the pure moisture of divine inspiration renders more fertile the garden within our hearts.

[64] Bernard of Clairvaux, deeply inspired by the Song of Songs, wrote a magnificent commentary, delivered in 86 individual sermons. See *The Song of Songs, Commentary on the Book of Canticles or the Song of Songs* by Roland E. Murphy (Minneapolis, MI, Augsburg: Fortress Press, 1990), title page, as cited by Cynthia Bourgeault in *The Meaning of Mary Magdalene*, op.cit, p. 201.

If I speak in the tongues of men or of angels, but do not have love,
I am only a resounding gong or a clanging cymbal.
If I have the gift of prophecy
and can fathom all mysteries and all knowledge,
and if I have a faith that can move mountains,
but do not have love, I am nothing.
If I give all I possess to the poor and give over my body to hardship
that I may boast, but do not have love, I gain nothing.
Love is patient, love is kind.
It does not envy, it does not boast, it is not proud.
It does not dishonor others, it is not self-seeking,
it is not easily angered, it keeps no record of wrongs.
Love does not delight in evil but rejoices with the truth.
It always protects, always trusts, always hopes, always perseveres. . . .
these three remain, faith, hope, and love. But the greatest of these is love.
[Bible, I Corinthians 13:1–7; 13]

As Shams of Tabriz encourages,

> The faith of the faithful must be so strong in certainty that they are able to pass over the mountain, so that they may see the seven-headed lion and grab it by its ears, and so that they might not suffer, because of the strength of their faith and love of the light of day. Faith and love turn human beings into heroes; they remove all fear.[65]
>
> A special sign of the mystic is that he never tires of talking about his Friend and can never have enough of that friendship.[66] . . . The distinguishing signs of a mystic are three: a heart occupied by the thought of God, a body that serves God, and an eye that attempts to see God.
>
> If a mystic gives his or her heart, he or she will receive love like those described in the Qur'an: *People whom He loves and who love Him* [5:54]. I

---

[65] Shams of Tabriz, *Rumi's Sun*, op. cit., p. 129.

[66] We are so grateful to so many dear ones of heart in this world, especially in Turkey, who have shared so deeply of Spirit, may God bless them all abundantly; for our friend, Dr. Refik Algan (who introduced us to Hoca Cahit Goskan and many others), who shared so much from his heart that has elucidated our way, and with whom we were able to bring forth the words of Hazrati Shams of Tabriz in *Rumi's Sun*, for all of which we are eternally grateful.

have seen nothing more beautiful than humility. . . . Keep your religion through generous kindness and good character. One cannot escape death—the human being's destiny is always with him or her.[67]

After the Ascension of Jesus, the oldest traditions of Irenaeus and Eusebius of Caesarea relate that St. John journeyed to Ephesus; it is understood by many that he brought Beloved Mary, his adopted mother, there with him. Paul had earlier journeyed there to teach, so there was already a small community of those following the teachings of Jesus to receive them. It was here that the Apostle John also is thought to have been laid to rest in his elder years; his tomb is said to be located in the former Basilica of Saint John in Seljuk, just above Ephesus.[68] The existence of this major church of St. John and the early Church of Mary built nearby, one of the first dedicated to her, lend a foundation to the traditions of Beloved Mary having lived in the hills of Ephesus and the continued blessing of her loving presence there.

The Church of Mary in Ephesus is one of the "Seven Churches of Revelation," also known as the "Seven Churches of the Apocalypse" and the "Seven Churches of Asia"—seven major churches of early Christianity, as mentioned in the Book of Revelations of the New Testament of the Bible—all of which are located in what is now Turkey, the land of so many of the stories of early Christianity. This church dedicated to Beloved Mary, which dates to the early fifth century CE, was built within the southern portico of the remains of an early Roman temple sanctuary, a basilica-like building that had been abandoned around the third century CE, known as the "Hall of the Muses."[69] It is said that

---

[67] Shams of Tabriz, *Rumi and His Friends*, op. cit., section 526 II, 526 IIIb: pp. 279, 280.

[68] In the continuing persecutions by the Romans, John was later exiled to the island of Patmos, where some say he wrote the Book of Revelations, but he returned to Ephesus in his old age and died there, sometime after 98 CE, during the reign of Trajan. It is thought that John was the youngest of the apostles and had outlived the others. The Basilica of St. John was built over his tomb by Byzantine Emperor Justinian in the sixth century.

[69] Ephesus had long been famous for the nearby Temple of Artemis completed around 550 BCE, which became known as one of the "Seven Wonders of the Ancient World." Artemis (Diana) had long been revered there; the awareness of the feminine was vibrantly strong. Around the time of Christ, as capital of

the Council of Ephesus of 431 CE was held within it; *The Acts of the Council of Ephesus*, a record of the convocation, states that the sessions transpired in "the church named for Mary." In around 500 CE, the church of Beloved Mary was expanded into a magnificent cathedral; it was rebuilt several times. The apse and some of the pillars remain. In the central baptistry, there was a large pool where supplicants could be completely immersed, blessed with water, with Light, with Love, as their hearts turned to God.

*One Day you will see the faithful men and the faithful women,*
*how their Light runs forward before them and to their right:*
*"Good news for you today:*
*gardens beneath which running waters flow, where you may live—*
*this, this is the highest achievement!"*
[Quran, *Surah al-Hadid* 57:12]

*O humankind! A manifestation of the Truth has now come to you*
*from your Sustainer, and We have sent to you a clear light.*
*And as for those who have attained to faith in God and hold fast to Him/Her—*
*He/She will cause them to enter into His/Her Compassion*
*and His/Her abundant blessing,*
*and guide them to Himself/Herself by a straight way.*
[Quran, *Surah an-Nisa* 4:174–5]

It is said that Beloved Mary journeyed a while with John, beloved disciple to whom she had been entrusted in mutual care. Enroute to Ephesus they may well have passed through Damascus, where five hundred years later Emperor Justinian so strongly experienced her presence.

When visiting a dear friend in Damascus some years ago, we were encouraged to visit Saydnaya ("Our Lady"), a town nearby, where a beautiful Orthodox Christian convent, originally built by Justinian,

---

proconsular Asia, Ephesus was second in importance only to Rome.

The city was later destroyed by the Goths, in 263 CE, but much was rebuilt by Emperor Constantine. In the fifth and sixth centuries, Ephesus was the second most important Byzantine city, after Constantinople. Eventually, largely due to deforestation and overgrazing, the harbor filled in with sediment and the coastline shifted almost two miles away from the formerly coastal sites. Some say that the Gospel of John was written while he was in Ephesus, around 90 CE.

continually welcomes multitudes of Christians and Muslims who come to honor the Virgin Mary and to receive healing there, offering gratitude in abundant prayer. On the northern outskirts of Damascus, Syria, this community, like nearby Maaloula, is one of the few in the world where Aramaic is still spoken, amid the Arabic.

It was around 547 CE that the Monastery of "Our Lady" was established by Justinian I. He was leading his army through the region and had encamped in the Syrian desert but soon ran out of water; they were growing quite distressed with thirst. Suddenly, the emperor caught sight of a deer and chased after it. When the deer seemed nearly exhausted it halted atop a rocky mound, revealing nearby a spring of clear, fresh water. The deer then transformed into an icon of Beloved Mary radiating Light, and Justinian heard her voice saying, "Build a church for me here on this hill."

Immediately, he ordered a church to be designed, but the royal engineers couldn't agree on how to construct it there. Finally, one night, the emperor had a dream in which he saw the deer and the Virgin once again, and she inspired in him a beautiful design which he then had built upon the hill—the Monastery of Our Lady still stands there. Though damaged during the recent war in Syria it is being rebuilt, one of the most ancient monasteries in the world.

Within its inner sanctum abide many early icons, including an early replica of the icon of *Our Blessed Lady* by St. Luke, known as *Shagoura* in Syriac, *Shahira* in Arabic, ("The Illustrious One"; *Shagoura* also has the meaning of "The Source") an icon that, it is said, was brought from Jerusalem to Saydnaya by a Greek at the time of Theodore, in the eighth century CE. Women of all faiths visit there to pray for the blessing of conception.[70] The

---

[70] Since the Middle Ages, pilgrims have come to The Convent of the Virgin Mary enroute to the Holy Land of Jerusalem to offer prayers and receive the blessing of Beloved Mary (Maryam). Saydnaya rises on the slopes of Mount Qalamoun about twenty-five kilometers north of Damascus; the surrounding town was renowned among travelers for its beauty. Beneath the convent wells continue to supply water for nourishment of the nuns and the gardens. Local tradition relates that "Saydnaya" also holds the meaning of "Halting-place of the gazelle." In current times, the *Shaghoura* icon is kept out of view, in a niche behind a curtain beside which are many relics and gifts in recognition of healings that have transpired. The chapel with low vaulted ceiling is veiled in semi-darkness, though always lit by numerous candles. One of the first written accounts of a visit in the chapel is by a pilgrim

icon of Beloved Mary is hidden behind a silver filigree grill in the Orthodox convent chapel, which is always lit with numerous candles and oil lamps suspended from the ceiling. Since medieval times, the icon has been known to ooze a healing oil, long treasured for its healing capacities by Muslims as well as Christians, and even in earlier eras, by Jews.

When our daughter was young, she continually had painful ear infections, nothing really seemed to help. My husband Kabir and I visited the blessed chapel of Our Lady with a friend from Damascus. We, too, as others, removed our shoes upon entering—even as it is also a practice in Islam before one enters a mosque. This practice of Moses before the Presence of God is remembered with a verse of Exodus gracing the doorway there: "Put off your shoes from your feet, for the place whereon you stand is holy ground."[71]

The nuns offered us a little packet with a piece of cotton soaked with the healing oil, their gift of remembrance to pilgrims. We offered a prayer and brought back some of this healing oil for our daughter. I told her about Saydnaya, this sanctuary of Beloved Mary— with whom she has always had a special connection—and gently swabbed her ears with the oil. The ear problem abated and did not return.

It was the Feast of Beloved Mary's Nativity, September 8, that Justinian dedicated the completed convent. Since then Christians, and soon thereafter, Muslim pilgrims as well, have continually arrived at the monastery to honor Our Lady of Saydnaya. For centuries now it has been

---

named Giraud in 1175 CE; he describes how on the day of the Nativity celebration of Beloved Mary, September 8th, and on the Feast of her Assumption, Muslims as well as Christians thronged the chapel in prayer. See https://www.antiochpatriarchate.org/en/page/our-lady-of-saydnaya-patriarchal-monastery/146/.

[71] Bible (Torah), Exodus 3:5. There are particular places on this earth that have gathered resonance from holy beings and from immense prayer that has occurred there. We honor these sacred spaces.

It is sometimes forgotten that in the teachings of Islam, the earth itself is considered sacred, and that we are guardians of its many blessings; one may offer one's ritual prayer upon a natural space of earth even as upon a prayer carpet. And if no water is at hand to make one's ritual ablution, one may use clean sand instead, with intention. We understand now how silica conducts, so we can understand even better the wisdom of this—how sand as well as water can adjust electromagnetism of the surface of the body, refreshing us so that we may more deeply enter prayer.

a place of healing through the heart of her grace and the healing power of God, a place where both Christians and Muslims visit to offer prayers throughout the year; for Eastern Orthodox Christians a pilgrimage there, considered the second most holy site of their faith, is honored in importance second only to a pilgrimage to Jerusalem. Countless offerings displayed on the walls attest to the many miracles of healing with which her faithful visitors, both men and women, have been blessed, when they have been called to be present here in prayer.

The call of God, whether it is veiled or unveiled,
bestows that which He bestowed on Mary
from His heart.
Death's decay is just underneath your skin;
turn back from nothingness,
listen to the voice of the Friend!
Absolutely, that voice is God's
even though it may come
from the throat of His servant.
God has said to the saint,
"I am your tongue and eye; I am your senses;
I am your good pleasure and your wrath.
Go, for you are one whom God describes as,
'By Me he (or she) hears and by Me he (or she) sees.'
You are the Divine consciousness itself.
How could it be right to say,
'You are the possessor of consciousness'?
Since you have become, through bewilderment,
'He that belongs to God,'
I am yours, for, as it is said,
'God shall belong to him.'"[72]
[Rumi, *Mathnawi* I: 1934–39]

Rumi refers here to a famous *Hadith Qudsi* (a saying of God conveyed through the Prophet Muhammad external to the Quran). God says, "When my faithful servant draws near to Me through his or her voluntary

---

[72] This is also a *Hadith Qudsi*: "He that belongs to God, God shall belong to him" (*Man kana lillahi kana 'llahu lahu*).

devotions, then I love him/her and I become the ear with which he or she hears, the eye with which he or she sees, the tongue with which he or she speaks, the hand with which he or she grasps, the foot with which he or she walks."

*God guides unto His/Her light he/she who wills to be guided;*
*and so God propounds parables unto people,*
*since God has full knowledge of all things.*
*In the houses of worship which God has allowed to be raised so that His Name may be remembered in them,*
*there are such as extol His limitless glory at morn and evening—*
*people whom neither business nor striving for profit*
*can distract from the remembrance of God,*
*and from constancy in prayer,*
*and from charity . . .*
*for God grants sustenance unto whom He/She wills, beyond all reckoning.*
[Quran, *Surah an-Nur* 24:35–38]

The prophet or saint drawn near sees with the Light of God, even as was Muhammad's experience in his *Miraj*,[73] into the Presence of God:

*His heart didn't contradict what he saw . . .*
*the eye did not waver, nor yet did it stray:*
*truly did he see some of the most profound of his Sustainer's symbols*
[Quran, *Surah an-Najm* 53:11; 17–18]

In such moments of deep immersion with Spirit, the light is known as brilliant.[74]

---

[73] It is said after he journeyed to Jerusalem on the female mythical creature Buraq, Prophet Muhammad rose through the heavens until he neared the Divine Throne where Angel Gabriel could no longer accompany him. He went alone into the Presence of God, two bow lengths or nearer (Quran, *Surah an-Najm*, "The Star." 53:9), closer than the brow . . . face to Face, with unwavering gaze.

It is understood that every prostration of prayer has the potential to be a *Miraj* into the Presence of God—continually, that Reality is inviting us to come near.

[74] In the Brilliance of the Light of God, the individual "face" disappears. *Everything is perishing except the Face of God* (Quran, *Surah al-Qasas* 28:88). Out of respect for that immersion in Spirit and the major tenet of Islam attesting to the Oneness of God (*La illaha il Allah*, "There is no god but God, no reality but the

*Miraj of the Prophet Muhammad*
*Illustration from the* Khamsa *of Nizami created (1539–43* CE*)*
*for the Persian Shah Tahmasp I, showing Chinese-influenced clouds and angels*

---

Reality") Islamic artists avoid rendering the face of the Prophet Muhammad. The Light shines forth.

*Madonna of Tenderness (*Eleusa*)*
*Painted within the "Flame" of the Bodhi Leaf of Light, India*[75]

Within Damascus itself, St. Mary's Cathedral, one of the oldest Greek Orthodox churches, is the seat of the Greek Orthodox Church of the Antioch region. The church was built in the second century CE, not long

---

[75] A Madonna of the *Eleusa* style (from the Greek for "tenderness, showing mercy"), similar in style to an icon at the entrance to our Lady of Saydnaya Convent, and one treasured in the Church of Mary in Damascus. There are several major styles of icons of Our Lady patterned on the original icon said to have been painted by St. Luke: "Our Lady of Wisdom Enthroned" (like the Madonna of Hagia Sophia), "She Who Shows the Way" (like "Our Lady of Czetochowa"), and "Our Lady of Tenderness" (*Eleusa*). The Bodhi leaf carries sacred meaning for those of the Buddhist path, as it is of the tree at the foot of which the Buddha attained enlightenment (see pp. 384–86 with n. 60), so this particular rendering, crafted in India, carries an enriched meaning.

after Beloved Mary may have passed that way while journeying with John. Sacred Tradition holds that the icon known as *Eleusa* within it, the "Virgin of Tenderness" and *Hodegetria*, "She who Shows the Way," are also patterned after icons that came originally from the hand of St. Luke, even as the *Shahgoura* icon of Saydnaya.

Luke, a physician and a painter from Antioch,[76] had been inspired by the teaching of Paul and soon became a follower of the teachings of Jesus. It was on the road to Damascus that Paul himself had experienced a sudden turning of heart, his "conversion" experience of enlivening Spirit, when he was overwhelmed by the light.[77] Antioch and Damascus were ancient centers of learning, and tradition indicates that Luke was quite well-educated, particularly in medicine. He is known by Christians as the author of the Gospel of Luke and of the Acts of the Apostles of the Bible. It is from beautiful verses of Luke's Gospel that hearts have been inspired

---

[76] The city of Antioch, within the boundaries of ancient Syria, is now within the country of Turkey. It was in Antioch that Paul and the followers of Jesus are first referred to as "Christians," by King Agrippa (see the Bible, Acts of the Apostles 26:28).

[77] A Jewish Roman citizen, a Pharisee, Paul had at first personally persecuted the followers of Jesus, whom he would have viewed as aberrant Jews and threatening to the State, until he, himself, (at about age 27) experienced a burning light and a deep change of heart on the road to Damascus. As he later said to King Agrippa, "Why should it be thought a thing incredible with you, that God should raise the dead?" (Bible, Acts of the Apostles 26:8). He related further to him:

I journeyed to Damascus with the authority and commission of the chief priests.
At midday, O king, I saw on the way a light from heaven,
brighter than the sun, that shone around me and those who journeyed with me.
And when we had all fallen to the ground,
I heard a voice saying to me in the Hebrew language,
"Saul, Saul, why are you persecuting me?"
. . . And I said, "Who are you, Lord?"
And the Lord said, "I am Jesus whom you are persecuting.
But rise and stand upon your feet, for I have appeared to you for this purpose,
to appoint you as a servant and witness
to the things in which you have seen me and to those in which I will appear to you,
delivering you from your people and from the Gentiles
—to whom I am sending you to open their eyes,
so that they may turn from darkness to light."
[Bible (ESV), Acts of the Apostles 26:12–18]

to render canticles for singing in the liturgy of the "Hours" of Beloved Mary—the *Benedictus*, the *Magnificat*, and the *Nunc Dimittis*. These are sung daily in remembrance in churches, convents, and monasteries around the world.

Tradition relates that it was while Luke was in the presence of Beloved Mary that he painted his icon of remembrance of her, upon a wooden cedar panel that had been part of a table crafted by Jesus, during his time in Nazareth in the workshop with dear Joseph. While Luke painted, he absorbed all that Beloved Mary related of the passages of her life, and that of Jesus and his followers. It is told that this was while Beloved Mary was staying with the Apostle John in about 60 CE. Though Luke was not among the community while Jesus was present, he devotedly gathered accounts from Beloved Mary and the Apostles, rendering them into his gathering of the "Good Word" and the "Acts of the Apostles." Many of the most beloved parables, the teaching stories of Jesus, are related by Luke; he highlights the important role of women and the pivotal importance of love for the poor and the flowing of mercy. It would seem that he was profoundly influenced by the moments he spent with Beloved Mary.

There are several legends as to the further home of the icon painted by Luke. Perhaps he painted several similar ones as a painter might, in repeated attempts to fully capture the radiant presence of Beloved Mary, hearkening back to the moments of her youth and her newly awakened motherhood. After having been lost for over two hundred years, one painting it is told was found by St. Helena, the mother of Constantine,[78] in 326 CE when she was in Jerusalem on pilgrimage and searching for the remains of the Holy Cross. It is related that she brought the icon back to Constantinople and gave it to her son, along with fragments of the Cross. It is said that it was then later brought to Rome, where it became known as *Salus Populi Romani* ("Protectress of the Roman People") and has resided within the Basilica of Santa Maria Maggiore for over seventeen hundred years. Another story relates that the icon of Beloved Mary made its way to what is now Poland where, having been darkened by age, it has been known for centuries as the Black Madonna, "Our Lady" of Czestochowa.[79]

---

[78] See p. 362, n. 18 of this text.

[79] See p. 223–24 of this text.

Many other icons adorn the walls of the chapel of Saydnaya, darkened with age and the soot of candles lit continuously for centuries. One of the few icons still visible depicts Beloved Mary with a man kneeling beside her wearing a green robe and turban whom local tradition identifies as Sultan Baybar or the brother of Saladin, Ayyubid Sultan al-'Adil. Another of the most precious liturgical objects, especially used after the office of Good Friday, is an epitaphios embroidered tapestry depicting the "Placing in the Tomb." The inscription is in Russian. Christ lies at the center of the composition, enshrouded in white, his eyes closed and hands folded, his head surrounded by radiant light. Around him are gathered the women in golden gleaming clothing against the dark background: Mary Magdalene, Mary, mother of James and Joseph, the wife of Zebedee, and Beloved Mary, depicted as she often is with stars adorning her golden mantle. Of the four women and two men who are near—the men depicted it seems representing St. John the Evangelist and Joseph of Arimathea—Beloved Mary is the only one with open eyes, as though she alone is aware of the full meaning of the moment, and is accompanied by two angels in white who also are keeping watch.[80]

The *Salus Populi Romani* icon of Beloved Mary attributed to St. Luke continues to abide at the Shrine of Our Lady Protectress of Rome, Santa Maria Maggiore.[81] The original basilica of Beloved Mary there was built about 350 CE; it was first called "Santa Maria ad Nives" because of the legend that the outline of the church building Beloved Mary was requesting had appeared drawn there in snow on the Esquiline Hill on a warm summer day. Whenever there has been danger to the city, citizens of Rome stream to the basilica to abide within Beloved Mary's protective grace.

St. Hildegard of Bingen spoke of Beloved Mary as a mirror, indicating how within her being one can see the pure reflection from Non-existence, of Divine Reality, and catch a glimpse of that Reality within oneself. She was that rare clear mirror of whom Rumi spoke, reminding us of our need to find such a mirror of the true self abiding within us. Then we, like Beloved Mary, might open to the life and light-giving sustenance pouring from the Divine Reality:

---

[80] See https://www.antiochpatriarchate.org/en/page/our-lady-of-saydnaya-patriarchal-monastery/146/.
[81] See p. 77 with n. 9 of this text.

How, I wonder, shall I behold my own face,
so as to see what complexion I have and whether I am like night or day?
For a long while I was seeking the image of my soul,
but my image was not reflected by anyone.
"After all," I said, "what is a mirror for?
It is so that everyone may know what and who he or she is."
The mirror of iron is but for husks;
the mirror that shows the heart is extremely rare.
The soul's mirror is nothing but the face of the friend,
the face of that friend who is of the land Beyond.
I said, "O heart, seek the Universal Mirror, go to the Sea:
this business will not succeed by means of a river."
In this quest your servant at last arrived at your abode,
as the pains of childbirth drew Mary to the palm tree.
When your eye became an eye for my heart,
my blind heart became drowned in vision.
I saw that you are the Universal Mirror eternal:
I saw my own image in your eye.[82]
I said, "At last I have found myself:
in his eyes I have found the Shining Way."
My false instinct said, "Beware! That is just your illusory image;
distinguish your essence from illusion";
but my image spoke from your eye:
"I am you and you are I in perfect oneness;
for how should an illusion find the way into this illumined eye
that never ceases contemplating the Divine Reality?"
[Rumi, *Mathnawi* II: 92–104]

On the Mount of Olives, near the cave of the Holy Sepulchre, the Church of the Ascension is located over a site believed to be the earthly spot from which Jesus ascended into heaven following the Resurrection; a stone slab bears the mark of what is known as his footprint. The first

[82] It seems Rumi is speaking here of his beloved friend Shams of Tabriz, who for Rumi was the perfect mirror of his deepest soul through which he witnessed the Divine Reality. Through the eye of the saint, our own vision is expanded. See also the Virgin of Guadalupe, p. 358, n. 13 of this text.

church was erected there a few years after the visit of the pilgrim Egeria,[83] around 392 CE, by Poimenia, a noble lady from the Roman imperial family whose heart had been illumined by the teachings of Jesus.

Just nearby is another burial crypt revered by all three Abrahamic faiths as the burial place of a devoted woman. It is the revered seventh-century-BCE prophetess Huldah[84] whom Jews believe to be buried there. Christians believe it to be the tomb of the fifth-century-CE St. Pelagia, a beautiful former courtesan whose turning of heart upon hearing the preaching of Bishop Nonnus caused her to give up her former life. After giving away all her possessions, disguised as a monk, she lived in the desert as a hermit until just before her passing; she became renowned as Pelagia of Antioch.[85] Some Muslims maintain that the eighth-century mystic Rabi'a al-'Adawiyya rests in this tomb. However, Muslim scholars clarify that rather than Rabi'a al-'Adawiyya (who lived in what is now Iraq), it is Rabi'a bint Ismail, or "Rabi'a of Syria" as she was also known, who rests on the Mount of Olives in this cave of blessing and silent retreat of the heart. This Rabi'a was also a renowned Sufi teacher, of both men and women. A noble woman of Syria, she had used her wealth to support her husband, the Sufi teacher Ahmad ibn Abi al-Hawari, and his companions. Her husband often acknowledged her superiority in spiritual matters. He recounts how one day he called to her, but received no response; an hour later she told him, "My heart was so filled with the joy of God that I could not answer you." He further relates: "Once when I was engaged in performing the prayers of the night vigil, I remarked to Rabi'a that I never saw anyone remain so concentratedly awake as she. Rabi'a replied, 'God be glorified! Do not speak like this. I am called, I arise.'"[86]

---

[83] When Egeria visited, the Ascension was celebrated on an open hillside near the cave; the church had not yet been built.

[84] The Jewish Prophetess Huldah ran a school for women in Jerusalem; she is known to have exhorted the Jewish women to repent, to love God.

[85] A monk of the community of Nonnus later heard of a holy man named Pelagius and traveled to Jerusalem to pray with him. His heart called him to return a few days later, but he found that Pelagius had died. Assisting in preparing the monk for burial, he discovered "Pelagius" was actually Pelagia, a saintly woman.

[86] Dr. Javad Nurbaksh, *Sufi Women* (New York: Khaniqahi Nimatullahi Publications, 1980), p. 81, as quoted in Camille Helminski, *Women of Sufism*, op. cit., pp. 35–36.

The teachings of another of the Christian Desert Mothers, Amma Syncletica (270–350 CE), resonate so beautifully with the discerning teachings of the Khwajagan, reminding us that across traditions certain practices are essential, foundational. Indications are everywhere that, rather than outer appearances of piety, our inner attitudes and focus are what counts.

> There are many who live in the mountains and behave as if they were in the town; they are wasting their time. It is possible to be a solitary in one's mind while living in a crowd; and it is possible for those who are solitaries to live in the crowd of their own thoughts.[87]

Yet another of the Desert Mothers, Amma Theodora, reflected: "Neither asceticism, nor vigils, nor any kind of suffering are able to save. Only true humility can do that."[88] In Oneness we are created, in Oneness we return. We begin to recognize that countless beings of Spirit have come before us and, God willing, will continue to come after, and that all are held in the Encompassing Vastness of Reality, of Truth:

*In the Name of God, the Infinitely Compassionate and Most Merciful:*
*Consider the fig and the olive,*
*and Mount Sinai,*
*and this city of security!*
*Truly, We have created human beings in the most beautiful proportion.*
*Then We reduce them to the lowest of the low—*
*except those who have faith and do the deeds of wholeness and reconciliation:*
*For they shall have an unceasing reward!*
*What, then, could from now on cause you to deny this Way?*
*Is not God the Wisest of judges [the Most Healing of healers in wisdom]?*
[Quran, *Surah at-Tin*, "The Fig," 95:1–8, complete]

Some understand that "fig" here refers to Abraham, "olive" to Jesus, "Mt. Sinai" to Moses, and "the city of Security" to Mecca and Muhammad, may great peace and blessing be upon them all. These aspects are also understood to be a part of every human being, even in our physical form: the "fig" as symbolic of the brain, the "olive" symbolic of the

---

[87] See John Chryssavigis, *In the Heart of the Desert: the Spirituality of the Desert Fathers and Mothers,* revised ed. (Bloomington, IN: World Wisdom, 2008), p. 30.
[88] Ibid, p. 73.

eye, "Mt. Sinai" symbolic of the third eye of the forehead, and the "city of security" as the heart: *Whoever enters it finds tranquility* (Quran, *Surah al-'Imran* 3:97).

In utmost humility, to enter "the City of Security," Muslims strive to prepare for the Hajj, the pilgrimage to Mecca, by rectifying whatever may need to be addressed in their own lives and families, and as is possible in their extended communities, as though preparing for their own death, preparing to meet their Sustainer, "the Wisest of Judges." One could say the climax of the Hajj rituals in Mecca is the moment when everyone gathers, bowing and prostrating in prayer before God, on the plain in the desert around Mt. Arafat. And despite the crowds, as though alone, it is a moment of intimacy of the soul with God. Even as Rumi describes the practice of a prophet:

The person of the prophet sits here,
while his other body is in heaven, like the moon.
This mouth of his discourses with those beside him,
while that mouth intimately whispers with the Beloved.
His outward ear apprehends these words,
while his spiritual ear draws close the mysteries of Being.
His outward eye apprehends human forms and features,
while his inward eye is dazzled by the Face of that Friend.
Here his feet stand evenly in the row of worshippers within the mosque,
there he circumambulates the heavens.
Every part of him is reckoned in this way:
here within Time, there Eternity's companion.
[Rumi, *Mathnawi* V:3601–06]

Climbing to the top of Mt. Arafat when possible, pilgrims offer supplications near the mountain all afternoon until sunset, pausing in an eternal moment. It is here that the Prophet Muhammad gave his farewell sermon before his passing; tradition also relates that it was here that Adam and Eve were re-united after the long journey of the soul—where the feminine and masculine principles re-coalesced in full and true self-knowledge within God, within the Oneness.[89] And so this pinnacle of Arafat ("gnosis"—

[89] It is in the surah of *al-A'raf*, the *surah* of the heights of gnosis, that we are given the beautiful verse of the original union which is now restored:

*It is He/She who created you from a single soul and likewise his mate of like nature,*

derived from the same root as *Arif* meaning "Knower") is also referred to as Jabal-ur-Rahma, the "Mountain of Mercy."

Though many of the rituals of the Muslim pilgrimage may be enacted in one's own time within the days of Hajj, this important moment must be observed all together, by all who are endeavoring to complete the Hajj, on the afternoon of the ninth of the month of Dhul Hijjah, this "Day of Arafat." After the source of water (the Zamzam) has been found, the Source of the sustenance of life has been recognized, one is ready to climb the mountain of the self, and through God's grace—if He/She so wills, for He/She is the Sustainer of all things, and the One who unifies and resurrects in His/Her Light and Everlivingness—to comprehend unity within one's self. To fulfill the Hajj, a pilgrim must remain within the precinct of Arafat from noon until after the sun sets. One spends the day in the fullness of the sun's light here. This is the W*aquf*, the "Standing," the halting, the symbolic retreat (*khalvet*) of the pilgrimage. As throngs cluster upon the mountain, even one minute on the mountain is enough to satisfy one's obligation for the *Hajj* (if one has also donned the *ihram* —ritual white clothing, after "intention" and purification—and made the circumambulation, the other two obligatory actions of the *Hajj*), but if one is able to stay longer in meditation, even in the midst of crowds, all the better. This is the day of heights, the day of gnosis, of the realignment of the masculine and feminine principles, of power and beauty, the day of Union. And opening from these moments of union, one then returns to offer farewell circumambulations (*tawafs*) around the Kaaba and to gather water from the Zamzam spring to bring home for healing and blessing. It is a day of forgiveness and of gratitude, of immersion in Spirit.

The lover hotly pursues the beloved:
when the beloved comes, the lover is gone.
You are a lover of God, and God is such
that when He/She comes not a single hair of yours remains.
At that look of His/Hers a hundred like you vanish away.
I think you are in love with nothingness.
You are a shadow and in love with the sun.

---

*in order that he might dwell with her (in love).*
[Quran, *Surah al-A'raf* 7:189]

When the sun comes, the shadow quickly disappears.
[Rumi, *Mathnawi* III: 4620–23]

Beloved Mary's place of farewell is considered by many to be the "Nightingale Mountain" (Bulbul Dag) above Ephesus.[90] Even as the nightingale sings of the rose, many pilgrims, both Muslim and Christian, make their way there throughout the year in remembrance, to immerse within the fragrance of her presence in prayer. It was in the fourth century CE that the tradition of her abiding there in her elder age was first recorded by Epiphanius of Salamis; the Ephesus tradition was reinvigorated through the visions of the Augustinian sister, Blessed Anne Catherine Emmerich (1774–1824 CE).

In her visions, Anne Catherine Emmerich, who had been bedridden due to extended illness, recounted the last days of the life of Jesus, and details of the life of Beloved Mary. Anne Catherine had become known in Germany as a mystic, referred to by some as "the pious Beguine," and many people came to visit her. One of her visitors, Clemens Brentano, a writer, in whom she confided some of her experience, was so taken with the power of her visions that he returned every day for five years to transcribe them. After Anne Catherine's death, he published a book based on his transcriptions; a second book was published based on further notes of his after his own passing. Modern archaeological discoveries have confirmed many of the references she made to local customs and details of life at the time of Christ.

Ven. Anne Catherine described how Mary did not live in Ephesus itself, but in the nearby hills above it where the Apostle John had built a little stone house for her, to the left of the road from Jerusalem that sloped steeply towards Ephesus.

> Before John brought the Blessed Virgin to this settlement, he had built for her a dwelling of stone very similar to her own at Nazareth.[91]

> As a rule, they lived at a quarter of an hour's distance from each other. The whole settlement was like a scattered village. Mary's house was the only one built of stone.[92]

---

[90] The city of Ephesus was a major trade center of the East, partially due to its large harbor; it had the largest population density after Antioch. The current Turkish town of Seljuk, above which is *Bulbul Dag*, is about 7 km from Ephesus.
[91] *The Life of Jesus Christ*, op. cit., Vol. IV, p. 451.
[92] Ven. Anne Catherine Emmerich, *The Life of the Blessed Virgin Mary*, op. cit., p. 348.

Tradition relates that John, thought to be the youngest of the Apostles, lived in Ephesus many years, after traveling there with Beloved Mary.[93] The former Basilica of St. John in nearby Seljuk is considered to be the location of his tomb. The basilica Church of the Virgin Mary established in Ephesus in the third century is also regarded as attesting to the presence of Beloved Mary in these nearby hills.

Ven. Anne Catherine described details of the house: "that it was built with rectangular stones, that the windows were high up near the flat roof and that it consisted of two parts with a hearth at the center. . . . She further described the location of the doors, the shape of the chimney, etc."[94]

On October 18, 1881, a French priest, the Abbé Julien Gouyet journeyed to Ephesus to seek out Mary's House, with the description from the book by Brentano (that was based on his conversations with Ven. Anne Catherine Emmerich) as his guide. He did indeed discover a small stone building on a mountain there overlooking the Aegean Sea, high above the nearby ruins of ancient Ephesus, in what is now Turkey. He believed it was truly the house where the Virgin Mary had lived the last years of her life. Not much attention was paid to his discovery.

About ten years later though, two Lazarist priests were drawn to follow the same description of Ven. Anne Catherine's to seek it out. Locals tell the story of how these two were wandering in the hills, attempting to follow her indications, longing to see Beloved Mary's house, when they became thirsty and inquired of a woman working in a field if there might be water anywhere nearby. They were told, "Oh, yes . . . the spring by Mary's House is just over there." Struggling still to find it, they at last

---

93 Though some traditions, including those shared by Maximus, relate that after a while living in Ephesus with John, Beloved Mary turned back to minister to those in Jerusalem, remaining there under the wing of James (step-brother of Jesus), son of Joseph, the tradition of her abiding in Ephesus until her Dormition and Assumption is now widely accepted. Some traditions relate that the apostles would return each year to take counsel with her, except for Thomas who had journeyed the most distantly, to India. Tradition relates that John outlived all the other apostles, and that later, after having been exiled to Patmos, he returned again in his old age to Ephesus where he passed from this earthly life in 98 CE. The early bishop, Irenaeus (125–202 CE) from nearby Smyrna (now Izmir) writes of "the church of Ephesus, founded by Paul, with John continuing with them until the times of Trajan." See Robert M. Grant, *Irenaeus of Lyons*, (London: Routledge, 1997), p. 2.

94 See AnneCatherineEmmerich.com.

noticed tall trees, plane trees and a poplar, and realized the trees were guiding them. And so they, too, came to discover the ancient stone chapel on the hill on July 29, 1891. These devoted ones, Father Poulin and Father Jung, who were from Smyrna, learned that the little stone building, whose roof was then in ruins, had long been venerated by the people of nearby Sirince (Kirkindji), a mountain village whose inhabitants were descended from the early Christians of Ephesus. This "Doorway to the Most Holy" (*Panaya Kapulu* or *Panaghia Capouli*), understood by the people of Sirince as another name of blessing of Beloved Mary, is the name long given by local Christians to the "House of Mother Mary," Maryem Ana Evi in the Ephesus hills. Father Poulin related, "Since time immemorial they had come on a pilgrimage to this place, every year, particularly in mid-August in memory of the Holy Virgin's death."[95]

Before long, Sister Marie de Mandat-Grancey was named Foundress of Beloved Mary's House by the Catholic Church and was tasked with restoring and preserving it and the surrounding areas, which was soon accomplished.[96] Beloved Mary's quiet abode continues to be visited often by pilgrims of many faiths (including several popes), and especially on the 15th of August, the date Christians celebrate Beloved Mary's Dormition and Assumption.

The little house has two main rooms, after the entry, a larger room for prayer that is now the chapel, and to the right a smaller room where

---

[95] P. Eugene Poulin, *The Holy Virgin's House, the True Story of its Discovery* (Istanbul: Arikan Yayinlari, 1999), p. 59. *The Holy Virgin's House* is an autobiographical account by a priest, Father Eugene Poulin, of his experience in the rediscovery of Beloved Mary's abode on Bulbul Dag. Originally quite skeptical of Ven. Anne Catherine's visionary account, Father Poulin was drawn to discover its veracity and confirmed the felicity of her visions. He then assisted in encouraging the Catholic Church officials to acknowledge *Panaghia Capouli* as Meryem Ana Evi, the abode of Beloved Mary.

[96] A few years after it was located, archeological excavations were begun on the site: "In 1898, architect M. Carré, who was put in charge by the French Government came from Konstantinopolis (Istanbul) in order to make a meticulous analysis of the House. In his report he wrote the House dates back to 'the first centuries' however he explained unofficially that it can be from the first century." See E. Poulin [Gabrielovich], *Un dernier mot sur le lieu où est morte la Sainte Vierge*, s.e (Smyrne: 1921), p. 37. As cited at https://www.hzmeryemanaevi.com/en/monastery-water-supply-hiking/

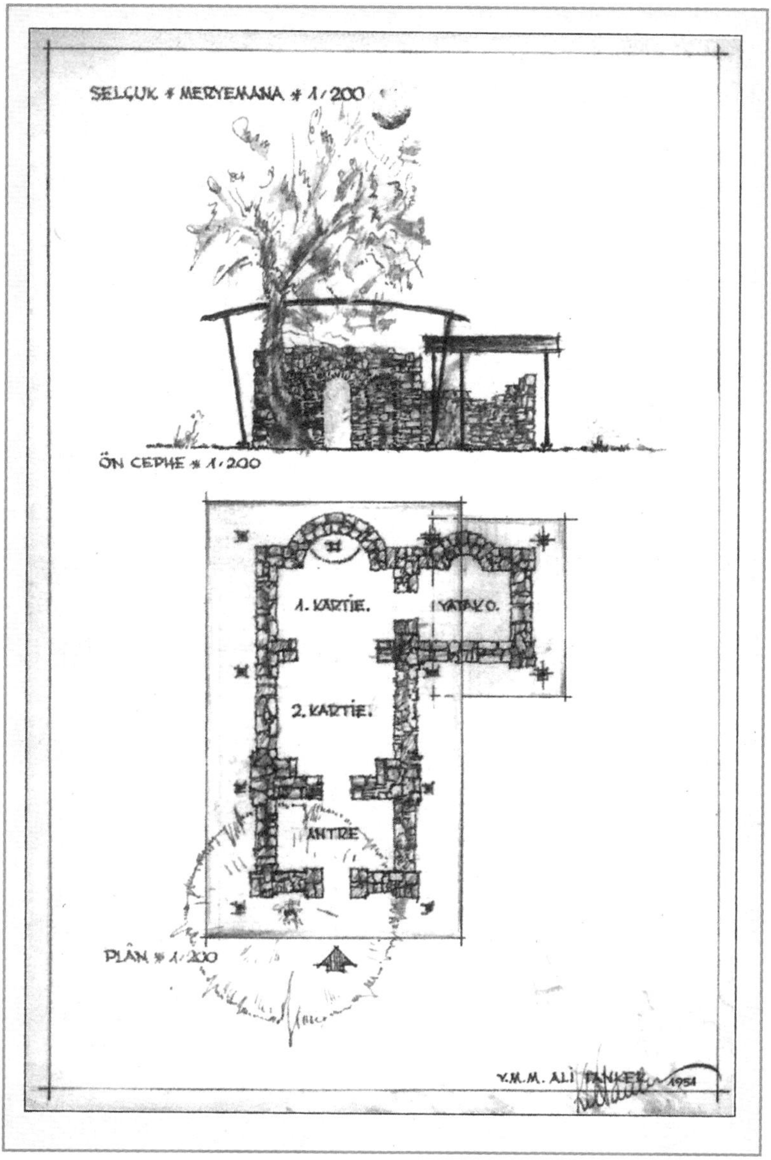

*Meryem Ana Evi*
The Holy Virgin's House, the True Story of Its Discovery
*(Rendering drawn of it when discovered by P. Eugene Poulin)*

it is said Beloved Mary rested and which had a channel of water flowing through from a spring beneath it. Outside the little stone house, just down the hill a bit, is the "wishing wall" where pilgrim visitors have tied prayers and requests written on small pieces of paper or cloth. Just nearby is the fountain of the spring of healing water that is gathered by pilgrims to bring home for blessing.

When a spring gushes from a rock,
the rock disappears in the spring.
After that, no one calls it a "stone,"
seeing such pure water gushing forth.
Know that these bodies are vessels
valued for what God pours through them.
[Rumi, *Mathnawi* V: 3283–85]

Meryem Ana Evi is now recognized by many as Beloved Mary's final abode, one of the most renowned sites in the world that is dedicated to her. We have visited dear Beloved Mary's house many times now, over the forty years we have been journeying to Turkey. For those journeying with us it has always offered refreshment of Spirit, a gracious haven of Peace, this garden of beautiful silence to which the spirit of Beloved Mary welcomes all.

*Those who have attained to faith and do righteous deeds—*
*and We do not burden any soul*
*with more than it is well able to bear—*
*they will be companions of the Garden, there to dwell,*
*after We shall have removed whatever unworthy thoughts or feelings*
*may have been lingering in their hearts.*
*Running waters will flow at their feet;*
*and they will say: "All praise belongs to God, who has guided us here;*
*for certainly we would not have found the right path*
*unless God were our guide!*
*Truly, our Sustainer's messengers have told us the truth!"*
*And a voice will call out to them:*
*"This is the Garden which by virtue of your deeds has come to you."*
[Quran, *Surah al-A'raf* 7:42–43]

Father Tarcy Mathias, careful guardian of the heart of Mother Mary's House (Meryem Ana Evi), often shared with us his deep experience of Beloved Mary's Presence there. A Capuchin (Franciscan) priest, he himself was from India, where he had studied devotedly in his younger years with Brother Bede Griffiths,[97] and he also was a lover of Mevlana Rumi. One year when we visited, Father Tarcy told us of how a great fire had threatened the area that year and all devoted to the care of Meryem Ana Evi were concerned that it would consume the sacred site, but they witnessed, as they watched through the hours, how the fire stopped at the borders of the sanctuary; where there were images of Mary standing in blessing, the fire turned back, and the sanctuary hill was preserved. It was not long before the surrounding hills were again verdant. As he related:

> Mary, the cosmic and universal Mother, is present here in a very special way. . . . There are two traditions concerning the last years of Mary's life. Some say that she came to Ephesus with St. John, but then returned to Jerusalem and died there. The far greater weight of belief, however, is that Mary lived the last years of her life in the house built for her by St. John on the hills near the ancient city of Ephesus. She lived silently and in prayer, but always ready to help as a Mother. She is believed to have died in Ephesus and that the Assumption took place here. . . . Meryem Ana Evi was and is the House of Mary, a Spirit filled person.[98]

She understood that her life was a destiny of Love, to which she said, "Yes!" with the whole of her heart, glorifying God, with every breath.

> Know that the wheeling heavens are turned by waves of Love:
> were it not for Love, the world would be frozen, stiff.
> How would an inorganic thing transform into a plant?
> How would living creatures sacrifice themselves

---

[97] Brother Bede Griffiths (1906–1993) was a towering heart of early interspiritual vision who fostered in many a love of the One. His later home was in Shantivanam ("forest of peace"), India. As he said in his introduction to *Universal Wisdom* (1994): "This is the destiny of all humanity, to realize its essential unity in the Godhead, by whatever name it is known, to be one with the absolute Reality, the absolute Truth, the infinite, the eternal Life and Light." See http://www.theinterfaithobserver.org/journal-articles/2017/10/4/bede-griffiths-interfaiths-interspiritual-pioneer.

[98] From "Meryem Ana Evi, House of the Blessed Virgin Mary" offered by Father Tarcy Mathias, Meryem Ana Evi, Ephesus, Selcuk, Izmir, Turkey 2004.

to become endowed with spirit?
How would the spirit sacrifice itself for the sake of that Breath
by which Mary was made pregnant?
Each one of them would be unyielding and immovable as ice:
how could they be flying and searching like locusts?
Every one is in love with that Perfection
and hastening upward like a sapling.
Their haste implicitly is saying, "Glory to God!"
They are purifying the body for the sake of the spirit.
[Rumi, *Mathnawi* V, 3854–59]

Father Tarcy further relates:

> More than a million visitors a year are said to come to the shrine of Meryem Ana Evi, the House of Mother Mary near Ephesus in Turkey. In official documents of the government, the site is referred to as a museum or a monument. To the visitors—whatever be their nationalities, cultures, languages, or religions—it is a sacred place, sacred in the basic and fundamental sense of the word.
>
> Not infrequently, one sees a person—man or woman, young or old—deeply moved emotionally, very often in tears. One feels like asking, "Why are you weeping? Are you sad?" The answer comes: "No, I am not sad. I feel greatly touched; I feel something special, a peace, a joy, a warm welcome, a happiness. I feel like staying here." Others say, "This is a special place; this is a sacred place. I feel the presence of Mary, our Mother. She has certainly lived here."
>
> Whatever the religious attitude of those who visit, all feel an intimate and warm welcome inside this poor house. They feel free and relaxed. Young lovers experience deeper and richer meaning in their mutual love, and they symbolize it by their tears of joy, and by lighting and joining two candles together. Who could be a better guide to a life of love than Mary, whose life was filled with the Holy Spirit of Love . . . ?
>
> Another important aspect of Meryem Ana Evi is the value and importance given by our Muslim sisters and brothers to this place. It is interesting to note that in the Holy Book of the Quran only one woman is mentioned [by name], and that about thirty times. She is Mary, the Mother of the Prophet Jesus—accepted by Muslims as one

> of the greatest prophets. When our Muslim sisters and brothers come to Meryem Ana Evi, they come not as tourists or just visitors. They come to pray, in perhaps the only place in the world where people of these great religions—Islam and Christianity—can pray together without regard to their differences . . .
>
> Mary teaches people here that every true religion should lead people towards acceptance, tolerance, unity, and service towards one's neighbor—whatever be his or her religion. A religion which distinguishes and divides, which leads toward fundamentalism and hatred of others, can never be the practice of a true religion. Here, Mary teaches that every true religion teaches its followers how to love and serve one another.
>
> Why is all this felt here in Meryem Ana Evi? The answer is simple. A deep and personal spirit is felt in this place. It is sensed and experienced here because a person rich in the spirit of love, unity, prayer, sacrifice, welcome, tolerance, and acceptance has left that spirit here. That person is a woman and a mother. . . . This is the house where Mary lived and lives."

We visited with Father Tarcy for a number of years whenever we were able to journey to Meryem Ana Evi, until his health declined, and following a serious heart episode he sadly was retired to Italy for more extensive care, but sorely missing the Presence of Beloved Mary within whose sanctuary he had been sustained for so long, surely joining her fully in Spirit when he passed in 2010. We had corresponded for several years, and I treasure the letters he wrote. Among them was this letter he sent not long after one of our visits, after we had mailed to him a copy of the newly published volume of *Rumi's Sun, The Teachings of Shams of Tabriz*. We hold him dearly in our hearts and are ever sending love, from this world to the next.

Adjacent to the little stone chapel house of Meryem Ana Evi, a cave was more recently excavated where it seems that Beloved Mary retired for even deeper immersion in prayer, even closer with the earth. It is here, within this cave that some say St. John wrote his Gospel. In this simple abode near Ephesus, the Presence of Beloved Mary joins both worlds, ancient and modern, Christian and Muslim, heaven and earth in a restorative silence and a "feast of Light."

FAX TO No: 001-831-6853977

MERYEM ANA EVI
35922 - SELÇUK, TURKEY
Tel: 0090-232-894 1014
Fax: 0090-232-8941006

My very dearest Camille and Kabir

The book that you sent with so much love "Rumi's Sun" has just come in and with a heart full of joy and gratitude, I say "Thank you" and may the All Powerful omnipotent one who always widen our hearts bless you in His own abundant way. The book coming, as it is during Holy week, is and always be a 'Easter gift'. Thank you once again. Understandably I glanced through the whole book though it was difficult to do it so fast and liked it so much. The contemplative cover picture is really wonderful.

Let me wish you a very Happy and Holy Easter - a feast of hope, a feast of light, a feast of life. Let us pray for one another - and I depend so much on your love and prayer - that we may understand the mystery of our individual life in the mystery of the Eternal Life of the Risen Lord present in our hearts.

Hope you have received my last letter with a picture. With much much love and ever so grateful for the blessing you are to me

Love and wishes to all in the family

your loving brother
Fr. Tarcy

*Dear Father Tarcy's Letter*[99]

---

[99] Transcription of dear Father Tarcy's letter:

My very dearest Camille and Kabir,

The book that you sent with so much love "Rumi's Sun" has just come in and with a heart full of joy and gratitude, I say "Thank you" and may the All Powerful omnipotent one Who always widen[s] our hearts bless you in His own abundant way. The book coming, as it is during Holy Week, is and always [will] be a[n] "Easter gift." Thank you once again. Understandably, I glanced through the whole book, though it was difficult to do it so fast and liked it so much. The contemplative cover picture is really wonderful.

Let me wish you a very Happy and Holy Easter—a feast of hope, a feast of light, a feast of life. Let us pray for one another—and I depend so much on your love and prayer—that we may understand the mystery of our individual life in the mystery of the Eternal life of the Risen Lord present in our hearts.

Hope you have received my last letter with a picture. With much much love and ever so grateful for the blessing you are to me. Love and wishes to all in the family.

Your loving brother, Fr. Tarcy

(Transcribed with love from one who remembers him. *Al-Fatiha.*)

*Those who have a turning of heart and come to faith*
*and do the deeds of wholeness and reconciliation:*
*these will enter the Garden, and will not be wronged in any way—*
*Gardens of Eternity, those which the Most Gracious*
*has promised to His/Her servants in the Unseen:*
*for His/Her promise must be fulfilled.*
*They will not hear any empty talk there*
*but only greetings of peace;*
*and there they will receive their sustenance, morning and evening.*
*Such is the Garden which We bestow as an inheritance*
*to those of Our Servants who are conscious of Us.*
*[The angels say:] "We descend by command of your Sustainer alone:*
*to Him/Her belongs what lies open before us*
*and what is behind us and what is in between.*
[Quran, *Surah Maryam* 19:60–64]

*Meryem Ana Evi*

## *Beyond Sustenance*

Mary,
you have gathered us close,
again and again.
We rest in your arms,
embraced with the stars
amid the heavens
and know the Eternal
Forgiveness
for our fragility of being
by which we sometimes stumble
in our ineptitude,
and yet
we also know
Eternal strength and Power
that supports our very bones
in these moments walking on this earth,
through the valleys
and over hills.
Over all, blue sky
spreads out to silent darkness,
vast spaces
where energy flows
beyond our eyes and ears
but perceived by heart—
these hearts that can reflect
the firmament
and know the Truth
of the exquisite Beauty of Creation
and of Love
and all Your Names, O God,
as You sprinkle them so generously

among us,
dancing through us every night and day,
dearest Mother/Father/Source—
we bow and prostrate,
rise, and dance
within Your Glory
that pours through everything.
Keep opening our eyes,
our ears, our hearts
to witness Your Eternal Beauty
now
and now
and now.
*See how God grants sustenance*
*to whom He/She wills, beyond all reckoning.*[1]

[1] Quran, *Surah al-'Imran* 3:37.

# XII. TWELFTH STAR OF BLESSING

## *Tranquility of Spirit*

# *Tranquility of Spirit*

*Truly in the remembrance of God, hearts find tranquility.*
[Quran, *Surah ar-Rad*[1] 13:28]

*On the Day of Recognition God will say:*
*"Today, their truthfulness shall benefit*
*all who have been true to their word.*
*Theirs shall be gardens through which running waters flow,*
*there to dwell beyond the count of time;*
*well-pleased is God with them,*
*and well-pleased are they with Him/Her: this is the ultimate success."*
[Quran, *Surah al-Maida* 5:119]

The completion of *Surah al-Maida* conveys the recognition of a true alignment with the "word" of being opening the doorway into the Garden. And Beloved Mary, she who had been so completely true to her Word, so completely in alignment, was called home, as Maximus relates, in her eightieth year. This beloved one, who in her elder years slept little, whose pillow was a stone, had nurtured so many and prayed for all. According to Maximus her "mercy was not only toward loved ones and acquaintances but toward strangers and enemies, for she truly was the mother of the merciful one; she was the mother of the benevolent one

---

[1] This *surah*, like so many others, takes its title from a particular meaningful word within the *surah*, in this case, the word "thunder," indicative of God's creative powers observable through the manifestations of nature.

"The main theme of this *surah* is God's revelation, through His prophets, of certain fundamental moral truths which [the human being] may not neglect without suffering the natural consequences of such a neglect . . . just as a realization of those moral truths by those 'who are endowed with insight . . . [and] are true to their bond with God' (verses 19–20) invariably causes them to 'find inner happiness and the most beauteous of all goals' (verse 29) . . ." See Muhammad Asad, *The Message of the Qur'an* (introduction to *Surah ar-Rad*).

and the lover of humankind."[2] And even as her beloved Sustainer, "Who makes the sun to shine on the good and the evil and sends rain on the righteous and sinners" (Bible, Gospel of Matthew 5:45),

> [Beloved Mary] was the mother of the poor and the needy. . . . So greatly was she magnified she became greater than all, as the sun is brighter than the stars.[3]

Beloved Mary disappeared within the brightness, the Light of God that had so long been her sustenance, held in luminosity of Spirit and yet reappearing through grace to hearts waiting to hear of Love, of Life, of Truth, of the possibility of resurrection from the grave of the bodily discomfiture into that Continually Creative Light, merging through the darknesses to rebirth Love again and again. She knew and taught, and still teaches, how to take refuge in the Beloved, even as Mevlana Rumi remembers her in his *Mathnawi*:

When something makes you rejoice in this world,
consider at that moment the parting from it.
Many have been gladdened by what made you glad,
yet in the end, like the wind, it escaped.
It will escape from you, too: don't set your heart upon it;
escape from it before it flies from you.
Before everything you own slips away,
tell the material world, like Mary:
"I take refuge from you with the Merciful."[4]

---

[2] Maximus, *The Life of the Virgin,* op cit. p 129.

[3] Ibid. Her radiant and generous being reminds us of the "Seven Counsels" of Mevlana Rumi:

In generosity and helping others, be like a river.
In compassion and grace, be like the sun.
In concealing others faults, be like the night.
In anger and fury, be as though you had died.
In modesty and humility, be like the earth.
In acceptance, be like the sea.
Appear as you are or be as you appear.

[4] Quran, *Surah Maryam* 19:18. (The response of Beloved Mary to Angel Gabriel's sudden appearance.)

In her chamber Mary saw something that quickened her heart,
a life-increasing, heart-ravishing one—that trusted spirit arose
from the face of the earth like the sun
and the moon, from the East,
like beauty unveiled.
Mary, who was undressed, began to tremble,
fearful of the evil that might be with it.
This kind of thing could cause
Joseph to slice his own hand, like the women of the court.[5]
Like a rose, it blossomed in front of her,
like a fantasy that lifts its head in the heart.
Mary left herself, and in this selflessness
said, "I will leap into God's protection,"
because that pure-bosomed one
was accustomed to flying to the Unseen.
Since she knew this world is a temporary kingdom,
she had built her fortress in Holy Presence,
so that in the hour of death
she would be invulnerable, strongly held.
She saw no better fortress than the protection of God;
she had made her home near His/Her Stronghold.
[Rumi, *Mathnawi* III: 3697–3711]

Beloved Mary had early grasped *the most trustworthy handhold which shall never give way* (*Surah al-Baqarah* 2:256). Within the depths of silence, deepest prayer, and contemplation, she had made her home near her Beloved Sustainer. On Bulbul Dag ("Nightingale Mountain"[6] —named in remembrance of the nightingales there bursting with song, in love with this Rose) dwelt Beloved Mary, the beloved Rose of God, whose holy being has fragranced the ages, continuously. The Christian Benedictine abbot,

[5] This is a reference to the Prophet Joseph whose countenance of grace caused the women of the court who were dining with Zulaikha, wife of Potiphar, to cut their hands in distraction when suddenly faced with the intensity of his radiant beauty. (See Quran, *Surah Yusuf*, "Joseph," 12:30–31.)
[6] Though nightingales have a rather "ordinary" appearance, their song is one of the most beautiful and most complex verbal sounds of the animal kingdom.

Engelbert of Admont (d. 1331 CE)[7] began every stanza of the psalter of prayer he composed with "*Ave, Rosa*" in remembrance of Beloved Mary:

> Hail Rose, flower of summer, O Mary, sweet abode of the living light!
> Hail, Rose, exceptional exemplar and canon of maidenly restraint!
> Hail Rose of vernal dew, the dew of Divine love wholly you bestowed!
> Hail, Rose of Paradise, through whom all disease is erased![8]

There is a beautiful saying of the Prophet Muhammad that reminds us of the depth of God's love that belongs to those who join together in that Love, immersing together within the Unitive, Infinitely Loving Presence of the Divine Reality:

> God, Most Exalted, said, "My love belongs by right to those who love one another in Me, to those who sit together in Me, to those who visit one another in Me, and to those who give generously to one another in Me."[9]

---

[7] Engelbert of Admont was a follower of the Order of St. Benedict. St. Benedict (480–547 CE) had encouraged dividing one's days of practice into three roughly equal portions: five to six hours of prayer, five hours of manual labor in garden or field or kitchen or craft, and four hours of scriptural reading and study. Engelbert, one of the most learned men of his era, is perhaps best known for his political treatise: *De ortu, progressu et fine Romani imperii*, which included the following of two key political principles: a ruler must be a learned man and his sole aim must be the welfare of his subjects. He was also the author of the *Treatise of the Graces and Virtues of the Blessed Virgin Mary* (*Tractatus de Gratiis et Virtutibus B. M. Virginis*), published in B. Pez, *Thesaurus Anecdotorum Novissimus* (Augsburg: 1721), in which, in Part III, ch. 6, he reflects:

> The Blessed Virgin, alone among us, alone among all, because she was worthy of it, was chosen in advance and consecrated [ordained] above every part and priestly grace for this function: to conceive the body of the Lord through the operation of the Holy Spirit and form in herself by her own proper action, not just bread and wine, but her own virginal body and blood, . . . and to engender it and touch it and envelop it with her limbs and to nourish it until finally, standing upright next to the cross, at the same time when her son [was making his sacrifice], she offered for us to God the body itself of her son; and through her compassion she joined to it her own body and soul according to the words of Luke 2:35: "A sword of pain will pierce your soul."

[8] See *Mary and the Art of Prayer*, op. cit., p. 91.

[9] *Hadith* of the Prophet Muhammad (conveyed by Mu'adh ibn Jabal; see Malik).

Surely Beloved Mary would have encouraged such immersion in that Loving Presence of God, together, quietly, gently, in lived prayer and surrender, for anyone who visited her, or still visits her, that all might be resurrected within that Pure Love. Perhaps it was her being that inspired Paul to pour forth the beautiful passage in regard to Love of I Corinthians 13.[10] Over the unfolding centuries, she has appeared to people all over the world to encourage the aliveness of Love among us.

One of the most renowned appearances of Beloved Mary, the first recorded in the Western hemisphere, was her visit in 1531 CE with a humble shepherd in his late fifties, a simple man, named Juan, of central Mexico who was of Aztec heritage. His heart had opened to the teachings of Christianity through the words of preachers who had come with the Europeans arriving in the sixteenth century. One day on his way to a nearby Christian chapel, as he passed Tepeyac Hill, he suddenly beheld a beautiful lady surrounded by a ball of light more brilliant than the sun. She spoke to him in his native language of Nahuatl. Her first words to him were, "My dear little son, I love you." She went on to tell him her name: "the Virgin, Mary." She instructed him that she wished for a church to be built in that place where people might experience her compassion:

> "All those who sincerely ask my help in their work and in their sorrows will know my Mother's Heart in this place. Here I will see their tears; I will console them and they will be at peace."

She requested of him that he go to the bishop in Tenochtitlan to convey her message. Though he had never been there, he immediately followed her direction. Bishop Fray Juan de Zumárraga and his servants gave Juan a dubious welcome. He returned to the hill, where he found Beloved Mary waiting. He begged her to send someone more effective. She responded:

> "My little son, there are many I could send. But you are the one I have chosen."

She asked him to return to the bishop with her request. The next day, a Sunday, after waiting for hours, he again gained an audience with the bishop who listened once again to his story and requested that he ask the

---

[10] See p. 322 of this text.

lady for a sign of proof that she was indeed Beloved Mary. He returned a third time to the Hill where he found the lady waiting for him. She told him not to worry, but to return the next day. Juan's uncle suddenly became gravely ill and he needed to stay near to care for him and so missed the meeting. Two days had passed, when his uncle was hovering on the verge of death and Juan left him to bring the priest for his last rites. On the way he again encountered Beloved Mary, awaiting him. In this fourth meeting with her she spoke so gently to him:

> "Do not be distressed, my littlest son. Am I not here with you who am your Mother? Are you not under my shadow and protection? Your uncle will not die at this time. There is no reason for you to engage a priest, for his health is restored at this moment. He is quite well. Go to the top of the hill and cut the flowers that are growing there. Bring them then to me."
>
> While it was freezing on the hillside, Juan obeyed Mary's instructions and went to the top of the hill where he found a full bloom of Castilian roses. Removing his tilma, a poncho-like cape made of cactus fiber, he cut the roses and carried them back to Mary. She rearranged the roses and told him:
>
> "My little son, this is the sign I am sending to the Bishop. Tell him that with this sign I request his greatest efforts to complete the church I desire in this place. Show these flowers to no one else but the Bishop. You are my trusted ambassador. This time the Bishop will believe all you tell him."[11]

Juan was impressed with the beautiful roses in the midst of winter and straight away went again to the bishop and told him the story, opening his *tilma* to show him the roses. Yet it was the *tilma* itself that stunned the bishop. Where the roses had lain upon it, an image of Beloved Mary shone forth—she was standing before the sun, completely illuminated, her feet resting upon the horns of the crescent moon held by an angel.

A great sign appeared in the sky, a woman clothed with the sun,
with the moon under her feet,

---

[11] See https://www.catholic.org/about/guadalupe.php and also https://olg.cc/about/about-our-patroness/our-ladys-image-on-the-tilma/ (accessed April 28, 2020).

and upon her head a crown of twelve stars.
[Bible, Revelation 12:1]

In the image emblazoned upon the *tilma*, her gentle face shone with the radiance of a loving mother, and she wore a black band around her waist, an indication that she was with child, just as Juan had described the beautiful presence of the lady whom he had met.

The next day Juan took the bishop to the hill; he then went to see his uncle whom he found had indeed been restored to health. His uncle told him how he had been visited by a lovely lady shining with light who had said she had sent his nephew to Tenochtitlan with her picture; she had told his uncle that she could be known as "Our Lady of Guadalupe."

The *tilma* itself survives in the church of "Our Lady of Guadalupe," now large enough to hold ten thousand congregants at once. Hanging in a frame over the altar, it has been through many stresses over the years, fires and floods; even after a bombing of the church altar in 1921 when the cast-iron cross and the stone altar rail were badly damaged, the *tilma* remained intact and no one was injured.[12] The tilma has been scientifically examined and yet scientists have been unable to determine the method used to create it or to explain its longevity. Though usually fiber made from the cactus filaments would have deteriorated in 20 to 60 years, after 450 years the *tilma* still holds the beautiful image of "Our Lady."[13]

Countless pilgrims continually come to visit and offer prayers with "Our Lady of Guadalupe," especially on the remembrance day of her first appearance to devoted Juan, December 12. When my husband Kabir and I were in Mexico, we also once visited and stood alongside Christians in prayer. We were surprised to see people lifting their hands in a manner in which we had never seen Catholics praying together (even Kabir who was raised Catholic). However, it was a manner that was very familiar to

---

[12] Whatever political opinions or actions may be circulating, Beloved Mary's presence seems to lend a protective radiance; her heart is ever open.

[13] When skilled scientists have examined it in recent decades, they have found the main original image to be smooth, as though like a photograph (though it was made centuries before the photographic process was invented); no brushstrokes can be seen even at a microscopic level. Upon careful magnified examination it has been noticed that reflected within the pupil of her eye is an image of Juan standing before her.

*Our Lady of Guadalupe Tilma, 1531* CE

us both from praying in the Middle East, standing alongside Muslims who naturally raise their hands held before them, open in prayer, as they recite by heart the *Fatiha*, the opening chapter of the Quran, an integral part of prayer for Muslims on many occasions and throughout the day. Hands are opened as though to catch the blessing of the words, as they waft through the air, and reflect them back upon the body and the soul. Perhaps some of those present here adapted this from the "orans" posture of priests offering prayer on behalf of the community, but perhaps some of those present might also have inherited a familiarity with this more intimate prayerful gesture from ancestors of earlier Spanish generations who had come to this land now called "Mexico" carrying Muslim heritage from ancient Andalusian Moorish roots. Some of the place names in Mexico still carry Arabic designations converted to Spanish resonance, such as the city of Guadalajara, one of the largest in Mexico, established in 1542 CE—its name derives from the Arabic *Wadi al-Hajarah* which means "River Valley of Stone." One of the largest and most navigable rivers in Spain, the Guadalquivir, continues to carry its Arabic name: from *Wadi al-Kabir*, "The Great River." Similarly, some say the name "Guadalupe" is derived from the Arabic phrase *Wadi al-Lubb* ("Hidden River"); even so, Beloved Mary is a "hidden river" of beneficence continually flowing.[14]

Continually we are all so much intertwined and can learn so much from each other's experience. One of the oldest fountains in Chiapas, Mexico, in Chiapa de Corzo, "La Coronna," was built by the Dominican friars in the sixteenth century, constructed with beautiful buttressed arches, built on an octagonal base, in the Mudejar (Moorish) style. From the Muslim "Moors" of Iberia they had learned how to bring sustaining water to their towns; the Moorish people had created renowned gardens with fountains, like those of the magnificent Alhambra in Granada, now a part of Andalusian Spain.

A passage in the Gospel of Mary Magdalene reminds us of how we are all so intertwined in this life and yet, we will return to the root of our nature:

> All of nature with its forms and creatures exist together and are interwoven with each other. They will be resolved back, however, to their own proper origin, for the compositions of matter return to the original roots of their nature. Those who have ears, let them hear this.
>
> [Gospel of Mary Magdalene, Dialogue 1][15]

The Assumption of Mary, celebrated generally on August 15th, is the fourth "Glorious Mystery" of the Rosary, and her Coronation, celebrated a week later on August 22nd has become the completion, the fifth "Glorious Mystery" of the Rosary. Within both Christian communities of West and East, Catholic and Orthodox, it is taught that Beloved Mary was taken up body and soul into Heavenly Glory and crowned with stars,

---

[14] The name "Guadalupe" some say may also be the Spanish version of a Nahuatl name for a goddess of fertility, "Coatlaxopeuh." Both meanings intertwine.

[15] *Gospel of Mary Magdalene*, Dialogue 1, as quoted in Cynthia Bourgeault, *The Meaning of Mary Magdalene*, op. cit., p. 46.

returned to the root of her being, into the presence of her Lord. Many Muslims also acknowledge her holy Assumption.

While some may still say this occurred in Jerusalem,[16] most now acknowledge her Assumption as taking place near Ephesus. Archaeologists have discovered tomb ruins with accompanying traditions of Beloved Mary's passing in both places, but no relics of her beloved body in either place. By the early eighth century, her "Assumption" was well accepted; John of Damascus wrote: "Mary died in the presence of the Apostles, but her tomb, when opened, upon the request of St. Thomas, was found empty; and so the Apostles concluded that the body was taken up to heaven." Recently, Syriac manuscript fragments relating the Assumption of Mary have been discovered that date to as early as the third century CE and speak of it as though it was widely known. The Assumption of Mary has often been symbolically depicted by a Madonna holding a three-petaled blue and golden *fleur-de-lys*,[17] reminiscent of the heavens and of the traditions of her empty tomb being filled with lilies and roses.

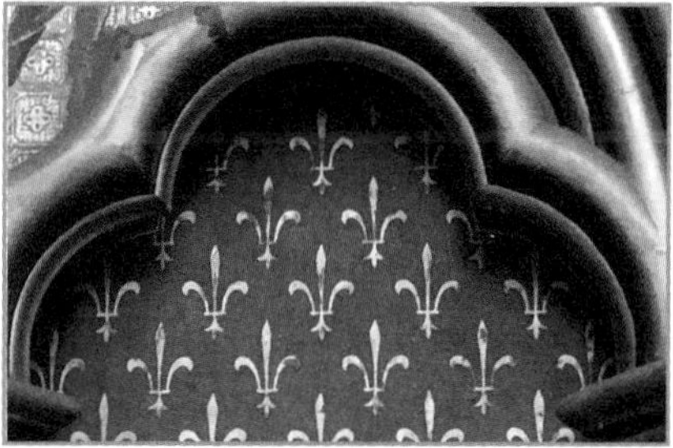

*Fleur-de-lys detail, Sainte-Chapelle, Paris*[18]

[16] The Church of the Sepulchre of Saint Mary is located over what some have believed was her tomb in the Kidron valley at the foot of the Mount of Olives in Jerusalem.

[17] The *fleur-de-lys* has also been used to symbolize the royalty of French kings and queens who claim their descent through the Merovingian line which some say descends from the child of Jesus and Mary Magdalene who came to what is now France with her mother so very long ago (see p. 437 of this text). One may also recognize within the form of the *fleur-de-lys* a stylized bee, symbolic of divine royalty and the blessing of fertility, and long associated with Mary Magdalene.

[18] One of the special beauties of visiting Paris is to visit Sainte-Chapelle, built by

Recognizing how much most of us are "intermixed" in this life, both spirit and clay within one being, often prickly thorns more evident among the roses,[19] Mevlana Rumi encourages us to return to the "root of the root" of ourselves now, to unveil that Source of Light within us, here, in this life:

> You are born from the children of God's creation,
> but you have fixed your sight too low.
> How can you be happy?
> Come, return to the root of the root of your Self.

---

sainted French King Louis IX together with his beloved mother, Queen Blanche of Castile (see Appendix I, p. 418 for her "Song for the Virgin Mary" with original Old French on p. 417), adjacent to what was their royal abode on the Isle de la Cité. It was completed in 1248 CE to house numerous precious relics, including what was reputed to be the Crown of Thorns and a portion of the True Cross found by Helena in the fourth century, for which Louis paid a vast sum to the Byzantines. Louis and Blanche had been instrumental in initiating the seventh crusade to the Holy Land, and she and his father had been leaders in the earlier crusade against the Cathars; one wonders if Blanche might have had a change of heart in her elder years, as witnessed by her song of Love, yet we recognize that we are all "intermixed" during our life in this world, sometimes limited in our vision, while holding within ourselves blind spots side-by-side with illuminated inspiration, all on a journey of return to wholeness and complete "soundness" of heart within the One Heart. Both Blanche and Louis had also overseen the building of the incredibly beautiful Notre Dame cathedral and were devoted to "Our Lady." See Extended Context Notes in Appendix, Star XII, 1.

[19] See ghazal 2381 of Mevlana Jalaluddin Rumi, excerpted here from "Intermixed" in *Love's Ripening, Rumi on the Heart's Journey*, translated by Kabir Helminski and Ahmad Rezwani (Boston, MA: Shambhala Publications, 2008), pp. 22–24:

> See how love intermixed with the lovers.
> See how the spirit and the clay are intermixed.
> How often are you going to see this and that, good and evil?
> Look at the end and see how this and that are intermixed.
> How long will you say the "known" and the "unknown"?
> See that both are intermixed.
> How often do you say this world and the next?
> See that the two are intermixed. . . .
> What a King He is! In this garden, by His grace,
> thorns and flowers intermix.

Although you are a talisman protecting a treasure,
you are also the mine.
Open your hidden eyes
and come to the root of the root of your Self.

You were born from a ray of God's majesty
and have the blessings of a good star.
Why suffer at the hands of things that don't exist?
Come, return to the root of the root of your Self.

You are a ruby embedded in granite.
How long will you pretend it isn't true?
We can see it in your eyes.
Come to the root of the root of your Self.[20]

Over the centuries, Beloved Mary has reached out to people everywhere, to many hearts around the world, calling each to recognize the root of the soul in the Mystery of Love.

Though the tree drinks from hidden roots,
we see the display of its branches.
Whatever the earth took from heaven,
it yields up honestly in spring.[21]

Many find that through the recitation of the prayers of the Rosary, in all its different forms, Beloved Mary accompanies the heart, directing a Way as we make this journey of the soul, back to God. The twelve passages or *Aves* of the Crown Rosary, are traditionally prayed in three groups of four "Hail Mary" prayers, each group also beginning with an "Our Father" (the Lord's Prayer) and ending with a "Glory be!"

## *Hail Mary*

Hail Mary, full of grace, the Lord is with you!
Blessed are you among women,
and blessed is the fruit of your womb, Jesus.

---

[20] Excerpt from "The Root of the Root of Your Self," *The Pocket Rumi,* op. cit., p. 26.
[21] Excerpt from "Love is a Stranger," ibid., p. 28.

Holy Mary, Mother of God, pray for us sinners,
now and at the hour of our death.
Amen.[22]

As the beads are "told," passing through the hands, such an ancient practice of prayer, the passages of Beloved Mary's journey are remembered—the blessings of her whole-hearted devotion to God; her most blessed pregnancy; her journey with beloved Joseph, her pure, supportive husband, and how she bore her son for nine months and journeyed with him; how she nursed him, enveloping him with love; and how Jesus received teaching from her, through her, and how through the blessing of the Holy Spirit she was a living temple of Grace radiating blessings upon all.

Using beads to accompany and focus prayer has long been a practice of devotion in many cultures.[23] The English word "bead" derives from *bede*, the Old English word for "prayer." The Roman Catholic Rosary (*Rosarium* in Latin, meaning "rose garden") is usually 59 beads; the Eastern Orthodox use a prayer rope of 100 knots. In Islam, *tasbih*[24] are strings, usually of 99 beads completed with one large bead, used for chanted remembrance of one of the Ninety-Nine Names of God or simply "Allah."

---

[22] Many chant the "Hail Mary" in this way; many also are moved to offer it in full-hearted song. One of our favorite recordings of an *Ave Maria* in song can be found at https://www.youtube.com/watch?v=66zUY8UZn4M (accessed June 21, 2021).

[23] From the sixteenth century onwards, rosary recitations have also often included "picture texts" that assisted meditation. Such imagery continues to be used to depict the mysteries of the rosary, even as in Buddhism one may meditate upon a mandala to focus the attention. Hindus and Buddhists have also long used a *japa mala*, a string of 108 beads, held together through a single larger bead known as *meru* ("mountain" or "teacher"), often tied with a tassle, to count repetitions of a mantra (a holy phrase of remembrance) and to assist in being attentive to each breath in meditation. The earliest usage of prayer beads probably goes back to Hindu practice in India; Buddhism, as it evolved, included this practice. The word *mala* in Sanscrit means "a garland." Through this garden of remembrance, one aims to achieve the realization—*samadhi*—of the interconnectedness of all things, as part of the all-pervading Divine Essence.

[24] *Tasbih* derives from the word *subhan*, "glory and praise" to God, which also has the meaning of "to travel swiftly," indicating how our praise of God carries us swiftly into that Holy Presence.

According to the Dominican tradition, the Rosary prayer was gifted to St. Dominic, the inspirer of their Order, by Beloved Mary when she appeared to him in the church of Prouille, France, in 1214 CE and encouraged him to recite and share the Angelic Psalter, a rosary of 150 Hail Mary's.[25] The practice of the Rosary prayers was also transmitted by Brother Alanus de Rupe, another Dominican, beginning in 1460 CE, following a vision he had that encouraged its use and intimating fifteen promises from Beloved Mary regarding its benefit and blessing. St. Louis de Montfort, another Catholic priest (1673–1716 CE) devoted to Beloved Mary who encouraged the Rosary Prayers, wrote two books instructing people in meditation with the Rosary, *God Alone* and *Secret of the Rosary*, within which he reminded the faithful of the importance of purity of intention and attention in prayer. Rosary prayers have also been encouraged by the Franciscans[26] since the fifteenth century in the form of the Crown Rosary. Though the origin of the rosary prayers has been attributed to a number of the devoted who deeply felt the balm of her presence, it is also acknowledged by many that the use of the Rosary in remembrance of Beloved Mary has been in practice in some form since the 800's CE. Based on the process of *Lectio Divina*,[27] these prayers have long been a source of blessing for the deepening of meditation and contemplation. As Padre Pio,[28] a

---

[25] St. Dominic emphasized a way of simplicity, humility, and charity, and encouraged prayer, study, and preaching of the Word. He would not sleep on a bed, but rather on the ground. When he reached the edge of a town, he would remove his sandals and walk barefoot as he entered. As he walked, he prayed continually, or taught those near him as he walked. Rosary devotions had existed before his time, but it is told that he introduced this extended form. Another Dominic, Dominic of Prussia, a Carthusian monk (1384–1460 CE), is also known for spreading the use of the rosary, a rosary of fifty Hail Mary's each followed by a reference to a moment in the life of Christ, son of Beloved Mary.

[26] See p. 18 of this text.

[27] "Lectio Divina, literally meaning 'divine reading,' is an ancient practice of praying the Scriptures. During Lectio Divina, the practitioner listens to the text of the Bible with the 'ear of the heart,' as if he or she is in conversation with God." See https://www.contemplativeoutreach.org/lectio-divina-contemplation/ (accessed May 13, 2021).

[28] St. Padre Pio was an Italian priest born in 1887 who was known for his charity and love for all around him. He had joined the Capuchin Order, becoming a priest in 1910, and dedicated himself to extreme poverty, strictness, and simplicity,

rosary devotee, once said, "Through the study of books one seeks God; by meditation one finds Him."

In recent centuries, the spread of the devotion to the Rosary prayers was encouraged further by the appearance of Beloved Mary holding a rosary at Lourdes, France, in 1858 CE and in Fátima, Portugal, in 1917. Near Lourdes, in a cave grotto, she appeared to Bernadette Soubirous, an illiterate, teenage village girl, as she was out collecting firewood with her sister. The beautiful lady indicated to Bernadette where a hidden spring was near, and told her to drink from it. When word of repeated appearances spread, pilgrims began to arrive and miraculous healings to occur; the flowing water continues to be treasured. It is interesting to note that the shape of the cave around Beloved Mary's illuminated presence there, remembered now with the placement of a statue, evokes the *vesica piscis* shape of the Virgin of Guadalupe *tilma*, the shape of the seed, the basic structure underlying the "Flower of Life." In 1917, during Beloved Mary's appearance to three Portuguese children in the village of Fátima in west-central Portugal, she again appeared enfolded in brilliant white, holding a rosary, and referred to herself as "The Lady of the Rosary." For the blessing of her presence there, she has also come to be known as "Our Lady of Fátima."[29]

So many others have felt the blessed support of her presence, in many regions of this world. St. Thomas Aquinas[30] and St. Bernard

---

living as closely to St. Francis' ideals as possible. Like St. Francis, he too experienced the stigmata wounds, beginning in 1918 until just before his death in 1968, when as miraculously as they had come, they disappeared.

[29] See pp. 374–76 of this text.

[30] St. Thomas Aquinas (1225–1274 CE) is considered to be one of the greatest Catholic theologians and philosophers, one of the now 36 "Doctors of the Church." Among the 36, the list also now includes four women: Catherine of Siena, Teresa of Ávila, Thérèse of Lisieux, and Hildegard of Bingen. St. Thomas encourages prayer to Mary: "for in every danger you can obtain salvation from this glorious Virgin [and] in every work of virtue you can have Mary as your helper [for] she truly says of herself, 'I am the Mother of fair love, and of fear, and of knowledge, and of holy hope, in me is all grace of the way; in me is all hope of life and of virtue' [Ecclesiasticus 24:24–25]."

See St. Thomas Aquinas, *Meditations*, selected by P. D. Mezard, O. P., adapted and translated by E. C. McEnery, O. P., new and revised ed. (Columbus, Ohio: College Book Co., 1941), 103. The selected meditations are mostly from the

*Our Lady of Lourdes, remembered at Lourdes, France*

of Clairvaux[31] were both devoted to Beloved Mary. St. Bernard counseled:

> Look to the "Star of the Sea," call upon Mary . . . in danger, in distress, in doubt, think of Mary, call upon Mary. May her name never be far from your lips, or far from your heart . . . If you follow her, you will not stray; if you pray to her, you will not despair; if you turn your

---

*Summa* as well as from his *Commentary on the Angelic Salutation, Namely, The Hail Mary!*, and his *Commentaries on Sacred Scripture.*

[31] Saint Bernard (1090–1153 CE) founded the monastery of Clairvaux (Claire Vallée) in 1115 and revitalized Benedictine monasticism through the newly awakening Cistercian Order. Considered to be one of the foremost "Doctors" of the church, Bernard preached an immediate faith for which Beloved Mary was the inspiration. He encouraged silence, humility, and purity of heart in emulation of her devotion. At the Council of Troyes in 1128, Bernard presented the outline of the "Rule of the Knights Templar" which became the ideal of Christian nobility; his work assisted in inspiring the building of the magnificent cathedrals dedicated to Beloved Mary.

> thoughts to her, you will not err. If she holds you, you will not fall; if she protects you, you need not fear; if she is your guide, you will not tire; if she is gracious to you, you will surely reach your destination.[32]

He said of her further: "In you and for you and from you the kindly hand of the Almighty recreates everything that He has created."[33] And so Bernard would contemplate Mary to learn how to let himself be restored, to be recreated by God.

As Maximus expresses it in *The Life of the Virgin*: "Mary is a Divine gift to humanity and an offering from humanity to God."[34] Even so, the Quran also encourages "*zhikr* Maryam" (*wazhkur fee al kitabi Maryam—Surah Maryam* 19:16); immerse in her presence. Muslims are also encouraged to extend greetings and ask for blessings for Prophet Muhammad. Not only for his sake or for Mary's sake is this done, but because they are channels to the Sea of Divine Grace; when we look to them, through them, we discover God's glory.

Open a window towards God
and begin delighting upon the Face.
The whole business of Love is to make this window in the heart.
For the breast is illumined by the Beauty of the Beloved.
[Rumi, *Mathnawi* VI: 3095–97]

No sound of clapping comes forth from only one hand.
The thirsty man is moaning, "O delicious water!"
The water is calling, "Where is the one who will drink me?"
This thirst in our souls is the magnetism of the Water:
We are Its, and It is ours.
[Rumi, *Mathnawi* III: 4397–99]

Al-Qushayri in his *Risalah* has advised: "Moments belong to those who have hearts, states (*hal*) belong to those who have spirit (*ruh*), and inspirations belong to the people of inner being (*sirr*, "the inner secret"). The

---

[32] Bernard of Clairvaux, also sometimes referred to as "The Troubadour of Mary," exalts her in this homily in Praise of the Virgin Mother: *Hom. II super Missus est*, 17: *PL* 183, 70–7.

[33] *In te et per te ed de te benigna manus omnipotentis quidquid creaverat recreavit.*

[34] Maximus, *The Life of the Virgin*, op. cit., p. 132.

Sufis have said the best act of worship is to count the breaths along with God Glorified and Exalted."

*Say: "Truly, God's guidance is the only guidance:*
*and so we have been called to surrender ourselves*
*to the Sustainer of all the worlds,*
*and to be constant in prayer and conscious of Him:*
*for it is to Him that we shall be gathered together."*
*And He it is who has created the heavens and the earth*
*in accordance with an inner Truth*[35]*—*
*and the Day He says, "Be," it is.*
*His word is the Truth.*
*And His will be the dominion*
*on the Day when the trumpet of resurrection sounds.*
*He knows all that is beyond the reach of a created being's perception,*
*as well as all that can be witnessed:*
*for He alone is Truly Wise, All-Aware.*
[Quran, *Surah al-An'am* 6:71–73]

*O Humankind!*
*Worship your Sustainer,*
*who has created you and those who lived before you,*
*so that you might remain conscious of the One*
*who has made the earth a resting-place for you and the sky a canopy,*
*and has sent water down from the sky*
*and with it brought forth fruits for your sustenance:*
*then don't claim that there is any power that could rival God,*
*when you grasp the Truth.*
[Quran, *Surah al-Baqarah* 2:21–22]

When we "grasp the Truth", we become alive, through the awareness of the Divine Reality, and are enabled to see how that Reality permeates everything and activates, enlivens the continued unfoldings of Being. Even as it says in the Quran, *the future belongs to the God-conscious*!

*As for that [happy] life in the hereafter,*
*We grant it [only] to those who do not seek to exalt themselves on earth,*

---

[35] See also Quran, *Surah Yunus* 10:5.

*nor yet to spread corruption:*
*for the future belongs to the God-conscious.*
[Quran, *Surah al Qasas* 28:83]

What might it mean to be "God-conscious"? Perhaps to have an intrinsic awareness of the inspiration of all things, all Being—beyond names or labels—that Oneness that comprehends all tongues, knows all peoples, every individual, by heart, and is the Source of the emerging "greenness" of all creation.

*You are the One who causes the seeds and kernels to split open*
*and the plants to sprout forth.*[36]
[Quran, *Surah An'am*, "Cattle," 6:95]

Now the parable is this: The seed is the word of God.
[Bible, Gospel of Luke 8:11]

Jesus (the "Word" of God) is recorded as saying, "I am come so that they might have life and have it more abundantly" (Bible, Gospel of John, 10:10). Hildegard of Bingen, the great Christian mystic, speaks of that Force of fertile greenness:

O most powerful path
that has entered into everything
the heights, the earth, and the depths,
you fashion and gather everything
around you:
clouds float, air streams,
stones become wet,
waters create rivers
and the earth perspires greenness.[37]

This is echoed by the eighteenth-century Christian theologian William Law:

---

[36] *Faliqul habbi wan nawa.* In Arabic, the words for "seed" (or "kernel") and "love" come from the same root: *ḥā bā bā*.

[37] Hildegard von Bingen, *Writings of Medieval Women*, translated by Marcelle Thiebaux (New York: Garland Publishing, 1994).

> This world, with all its stars, elements, and creatures, is come out of the invisible world; it has not the smallest thing or the smallest quality of anything but what is come forth from thence.[38]

We can recognize that this is also expressed in the ancient text of the Hindu faith, the Upanishads:

> The Imperishable is the Real. As sparks fly upward from a blazing fire, so from the depths of the Imperishable arise all things. To the depths of the Imperishable they again descend. Self-luminous is that Being, and formless. He dwells within all and without all. . . . From [Him] are born breath, mind, the organs of sense, ether, air, fire, water, and the earth, and [He] binds all these together.[39]

The Quran, also, encourages us to read the "Book of Nature," including the book of our own self, to look within and all around us, to see the *Truth.* It is understood that we cannot "own" Truth, but we can reflect it, we can Be[40] it. We can become the Word we are as spoken by God, *"Be!" and it is*—this Breathing that permeates all that is. Throughout the ages, mystics of all traditions have recognized this. When we are surrendered to that Truth that is at the core of all that exists, all our actions may become in consonance with the Divine Order and Will. Surely Beloved Mary was instructing Jesus, her beloved son, and those around her, by being this emanence of Spirit in presence here, together with him. It would seem that the more people are able to recognize this unitive thread that ties us all together, the greater the possibility for peace—within ourselves and within this world in which

---

[38] William Law (1686–1761 CE), *Selected Mystical Writings*, quoted in Whitall Perry, *A Treasury of Traditional Wisdom* (London, 1971), p. 26. Law's mystic and theological writings influenced Enlightenment thinkers and evangelicals of his era, as well as, with *A Serious Call to a Devout and Holy Life* (1729), the philanthropist and leading proponent of the abolition of the English slave trade, William Wilberforce.

[39] Mundaka Upanishad, II, i: 1–4, as reprinted in *Seeing God Everywhere,* edited by Barry McDonald (World Wisdom, 2003), p. 33. The Upanishad texts were composed by Indian Vedic sages circa 800–400 BCE.

[40]
*For He is the Creator Supreme in skill and knowledge!*
*His Being alone is such that when He wills a thing to be,*
*He but says to it, "Be"—and it is!*
[Quran, *Surah Ya Sin* 36:81–82]

we live. We may each have different names for the Divine Reality, but how could we ever fully name that One who cannot be fully named; though we may approximate, how could we ever fully designate the Source of All Being, especially in any way that would negate another, for truly, we are all in this together: *We have created you [all] from an inner Truth* (Quran, *Surah al-An'am* 6:73).

It feels as though Beloved Mary intrinsically knew this, that she was purely Being in herself, True, and from this deepest Truth breathed through her, gave birth, from the breath of God, breathing Love. Through the eye of her heart, it is possible to see our own shining self, and smile in recognition, feeling that Love. Every soul has an intrinsic need to be known. When we experience our souls as being seen by God, perhaps through the eyes of one of His/Her saints, the soul comes to recognize its own True self and can rest in that Powerful Beauty.

We may contemplate all of creation as symbols—knowing that in contemplating them, in looking through the essence of each thing, each "being" that exists, we may contemplate the Divine; but little by little we, also, come to comprehend that "God" is looking back at us.[41] As the Prophet Muhammad, peace and blessings upon him, indicated, "Pray to God as if you saw Him, because even if you don't see Him, He sees you."

Mevlana Jalaluddin Rumi spoke of this Mysterious Beauty in his discourses:

> Because there is nothing more beautiful than You, I have brought You a mirror so that You can see Your face reflected every moment!
>
> What does God not have? What does He/She need? One must take a polished heart to God so that He/She can see Himself/Herself in it. "God does not look at your forms or at your deeds, but He/She looks at your hearts" [*hadith* of Muhammad].
>
> The city of your dreams
> you found lacking nothing save noble human beings.
> [Al-Mutanabbi]
>
> In a city where you find all the beauties, pleasures, delights and various adornments of nature, you won't find an intelligent person.

[41] See p. 284 of this text regarding *gorushmek*. Surely beloved Mary taught this in every moment of her being: Seeing, being seen.

The Virgin *by Joseph Stella*

Would that it were the other way around! That city is the human being. If it has a hundred thousand accomplishments but not the intrinsic meaning, it would be better for it to be in ruins. If it does have the intrinsic meaning, no matter that it have no external embellishments. The *mysterion* must be there for it to flourish. In whatever state man may be, his *mysterion* is concerned with God, and his external preoccupations in no way hinder that inner concern. In whatever state a pregnant woman may be—war or peace, eating or sleeping—the baby is growing, is being strengthened, and is receiving sensations in her womb. . . . Humankind likewise is "pregnant" with that *mysterion. But the human being undertook [the faith]: truly he/she was unjust to himself/herself, and foolish* [33:72], but God does not leave a person in his/her injustice and foolishness. If out of the human being's apparent burden come companionship, sympathy, and a thousand acquaint-

> ances, then consider what marvelous friendships and acquaintances will issue out of the *mysterion* to which the human being gives birth after death. The *mysterion* is necessary in order for a human being to flourish. It is like the root of a tree: although it is hidden from view, its effects are apparent on the branches. Even if one or two branches break off, when the root is strong the tree will continue to grow.[42]

And in that growth, as we extend more and more truly into the depths of our rootedness, and open our arms to the embrace of the Sun and Rain of Reality, through the grace of that Ever-Generous Source, we may come to fulfill the *Hadith Qudsi* conveyed by Muhammad: God says,

> When My faithful servant draws near to Me through his or her voluntary devotions, then I love him/her and I become the ear with which he/she hears, the eye with which he/she sees, the tongue with which he/she speaks, the hand with which he/she grasps, the foot with which he/she walks.[43]

When we are in connection with the root, the sap flows, and all that is experienced can be recognized as sacred, a gift from the Divine Reality. We recognize the communication of the Unseen permeating our existence.

It is interesting to note that one of the most renowned of the ten appearances officially recognized by the Catholic Church as truly miraculous "Marian Apparitions" is the appearance of Beloved Mary as "Our Lady of Fátima." When Beloved Mary appeared to the three children in Portugal in 1917, near the small village of Fátima, named after the Prophet Muhammad's daughter, the appearance was subsequently witnessed again by tens of thousands of people. Since that event, numerous Christians worldwide address the Virgin Mary in prayer as "Our Lady of Fátima," further interweaving hearts of the Abrahamic faiths.

On May 13, 1917, at Cova da Iria, in Fátima, Portugal, the Virgin Mary appeared to three young children while they were tending sheep on the hillside. They had bent to look into a well located on the family property, when they saw in the water an apparition of a beautiful woman with a rosary in her hand. Suddenly sensing a storm bursting over them,

---

[42] Mevlana Jalaluddin Rumi, *Fihi ma Fihi*, Discourse 50, *Signs of the Unseen*, op. cit., pp.195–96 (adapted by the author).
[43] This *hadith* is noted in the *hadith* collection by Bukhari. See p. 453 of this text.

*Our Lady of Fátima*

and seeking shelter from the rain among the trees they again saw her, hovering in the air above a tree, within a beautiful ball of light; they heard her reassure them not to fear, saying to them, "I come from heaven."

This vision of Beloved Mary had been preceded by visits to the children from angelic presences in the spring of 1916, when Lúcia Dos Santos was nine years old and her cousins Francisco and Jacinta Marto were eight and six. The Angel of Peace had prepared them. His luminous presence, Lúcia described as "like snow that the sun shines through until it becomes crystalline."[44] This brilliant presence had told them who he was and encouraged them not to fear but to pray with him. Kneeling on the ground, he prostrated himself until his forehead touched it, saying:

"My God, I believe, I adore, I hope, and I love You! I beg pardon of You for those who do not believe, do not adore, do not hope, and do

---

[44] William Thomas Walsh, *Our Lady of Fátima* (New York: Image Books, Doubleday, 1990), p. 36.

not love You!"[45] Lúcia later wrote, "It was so intense that we were almost unaware of our own existence for a long space of time."[46] They continued praying in this way.

Then in mid-May when again they returned to the hill, flashes of light had preceded Beloved Mary's arrival. Lúcia described her appearance as "a Lady all of white, more brilliant than the sun dispensing light, clearer and more intense than a crystal cup full of crystalline water penetrated by the rays of the most glaring sun."[47] Beloved Mary encouraged them to pray the Rosary to assist in the ending of World War I, to pray for peace, and gave instruction in what would become known as the "Decade Prayer." Over the next few months, Beloved Mary appeared to the children six times, on the thirteenth of each subsequent month; the completion visit was to be on 13th of October.

As word of the appearances spread, thousands of people gathered to accompany the children each month, until for this last visit 70,000 people came together, awaiting in prayer as the rain poured down that day. Suddenly, they witnessed the sun emerge, spinning, radiating bands of light that colored the clouds, the sky, the trees, and everyone gathered there. Then for some moments the sun stilled, and again it began to whirl down through the sky as though it would fall upon them; people fell to their knees in intensified prayer. The children saw again Our Lady dressed in white like a brilliant sun herself, with a mantle of blue, communicating with them by heart. The sun then returned to its place in the heavens and people began to realize that their clothing had completely dried.

On the 17th of October, *O Dia*, a major Lisbon newspaper, reported the following:

> At one o'clock in the afternoon, midday by the sun, the rain stopped. The sky, pearly gray in color, illuminated the vast arid landscape with a strange light. The sun had a transparent gauzy veil so that eyes could easily be fixed upon it. The gray mother-of-pearl tone turned into a sheet of silver which broke up as the clouds were torn apart and the silver sun, enveloped in the same gauzy gray light, was seen to whirl and turn in the circle of broken clouds. A cry went

---

45 Ibid.

46 Ibid., p. 37.

47 Ibid., p. 50.

> up from every mouth and people fell on their knees on the muddy ground. The light turned a beautiful blue as if it had come through the stained-glass windows of a cathedral and spread itself over the people who knelt with outstretched hands. The blue faded slowly and then the light seemed to pass through yellow glass. Yellow stains fell against white handkerchiefs, against the dark skirts of women. They were reported on the trees, on the stones and on the serra. People wept and prayed with uncovered heads in the presence of the miracle they had awaited.[48]

The village of Fátima soon became a pilgrimage site and in the 1920's a chapel dedicated to Beloved Mary, "Our Lady of Fátima" was built there. Bishops and Popes have declared the genuineness of the miracles that occurred there, and every year thousands make the annual pilgrimages to celebrate her appearances on the thirteenth day of each month from May to October. Though the rosary had been devotedly used with prayer for centuries, this Marian Apparition also became known as "Our Lady of the Rosary" because of her encouragement of its use. How remarkable that Beloved Mary should appear in a town called "Fátima", as though Mary herself was demonstrating how close in spirit she and Fatimah are.

Fatimah, may God preserve her secret, the youngest daughter of Muhammad and his beloved wife Khadijah, may peace and blessings be upon them both, was known among the early Muslim community as the "Resplendent One" (*az-Zuhra*) because of her luminous face which seemed to radiate light.[49] It is said that when she stood for prayer, the *mihrab* would reflect the light of her countenance. She was also called "*al-Batul*" (the "Virgin", the "Devoted One") because of her asceticism and devotion. She spent a great deal of her time in prayer and worship[50] and recitation of the Quran, in fasting, and in service to the growing Muslim community. She was five years old at the time of the opening of Muhammad's prophethood, was the youngest "Muslim," and so grew up under the dynamic influence of the new Message that was being conveyed,

---

[48] https://www.ewtn.com/fatima/sixth-apparition-of-our-lady.asp and http://francismary.org/miracle-of-the-dancing-sun-at-fatima-eye-witness-accounts/ (accessed April 28, 2020). See Extended Context Notes in Appendix, Star XII, 2.

[49] See "Fatima bint Muhammad" in Alim 6.0 (educational software).

[50] *Ibadah*: "worship and servanthood."

along with her sisters Zaynab, Ruqayyah, and Umm Kulthum, and their beloved mother Khadijah.

Though Muhammad (peace and blessings be upon him) had previously been quite beloved by the people of Mecca as one of the most trusted and respected men, of the noble Quraysh tribe, and his dear wife Khadijah was one of the most respected among the noble women of Mecca, once he began sharing the revelations he was receiving, the family were shunned; garbage was thrown upon him and people jeered at him continually. Even so, little by little some hearts among the people of Mecca were drawn to the truth of the message he was conveying. These, too, were ostracized, and as the community of the faithful gained momentum, a boycott was placed upon them all; ostracized, food, and even water, became scarce for them. Occasionally someone would take pity and send a camel laden with supplies in their direction. Fatimah was about sixteen when, due to the harsh measures of the boycott, her beloved mother Khadijah died. She witnessed her older sisters' health also fail. From the extent of her love and affection for her father, and the fact that she was always with him and trying to defend him, just as a mother guards her child, even so she became known as *"Umm Abiha"* ("Mother of her Father") by the *sahaba* ("close companions") and later scholars. The Prophet Muhammad would say, "Fatimah is a part of me."

After some years of persecution, when she was eighteen, they emigrated to Medina, invited by the tribes there to come in refuge.[51] The Prophet Muhammad was of the last to leave Mecca, after the rest of the community had safely departed. When word reached the Muslims in Medina that he was approaching, the community came out to welcome him. The women stood on the rooftops with their hand drums waiting for him, and, when he was perceived, burst forth in song—"*Tala'a al Badru 'Alaynaa*" ("The full moon has ascended!")—a song that is still much beloved.[52] Surely Fatimah was among them, singing with joy, and of the first to greet him.

Fatimah was then married to Ali, the cousin and close companion of Muhammad, whom he had also raised within their own household. Slowly the community developed and the numbers of the faithful swelled; many of the poor and former slaves joined the community. Known for

[51] See p. 132 and p. 423 of this text.

[52] See *Tala'a al Badru*, in "Songs of Love," p. 420.

her refined manners and gentle speech, Fatimah is remembered as being especially kind to the poor and indigent folk; none who came to her door ever went away empty handed. So compassionate was she that she would often give all the food she had to those in need even if she herself remained hungry. The name "Fatimah" also has the meaning of "one who abstains" as well as "one who weans a child."

Over the subsequent years, she and Ali had four children: two boys, Hasan and Husain, and two girls, Zaynab, and Umm Kulthum. Imam Husain would later remember, "I often witnessed my mother absorbed in prayer from dusk to dawn." During the days, she would grind grain, fetch water from the well, and cook their meals. As her health had been greatly weakened by the years of deprivation of the boycott, she began to tire more quickly. Ali, who labored carrying water, suggested she go to her father to ask for someone to assist them. She started to go, but she got only partway there before she was overcome and felt she couldn't ask, so she returned home again. Ali inquired what happened. She said, "I just couldn't quite bear to ask." So, he said, "Perhaps you should try again." So she went back, and this time she spoke to her father and asked if they might have someone to help them with their work. He paused and said, "You know, there are poor people who need help more, and especially the *ahli suffa* ['people of the bench']." These were those who remained immersed in prayer on a bench platform near the mosque, who are referred to as some of the earliest Sufis, the early mystics of Islam.

Fatimah recognized the truth of what he was saying and quietly returned home, but later that evening there was a knock on the door of their hut, and she and Ali heard the voice of the Prophet Muhammad. They called to him to enter, and when they started to rise, he said, "No, please just stay as you are." He continued, "Would you like to know something that would be of even more help than the support for which you asked?" They responded, "Of course." And so he recommended that they recite thirty-three times each: *Subhanallah* ("Glory be to God"), *Alhamdullilah* ("All Praise be to God"), and *Allahu Akbar* ("God is Greater") before going to bed.

Ali, who outlived Fatimah by many years, later related that he never once missed offering this recitation from then on for the rest of his life, and he spoke of what a support it was. This recitation continues to be offered by many Muslims after every ritual prayer, and it is often referred to as

*Hand of Fatimah Blessing*

the "*Tasbih* of Fatimah", counted by hand with the fingers or with accompanying prayer beads. Fatimah's blessing continues to this day, and is also remembered within the beautiful tradition of the "Hand of Blessing."[53]

---

[53] There is a great use of the intertwining of calligraphic, geometric, and floral forms of nature to symbolize the infinitude of the Divine. Within some schools of Islamic thought, human representation is discouraged, and especially the facial features of the Prophets and sometimes the saints, are not rendered in particulars, but rather represented with Light.

Many versions of this symbol of Fatimah's blessing adorn doorways, rooms, and vehicles, and are also worn as protection, on clothing or incorporated into jewelry, throughout the Middle East and around the world. (See also p. 134 of this text.) For some, the Hand of Fatimah is also a reminder of the five daily prayer remembrances and the "Five Pillars" of Islam—the profession of faith (*shahada,* witnessing to the Divine Reality and Muhammad, peace and blessings be

When her beloved father, Prophet Muhammad died, Fatimah was 28; it was she who offered his eulogy to the community. She opened with these words:

> Praise to Allah for that which He bestowed. We thank and praise Him for all that which He inspired and offered, for the abundant boons which He initiated, the perfect grants which He presented. Such boons are too many to compute, too vast to measure. Their limit is too distant to grasp. He commended them (to His creatures) so they would gain more by being grateful for their continuity.
>
> He ordained Himself praiseworthy by giving generously to His creatures. I testify that there is no God but God, the One without a partner: sincere devotion is its interpretation, the hearts guarantee its continuation, and in minds and hearts is its perpetuation. He is the One who cannot be perceived with vision, nor can He be described by any tongue, nor can the imagination encompass how He is.

One morning, less than six months after the Prophet's passing, Fatimah smiled, knowing her moment had also arrived. She bathed her children, made her ablutions, and lay to rest under the open sky of the courtyard of their little abode. She called for Ali and commended their children to his care, and with one last breath of Love returned to her Lord.

It is related that Prophet Muhammad before his own death had told his daughter Fatimah, "You shall be the most blessed of women in Paradise, after Mary." And now, Beloved Mary is well-known around the world as "Our Lady of Fátima." Surely Beloved Mary's appearance at Fátima, Portugal, is a renewed sign for the unity of spirit among Muslims and Christians, a gift from this Mother of Spirit who continues to bring together people of varied cultures, times, and place.

In earlier centuries, Portugal and Spain had long been lands of intermingled Christians and Muslims, who shared the love of Beloved Mary. Alfonso X (1252–1284 CE), *El Sabio* ("The Wise"), co-authored the vast collection of *Cantigas de Santa Maria* (*Songs to the Virgin Mary*),[54] one of the

---

upon him, as God's messenger), prayer (*salaat*), fasting (*sawm*), charity (*zakat*), and pilgrimage (*Hajj*)—that together bring blessing for one's life, here and hereafter. And at the center is the "Eye of God."

[54] See "The Oxford Cantigas de Santa Maria" database, http://csm.mml.ox.ac.uk/ (accessed April 21, 2021), and http://cantigasdesantamaria.

first works to be written in the vernacular Galician-Portuguese language, including 420 poems with beautifully illuminated musical notation, many regarding the miracles of Mary, including his own healing through Beloved Mary at what became known as "Puerto de Santa Maria" ("The Doorway of Saint Mary"). He established his own *scriptorium* in Toledo, with Muslim, Christian, and Jewish scholars assisting in translation of important texts, many of which had been preserved for years in Arabic; this was a major source of dissemination throughout Europe[55] of these treasures of ancient knowledge including medical theory and astronomy. Though he may not have fully comprehended the extent of the love of Beloved Mary in the heart of a Muslim, he acknowledged her capacity to come to the aid of anyone who sincerely called upon her, no matter what their faith. As well as scholars, he employed Christian, Muslim, and Jewish poets, artists, and musicians; under his auspices the Mary songs were gathered, some of his own composing, offerings of love to the one to whom he was devoted.

In those eras, devotion to the Virgin Mary went hand-in-hand with the revalorization of beauty—the honoring of the feminine, restoration of human dignity and the principles of chivalry, of "right action." In the legal code Alfonso established, *Las Siete Partidas*,[56] he was also influenced by Islamic practice and ideals, including principles of chivalrous behavior (*futtuwah*) and careful cleanliness as preparedness for prayer that were embedded in Islamic culture.

In those "Middle Ages," one of the most important pilgrimage sites in all of Europe was Rocamadour, a cliffside oratory dedicated to

---

com/ as well as https://www.oxfordbibliographies.com/view/document/obo-9780195396584/obo-9780195396584-0210.xml (accessed December 20, 2018).

[55] It was through sharing knowledge with his sister, Eleanor of Castile, Queen of England, the beloved wife of Edward I, that many of these works found their way into England and European courts. Well-educated, Eleanor could herself read and write, at a time when even kings were still illiterate. Her own love of knowledge was so passionate that she maintained her own *scriptorium*, the only one in all of northern Europe at that time.

[56] Perhaps Alfonso's devotion to Beloved Mary also inspired the composition of the legal code he established in his efforts toward greater universal justice for his people, including greater rights for women. Known as *Las Siete Partidas*, these principles are part of the foundation of the laws of Spain and were also incorporated into the early legal structure of the United States of America. See Extended Context Notes in Appendix, Star XII, 3.

Beloved Mary.[57] In 1166 CE, in a cliff opening, the ancient body of a man was found that was incorrupt and around whom miracles began to occur. Tradition relates that the body of the hermit discovered there was that of St. Amadour who had been a disciple of Jesus.[58] It is said that Beloved Mary had sent him to France where he became a hermit in the mountains, anchoring the rocks of the mountainside in prayer, and so this mountain oratory had become known as "Roc Amadour." Some say that while there he carved a wooden statue of Beloved Mary, a Madonna enthroned in wisdom, in remembrance, by this lover (*amadour*) of God. Many miracles have occurred there over the centuries in relation to this simple wooden statue and the loving presence of Our Lady.[59]

This ancient statue of Our Lady, the Black Madonna of Rocamadour, and the renowned statue, sculpted in Japan in the seventh century, of Maitreya Buddha—which suddenly presented itself for the first time into our awareness as we began to complete this chapter of the journey with Beloved Mary, as though at her invitation—bear such a striking resemblance to each other, not just in facial features, but even more impressive in the similarity of their presence, the inner attunement conveyed. December 8, the day Roman Catholic Christians observe the feast day of the Immaculate Conception of Mary, is also commemorated by Buddhists as Bodhi Day,

---

[57] During the Middle Ages, Rocamadour was one of three prominent pilgrim destinations along with the Holy Land and Santiago de Compostela located in what is now Spain. (Santiago de Compostela is where St. James the Greater, apostle of Jesus, was buried, whose tomb was rediscovered in the ninth century. The town grew up around it and walking journeys along the Camino de Santiago from France, over the Pyrenees 760 km to Santiago, have been endeavored for centuries by pilgrims who carry the symbol of the scallop shell, from the sea.)

[58] Some traditions relate that "St. Amadour" was Zacchaeus, a disciple of Jesus, mentioned in the Gospel of Luke 19:1–10, and that his wife was Veronica, who attempted to relieve the suffering of Christ by soothing his face as he was carrying his cross. It is said they journeyed together to France and that it was after her passing that St. Amadour became a hermit in the hills and built his oratory dedicated to Beloved Mary, that he might immerse in prayer, in the heights where eagles soared.

[59] *Our Lady of Rocamadour*, carved simply in walnut wood, tradition says was originally carved by St. Amadour, in the first century CE; the beloved statue on the following page, a copy some say of a lost original, has been dated to at least the thirteenth century.

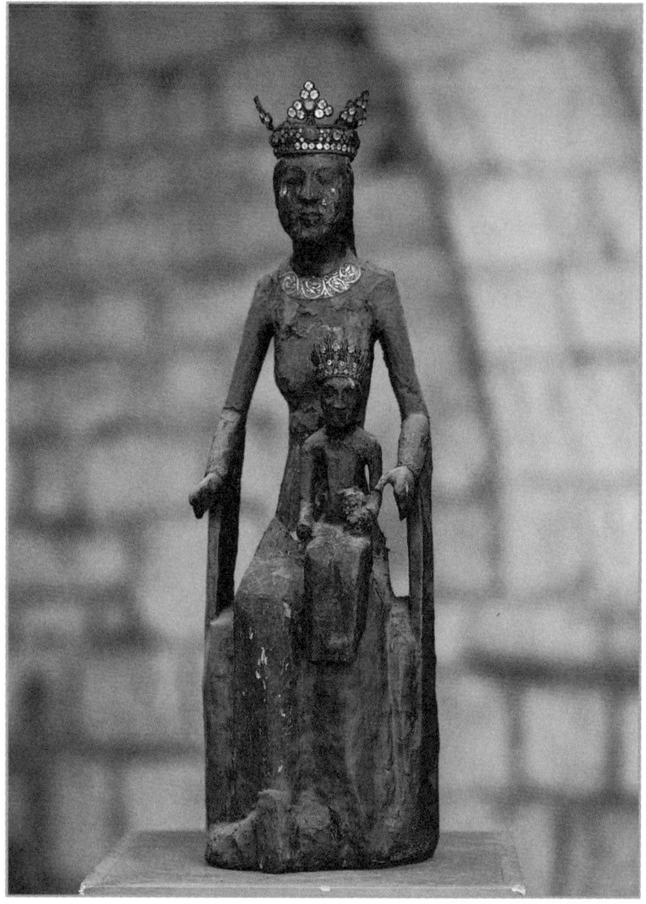

Our Lady of Rocamadour

the day when Siddhartha Gautama became enlightened and began to be known as the "Buddha." The title "Buddha" means "Awakened One."[60] It

[60] About 2,500 years ago, in approximately 500 to 400 BCE, the young Indian prince, Siddhartha (a Sanskrit name meaning "he who achieves his aim") left his palace and chose to live as an ascetic; still not achieving his aim, he then chose to leave behind even the ascetic life to meditate underneath a Bodhi tree (see p. 330, n. 75 of this text), vowing to remain there until he found true enlightenment. He experienced an intense inner journey that tested him to his very core

Miroku (Maitreya) in Meditation
*Gilt bronze, Japanese, Asuka period, seventh century* CE.

---

until at last he was able to see how everyone and everything is connected, interdependent. His enlightenment, often depicted with a radiant lotus rising from his crown chakra (see p. 252 and p. 435 of this text), brought him the realization of the "Four Noble Truths" (there is suffering; there is the arising of suffering; there is the cessation of suffering; there is a path to the ceasing of suffering) and the "Eight-Fold Path" (as a way of perfection and freedom from suffering). See Extended Context Notes in Appendix, Star XII, 4.

In the Buddhist tradition, it is understood that Buddhas, "Awakened Ones," are not reborn after they die, but rather enter a state of nirvana ("passing away," beyond suffering), in a manner similar one might consider to the Assumption

seems it is more than coincidence that these two beings of light share this day of celebration.

Within the Mevlevi Sufi path, in the dervish lodge or *tekkye*, if there were a need to awaken a sleeping person, in order not to startle the person, one would go slowly near his or her bed, tap lightly on the pillow with the tips of one's fingers, and then softly call, "*Agah ol, erenler*" ("Be aware, O attained ones"). This phrase *Agah ol* has the meaning of "come to yourself," or "awaken your consciousness," even as was the practice of Buddha—awaken! Awaken to the Light!

Our original food is the light of God.<br>
Living on material food alone is not for us,<br>
but some disease has caused<br>
our minds to fall into this delusion

---

of Christ. The next "Buddha" who was expected to come was to be known as Maitreya (derived from the Sanskrit word *maitri,* meaning "friendship"). Some feel Jesus, the Messiah, might have been this next Buddha. It was foretold of Maitreya that his followers would lead the holy life of oneness under his guidance.

There are some who consider that Jesus might have journeyed to India during the silent years, as trading caravans frequently went there from the Holy Land, traveling along the silk routes. As we have mentioned, spikenard was one of the precious commodities conveyed. It is also noted in the Gospel of John that Apostle Thomas was late returning at the time of the passing of Beloved Mary because he had been in India. One might even consider that the Maitreya Buddha of Compassion, the one renewing the teachings of the "Awakened One," bringing the community into Oneness, would be a being similar to Beloved Mary herself—overflowing with compassion, quietly present, radiant. There is also within Buddhism a comprehension of the feminine aspect of this bodhisattva as Avalokiteshvara (also known as Guanyin), the bodhisattva of Infinite Compassion and Mercy (see illustrations on pp. 384–85 and p. 302).

The Bodhi Tree ("Tree of Awakening") was an ancient, sacred fig tree belonging to the *ficus religiosa* family. The descendent of the original tree of the Buddha continues to grow in the spot of the Buddha's Awakening at the Mahabodhi ("Great Awakening") Temple in Bodh Gaya, India. The Bodhi tree leaves are heart-shaped; it is a favorite leaf chosen by painters for illumination, as with the beautiful *Eleusa* icon of Beloved Mary.

Some of the teaching stories of the lives of the Buddha have been beautifully retold for children by a Sufi woman of the twentieth century, Noor Inayat Khan, in *Twenty Jataka Tales.*

that day and night we should eat only that food.
We become spiritually pale, weak, and faint:
where is the food of *heaven's starry tracks*?[61]
That is the food of the chosen,
food eaten without fork or throat.
[Rumi, *Mathnawi* II: 1083–86]

Mouthfuls of food are the gift of every tree bearing fruit,
but the gift of a throat is from God alone.
He bestows a throat on the body and the spirit;
He gives an appropriate throat to every part of you.
[Rumi, *Mathnawi* III:17–18]

We are so graced to be able to catch the Light, to catch the fragrance of roses, to be nourished in so many ways. Even as roses are everywhere in the stories and appearances of Beloved Mary, roses also blossom throughout moments of the Mevlevi tradition that opened with the example of Mevlana Jalaluddin Rumi. Even if one visits his tomb now in Konya, one passes through a garden of roses, in this land of Anatolia (land "full of mothers") that bursts forth with roses everywhere in the spring. The fragrance of roses has also long been associated with saints in the Islamic tradition.

One of Mevlana's chief disciples was Fakhr an-Nisa. She was known as the saintly Rabi'a[62] of her age, in that era of the thirteenth century. Some years ago, for various reasons of renovation and road rerouting, it was decided to reconstruct her tomb. As our Shaikh Suleyman Hayati Dede was then the acting spiritual head of the Mevlevi order in Konya, he was asked to be present when she was exhumed. He told of how, when

---

[61] Quran, *Surah adh-Dhariyat* 51:7.

[62] As the mystical side of Islam developed, it was a woman, Rabi'a al-'Adawiyya (717–801 CE), who first clearly expressed the relationship with the Divine in the language we have come to recognize as particularly Sufic, by referring to God as "the Beloved." Rabi'a was the first human being to speak of the realities of Sufism with a clear language that anyone could understand. Though she experienced many difficulties in her early years, Rabi'a's starting point was neither fear of hell, nor desire for paradise, but only love. Her method was love for God because "God is God; for this I love God . . . not because of any gifts, but for Itself." Her aim was to melt her being in God. According to her, one could find God by turning within oneself.

her body was uncovered, it was totally intact even after seven hundred years, and the fragrance of roses filled the air.

Within the Mevlevi Tradition, the mystic path founded upon the example of Mevlana Jelaluddin Rumi, women have always been deeply respected, honored, and invited to participate in all aspects of the spiritual path; there have been female Mevlevi shaikhas (spiritual teachers) who have guided both women and men. Mevlana himself had many female disciples, and women were also encouraged to participate in *sema*, the musical whirling ceremony of the Mevlevis. *Sema* or *sam'a*, means "listening." *As-Sami* is a name of God, the "All-Hearing." The term was adopted by Mevlevis to refer to the sacred whirling ceremony, which also is called a *mukabele*, or "meeting face to face," reminding the soul of the meeting with God, and the possibility of seeing the Divine, the Light of God, within all.

A story is told of one particular gathering filled with the fragrance of roses. At the time of Mevlana, on Thursday evenings, all the noble ladies of Konya would go to the house of the Sultan's representative, Aminuddin Mika'il, for a gathering led by his wife. They begged her to invite Mevlana, because they knew that he held her in special regard and referred to her as *Shaikh-i Khawatin*, "Spiritual Director of Ladies." When this gathering had begun and everyone was concentrated in tranquil presence (*huzur*), Mevlana, himself, without anyone informing him of the request, arrived just after the night prayer, all alone.

He sat down in the middle of the ladies who made a circle around him; the husbands formed a protective circle outside, engaging together in spiritual conversation. Inside, at the center of the circle, until the middle of the night, Mevlana shared divine insights, secrets of Spirit (*Ruh*), and moral council; the dear ladies scattered rose water and cast rose petals over him as keepsakes of blessing, and then he began to whirl in *sema* until just before the dawn prayer.

The beautiful rose windows of the Gothic cathedrals of the Middle Ages, most of which were dedicated to Beloved Mary, were transparent to the dancing light. Over the centuries, numerous churches and cathedrals have been built and dedicated in honor of Beloved Mary, on every continent now, including Antarctica. The iconic Notre Dame ("Our Lady") Cathedral in Paris is anchored with twin towers and opens to the light through a stunningly beautiful rose window.

Another of the first to include such a rose window was the Cathedral of Chartres in France, where the veil (*Sancta Camisa*) of Beloved Mary rests. It is told that this relic of the "Veil of Mary" had come into the hands of Byzantine Empress Irene, who gifted it to Charlemagne. In 876 CE, his grandson, Charles the Bald, gave it as a gift, wrapped in Damascene silk, to Chartres Cathedral, dedicated to "Our Lady." It is said to be the cloth Mary was wearing when she gave birth to Jesus, that has brought blessing to many over the centuries. Mary, herself, was said to have been a weaver of cloth from the time she was serving in the Temple. There is a long tradition among women of the Holy Land, whether Jewish, Christian, or Muslim, of offering prayers, moment by moment, breath by breath, while spinning, weaving, sewing, and embroidering, imbuing the fabric with prayer.

Current scholarship is acknowledging that the Gothic style of cathedral building may actually have been based on Islamic building techniques brought back from the Holy Land in the thirteenth century, and from the architectural mastery manifest in the Grand Mosque in Cordoba, Spain (just as it is now being remembered that the troubadour traditions of Europe also developed from Sufi poetry to the Beloved, that was carried into Europe from journeys to the Holy Land and from the Moorish culture of Spain). Rose windows with tracery comprised of overlapping arcs like flower petals were opened, often in the main entry wall, to illuminate the inner sanctuary, awakening remembrance of "Our Lady of the Rosary." As the architectural possibilities developed into Rayonnant and Flamboyant Gothic, the windows became more complex with "flames of light" within the rose; many of the largest windows, like those in Sainte-Chapelle and the Cathedral Basilica of Our Lady of Amiens hold such beauties in remembrance of Beloved Mary. A contemporary poet of that era, Dante Alighieri, praised Beloved Mary as the "Rose in which the word of God became flesh."[63]

---

[63] Dante Alighieri (1265–1321 CE), *Paradiso,* 23:73–74. The third, completion portion of his epic poem, *The Divine Comedy*, the *Paradiso* begins with the lines:

> The glory of the One who moves all things
> permeates the universe and shines
> in one part more and in another less. [1:1–3]

The poem climaxes with a beautiful vision of an immense white rose emerging from a ray of heavenly light, with the Virgin Mary at the center. It closes with

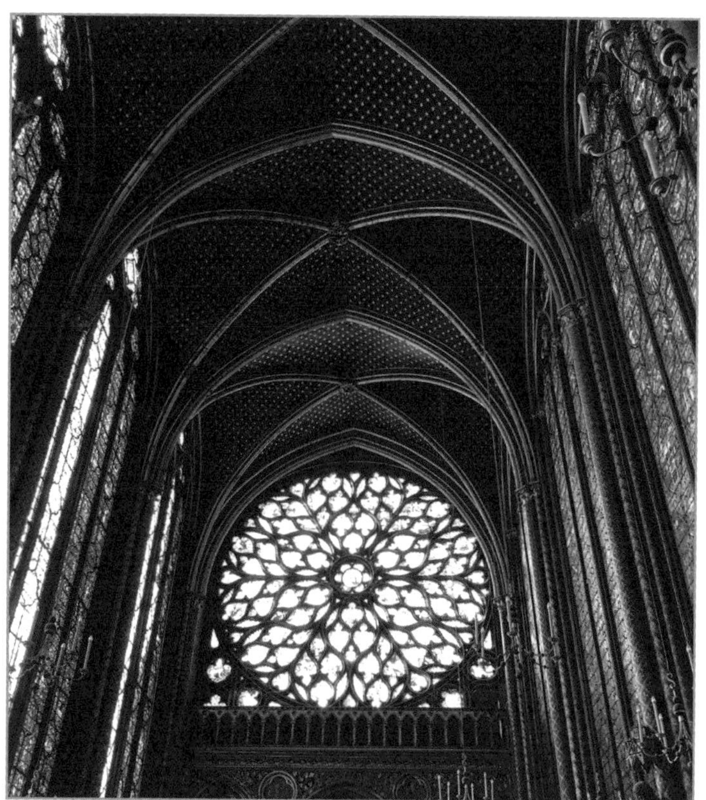

*Rose and Illuminated Windows Amid Starry Heavens*
*Sainte-Chapelle, Paris*

From within the fertile darkness the Light emerges, as though radiating through the Mystery of Beloved Mary's heart. Christian practitioners are often encouraged, "When you arise at night to praise God, recite the matins with such devotion as if you were there at the birth of Jesus"— it is believed to have taken place within that darkness, before the dawn.

As it is said in the Quran, arising at night to offer prayer is of stronger energy, efficacious to the heart and soul, when the mind is more still and open to the intimate whispers of God.[64] Muslims are encouraged to watch for "The Night of Power," like the night of the first opening of

---

remembrance of the reality that all is returning to the One Creator.

[64] Quran *Surah al-Isra'* 17:78–80:

the revelation of the Quran, that took place within the fasting month of Ramadan, when the angelic realms and the supportive presence of the prophets and saints are near, in beautiful friendship of Spirit. It is within *Surah Maryam*, she who held so much within her vast heart, that a beautiful verse occurs encouraging remembrance of many of the prophets, holding their presences within our hearts, even as did Muhammad:

*And call to mind [zhikr],[65] through this divine writ, Moses—*
*behold, he was a chosen one, and was a Messenger of God, a Prophet.*
*And We called upon him from the right-hand slope of Mount Sinai*
*and drew him near in mystic communion,*
*and out of Our grace, We granted unto him his brother Aaron,*
*to be a Prophet [by his side].*
*And call to mind [zhikr], through this divine writ, Ishmael.*
*Behold, he was always true to his promise, and was a Messenger, a Prophet,*
*who used to enjoin upon his people prayer and charity,*
*and found favour in his Sustainer's sight.*
*And call to mind [zhikr], through this divine writ, Idris.*[66]

---

*Be constant in prayer from the time when the sun has passed its zenith till the darkness of night,*
*and [be ever mindful of its] recitation at dawn:*
*for, behold, the recitation at dawn is indeed witnessed [by all that is holy].*
*And rise from your sleep and pray during part of the night [as well], as a free offering,*
*and your Sustainer may well raise you to a glorious station.*
*And say: "O my Sustainer!*
*Cause me to enter [upon whatever I may do] in a manner true and sincere,*
*and cause me to leave [it] in a manner true and sincere,*
*and grant me, out of Your grace, sustaining strength!"*
[Quran *Surah al-Isra'* 17:78–80]

See also Quran, *Surah ad-Dhukan* 44:1–9 and *Surah azh-Zhariyat* 51:15–21 in Extended Context Notes in Appendix, Star XII, 5.

[65] *Zhikr*, i.e. "chant, bring to heart, keep in remembrance, be in Presence with."

[66] Many of the classical Quranic commentators identify the Prophet Idris (also mentioned in Quran 21:85) with the Biblical Enoch (Genesis 5:18–19 and 21–24). Others of the earliest Quranic commentators determined that "Idris" is another name for Ilyas (Greek "Elias" and Hebrew "Elijah" in the Bible). See Quran 37:123 and the Bible I Kings 17 ff. and II Kings 1–2. Both Enoch and Elijah are Hebrew prophets especially renowned for Truth.

*And Zachariah and John and Jesus and Elijah, they were all from among the righteous.*
[Quran, *Surah al-An'am* 6:85]

*Behold, he was a man of truth, a Prophet,*
*whom We exalted to a lofty station.*
*These were some of the prophets upon whom God bestowed His blessings—*
*of the seed of Adam and of those whom We caused to be carried with Noah,*
*and of the seed of Abraham and Israel,*
*and all among those whom We had guided and elected;*
*whenever the messages of the Most Gracious were conveyed unto them,*
*they would fall down in worship, prostrating themselves and weeping.*
*Yet they were succeeded by generations who lost all [inclination to] prayer*
*and followed their own lusts; and these will, in time, meet with utter disillusion*
*Those who turn in remorse and have faith*
*and do the deeds of wholeness and reconciliation:*
*these will enter the Garden, and will not be wronged in any way—*
*Gardens of Eternity,*
*those which the Most Gracious has promised to His servants, in the Unseen:*
*for His promise must be fulfilled.*
*They will not hear any empty talk there*
*but only greetings of peace;*
*and there they will receive their sustenance, morning and evening.*
*Such is the Garden which We bestow as an inheritance*
*upon those of Our Servants who are conscious of Us.*
*[The angels say:] "We descend by command of your Sustainer alone:*
*to Him belongs what lies open before us*
*and what is hidden behind us and what is between;*
*and your Sustainer never forgets,*
*the Sustainer of the heavens and of the earth*
*and of all that is between them.*
*So worship Him and be constant and patient in His worship."*
[Quran, *Surah Maryam* 19:51–64]

It is to children especially that Beloved Mary has been appearing in recent centuries,[67] perhaps because they are less dominated by the world

[67] Another beloved "Marian Apparition" that is still awaiting full recognition, is the appearance of Beloved Mary at the small village of Medjugorje in Bosnia-Herzegovina. Beginning in 1981, over the course of a number of years, six other children experienced the blessing of Beloved Mary's presence. Daily, she spoke to the children through the window of their hearts:

and more clearly able to hear her by heart. They have witnessed her as a beautiful presence, conveying messages of remembrance, to re-educate, and encourage people everywhere to re-center our lives in the Divine Reality, even as in the above passage from *Surah Maryam* that arrived through the heart of the Prophet Muhammad. Prophet Muhammad himself had such great love and respect for Mary that he is recorded as saying she will lead the souls of the blessed to Paradise. Another much beloved *hadith* of Muhammad is:

> The most noble women of humankind are Mary, mother of Jesus, Asiyah, the wife of Pharaoh, Khadijah bint [daughter of] Khuwaylid, and Fatimah, daughter of Muhammad.[68]

There are numerous versions of this *hadith* emphasizing his recognition and love for these four holy women. In another version it is related:

> It was narrated from Anas ibn Malik that the Prophet (peace and blessings of God be upon him) said: "Sufficient for you among the women of the worlds are Maryam the descendant of 'Imran, Asiyah the wife of Pharaoh, Khadijah bint Khuwaylid, and Fatimah bint Muhammad."[69]

How extraordinary and mysterious. An intimation comes to the heart of a human being and something is conveyed. It is noteworthy to recognize here that rather than naming women only of his own community or immediate faith, Muhammad reached back to first include and honor

---

"I have come to tell the world that God exists. He is the fullness of life."

Many beautiful messages have been conveyed over the years of their experience of her presence with them. The validity of the miracles is still being weighed by the Church, but the core of the message remains a blessing and encouragement to Peace within oneself in alignment with God and so within the world. A main theme is that there is only one God, one faith. "In God there are no religions, there are no divisions, but it is human beings who have made divisions." Or as Mevlana Rumi also relates, based on Quranic understanding:

Every prophet and every saint has a way, but all lead to God.
All ways are really one.
[Rumi, *Mathnawi* I: 3086]

68 See Muslim Sahih 4:1886–87; 2430–31.

69 *Hadith* conveyed by Anas ibn Malik in collections of Tirmidhi (narrated and classed as *saheeh* [sound] by al-Tirmidhi, 3878).

Beloved Mary, she of most pure spirit, so open in receptivity, and so strong in her devotion, who gave birth to the "Word of God," Jesus (Isa), the "Messiah". And then the expanse of his heart opened to further remember Asiyah—adoptive mother of Moses[70]—who stood up for love and recognition of the true spirit apparent to her within the Hebrew infant Moses, valiantly protecting this future prophet in the face of Pharaoh's forces of egoistic tyranny; even so, Muhammad's own wife, Khadijah, recognized the truth of Muhammad's own being and steadfastly stood in support of his prophethood in the face of intense persecution as the years unfolded. Prophet Muhammad's youngest daughter, Fatimah, she of radiant light, the "Resplendent One," also revered and devotedly cared for her father as a Messenger of Truth. Mother, adoptive mother, wife, and daughter—of Christianity, Judaism, and Islam—are woven together in the roles of womanhood, beyond time, in the depth of their love and the honoring of Spiritual Reality.

With these words, the Prophet Muhammad was once again affirming the unity of the faith in the *Deen al-Hanifa,* the "Path of Rectitude" of Abraham.[71] He was acknowledging that faith is a matter of heart and inspiration, not the upholding of the status quo, and especially not of oppressive authority. He reached out to include those who stood up for Truth despite the prevailing norms, spanning vast eras and cultures. He included women who on the surface of things one might see as opposites: Beloved Mary, dedicated to God and immersed in remembrance and prayer since birth, with the wife of a pharaoh, a well to-do aristocrat accustomed to great luxury, who nevertheless could turn from the impetus of egoic heedlessness to recognize, nurture, and support a prophet not of her own blood nor

---

[70] In the Quranic version of the story, it is Pharaoh's wife, rather than his daughter, who discovers the infant Moses at the side of the Nile and brings him home to the palace, persuading her husband that they might raise him as their own.

[71] Quran, *Surah al-Baqarah* 2:130–132:

*And who, unless he be weak of mind, would want to abandon Abraham's creed,*
*seeing that We have indeed raised him high in this world,*
*and that, truly, in the life to come he shall be among the righteous?*
*When his Sustainer said to him, "Surrender yourself unto Me!" – he answered,*
*"I have surrendered myself unto [You,] the Sustainer of all the worlds."*
*And this very thing did Abraham bequeath unto his children, and [so did] Jacob:*
*"O my children! Behold, God has granted you the purest faith;*
*so do not allow death to overtake you before you have surrendered yourselves unto Him."*

even of her own people, but of the enslaved Hebrews. In the personage of Beloved Mary, one might recognize an unwed mother who nevertheless deeply and intimately trusted in her Lord, and in Asiyah, an adoptive mother, who recognized the consanguinity of Spirit fluid in all beings.

*Those who are true to their bond with God*
*and do not fail in their pledge;*
*those who keep together what God has commanded to be joined,*
*and stand in awe of their Sustainer and the awesome reckoning to come;*
*those who patiently persevere seeking the Face of their Sustainer,*
*and are constant in prayer,*
*who distribute secretly and openly*
*from what We have given them for their sustenance,*
*and turn away evil with good:*
*for these is the fulfillment of the ultimate Abode—*
*gardens of endless bliss—which they shall enter*
*together with the righteous among their parents,*
*their spouses, and their offspring,*
*and angels shall greet them from every gate:*
*"Peace be with you for having patiently persevered!*
*Then how excellent is the final dwelling-place!"*
[Quran, *Surah ar-Rad* 13:20–24]

*Moses said unto his people: "Turn unto God for aid,*
*and have patience in adversity. Truly, all the earth belongs to God:*
*He gives it as a heritage to such as He wills of His servants;*
*and the future belongs to the God-conscious!*
[Quran, *Surah al-A'raf*, "The Faculty of Discernment," 7:128]

Asiyah, she of deep heart, tried to counsel Pharaoh. The name, "Asiyah" given to this woman of ancient Egyptian roots also has the meaning of "one who tends to the weak and heals them." Mevlana Rumi shares a version of Asiyah's wise plea attempting to call her husband to that "God-consciousness," away from his own self-adulation:

Pharaoh told Asiyah of what Moses had said.
She said, "O black-hearted one, surrender your soul to this!
Behind these words of Moses is God's Grace:
quickly, delight in that flowing, O virtuous king!

The time of sowing has arrived, and such a sowing of abundance!"
With these words, she wept and encouraged him.

She jumped up from her place and said, "O, how you are blessed!
O poor bald man, a sun has come as a crown for you!
A cap hides the fault of a hairless head,
especially when that cap is the sun and the moon.
In the chamber where you heard this offer,
why didn't you say 'Yes,' singing a hundred praises?
If these words of Moses had pierced the ear of the sun,
the sun itself would have descended in hope of this grace.
Do you understand at all what this promise, this gift is?
God is showing his care for Satan.
When that Gracious One called you back so kindly,
it's amazing that your heart remained unmoved,
that it didn't burst open, so that by means of your heart,
you might gain felicity in both the worlds.

The heart that bursts open for the sake of God's portion
eats fruit in both worlds, as martyrs do.
It's true that heedlessness and blindness also manifest God's Wisdom,
so that the heedless one might endure, but why be this heedless?
Yes, heedlessness also manifests Divine Abundance and Wisdom,
so that one's business may not suddenly fly out of one's hand;
but not heedlessness so great that it becomes an incurable festering,
a poison for the spirit and intellect of he who is ill.

Who, really, can find bazaars like this—
where with a single rose you are buying whole gardens of roses;
where a hundred orchards are offered in exchange for one seed,
a hundred mines in exchange for one coin?
'He belongs to God' [*Kana lillah*] is the giving of that coin,
so that 'God belongs to him' [*kana 'llah lahu*] may fill your hand;
for this weak, unstable 'he' [*hu*] was brought into being
by the abiding *Hu* of God.

When the *hu* that passes away surrenders itself to Him,
it becomes everlasting and never dies.
It's like a drop of water afraid of earth and wind
since by these two it perishes.

When it leaps into the Sea, its source,
it's delivered from the heat of the sun, from wind, from earth.
Its form disappears within the Sea,
but its essence is forever abiding and good.

Listen, O drop, give yourself up without regret,
and in exchange gain the Ocean.
Listen, O drop, bestow upon yourself this honor,
and in the arms of the Sea be secure.
Who indeed should be so fortunate?
An Ocean wooing a drop!
In God's name, in God's name, sell and buy at once!
Give a drop, and take this Sea full of pearls."
[Rumi, *Mathnawi* IV: 2597–2622]

How wondrous to be a drop wooed by an Ocean! Beloved Asiyah continues:

"In God's name, in God's name, don't delay;
these words of Moses come from the Sea of Grace.
Any other grace vanishes before this Grace,
that one of the lowest of the low
could ascend to the Seventh Heaven.
Pay attention, for a marvelous falcon has come to you;
no seeker will ever find it by searching."
[Rumi, *Mathnawi* IV: 2623–25]

Continually God is calling to us, through the being and voices of devoted women and men and through the God-consciousness awakening within our own hearts.

*And God sets forth as an example to those who have faith*
*the wife of Pharaoh:*
*witness, she said: "O my Sustainer!*
*Build for me in nearness to You a mansion in the Garden*
*and save me from Pharaoh and his actions*
*and save me from those who do wrong";*
*also Mary, the descendant of 'Imran, who guarded her chastity,*
*and We breathed into her of Our spirit,*

*and she witnessed to the truth of the words of her Sustainer*
*and of His revelations and was one of those devoted.*
[Quran, *Surah at-Tahrim* 66:11–12]

The prophets are human beings because of this,
so that humankind, through likeness of the prophets with them,
might be saved from the water-spout's edge.
So the Prophet called himself *a man like you,*
that you might come to the one who is like you and not be lost;
for similarity is a wondrous attractor.
Wherever there is a seeker, her like is calling her.
[Rumi, *Mathnawi* IV:2669–71]

We can understand all this as a story within the human heart, the forces of ego within ourselves that refuse to listen, and yet the voice of the inner heart calling us to awaken, even as Shams of Tabriz encourages us—to recognize that all is within:

> See everything within yourself: Moses, Jesus, Abraham, Noah, Adam, Eve, Asiya, Khidr, Elias, Pharaoh and Nimrod, are all within you. You are an infinite universe; what are the earth and the skies in comparison? Didn't God say: "My heavens and My earth cannot contain Me, but I can be contained within the heart of a faithful servant of Mine"? You will not find Me in the heavens; you will not find Me on the Throne![72]

The body, like a mother,
is pregnant with the spirit-child:
death is the labor of birth.
All the spirits who have passed over
are waiting to see how that proud spirit shall be born.
[Rumi, *Mathnawi* I: 3514–15]

As the Prophet Muhammad said, "He who knows himself knows his Lord." It is Love that carries and sustains us through this process. The door of the heart will finally open only with Love, because—though knowledge may be important and can assist in our discrimination along

[72] *Rumi's Sun*, op. cit., p. 341.

the way, and may help us to reach the threshold—it is ultimately through Love that we are brought into unity of Being.

If from bewilderment, this intellect of yours flies out of your head,
every tip of your hair will become a new knowing.
In the presence of the Beloved, the brain needn't labor;
for there the brain and intellect spontaneously produce
fields and orchards of spiritual knowledge.
If you turn towards that field, you will hear a subtle discourse;
in that oasis your palm tree will freshen and flourish.
[Rumi, *Mathnawi* IV, 1426–28]

Some verses attributed to Rabi'a al 'Adawiyya describe it:

Where a part of you goes, the rest will follow—given time.
You call yourself a teacher: therefore learn.

My soul, how long will you go on falling asleep
and waking up again?
The time is near when you will fall into so deep a sleep
that only the Trumpet of Resurrection
will have the power to wake you.

O God, the stars are shining;
all eyes have closed in sleep;
The kings have locked their doors.
Each lover is alone, in secret, with the one he [or she] loves.
And I am here, too: alone, hidden from all of them—
With You.[73]

Among the *Aves*[74] praising God and in remembrance of Beloved Mary, one psalter of prayer begins with a verse from the heart of the Prophet King David, ancestral forbear of Mary and Jesus, describing such a steadfast and open heart:

---

[73] Rabi'a al 'Adawiyya, excerpted from *Doorkeeper of the Heart*, translated by Charles Upton (Putney, VT: Threshold Books, 1988), pp. 39, 44, 52. Rabi'a is credited with being the first among Islamic mystics to speak of God as the Beloved, a languaging of our relationship with God that then more explicitly became an essential basis of much of Sufi thought and practice and poetry. (See p. 387 with n. 62 of this text.)
[74] See p. 165, n. 36 and p. 166; p. 313.

And he [or she] will be like a tree that is planted by running waters
which will give its fruit in its time.
[Bible, Psalms 1:3]

The accompanying *Ave* response continues:

Gate of Paradise, tree of life that I have lost,
through you,
for me already the fruit of salvation becomes sweet and grows.

Generation upon generation, from the first soul created, human beings have been turning to their Creator, to the Source of Life, for guidance, in recognition of the enlivening power of Primordial Love. For many hearts these days, Beloved Mary continues to be as a Tree of Life in the garden of Paradise, offering blessed, sweet fruit of untold nourishment from her beloved Sustainer, an open gateway to Grace.

It is said the Angel Gabriel again visited Beloved Mary in her elder years and announced to her the coming of the moments of her Dormition and return, and gave to her a luminous branch of a date palm in recognition.[75] She then knelt in prayer and it is told that all the trees standing nearby bent low to the ground in acknowledgement of her dear presence. It is related that then the Apostle John came, as she had called him by heart, her "son" from the moments of the cross. And she asked for assistance to prepare the house and to light candles. And then she consoled all who gathered, individually and collectively, greeting them each and all by heart, and said:

> "Rejoice, O blessed children, and do not make my Dormition a cause for grief, but be full of the greatest joy, for I am going into eternal joy, and may the grace and mercy of the Lord be with you always."[76]

Mary, Maryam, Myriam, however we may know her, is an exemplar of enheartened Spirit through whom we can recognize and nurture virtues

---

[75] The stories of Beloved Mary's Dormition and Assumption date back to the third and fourth centuries CE; such details are not present in the New Testament. One of the earliest written narratives so far discovered is *The Book of Mary's Repose* (*Liber Requiei Mariae*). These stories encompass the "Palm of the Tree of Life" tradition.

[76] Maximus, *The Life of the Virgin*, op. cit., p. 131

that are surely rooted within us, also, but may need our focused encouragement to foster.

> Through you we have learned courage in good deeds. Through you we have been given wisdom, humility, love, and every other virtue . . .
>
> O treasure house of all virtues! O facilitator of super-natural human nature, our joy, our life, glory and peace, victory and wisdom and sovereignty, gathering of every good thing, which no tongue can express, no mind can grasp, and no span of time can age![77]

She is the furrow sprouting forth the wheat that strengthens hearts.
She is the table bearing eternal delight . . .
She is the pillar of light leading and illuminating those in darkness . . .
She is the flower of incorruptibility . . .
She is the thickly leaved tree in whose shade the weary rest . . .
She is the door of great mystery.[78]

St. John of Damascus (646–674 CE) later described the apostles gathered around her and angelic singing as she was taken to be buried. Though many now remember Beloved Mary as experiencing her Dormition in Ephesus, some still say that Beloved Mary passed away in the upper room of the house of Cleophus, on Mt. Zion (where the Last Supper had been shared, and where they say the disciples later gathered), and that she was brought to the sepulcher of her parents, Joachim and Anna, in Gethsemane. Still others feel that Beloved Mary was laid to rest at the foot of the Mount of Olives, in the "Church of the Tomb of the Virgin Mary" in Jerusalem, in the Kidron valley.[79] Franciscans took over the guardianship of that church in the fourteenth century, and then, in the eighteenth century, the Greek Orthodox and Armenian Apostolic Church took over responsibility for it. Over the centuries, Syrians, Abyssinians, Copts, as well as Muslims have shared guardianship of the holy site—a

---

[77] Ibid., p. 156, 157.

[78] Ibid., p. 150.

[79] The round upper church there was destroyed and rebuilt several times over the centuries, but the earlier crypt, built into a cave and dating to the first century CE, has remained throughout and continues to be lit by numerous hanging lamps. The cave sanctuary has an altar to the east, and to the west is a stone platform where it is said the body of Beloved Mary once lay.

*mihrab* was added for Muslims in thirteenth century near Mary's sepulcher. Many Muslims honor this "Tomb of the Virgin Mary" especially because it is recorded that the Prophet Muhammad, during his Night Journey (*'Isra*) from Mecca to Jerusalem before his *Miraj*, witnessed a light over the "Tomb of the Virgin Mary" in Jerusalem.

Other Muslims of the Ahmadiyya branch of Islamic faith visit with Beloved Mary where they feel she rests, in the high hills of Kashmir, now a part of Pakistan, in a beautiful valley called "Muree," named for her. It is said that she journeyed there with Jesus, after the times of their persecution in the Holy Land, and that his tomb is also nearby in Srinigar; some Christians also hold to this belief and both sites have been venerated for centuries.

Whether told of Jerusalem or Ephesus, stories relate that dear Apostle Thomas, who had been away journeying in India, returned three days after Beloved Mary's passing and yearned to greet her. And so the apostles opened the tomb on the third day following her burial that he might do so and found it to be empty; all that remained was her veil, her shroud, the same garment in which she had birthed Jesus, along with her supportive girdle waist wrapping, cloths with which she had also enwrapped her holy infant.[80] The finding of the relics is a part of the Dormition traditions of

---

[80] Some say that Mary had gifted these pieces of clothing to women in service to her, and that they were later carried to Constantinople. Constantinople, in its golden age, hosted many churches and chapels dedicated to Beloved Mary; the three most renowned were the shrines of Chalcoprateia (which housed her girdle), near Hagia Sophia; Blachernae, where her *Sancta Camisa* was once housed; and Hodegetria, where the icon by St. Luke was once venerated. It is said all were established by "Blessed" Empress Pulcheria (398/399– 453 CE) , the sister of Theodosius II, and wife of Marcian (co-ruler with both in the fifth century). Later, Byzantine Empress Irene of Constantinople sent the *Sancta Camisa* as a gift to Charlemagne, whose grandson Charles the Bald donated it to Chartres Cathedral (see p. 389 of this chapter). It was thought to have been destroyed in a fire in 1194, yet three days later it was found miraculously unharmed.

The Holy Girdle (*Sacra Cintola*) is a camel hair belt that according to tradition was made and worn by Beloved Mary. Some relate that as she ascended into heaven, she bestowed it upon the apostles as a reminder for them. By the late Middle Ages it had been translated to Westminster Abbey, where many devoted to Beloved Mary came in pilgrimage to visit it in prayer over the centuries. Tradition now locates it since the fourteenth century in Prato, where a fresco attributed to Angiolo (Agnolo) Gaddi depicts the history of the *Sacra Cintola*. See

both Jerusalem and Ephesus. In the moment when they opened her tomb, it is said light and fragrance emerged, enveloping them all in grace.

> And the earth was made holy by her walking on the earth and by her placement in the tomb, and from the holy burial wrappings of her immaculate body. And the skies and all creatures receive grace from her invisible and eternal regard and generosity.[81]

In the return of her blessed soul to the heavenly abode, she was gifted with:

> good things that no eye has seen, nor ear heard,
> nor has entered into the human heart,
> which God has prepared for those who love him.
> [Bible, 1 Corinthians 2:9]

> God says, "I have readied for My righteous servants
> what no eye has ever seen,
> and no ear has ever heard, and no heart of man has ever conceived."
> [*Hadith Qudsi* recorded by Bukhari, Muslim, and Tirmidhi]

> *Truly, God has purchased of the faithful their lives and their possessions.*
> [Quran, *Surah at-Tawba* 9:111]

Jafar as-Sadiq, the saintly descendant of Prophet Muhammad, reflected "All beings belong to Him—so let not that which belongs to Him distract you from Him."[82] Even so, when we see through all to the Essence, we see to the Truth of all things. The motion of everything originates in that Essential Primordial Moment—Breath before breathing, of the Abode of Peace. In this world, we are restless, in motion, searching. There, there are only greetings of peace and nourishment of purity as we received aforetime, before our entry into this world, when we knew the "Yes!" of "Am I not your Lord?"

> *And whenever your Sustainer brings forth their offspring*
> *from the loins of the children of Adam,*

---

http://www.palazzopretorio.prato.it/en/museum/exhibition/enchantment-holy-girdle/ (accessed September 8, 2021).

[81] Maximus, *The Life of the Virgin*, op. cit., p. 142.

[82] Ibid., p. 49.

*He calls upon them to bear witness about themselves:*
*"Am I not your Sustainer?"—*
*to which they answer: "Yes, indeed, we do bear witness thereto!"*
[Quran, *Surah al-A'raf* 7:172][83]

Through this perception—our innate capacity to perceive the existence of the Supreme Reality, the Creative Source of all Being—the human being becomes perfected in the Light, illumined by the Light of God received through the self-disclosure of that Infinitude, developing the capacity to then illuminate others through the pouring forth of that Grace.[84]

O sun, though you disappear from earth's rose-garden,
in order to illumine another side of this world,
the Sun of Divine knowledge has no motion—
its place of rising is within the spirit and the mind.
A perfect Sun shines in the realm of Reality,
illuminating both day and night.
Come to the Sun's rising-place:
after that, wherever you go, you'll have that radiance.
After that, wherever you go will be the place of sunrise.
[Rumi, *Mathnawi* II: 42–46]

One might consider "Assumption to God" also as an inward journey, through inner realms—for with God there is no up or down—cycling into the Placeless, Timeless abiding. As we deepen in humility, we rise within that Presence, returning through that primordial connection,[85] in stalwart devotion and immersion in Spirit.

*O you who have faith!*
*celebrate God's praises, and do this often;*

---

[83] Muhammad Asad in his note to this verse reflects: "It is this instinctive cognition—which may or may not be subsequently blurred by self-indulgence or adverse environmental influences—that makes every sane human being "bear witness about himself" before God. As so often in the Qur'an, God's "speaking" and man's "answering" is a metonym for the creative act of God and of man's existential response to it." See Muhammad Asad, *The Message of the Qur'an.*

[84] See commentary by al-Nisaburi reflecting on the Light Verse in Extended Context Notes in Appendix, Star XII, 6.

[85] *Surah al-Alaq*, first *surah* revealed. See p. 106, n. 10 of this text.

*and glorify Him morning and evening.*
*He it is Who sends blessings on you as do His angels*
*that He may bring you out of the depths of Darkness into the Light:*
*and He is Full of Mercy to the faithful.*
*Their greeting on the Day they meet Him will be "Peace!"*
*And He has readied for them a most generous recompense.*
[Quran, *Surah al-Ahzab* 33:41–44]

The Prophets and saints assist us, over and over again; reminding us to "keep our connection"[86] with our Source, that the Garden of Love might spread throughout this world even now. And then, in those moments of grace, as Shams of Tabriz encourages us, we may pause, immersed within the fragrance of the Beloved:

> All words in the whole world belong to seekers, to those who search. And what is the sign of the One they are seeking? I am listening; you are listening.
>
> When weighing "The Truth Sought" with "God" one has to know the right moment to be able to reach that universe. In the end, where are you going? My graceful friend! What more can one say after this discussion?
>
> "May God be with you," I say.
>
> But this is not a wish for separation—it is a prayer, that the favor and help of God, and the friendship of the Master and the Truth who knows the secrets, might protect you.
>
> Stop, O my camel! Joy has come to its last degree; the work is finished; the way has come to an end. The earth has turned into a beautiful paradise. The time of celebration has come again, and things have been set right.[87]

*For those who have faith and do the deeds of wholeness and reconciliation*
*are Gardens as welcoming homes for that which they have done.*
[Quran, *Surah as-Sajdah* 32:19]

---

[86] *And keep your connection, and remain conscious of God, that you may attain felicity* (Quran, *Surah al-'Imran* 3:200). (*Yaa 'ayyuha alatheena amanuuisbiruu wasabiruu warabituu wattaquuAllaha la'alakum tuflihuun.*)
[87] *Rumi's Sun*, op. cit., p. 221.

And roses upon roses upon roses! The longest-living rose in this world abides beside a church, long dedicated to Beloved Mary; it has been sending forth rose blossoms for a thousand years, carrying her fragrance further into this world. This cathedral of the Assumption of Mary, Hildesheim Cathedal, Germany, was originally founded in 815 CE by King Louis the Pious (778–840 CE), the son of Charlemagne. It was expanded between 1010 and 1020, but later, after numerous renovations over the centuries, it was almost completely destroyed during an air-raid of the Second World War in 1945. Over that next decade, slowly, with much devoted love, it was rebuilt and is now a UNESCO world heritage site. People had despaired of the rose bush which had been burned to the ground, but it was not long before green shoots appeared, and as the wall was re-established, the rose again began to climb to fragrance the air with its blossoms. The rose bush rises again to a height of 33 feet and has been scientifically verified as being at least 700 years old. That spring of 1945, it resurrected with 25 new shoots, and in 1947, the first new blossoms opened; ever since then the number of blossoms has increased year after year as new branches stretch heavenward.[88]

A number of versions of the story of the establishment of the church are told, but at the center of all of them are Beloved Mary and the rose. One beloved story relates how King Louis was out hunting and became separated from his men and was lost without his mount in the forest. He walked until suddenly he came upon a mound covered with wild roses. He had with him a reliquary of relics of Beloved Mary which his heart called him to hang upon a branch of the wild rose; he then knelt in prayer for assistance until he fell asleep beside it. When he awakened, he saw that even though it was the middle of summer, the mound was covered with brilliant white snow. Even so, the rose bush had burst forth with blossoms, and the trees and grass were shining green. His reliquary had become fixed into the rose bush with ice in the midst of the heat of summer. He understood that here was intended to be an abiding place for prayer in remembrance,

---

[88] Each new branch was labeled with a little metal sign indicating the year in which it has appeared. Its fruit, the rose hips, are known to be of great benefit as a remedy for inflammatory diseases; these are particularly noted for their high vitamin C. Rose hips can be used for both a delicious marmalade and a healing and refreshing tea. The fragrance of rose oil is among the most healing of scents in creation and has long brought benefit in uplifting the spirits of the ill.

that the rose was sacred, and that he must build a chapel here for Beloved Mary. When he was then soon found, he immediately initiated the plan and placed the altar of the chapel dedicated to her Assumption just near the rose. The cathedral building continues to be widely renowned for this "Thousand-year Rose" (*Tausendjähriger Rosenstock*) that grows along the outer wall of the apse in the courtyard of the cloisters. After over a thousand years now, the fragrance of Mary's rose continues to waft into the air.

*To God belongs all that is in the heavens*
*and all that is on earth;*
*and all things are returning to God.*
[Quran, *Surah al-'Imran* 3:109][89]

Countless lessons await us, through this journey, every breath. Who are we, but the Beloved—a vibrant mirror of that Love, a bit of matter sown on the breeze, breathed by that Breath of the Beloved:

We seeded this earth
because of You.
Everything tells Your story;
everything lives in You.
The First, the Last,
the Hidden and the Manifest,
Your Names parse our substance
and our non-existence emerges in another realm.
You are *al-Warith.*[90]
We cannot say these words
without You.[91]

---

89 *Wa lillahi ma fissamawati*
*wa ma fil 'ard.*
*Wa ilallahi turja'ul 'umuur.*

90 *Al-Warith*, "The Inheritor of All," is one of the Ninety-Nine Names of God that are mentioned in the Quran, as are "The First" (*Al-Awwal*), "The Last" (*Al-Akhir*), "The Hidden" (*Al-Batin*), and "The Manifest" (*Az-Zahir*).

*Ya Warith, Ya Nur, Ya Wadud* ("O Inheritor of All, O Light, O Infinitely Loving One!") is a beautiful chant to hold by heart as a companion in these moments of recognition of our return to our Source.

91 Excerpt from *Exaltations*, forthcoming volume of the "Songs of the Soul" series by Camille Hamilton Adams Helminski.

*Truly, those who have faith and do righteous deeds*
*their Sustainer guides by means of their faith:*
*beneath them will flow rivers in Gardens of Bliss.*
*There they will call out:*
*"Glory to You, O God!"*
*and they will be answered with the greeting, "Peace!"*
*And the completion of their cry will be:*
*"Praise be to God, the Cherisher and Sustainer of all the Worlds!"*
[Quran, *Surah Yunus*, "Jonah," 10:9–10]

Beloved Mary is such a radiant exemplar for all human beings, in demonstrating a soul's complete receptivity to God and the channel of Love each soul might become when purely open to that Source. May we all be encouraged by her beautiful example and strong being, and may we, as she did with such devotion before the overwhelming Grace of Reality, in songs of praise with the roses, the birds, and the mountains, with all of creation,

Bow in worship, drawing ever near.
[Quran, *Surah al-'Alaq*, "The Connecting Cell," 96:19]

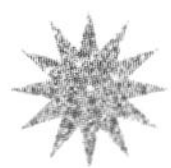

# *In the Name of All*[1]

Mary,
gentleness expounding,
waves of Mercy
upon the shore
of our being.

Who are we?
Who are you?
Spirit breathing,
being breathed.

A son arrived,
to you—a daughter;
Breath to breath,
hand to hand,
we hold each other—

the banks of a stream
leading
to the ocean,
sea to shining Sea.

Diamonds explode
in the Sun
of these hearts,
these minds
that would unearth
the songs

---

[1] Excerpt from *Exaltations*, "Songs of the Soul" series, Camille Hamilton Adams Helminski (forthcoming from Sweet Lady Press).

of Your Love,
O Cherisher of all!

Mine shafts
let in the light—
pierced
to the center.

Molten magma
bubbles up
and forms new promontories,
treasures for ferns
to kiss
in the bright morning.

Precious, virgin soil,
awaiting
Your creation,
with the spray of the sea
and the song of the birds,
already harvesting
nearby hills,
mountains of Your Making.

Up and down,
in and out,
You weave
Your tapestry
of Glory,
studded with gems
and tied
to the tent pegs
of Your Power
uniting
Heaven and Earth,
Inner and Outer.

"Peace,
a word . . ."[2]
from the Most Magnificent,
the Most Generous,
the Most Compassionate,
our Sustainer,
Most Merciful.

*Salaamun*
*qawlam*
*mir Rabb ir-Rahim.*[3]

*Subhanallah*
*Ya Rabb al-'Alameen,*[4]
of Paradise
and its fountains,
the Creator.
*Ya Khaliq, Ya Bari, Ya Musawwir,*
*Ya Awwal, Ya Akhir, Ya Warith.*[5]

---

[2] Quran, *Surah Ya Sin*, "O Thou Human Being!" 36:58.

[3] *"Peace!" A Word from the Sustainer, Most Merciful!* (Quran, *Surah Ya Sin*, 36:58).

[4] "Glory be to God! Sustainer and Cherisher of all worlds!"

[5] *Ya Khaliq* ("O Creator"), *Ya Bari* ("O Evolver and Patterner"), *Ya Musawwir* ("O Bestower of Form"), *Ya Awwal* ("O You Who Are the First"), *Ya Akhir* ("O You Who Are the Last"), *Ya Warith* ("O Inheritor of All").

*Hildesheim Rose of the Cathedral of the Assumption of Mary*
*(Oldest living rose bush on earth, reported to be 1,000 years old)*

# Rose Prayers

Upon the completion of a gathering for prayer and remembrance, traditionally a "rose" prayer (*gulbenk*) is offered; the prayer may take many forms, but the awareness of the opening of a rose of blessing is held, and sometimes, the fragrance of the rose can be perceived.

May this moment be blessed.
May goodness be opened and may all harm be dispelled.
May our humble entreaty be accepted in the Court of Honor;
may the Most Glorious God purify and fill our hearts
with the Light of His/Her greatest Name.
May the hearts of the lovers be opened.
May all our moments, our journeying be resplendent.
By the breath of our noble protector and guide Mevlana,

by the secret of Shams and Walad,
by the holy light of Muhammad, by the generosity of Imam Ali,
and the intercession of Muhammad, the unlettered prophet,
mercy to all the worlds,
and all the prophets and saints,
may we say Hu, Huuu.
[Mevlevi *Gulbenk*]

My Beloved speaks and says to me:
Rise up, my love, my fair one and come.
For, lo, the winter is past, the rain is over and gone.
The flowers appear on the earth;
the time of singing is come,
and the voice of the turtle-dove is heard in our land.
The fig tree puts forth her green figs,
and the blossoming vines give forth fragrance.
Arise, my love, my fair one, and come.
[Bible, Song of Songs of Solomon 2:10–13]

*And paradise will be brought near to the God-conscious,*
*no longer will it be distant:*
*"This is what was promised for you—*
*to everyone who would turn to God*
*and keep Him/Her always in remembrance—*
*who stood in awe of the Most Compassionate though Unseen*
*and brought a heart turned in devotion to Him/Her;*
*enter here in peace and security; this is the Day of eternal Life!"*
*There will be for them there all that they may wish*
*and yet more in Our Presence.*
*Bear then with patience all that they say*
*and celebrate the praises of your Sustainer*
*before the rising of the sun and before its setting,*
*and in the night also celebrate His/Her praises,*
*and at the end of prostration.*
*And listen for the Day*
*when the Caller will call out from a place quite near.*
[Quran, *Surah Qaf* 50:31–35;39–41]

## *Antiphon*
## *The Returning Sound*

Whispers arrive—
can we decipher
Your wish,
our destiny,
here and Hereafter?
You would have us know
how much we are loved,
not left unattended,
never alone.
Indescribable Goodness
is at hand;
angels hover
and all the relations,
trees and flowers
bend in adoration
with the moon and the stars—
Your sun rises in our heart,
and we know
this "we" and You
are One.

*There is no god, no reality, but Hu.*
*Everything is perishing except His/Her Face, the Face of Divine Reality.*
*To Him/Her belongs the Command, and to Him/Her will you all return.*

*La ilaha illa Hu.*
*Kullu shay-in halikun illa wajhah.*
*Lahul hukmu wa ilayhi turja'uun.*
[Quran, *Surah al-Qasas*, "The Story," 28:88]

# Appendix I

# *Songs of Love*

## *Song for the Virgin Mary*

Original in Old French, attributed to Blanche of Castile (1188–1252 CE)
Queen of France, mother of St. Louis

Amours, ou trop tart me sui pris
M'a, par sa signourie, apris,
Douce dame de paradis
Ke de vous voeill un cant canter.
Pour la joie ki puet durer
Vous doit on servir et amer.
Et pou çou ke nus n'a mespris
Tant vers vo fill, n'en fais, n'en dis,
S'il s'est en vo service mis,
Ke vous nel faciés racorder.
Pour la joie ki puet durer
Vous doit on servir et amer.
Virge Roine, flour de lis,
Com li hom a de ses delis
Ki de vous amer est espris,
Nus hom nel saroit reconter.
Pour la joie ke puet durer
Vous doit on servir et amer.
Mout fu li vaissiaus bien eslis,
Douce Dame, ou Sains esp(e)ris
Fu .ix. mois tous entiers nouris:
Ce fu vos cuers, Dame sans per!
Pour la joie ki puet durer
Vous doit on servir et amer.

Translation and score on following page by Camille Hamilton Adams Helminski in remembrance of Beloved Mary, eternally open-hearted, welcomer of hearts!

# *Song for the Virgin Mary*

Text: Blanche of Castile (13th century) poem in Old French
English translation by Camille Hamilton Adams Helminski

Music: Camille Helminski
Transcribed by Celil Refik Kaya
and Marianne Saint George

Love, by which I am cap-tured too late, by his mas - te - ry has taught me,
Sweet La-dy, of Par - a - dise, so I would sing a song a-bout you.
* Refrain
For the joy that can en-dure one should serve and love you.
And be-cause no one has so trans-gressed a - gainst your son,
in deeds or in words that if he en - gag - es in your ser - vice
might not find that all for-got - ten,
(Refrain)
*
Vir-gin queen, li - ly flower, what de-lights a man has, who is seized with love for you, no one could re - count.
(Refrain)
*
So well-chos-en was that ves - sel, Sweet La - dy, where Ho - ly Spir - it for nine months was com-plete-ly fed that was your heart O La - dy with-out peer!
(Refrain)
*

# L'chah Dodi

## Come, My Beloved

Sephardic Folk Tune
Text: Shlomo Alkabetz / Liturgy

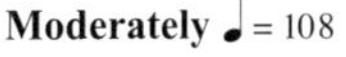

*L'chah dodi likrat kalah*
*p'nei Shabbat n'kab' lah.*
*L'chah dodi likrat kalah*
*p'nei Shabbat n'kab' lah.*

*Shamor v'zachor b'dibur echad,*
*Hishmi'anu el ha'meyuchad.*
*Adonai echad u'shmo echad;*
*L'shem ul'tiferet v'l'tehila.*

*Likrat Shabbat l'chu v'nelcha,*
*ki hi m'kor ha'bracha.*
*Me'rosh mi'kedem n'sucha;*
*sof ma'aseh b'mach'shava t'chila.*

*Hit'oreri, hit'oreri,*
*ki va orech, kumi uri.*
*Uri, uri, shir daberi;*
*k'vod Adonai alai'yich nigla.*

Beloved, come to meet the Bride;
beloved come to greet Shabbat.
Beloved, come to meet the Bride;
beloved come to greet Shabbat.

"Keep" and "remember": a single command
the One God invited us to hear;
the Eternal is One, God's Name is One;
glory and praise are God's.

Come my friend to meet the Sabbath,
forever a fountain of blessing.
Still it flows, as from the start:
the last of days, for which the first was made.

Awake, awake,
your light has come!
Arise, shine, awake and sing:
the Eternal's glory dawns upon you.

# *Tala'a al Badru*

Islamic Nasheed
Rast: Nay Dokah

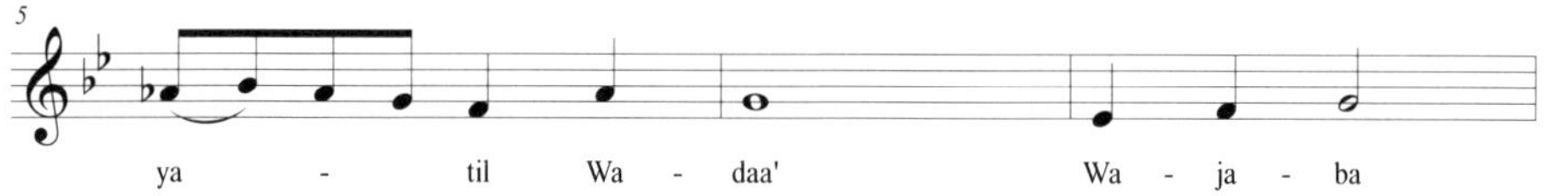


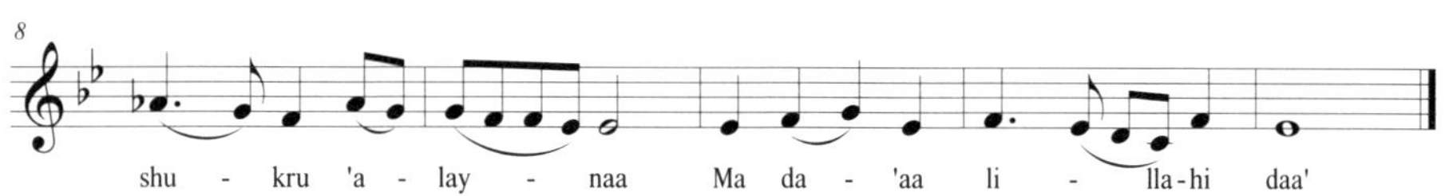


1. *Tala'a al Badru 'Alaynaa*
   *Min Thaniyyatil Wadaa'*
   *Wajaba shukru 'alaynaa*
   *Ma da'aa lillahi daa'*

1. The full moon has ascended
   over the valley of Wada'.
   Gratitude is essential for us
   when a caller calls us all to God.

2. *Ayyuhal mab'uuthu feena*
   *Ji'tta bil 'amril mutaa'*
   *Ji'tta sharraftal madeena*
   *Marhaban ya khayra daa'*

2. O you who have been chosen,
   you have come with a compelling command.
   You have come, honoring the city;
   O best of callers, welcome!

3. *Anta shamsun anta badrun*
   *Anta nuurun 'alaa nuur*
   *Anta misbaahu thurayya*
   *Yaa Habeebi Yaa Rasuul*

3. You are the sun, you are the full moon!
   You are light upon light!
   You are the lamp of Sirius.
   O my beloved, O Messenger of God!

# Appendix II

# *Extended Context Notes*

## *Introduction*

(p. xix, n. 4)

## *Story of Beloved Jochebed, Mother of Moses*

*We convey unto you some of the story of Moses and Pharaoh, setting forth the truth for people who have faith. Behold, Pharaoh exalted himself in the land and divided its people into castes. One group of them he deemed utterly low—he would slaughter their sons and spare only their women, for, behold, he was one of those who spread corruption on earth.*

*But it was Our will to bestow Our favor upon those who were deemed so utterly low in the land, and to make them forerunners in faith, and to make them heirs, and to establish them securely on earth, and to let Pharaoh and Haman and their hosts experience through those [children of Israel] the very thing against which they sought to protect themselves.*

*So We sent this inspiration to the mother of Moses: "Nurse, but when you fear for him cast him into the river, and do not be afraid or grieve: for We shall restore him to you, and We shall make him one of Our messengers."*

*Then Pharaoh's people caught him up: it was intended that he should be an adversary and a cause of sorrow to them, for Pharaoh and Haman and their hosts were erring people.*

*Pharaoh's wife said: "Here is a joy of the eye for me and for you: do not slay him. It may be that he will be of use to us, or we may adopt him as a son." And they did not perceive what was happening.*

*But an emptiness came to the heart of Moses' mother: she was about to disclose him had We not strengthened her heart so that she might remain one of faith. And she said to his sister, "Follow him."*

*So his sister watched him in the guise of a stranger, and they did not know. And We ordained that at first he should refuse to nurse until she said: "Shall I point out to you the people of a house that will nourish and raise him for you and be sincerely devoted to him?"*

*And so We restored him to his mother that her eye might be comforted, that she might not grieve, and that she might know that the promise of God is true; but most of them do not understand.*

[Quran, *Surah al-Qasas*, "The Story," 28: 3–13]

## *Star IV, 1*

(p. 54, n. 3)

A shoot will spring from the stem of Jesse;
from his roots a branch will bear fruit.
And the Spirit of the Lord shall rest upon him,
the Spirit of wisdom and understanding,
the Spirit of counsel and might,
the Spirit of knowledge and of the fear of the Lord:
And shall make him of quick understanding in the fear of the Lord:
he will not judge by what he sees with his eyes,
nor decide by what he hears with his ears:
But with righteousness he will judge the needy,
and with justice he will give decisions for the poor of the earth:
and he will strike the earth with the rod of his mouth,
and with the breath of his lips he will slay the wicked.
Righteousness will be his belt, and faithfulness the sash around his waist.
The wolf will live with the lamb,
and the leopard will lie down with the young goat;
the calf and the young lion and the yearling together;
and a little child will lead them.
The cow will feed with the bear; their young will lie down together:
and the lion will eat straw like the ox.
The nursing child shall play upon the hole of the cobra,

and the weaned child shall put his hand upon the viper's den.
They shall not hurt nor destroy on all My holy mountain:
for the earth will be filled with the knowledge of the Lord,
as the waters cover the sea.
[Bible, Isaiah 11:1-9]

## *Star V, 1*

(p. 81, 20)

The designation CE, stands for "Common Era." Formerly dates of our era were notated in the Western world as AD *Anno Domini*, "The Year of our Lord," to date events that occurred after the birth of Christ. Much of the civic world still dates their calendars in this way, by the Gregorian calendar which is solar based, though the reference is changed to CE. The Muslim calendar is lunar based and pivots around the *Hijrah*, the emigration of the Prophet Muhammad and his community from Mecca to Medina, for protection, in 622 CE as year 1 AH, when the community was formally established with the Jewish tribes of Yathrib as their hosts, who welcomed Muhammad's peace-keeping assistance. The Jewish calendar is lunisolar, keeping track of both lunar and solar cycles, and references 3761 BCE as year 1—the beginning of Creation according to Biblical years, as determined by Maimonides. Other faith traditions and cultures have other ways of reckoning time. Our concepts of time color our experience, our views of life; each calendar has its own special, holy, days of remembrance. God willing, one day, we will come to view every day and night as sacred.

Now await in patience the command of your Sustainer:
for truly you are within Our sight.
And celebrate the praises of your Sustainer whenever you arise,
and for part of the night also praise Him/Her
and at the retreat of the stars!
[Quran, *Surah at-Tur*, "Mt. Sinai," 52:48-49]

One may reflect upon all these happenings as actual history within time, of lives lived, of prophets and saints, even as some Christians may, as the birthing of the Divine within human form in this world, and yet one can also comprehend these "events" as metaphors of the journey of the soul and the unfolding of the Eternal in meaning. However one may find one's relationship with such a one as Beloved Mary, the ideal of "Mother"—of one who could so deeply listen and bring the fruition of compassion into this world—one can find within her story inspiration for Life. She cared not for her "good name" with the people, but rather her "good name" with her Sustainer, the Source of her sustenance, the Beauty of heart given her, a gateway to the Sea, and the Holy Sea of Love moving through her.

[Say: "Our life takes its] hue from God!
And who could give a better hue [to life] than God,
if we but truly worship Him?"
[Quran, *Surah al-Baqarah* 2:138]

## *Star V, 2*

(p. 82, n. 21)

Hannah Adams came to my awareness while researching family history, as a distant cousin of ours and, also, a distant cousin and friend of John Adams, second president of the United States, who invited her to use his library. Her father had been a bookseller before the Revolution. When book sales declined, he took in boarders from Harvard Divinity School to help make ends meet. Though she made lace to help support the family (her mother having died when she was twelve), her love was religion, and so when she could she would join the students for Latin and Greek lessons and little by little began her research into faith traditions which bore the amazing fruit of *A Dictionary of all Religions*, the first of its kind. She was the first American author to gain a livelihood exclusively from writing. Hannah so loved the pursuit of knowledge she once reflected, "My first idea of Heaven was of a place where we should find our thirst for knowledge fully satisfied."

## *Star V, 3*

(p. 91, n. 35)

Melchizedek was the King of Salem ("Peace"), also known as "Jerusalem" ("the Foundation of Peace"), the holy, wise, priestly king who blessed Abram and brought light to his heart: "Melchizedek said, 'Blessed be Abram by God Most High, Possessor of heaven and earth . . .'" (Bible, Genesis 14:18-19). It was Melchizedek who provided Abraham with food and wine (nourishment flowing from the Divine Reality), and it is said that Abraham later was known for never eating alone, but always inviting someone to his table (of spiritual fruits). Some say Melchizedek may have been identical with Shem, the son of Noah (who would have been approximately 465 years old when he and Abram met; Abram was then 75). It was Melchizedek who bestowed the priesthood upon Abram (whose name meant "high father"), in recognition of his noble character and steadfastness in the way of Truth, and helped to open the way to the moment when Abram's name was changed to Abraham:

> When Abram was ninety-nine years old the Lord appeared to Abram
> and said to him, "I am God Almighty; walk before me, and be blameless,
> that I may make my covenant between Me and you,
> and may multiply you greatly." Then Abram fell on his face.
> And God said to him, "Behold, My covenant is with you,
> and you shall be the father of a multitude of nations.
> No longer shall your name be called Abram,
> but your name shall be Abraham ["Father of many"],
> for I have made you the father of a multitude of nations.
> I will make you exceedingly fruitful, and I will make you into nations . . .
> [Bible (ESV), Genesis 17:1–3]

Some say Melchizedek passed Adam's robes to Abraham, and that it was Melchizedek's blessing that helped open such fruitfulness through Abraham with God's abundant Grace.

## *Star VI, 1*

(p. 106, n. 9)

Then Jesus was led by the Spirit into the desert to be tested by the devil.
And after fasting forty days and forty nights, he was utterly starving.
And drawing near, the Examiner said, "If you are the son of God,
tell these rocks to turn into bread."
He answered, "It is written: 'Humanity shall not just live on bread,
but on every word that comes from the mouth of God' [Bible,
Deuteronomy 8:3]."
[Bible (UNT), Matthew 4:1-4]

Then the devil took him to the holy city
and set him on the pinnacle of the temple
and said to him, "If you are the Son of God,
throw yourself down, for it is written:
'He will command his angels concerning you,'
and 'on their hands they will bear you up,
lest you strike your foot against a stone' [Bible, Psalms 91:11, 12]."
Jesus said to him, "Again it is written,
'You shall not put the Lord your God to the test'
[Bible, Deuteronomy 6:16]."
[Jesus references the Shema Yisrael in his next response:]
Again, the devil took him to a very high mountain and showed him
all the kingdoms of the world and their glory.
And he said to him, "All these will I give to you,
if you will bow down and worship me."
Then, Jesus said to him, "Begone, Satan! For it is written:
'You shall worship the Lord your God, and Him only shall you serve'
[Bible, Deuteronomy 6:13]."
[This is so similar to the quintessential statement of faith for a Muslim: *La illaha il Allah*: Declaring, "There is no god but God; there is no reality but the Reality" casting away any promptings of the tempting ego; then the illusory reality of the tempter vanishes and the angels arrive:]
Then the devil left him, and behold,
angels came and were ministering to him.
[Bible (ESV), Matthew 4:5-11]

Psalm 91 referenced in this passage from the Gospel of Matthew begins:

He who dwells in the secret place of the Most High
shall abide under the [sheltering] shadow of the Almighty.
I will say of the Lord, "He is my refuge and my fortress,
my God, in whom I trust."
[Bible, Psalms 91:1–2]

Rather than taking up the devil's temptation to prove his own specialness, like these words of the Psalms, Jesus steadfastly keeps his connection with God alone (Deuteronomy 6:13), for, as he would have been well aware, that Psalm of David continues:

Because he holds fast to Me in love, I will deliver him;
I will protect him, because he knows My Name.
When he calls to Me, I will answer him.
[Bible (ESV), Psalms 91:14-15]

## *Star VI, 2*

(p. 106, n. 10)

How amazing is the possibility of conception! A girl child is born with one to two million immature eggs already in her ovaries, eggs formed within her, while being still carried within her mother's womb, held generation by generation. Over the course of a girl's lifetime, month by month these are released, hundreds of thousands dispersed before she even reaches puberty. Until recently it was thought that the eggs with which one is born were all the eggs a woman would ever have, and that by middle age only a few thousand would be remaining (the ticking biological clock). Current studies have begun to indicate that, due to the development of stem cells within an ovary, it may in rare cases be possible that cells could emerge into a new egg during a woman's older life span (as occurred with beloved Anna, Mary's mother, and beloved Elizabeth). What an amazing creation we human beings are, both male and female, with such innate grace-full capacity for continued creation and nurturance!

## *Star VI, 3*

(p. 122, n. 1)

The "farthest" mosque, Al-Masjid al-Aqsa in Jerusalem, is the second oldest mosque (*masjid*, "place of prostration") in the world. This "Farthest Mosque" is located on the Temple Mount of Solomon (which it is said was constructed by Prophet Solomon around 950–970 BCE, rebuilt in 516 BCE, and further developed around 20 BCE by Herod). Around 530 CE, a Byzantine church dedicated to Our Lady (Mary) was constructed there, for she who had been so devoted to the Holy of Holies, and where her young son, Jesus (Isa) had been presented at the Temple. Later under Muslim auspices, the first simple structure of what developed into the Masjid al-Aqsa was begun around 638 CE upon the old ruins of that Byzantine church; adjacent to this early "Farthest Mosque," on the same Temple Mount, the golden Dome of the Rock was built in 691 CE over the rock upon which it is said the Prophet Muhammad stood before making his night journey through the heavenly realms into the Presence of God. Some say the octagonal plan of the Dome of the Rock was influenced by the Byzantine Church of the Seat of Mary (the *Kathisma* [Greek] or *al-Qadismu* [Arabic]), the first church dedicated to Beloved Mary in the Holy Land, built circa 451 CE, around the rock where it is said she sat down to rest while on the way with Joseph, along the route from Nazareth to Bethlehem (see pp. 76–79 of this text). Located on this mount sacred to all three Abrahamic traditions, Al Masjid al-Aqsa is also a metaphor for the "farthest mosque" in Paradise, the portal of intimate prayer with our Sustainer where "you" and "I" disappear in the Presence of the Beloved.

## *Star VII, 1*

(p. 127, n. 3)

After an extra two *rakah* (cycles of the ritual prayer) following the ritual night prayer (*isha salah*), in order to invite dream guidance through God's Grace, the Prophet Muhammad would offer this prayer:

### *Dream Prayer of Muhammad*

O my Allah,
I ask for goodness according to what You know to be good for me,
and I ask for strength from Your own strength.
I ask for abundance because Your strength is sufficient for everything
and my strength is not.
You know everything; I don't know;
it is You who knows perfectly all that which is hidden.
O my Allah! If this [thing I intend] is good for my religion, and my life,
and if the consequences of my deed will be good
according to Your knowledge,
make it easy for me to accomplish and make it fruitful,
otherwise if You know this endeavor is not good for my religion,
and my life,
and that the consequences of this endeavor would be harmful,
turn it away from me, and turn me away from it.
Give me what is good for me and make me accept it.
[*Hadith* 380; Bukhari, and Tirmidhi, Chapter 2]

## *Star VII, 2*

(p. 134, n. 14)

St. Catherine's monastery was built by Emperor Justinian I (483-565 CE) between 548 and 565, just after he built Haghia Sophia (between 532–537) in Constantinople (Istanbul). The monastery of St. Catherine's is one of the oldest functioning Christian monasteries in the world and houses the oldest continually operating library in the world; its doors have been open to seekers of knowledge since its dedication in the mid-sixth century. It is said the monastery chapel was originally ordered by the Empress Consort Helena, mother of Constantine the Great in 327 CE when she visited the holy mountain during her travels through the Holy Land. Among the many volumes and manuscripts the library houses (second only to the Vatican library in the treasures it holds), is the Biblical Codex Sinaiticus of 345 CE. This handwritten manuscript, written in Greek, contains the oldest complete copy of the New Testament. Among the other special manuscripts housed there is the earliest known travel journal, written in about 380 CE by a woman, Egeria (Aetheria or "Hegiras"), a pilgrim from the Iberian peninsula. While traveling for three years, sometimes mounted, mostly walking, she details her visits to many sacred places of the Holy Land, including this Mt. Sinai (Mt. Tur) where Moses had received the Ten Commandments. (Amid the handwritten text is an account written to her female friends which she closes: "But do you, ladies, light of my eyes, deign to remember me, whether I am in the body or out of the body.")

The monastery chapel, known as "St. Helen's Chapel," is built over the spot recognized as the place where Moses saw the burning bush—this *rubus sanctus* was transplanted just outside the chapel in the adjacent courtyard. The bush still growing there the monks believe to be the same bush that Moses witnessed with the fire of God's Presence. In remembrance of the humility of Moses in that moment, visitors are likewise asked to remove their shoes when entering this chapel, where a silver star marks the original rooting of the bush; the chapel itself is dedicated also to the remembrance of the Annunication of God's Word to Mary.

## *Star VIII, 1*

(p. 161, n. 29)

Rosh Hashanah is the beginning of the Jewish New Year, the holy day celebrated on the first day of the Hebrew month of Tishri (September or October). Ten days of repentance follow, culminating on the Day of Atonement (Yom Kippur). It is a time to reflect on one's life, to turn away from sin, and to affirm the doing of good deeds. Especially since medieval times (and the influence of the Zohar), many Jews on the first afternoon of Rosh Hashanah offer *Tashlich*—"casting off" of sins by walking to a flowing body of water and casting bits of bread into the water, symbolically casting their sins into the water to cleanse and carry them away, a process that also evokes remembrance of John the Baptist's ritual of immersion and the renewal of Spirit through Baptism. A prayer from Micah is often recited:

Who is like You, God,
who removes iniquity and overlooks transgression

of the remainder of His inheritance.
He does not remain angry forever because He desires kindness.
God will take us back in love;
God will cover up our iniquities,
You [God] will hurl all our sins into the depths of the sea.
Give truth to Jacob, kindness to Abraham,
like that You swore to our ancestors from long ago.
[Bible, Micah 7:18-20]

See Ariela Pelaia, "Tashlich: A Primary Ritual of Rosh HaShanah," *Learn Religions*, https://www.learnreligions.com/what-is-tashlich-2076496 (accessed June 19, 2021).

## *Star IX, 1*

(p. 180, n. 10)

## *Unity of Spirit*

The Quran indicates an ideal state as that of Adam and Eve in the Garden, two beings united as one. The ideal in Judaism, also, is expressed as one wife for one husband together, that the heart might not be divided or distracted, but unified in Spirit, as was encouraged also by the teachings of Jesus.

Though numerous instances of polygamy are noted among the people of the Old Testament of the Bible, King Solomon being an extreme example (and the numerousness of his wives being noted as a source of untold difficulty), the guidance of the Torah points towards monogamy. Within Christianity, there are also instances where it took many years for Christian leaders to adapt their tribal ways to the teachings of Jesus—among the early western converts to Christianity, King Clovis' son, the Frankish King Clothar I (497-561 CE) still took multiple wives as his right as a royal tribal leader. He was a Merovingian King who reigned over territory that is now within France. One of his wives, Radegund (520-587 CE), whom he had kidnapped, left him to become a nun; she established an abbey church in Poitiers, the first nunnery in Europe, and became the first saint of the Merovingians. They lived just before the time of Prophet Muhammad. One might consider that the Prophets demonstrate, by their behavior and their words, both lessons in what is beneficial as well as indications toward what may be detrimental to our spiritual wellbeing, the wellbeing of our bodies, hearts, and souls, showing us a way towards an ideal state for a human being.

Prophet Muhammad, (who himself was leading at a transitional epoch) was first married to one devoted and beloved wife, Khadijah, experiencing both a blessed monogamous marriage of twenty-five years of union and, after her passing, polygamous marriage with a number of women—partly to coalesce tribal alliances and to provide for women whose husbands had died during the persecution wars. The Quranic scripture, which was revealed amid this tribal society, replete at that time with multiple polygamy, then placed the limit of four wives for a man, if he could care equally for all, which it was also noted is almost impossible to do (see Quran 4:128-29), especially in regard to emotional support. One could view this as an indication that the best way forward was to leave behind the possibility of polygamy, and indeed when the Prophet's son-in-law, Ali, later considered taking a second wife, the Prophet Muhammad discouraged him from doing so, saying it would cause his daughter, Fatimah, unhappiness, and so Ali asked forgiveness of Fatimah for any pain he might have caused her in even considering it and returned his focused love to Fatima alone. Though subsequent generations may have made use of the allowance and even abused it, Muhammad's great-granddaughter, Aminah, for instance, availed herself of the possibility of monogamy; it is known that she specified it in her marriage contract. With the Quran, many rights of women were established for the first time among the pagan Arab tribes.

Though there are areas of the world where tribal practices still persist, monogamy is now the norm for Christians, Jews, and Muslims, and of course, secret relationships outside of a marriage, adulterations of that primary unitive commitment, are outlawed by the law of Moses, the "Ten Commandments," the Quran, and the teachings of Jesus and his followers. In the Gospel of Matthew 19:4-5 an indication is given: "And he answered and said, 'Have you not read that He created them from the beginning, made them male and female, and said, 'For this reason a man shall leave his father and mother and be joined to his wife, and the two shall become one flesh.'?"; see also 1 Corinthians 7:2, Ephesians 5:31, 1 Timothy 3:2: "A bishop (or an elder, a deacon) then must be above reproach, the husband of one wife, temperate, prudent, of good behavior, hospitable, apt in teaching."

About 1000 CE, marriage was declared forbidden for Roman Catholic priests—they were required to be celibate and devoted only to God and the church; however, Eastern Orthodox priests (also men) could continue to marry and were often strongly supported in their service by a devout wife. The Way of Muhammad had reaffirmed again the honoring of the Way of the Householder—recognizing marriage as a container for the development of Spirit. Even though some may be drawn to celibacy, and for some the way of marriage may not be gifted, it is a recognized joy for a couple to be supported in their love openly by a faith community and for their relationship to be of support to the community, encouraging the flowering of Spirit within the family and throughout a community.

In the Bible, both Old and New Testaments, the ideal for a new marriage is to build a foundation of happiness:

So husbands ought also to love their wives as their own bodies.
He who loves his own wife loves himself.
[Bible, New Testament, Ephesisans 5:28]

If a man has recently married,
he must not be sent to war or have any other duty laid on him.
For one year he is to be free to stay at home
and bring happiness to the wife he has married.
[Bible, Old Testament, Deuteronomy 24:5]

This principle is also true in Islam as indicated in the Quran, that couples might be "a garment" of blessing for each other:

*They are as a garment for you, and you are as a garment for them.*
[Quran, *Surah al-Baqarah* 2:187]

Though some, whether male or female, may find a committed relationship of marriage, and faithfulness to it, to be challenging, it is recognized as a crucible for the soul: "Marriage is half the faith" (*hadith* of the Prophet Muhammad). It is acknowledged in all the Abrahamic faiths that within marriage one has a precious and sacred opportunity to learn how to care for another soul, to support and be supported, to beautify the heart and the world, participating in the restoration of the Garden.

# *Star IX, 2*

(p. 305, n. 40)

## *Seven Stages of the Soul* (Nafs)

1. When the glimpse of the Essential first catches us, it pulls us from the state of *nafs-i ammara*, "the commanding, demanding self." Absorption with our particular, limited self and its grasping needs diminishes as we discover the existence of Eternal Wisdom and begin to be drawn home to our deepest, Essential Self.
2. When we begin to distinguish between that which is true and essential and that which is false, which inhibits and veils us from Truth, we witness our own shortcomings and begin to develop a conscience. This is the stage of the *nafs-i lawamma*, the "blaming, judging self," examining one's actions and heart in repentance.
3. Then a new vision opens for us and we come to the stage of *nafs-i mulhaima*, "the inspired self." New ways of being become apparent to us as we see by God's Light, by the Light of the Oneness with which we are still connected, and we cannot help but see that we are indeed a part of an integral living and flowing system. All of nature then reminds us of the Unity of all Being. Sometimes as it was for Mary of Magdala, it is a prophet or friend of God who, in a moment, reminds us, bringing us to Truth.
4. Our contentment with what we see then increases; here we come to the stage of *nafs-i mutmainna*, "the satisfied soul," for here we find that as it says in the Quran, *Truly in the remembrance of God, hearts find rest* (13:28).
5. Then the soul reaches the stage of *nafs-i radiye*, "the pleased soul"; that is not just satisfied, but pleased with that which its Source, God, bestows. One no longer attributes partners to God, one's own impulses are absorbed into the impulses of One's Maker and one acts in consonance with His/Her will.
6. Now it is that the soul becomes fully pleasing to God: the *nafs-i mardiye*, "the satisfying self"—one can more purely serve others, bringing the fragrance of Life, the Light of Life to others, and awakening the awareness of the Life-giving water within them.

7. Beyond this is the *nafs-i safiye*, or *nafs-i kamile*, "the purified or completed self" for whom there is no longer any separation. Empty of "self," open totally to the will of the Source, there is no longer a distinguishable self; there is only the Beloved, breathing, being breathed: *Wherever you turn there is the Face of God* (2:115).

## *Star IX, 3*

(p. 252., n. 57)

### *Fountains of Life*

When a baby is born, there are six places of flexibility in the bones of the head—allowing for growth and healthy development of the brain—still sensitive, and soft in the first months of life. There are four small fontanelles—two sphenoid and two mastoid— that close within two months, allowing for the settling of the bones of the head after birth; the larger, triangular shaped posterior fontanelle closes sometime between two and twelve months of age. The sixth and last fontanelle to close over, after twelve to eighteen months of being in this world, is the diamond shaped anterior "fontanelle", a "fountain" (whose rhythmic pulse can be visible). This "fountain" can also be experienced as a column of light through what some refer to in Hinduism and other eastern traditions as the "*Sahasrara* (crown) chakra,"—the "seventh chakra" (located just below the anterior fontanelle)—known also as the "Thousand-Petalled Lotus," and "Source of Light," because of the spiritual light that can radiate through it.

## *Star X, 1*

(p. 222, n. 5)

Praise befits you, our God, in Zion;
to you our vows will be fulfilled.
You who answer prayer,
to you all people will come.
When we were overwhelmed by sins,

you forgave our transgressions.
Blessed are those you choose
and bring near to live in your courts!
We are filled with the good things of your house,
of your holy temple.
You answer us with awesome and righteous deeds,
God our Savior,
the hope of all the ends of the earth
and of the farthest seas,
who formed the mountains by your power,
having armed yourself with strength,
who stilled the roaring of the seas,
the roaring of their waves,
and the turmoil of the nations.
The whole earth is filled with awe at your wonders;
where morning dawns, where evening fades,
you call forth songs of joy.
You care for the land and water it;
you enrich it abundantly.
The streams of God are filled with water
to provide the people with grain,
for that is how you have prepared the land.
You drench its furrows and level its ridges;
you soften it with showers and bless its crops.
You crown the year with your bounty,
and your carts overflow with abundance.
The grasslands of the wilderness overflow;
the hills are clothed with gladness.
The meadows are covered with flocks
and the valleys are mantled with grain;
they shout for joy and sing.
[Bible (NIV), Psalms 65]

The location of the church of "Holy Power" in Istanbul has been lost, but a sister church of Agia Dynamis ("Holy Power") in Athens, built in the sixteenth century over a temple to Hercules (the legendary hero renowned among Romans and Greeks for his strength, born of a human mother and the "Sky-Father God" Jupiter or Zeus), is dedicated to the Holy Power of the Virgin Mary. Pregnant women often frequent this church with prayers for strong children—another instance of ancient traditions being woven into subsequent devotions. The church dedication celebration for Agia Dynamis is in remembrance of the day of celebration of the birth of Beloved Virgin Mary (September 8).

## *Star X, 2*

(p. 228, n. 12)

According to the *Acts of Magdalene* (also known as *The Life of St. Mary Magdalene and of Her Sister Saint Martha*, compiled in the eighth or ninth century CE by Rabanus Maurus, archbishop of Mainz), Lazarus stayed in Marseilles, Mary Magdalene went to Aix-en-Provence with St. Maximin, and Martha settled in Tarascon. Ancient local traditions in France have long confirmed this. The church of St. Victoire in Marseilles was built over a natural cave that is honored as having been the refuge of Lazarus. Near Aix, the Basilica of Mary Magdalene at Saint-Maximin holds a relic of Mary Magdalene, and her cave at St. Baume has long been a place of pilgrimage. An ancient tradition tells of the miraculous cure of King Clovis, the first Frankish king to convert to Christianity, around 500 CE, after a pilgrimage to what has long been recognized as the tomb of St. Martha at Tarascon. Though there were early proponents of Christianity in the British Isles, it wasn't until the sixth century that this new expression of faith also became more embedded there, centered in "double monasteries"—a house of monks and a house of nuns, living alongside each other, coexisting in celibacy and presided over by an abbess; over the centuries, such abbesses became some of the most powerful women in Europe.

According to tradition, Joseph of Arimathea went on from Marseilles to Britain, and in particular to Cornwall and Glastonbury. Glastonbury traditions relate that Joseph of Arimathea had earlier brought the boy Jesus with him on one of his trading journeys to Britain and that they had lived together there for several years, while Jesus studied and prepared for his mission. Some say Joseph of Arimathea was Beloved Mary's uncle, so that he would have become Jesus' legal guardian upon the passing of her husband, Joseph, the beloved adoptive father of Jesus. If Joseph of Arimathea had been Jesus' guardian, and also a prominent trader in the Roman-British tin trade, it is quite possible he could have taken his nephew there with him. The belief that dear Jesus had spent time in England surfaces again and again throughout the culture, for instance in the poetry of the mystic English poet William Blake (1757–1827 CE) and in the Arthurian legends.

## *Star X, 3*

(p. 228, n. 13)

Now there stood by the cross of Jesus his mother, and his mother's sister,
Mary the [wife] of Cleophas, and Mary Magdalene.
[Bible, Gospel of John 19:25]

Among which was Mary Magdalene,
and Mary the mother of James and Joses,
and the mother of Zebedee's children.
[Bible, Gospel of Matthew 27:56]

There were also women looking on afar off:
among whom was Mary Magdalene
and Mary the mother of James the less and of Joses, and Salome.
Who also when he was in Galilee followed him and ministered unto him.
And many other women which came up with him unto Jerusalem.
[Bible, Gospel of Mark 15:40-41]

And Mary Magdalene,
and Mary [the mother] of Joses beheld where he was laid.
[Bible, Gospel of Mark 15:47]

And the women also which came to him from Galilee
followed after and beheld the sepulcher and how his body was laid.
And they returned and prepared spices and ointments;
and rested the Sabbath day, according to the commandment.
[Bible, Gospel of Luke 23:55-56]

And there was Mary Magdalene and the other Mary
[assumed to be Mary the wife of Cleophus, mother of James and Joses],
sitting over against the sepulchre.
[Bible, Gospel of Matthew 27:61]

## *Star X, 4*

(p. 231, n. 4)

Mary Dyer had left for England some weeks before her husband, William Dyer, who sailed later with Roger Williams to assist in petitioning for the charter of consolidation of the towns of Rhode Island. Rhode Island colony had recently been established by Roger Williams and his wife Mary, and the Dyers, and about ten other families as a haven from religious persecution. Mary Dyer is the only woman in the history of the United States of America to be martyred for standing for religious freedom—it was 1660 when she was hung on Boston Common by the Puritans, for promoting freedom of religious conscience. She went to her death with joy, witnessing to Truth, determined to honor the freedom of each soul to discover and relate to the Truth as he or she felt moved by the "Inner Light." The "Inner Light," that *Nur* within the heart of which she spoke, is so familiar to mystics of many faiths including those of the Sufi Way.

> This Inward Light may be briefly explained as follows: God is an indwelling Spirit, and humanity is his holy temple. His law is written upon the hearts of all men; and obedience to it will lead them into all truth, so far as religious truths are revealed to men. Through the operation of this law the soul of man is accessible to his Creator. It is the rule of life to which every one must subject himself [or herself], and out of which duty is evolved.

See Horatio Rogers, *Mary Dyer of Rhode Island The Quaker Martyr That Was Hanged On Boston Common, June 1, 1660* (Providence: Preston and Rounds, 1896).

The words she spoke as they were about to execute her are so reminiscent of the language of the Bible, the Quran, the *ahadith*, and Islamic mystics:

> This is to me the hour of greatest joy I ever had in this world. No ear can hear, no tongue can utter, and no heart can understand the sweet incomes and the refreshings of the spirit of the Lord, which I now feel.
>
> ~ Mary Dyer

Her death sent such ripples back to England that the newly restored king, Charles II, forbade further executions on religious grounds in the colonies, and the community of colonies, so rocked by these occurrences, began to be moved towards the stance of freedom for all religious inclinations. As she is quoted on the plaque below her commemorative statue near the Massachusetts State House in Boston, "My life not availeth me in comparison to the liberty of the truth."

In large part due to remembrance of her persecution and that of her two beloved friends in faith, William Robinson and Marmaduke Stephenson, who were hung in 1659 for also standing up for religious freedom, "Freedom of Religion" was incorporated as the First Amendment to the Constitution of the United States, and International Religious Freedom Day was established in 1998 to be commemorated each October 27 in honor of their sacrifice.

## *Star X, 5*

(p. 257, n. 66)

Regarding the "Fast of Ramadan," there are provisions of exception for the bodily fast for those who may be struggling with serious health issues (though it is also noted that the fast can be very beneficial for one's health), travelers, women whose blood is flowing with menstruation, pregnant women, and mothers who are nursing. However, as Shams of Tabriz once taught, these invitations to practice the five daily prayers and the fast are so that everyone of the whole community, not just those who might be by nature so inclined, might experience the taste of immersion in contemplation, as was experienced so completely by the Prophet Muhammad.

> The worship and work of Muhammad, may the Peace and Blessing of God be upon him, was immersion in Divine contemplation (*istighraq*). He said, "The work is the work of the heart, service is the service of the heart, and servanthood is servanthood of the heart."

(See *Rumi's Sun*, op. cit., p. 249.) The fast is meditation for the body. During the fast, one begins to recognize that perhaps more important than what is taken in through the mouth and the belly, or what is taken in through vibration upon the skin—the largest organ of the body—we are fed most deeply through the channels of breath, with fragrance, and through the subtle senses of the ears, the eyes, and the eye of the heart. Patience, perseverance, is elicited and watchfulness not just as to what one takes in, but also in regard to what goes out from one's self—one's words, one's actions, one's thoughts, ones intentions.

## *Star X, 6*

(p. 271, n. 86)

### *Witnessing Miracles*

In researching some family history of grandmothers long ago, I came across a surprising story regarding the step-father of another of the few ancestral grandmothers of ours whose name was Mary, this one on my mother's father's side. Among the Scottish and Irish colonists who first came to the shores of what is now America before the Revolutionary War, Rev. William Tennent, the step-father of Mary Noble, immigrated with his family from Ireland in 1705 when he was in his teens. Well-educated in the Presbyterian church, he later taught many of the promising young men of the late-eighteenth century at what was known as The Log College, soon to become Princeton University. Mary who came to live with him at the parsonage farm with her mother when she was ten years old must have also benefited from his instruction and kind presence. Rev. Tennent was someone of deep spirit who had himself passed through a very unusual awakening as a young man. Early in life he had been deeply impressed with a sense of the Divine and had determined to devote his life to the ministry of the Gospel. He engaged diligently in his studies and soon completed his course in languages, becoming particularly proficient in Latin. He then went to New Brunswick, NJ, to study theology under his brother, Gilbert, who was the preacher of the church there. While there he underwent a most miraculous experience; the story is told in the book "Log College" as follows:

> After a regular course of study in theology, Mr. Tennent was preparing for his examination by the Presbytery as a candidate for the gospel ministry. His intense application affected his health, and brought on

a pain in his breast, and a slight hectic. He soon became emaciated, and at length was like a living skeleton. His life was now threatened. He was attended by a physician, a young gentleman who was attached to him by the strictest and warmest friendship. He grew worse and worse, till little hope of life was left. In this situation, his spirits failed him, and be began to entertain doubts of his final happiness. He was conversing one morning with his brother in Latin, on the state of his soul, when he fainted and died away. After the usual time he was laid out on a board, according to the common practice of the country, and the neighborhood were invited to attend his funeral on the next day. In the evening, his physician and friend returned from a ride in the country, and was afflicted beyond measure at the news of his death. He could not be persuaded that it was certain; and on being told that one of the persons who had assisted in laying out the body thought he had observed a little tremor of the flesh under the arm, although the body was cold and stiff, he endeavored to ascertain the fact. He first put his own hand into warm water, to make it as sensible as possible, and then felt under and at the heart, and affirmed that he felt an unusual warmth, though no one else could. He had the body restored to a warm bed, and insisted that the people who had been invited to the funeral should be requested not to attend. To this the brother objected as absurd, the eyes being sunk, the lips discoloured, and the whole body cold and stiff. However, the doctor finally prevailed, and all probable means were used to discover symptoms of returning life. But the third day arrived, and no hopes were entertained of success but by the doctor, who never left him night nor day. The people were again invited, and assembled to attend the funeral. The doctor still objected, and at last confined his request for delay to one hour, then to half an hour, and finally to a quarter of an hour. He had discovered that the tongue was much swollen, and threatened to crack. He was endeavoring to soften it, by some emollient ointment put upon it with a feather, when the brother came in, about the expiration of the last period, and mistaking what the doctor was doing for an attempt to feed him, manifested some resentment, and in a spirited tone said, "It is shameful to be feeding a lifeless corpse!" and insisted with earnestness, that the funeral should immediately proceed. At this critical and important moment, the body to the great alarm and astonishment of all present opened its eyes, gave a dreadful groan and sunk again into apparent death. This put an end to all thoughts of burying him, and every effort was again employed in hopes of bringing about a speedy resuscitation. In about an hour the eyes again opened, a heavy groan proceeded from the body, and again all appearance of animation vanished. In another hour life seemed to return with more power, and a complete revival took place to the great joy of the family and friends, and to the no small astonishment and conviction of very many who had been ridiculing the idea of restoring to life a dead body.

Mr. Tennent continued in so weak and low a state for six weeks, that great doubts were entertained of his final recovery. However, after that period he recovered much faster, but it was about twelve months before he was completely restored. After he was able to walk the room, and to take notice of what passed around him, on a Sunday afternoon, his sister, who had stayed from church to attend him, was reading in the Bible, when he took notice of it and asked her what she had in her hand. She answered that she was reading the Bible. He replied, "What is the Bible? I know not what you mean." This affected the sister so much that she burst into tears, and informed him that he was once well acquainted with it. On her reporting this to the brother, when he returned, Mr. Tennent was found, upon examination, to be totally ignorant of every transaction of life previous to his sickness. He could not read a single word, neither did he seem to have any idea of what it meant. As soon as he became capable of attention, he was taught to read and write, as children are usually taught, and afterwards began to learn the Latin language under the tuition of his brother. One day, as he was reciting a lesson in Cornelius Nepos, he suddenly started, clapped his hand to his head, as if something had hurt him, and made a pause. His brother asking him what was the matter, he said that he felt a sudden shock in his head, and now it seemed to him as if he had read that book before. By degrees his recollection was restored, and he could speak Latin as fluently as before his sickness. His memory so completely revived, that he gained a perfect knowledge of the past transactions of his life, as if no difficulty had previously occurred. This event, at the time, made a considerable noise, and afforded, not only a matter of serious contemplation to the devout Christian, especially when connected with what follows in this

> narration, but furnished a subject of deep investigation and learned inquiry to the real philosopher and curious anatomist. . . .
>
> Many interesting anecdotes are recorded about Mr. Tennent in regard to his preaching, his manners, his dealing with men and his personal and spiritual experience, which may variously be described as . . . extraordinary, mysterious.

Rev. Tennent later married Catharine Van Brugh (the widow of John Noble), mother of Mary Noble, on August 23, 1738, and they lived happily together for almost thirty years until his passing, his life devoted to Spirit. The historical account of his experience was prepared by Hon. Elias Boudinot, LL.D. (the brother-in-law of Catherine, Mary Noble Cumming's daughter), a lawyer and member of the Continental Congress; the memoir of Rev. Tennent was first published in *The Assembly's Missionary Magazine* 1806, and has for centuries now been in the possession of the Historical Society of New Jersey. These quotations are from a book in which the story was published: *Log College* (Philadelphia: Presbyterian Board of Publication) by Dr. Archibald Alexander. Mary's daughter, Catherine, herself married a Presbyterian minister, Phillip Stockton, the "Revolutionary Preacher," brother of Richard Stockton, signer of the Declaration of Independence. Among such stories, one can witness how much Spirit was active in the formation of the free republic of the United States of America.

If you are born of Adam, sit like him
and behold all his progeny within yourself.
What is in the jar that is not also in the river?
What is in the house that is not also in the city?
This world is a jar, and the heart-spirit is like the river;
this world is the chamber, and the spirit is the wondrous city.
[Rumi, *Mathnawi* IV: 809-11]

# *Star XI, 1*

(p. 279, n. 1)

## Transfiguration *of Raphael*

*The Transfiguration* was known for centuries in the West as the finest painting in the world, one of the first paintings in oil, a technique that was for centuries thought to have originated in Europe during the Renaissance. Recent research has, however, discovered much earlier examples of oil paintings, created by Buddhist artists in caves in the Afghan region of Bamiyan from the fifth to the ninth centuries ce, painted with walnut and poppy seed drying oils. For many centuries, most artwork in Europe was religious in nature, commissioned by the Church, or wealthy nobility. Such monumental pieces as *The Transfiguration*, intended as an altarpiece, were a way of conveying the meanings of the Bible to the general populace who could not read. His earlier magnificent *Sistine Madonna*, commissioned by Pope Julius II, was completed in 1513 CE (when he was 30); the *Holy Family with Palm Tree* tondo is dated to 1506, when he was just 23.

It seems Raphael had been influenced by the *Apocalypsis nova* of Amadeus de Portugal (Amadeo Mendes da Silva), born 1420 CE in Morocco to Portuguese nobility, who, after being married at a very early age, had become a monk and then a Franciscan friar. (The oldest continually operating university in the world is in Fez, Morocco—Al Qarawiyyan—a mosque complex established and overseen in construction (while she was fasting) by a woman, Fatimah al-Fihri, in 859 CE, whose own wooden diploma was just rediscovered. For centuries it has been a place of knowledge where people of various faiths have gone to absorb wisdom; some even say that Gerber d'Aurillac (d. 1003 CE), who later became Pope Sylvester II, and is also the person who it is said introduced the use of Arabic numerals into Europe, studied there.) Amadeo's *Apocalypsis nova*, which takes the form of a conversation with Angel Gabriel, contains prophecies of the coming of a new pope, the "Angelic Pastor," who would endeavor with an emperor to restore harmony in the church and the world. Amadeo's sainted sister, Beatrice of Silva, was a Marian mystic and foundress of the monastic Order of the Immaculate Conception.

## *Star XI, 2*

(p. 297, n. 26)

Transliteration of "You are Joy" passage from Mevlana Jalaluddin Rumi's *Mathnawi* with the kind courtesy of Leila Bahreinian:

*Yaa elaahi! Sokkerat absaaranaa*
*Fa'fo annaa, usghelat awzaaronaa*

*Yaa khafeeyan! Ghad mala'ta-l-khaafeghayn*
*Ghad allavvat fawgha noor-o-l-mashreghayn*

*Anta serron kaashefo asraaranaa*
*Anta fajron mofajjer anhaaranaa*

*Yaa khafaa-o-l-zaat! Mahsoos-o-l-ataa*
*Anta ka-l-maa'e va nahno ka-r-rahaa*

*Anta ka-r-reehe va nahno ka-l-ghabaar*
*Takhtafe-r-reeho va ghobraahaa jahaar*

*To bahaaree maa cho baagh-e sabz-e khosh*
*Oo nahaan o aashkaaraa bakhsheshash*

*To cho jaani maa mesaal e dast o paa*
*Ghabz o bast-e dast az jaan shod ravaa*

*To cho aghli maa mesaal e een zabaan*
*Een zabaan az aghl daarad een bayaan*

*To mesaal e shaadi o maa khande-eem*
*Ke nateejey shaadee-ye farkhonde-eem*

*Jonbeshe maa har damee khod ashhad ast*
*Ke govaahe zo-l-jalaal e sarmad ast*

*Gardesh-e sang-aaseeyaa dar ezteraab*
*Ashhad aamad bar vojood-e jooye aab*

*Ey boroon az vahm o ghaal o gheel-e man*
*Khaak bar fargh-e man o tamseel-e man*

*Bande nashkeebad ze tasveer e khoshat*
*Har damat gooyad ke jaanam mafrashat*

## *Star XI, 3*

(p. 298, n. 27)

The blessings of salt: Sodium chloride, the most basic form of salt we ingest, keeps our bodies functioning—the chloride assists digestion and respiration, and sodium assists transport of nutrients and oxygen, for the functioning of nerves and muscle, especially the heart.

All salt comes from the Sea—its treasure may be apparent on the surface or it may be deeply buried from ancient shores. Certain places came to be valued for their wealth of salt deposits. There were once salt caravan routes even as there were silk routes, to trade in the precious commodity which in the sixth century was worth as much as gold. In 1352, Ibn Batuta, the greatest Arab-language traveler of the Middle Ages, who had journeyed overland across three continents—Africa, Europe, and Asia—wrote of visiting the city of Taghaza, entirely built of salt, including an elaborate mosque. For thousands of years salt provided the main means of preserving food, because salt preserves.

## *Star XI, 4*

(p. 315, n. 55)

When Black Elk was nine years old, he had fallen deathly ill, unresponsive, and it was several days before he came back to life. During that time he experienced intense visions, including that of a great tree of life encompassing the earth and all people, as well as teachings for the healing of his people.

The people of the Navajo (Diné nation) also offer a prayer that resonates deeply with this practice of the Khwajagan. And even as the Prophet Muhammad would offer the Light Prayer, as did Rumi every morning, the Native American peoples of the Navajo Diné nation would pray in a similar manner in recognition of the aliveness of all creation:

In beauty may I walk
All day long may I walk
Through the returning seasons may I walk
On the trail marked with pollen may I walk
With grasshoppers about my feet may I walk
With dew about my feet may I walk
With beauty may I walk
With beauty before me, may I walk
With beauty behind me, may I walk
With beauty above me, may I walk
With beauty below me, may I walk
With beauty all around me, may I walk
In old age wandering on a trail of beauty, lively may I walk
In old age wandering on a trail of beauty, living again, may I walk
It is finished in beauty.

## *Star XII, 1*

(p. 362, n. 18)

It is said the three petals of the *fleur-de-lys* represent purity, honesty, and wisdom, and both Blanche and Louis strove to humbly be exemplars; Blanche had carefully raised her son so that even at an early age he was humble, generous, and devoted to God. When he was king, he would say, "The peace and blessings of the realm come to us through the poor." He would daily feed beggars from his table, and he ate their leavings; he washed their feet, and ministered to the needs of the lepers.

Louis commissioned to be depicted within the stunning stained-glass windows of Sainte-Chapelle the story of the whole human journey from Adam and Eve until the moment of arrival of the holy relics within Sainte-Chapelle, their new home in France. Over the centuries, so many hearts have been uplifted by the beauty of the golden *fleur-de-lys* upon the fields of blue walls and the glorious blue stained-glass windows that soar to the heavens, letting so much soft light through the stone tracery of this slender oratory, a miracle of Gothic Rayonnant architecture. The lower supportive chapel is dedicated to Beloved Mary. Above the door, to the west, is a stunning rose window formed from multitudes of "petals" that depict stories from St.

John's Book of Revelations (in which the Beloved Lady is depicted standing before the sun, upon the moon, crowned by twelve stars shining).

## *Star XII, 2*

(see p. 377, n. 48)

The "Decade prayer", also known as "The Fatima Prayer," is recited at the closing of each ten repetitions of the "Hail Mary" prayers within the rosary practice: "O my Jesus, forgive us our sins, save us from the fires of hell, and lead all souls to Heaven, especially those in most need of Thy mercy." An *Ave* often sung in remembrance of Our Lady of Fátima:

*Ave María de Fátima.*
[Hail Mary of Fátima.]
*Ave, Ave, Ave María.*
*Ave, Ave, Ave María.*
[Hail, hail, hail, Mary.]
*El trece de mayo, la Virgen María*
[The thirteenth of May, the Virgin Mary]
*bajó de los cielos a Cova de Iría*
[below the heavens of the Cove of Iria]
*Ave, Ave, Ave María.*
*Ave, Ave, Ave María.*
*a tres pastorcitos la Madre de Dios*
[to three little shepherd children, the Mother of God]
*descubre el misterio de su corazón.*
[uncovered the mystery of her heart.]
*Ave, Ave, Ave María.*
*Ave, Ave, Ave María.*
*El Santo Rosario, constantes, rezad,*
[The Holy rosary, constantly pray]
*y la paz al mundo el Señor dará.*
[and peace to the world the Lord will give.]
*Ave, Ave, Ave María.*
*Ave, Ave, Ave María.*

*Hail Mary*

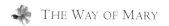

Hail Mary, full of grace, the Lord is with thee!
Blessed art thou among women,
and blessed is the fruit of thy womb, Jesus.
Holy Mary, Mother of God, pray for us sinners,
now and at the hour of our death.
Amen.

## *Star XII, 3*

(p. 382, n. 56)

The portrait of Alfonso continues to look out over the members of US Congress as one of the 23 people commemorated in marble relief over the gallery doors of the House Chamber for their work in establishing the principles upon which American law is based. In Part I, Title I, Law xi of *Las Siete Partitas*, he describes "What the Law-Maker Should Be":

> The law-maker should love God and keep Him before his eyes when he makes the laws, in order that they may be just and perfect. He should moreover love justice and the common benefit of all. He should be learned, in order to know how to distinguish right from wrong, and he should not be ashamed to change and amend his laws, whenever he thinks or a reason given him, that he should do so; for it is especially just that he who has to set others right and correct them should know how to do this in his own case, whenever he is wrong.

The *Siete Partidas* was woven with many threads, including principles from the Bible, from Aristotle, and Islamic law, as well as the writings of St. Thomas Aquinas, another soul much devoted to Beloved Mary.

## *Star XII, 4*

(p. 385, n. 60)

## *The Eightfold Path*

1. Right View: insight into the true nature of things (the "Four Noble Truths") and that all our actions have consequences and produce karma (a response, that we must work through in this life or the next).
2. Right Intention: adopting the way of the Buddha to follow the path towards enlightenment; avoiding attachment or any harmful intent.
3. Right Speech: purifying one's words; abandoning rude or hateful speech and lying.
4. Right Conduct: refraining from physical misdeeds—killing, harming, stealing, sexual misconduct are all prohibited; rather, manifest compassion.
5. Right Livelihood: avoid any trade that directly or indirectly might harm another; only own what is essential to sustain life.
6. Right Effort: release any disharmonious, unwholesome thoughts, desires, negative states; support and cultivate positive thoughts and states.
7. Right Mindfulness: always be conscious of what one is doing; maintain awareness of the body, feelings, and thought.
8. Right Concentration *Samadhi*: Practice meditation, striving for singleness, for a unification of the mind.

One witnesses in these principles both a resonance with the Ten Commandments of Moses (see p. 107 of this text) and the Sufi Laws of the Khwajagan (p. 315 of this text).

## *Star XII, 5*

(p. 391, n. 64)

Quran, *Surah ad-Dhukan* 44:1-9:

*By the Book that makes things clear—*
*We sent it down during a blessed night:*

*for We wish to give counsel.*
*In wisdom, that night the distinction between all things is clarified,*
*by command from Our Presence.*
*For We always are sending guidance*
*as a mercy from your Sustainer:*
*for He/She alone is All-Hearing, All-Seeing;*
*the Sustainer of the heavens and the earth*
*and all between them, if only you have inner certainty [nearness].*
*There is no god but He/She: it is He/She who gives life and gives death,*
*your Sustainer and the Sustainer of your earliest ancestors.*

And Quran, *Surah azh-Zhariyat* 51:15-21:

*Witness: the God-conscious will be amid gardens and springs,*
*taking joy in that which their Sustainer gives them*
*because before then they had lived a good life:*
*they would sleep only a little at night*
*and from the core of their hearts they would pray for forgiveness;*
*and of all that they possessed would grant a rightful share*
*to the one who asked and the one who was not able.*
*On the earth are signs for those with inner certainty,*
*just as within your own selves: will you not then see?*

## *Star XII, 6*

(p.. 404, n. 84)

Nizam al-Din al-A'raj al-Nisaburi (d. 1329 CE), a renowned Quranic scholar and astronomer, who assisted also in compiling the *hadith* collections, acquired respect at a young age because he did not indulge in backbiting, only speaking well of someone or not at all. (See al-Nisaburi, *Ghara'ib al-Quran,* vol. 18, p. 120, as quoted in *Sufi Commentaries on the Qur'an in Classical Islam*, op. cit., p. 128.) Reflecting on the Light Verse of the Quran and the "*Hadith* of Nearness"—"When my servant draws near to me"—Al-Nisaburi reminds us of what Beloved Mary knew so intimately, and so beautifully exemplified—God bestows *upon whom He/She wills, beyond all reckoning* (Quran, *Surah al 'Imran* 3:37):

The *niche* is the body, the *glass* is the heart, the *lamp* is the innermost heart (*sirr*), and the *tree* is the tree of spirituality (*al-ruhaniyya*) which has been created for subsistence (*baqa*) as has been described. The *oil* is the human spirit (*al-ruh al-insaniyya*) which is profoundly receptive to the light of gnosis (*'irfan*) and the *fire* is the fire of God's Self-disclosure (*tajalli*) and guidance in eternity. When it is combined with the light of the intellect (*'aql*) it becomes light upon light. When the *lamp* of the innermost heart (*sirr*) of *whom He wills* becomes illuminated by the light of timelessness, the *glass* of the heart and the *niche* of the body become illuminated. Their rays emerge from the aperture of the physical senses (*hawass*) and the earth of humanity (*al-bashariyya*) is illuminated, just as He said, *the earth will shine with the light of its Lord* (39:69). This is the station (*maqam*) of the *hadith* " I am his (or her) hearing, his (or her) seeing . . ."

*God is the Light of the heavens and the earth.*
*The parable of His light is,*
*as it were, that of a niche containing a lamp;*
*the lamp is enclosed in glass, the glass like a radiant star;*
*lit from a blessed tree—an olive-tree*
*that is neither of the east nor of the west—*
*the oil of which would almost give light*
*even though fire had not touched it: light upon light!*
*God guides to His light the one who wills to be guided;*
*and God offers parables to human beings,*
*since God has full knowledge of all things.*
[Quran, *Surah an-Nur*, "The Light," 24:35]

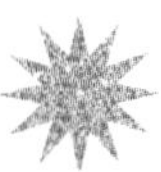

*"Notre-Dame"*
*Courtesy of Sanctuaire Notre-Dame de Rocamadour*
*(Photo gifted from the kind friends at the Sanctuaire on the Celebration Day of the Feast of the Coronation of Beloved Mary, August 22nd, just prior to sending* The Way of Mary *to press the week of her birthday celebration September 8th, 2021. As always, whether from within this world or from the next, her presence radiates blessing, with flowers and light.)*

# *Illustrations*

Cover illustration: Antique Quran opening page, from antique Quran graciously gifted by Renee Armand.

Frontispiece by Cara Grace Chadwick, © 2021.

Star motif heading each chapter: Quarta/Shutterstock.com.

"Rose of Love'ville Garden" in running header throughout: Photograph by Camille Hamilton Adams Helminski, © 2021.

## *Preface*

p. vii *Bismillah* calligraphy: Escondites assumed (based on copyright claims). Own work assumed (based on copyright claims), CC BY-SA 3.0, https://commons.wikimedia.org/w/index.php?curid=3696032.

## *Introduction*

p. xiii Twelve-pointed star: Adapted from existing artwork by Sweet Lady Press, 2021.

## *I. The Gift of the Conception of Mary to Anna, She Who Had Been Barren*

Sparrow page number ornament by Cara Grace Chadwick, © 2021.

p. 1 Bay laurel (*laurus nobilis*) illustration from *Medical Botany* (1836) by John Stephenson and James Morss Churchill: Rawpixel/Wikimedia Commons/ https://commons.wikimedia.org/wiki/File:Illustration_from_Medical_Botany,_digitally_enhanced_from_rawpixel%27s_own_original_plates_130.jpg#filelinks.

## *II. Within the Sanctuary*

p. 13 "Rose of Love'ville Garden" (also used as page number ornament throughout chapter): Photograph by Camille Hamilton Adams Helminski, © 2021.

## *III. Annunciation of the Word*

Dove page number ornament by Cara Grace Chadwick, © 2021.

p. 36 *Beloved Mary* by Cara Grace Chadwick, © 2021.

p. 43 Dove: Photo 114284355 © Alexander Potapov | Dreamstime.com.

## *IV. Magnificat, Mary's Song of Praise*

Madonna lily page number ornament by Cara Grace Chadwick, © 2021.

p. 51 Our Lady of Guadalupe (Virgen de Guadalupe) oil painting

(Spanish Colonial art) by Jose Antonio Robles, courtesy of Jose Antonio Robles at https://www.etsy.com/uk/shop/SacredArtByRobles?ref=l2-about-shopname.

p. 53 *Columbine:* Painting by Camille Hamilton Adams Helminski, © 2021.

p. 56 *The Visitation*: Angelico, Fra (1387–1455): Cortona Altarpiece showing the Annunciation, predella: the Visitation. Cortona, Diocesan Museum.© 2021. Photo Scala, Florence.

## *V. Birthing Jesus*

Frankincense leaves page number ornament: Illustration 96172402 © Roza D | Dreamstime.com.

p. 71 *Virgin Mary and Jesus* (old Persian miniature): Historic Images/ Alamy Stock Photo.

p. 87 "Methuselah" Judean Date Palm, germinated from 2,000 year-old seed found at Masada. By DASonnenfeld, own work, CC BY-SA 4.0, https://commons.wikimedia.org/w/index.php?curid=73559534.

p. 90 Frankincense: CPA Media Pte Ltd/Alamy Stock Photo.

p. 92 Myrrh tree: Vladimir Melnik/Shutterstock.com.

p. 94 Olive, *olea europaea.*: Florilegius/Alamy Stock Photo.

p. 94 The oldest known olive tree with an age of over 3,500 years old at Kavusi, Crete, Greece: Georgios Tsichlis/Shutterstock.com.

## *VI. Presentation of the Infant Jesus in the Temple: Forty Days of Love*

Olive branch page number ornament: Marharyta Art/Shutterstock.com.

p. 101 *Nativity*: Painting by Lee Adams. Courtesy of the Riverside Baptist Church, Jacksonville, Florida.

p. 118 "Chamber of Virgin Mary": Photograph by Rauf Gharib, courtesy of Rauf and Zakiyah Gharib.

p. 119 "Jesus' Cradle": Photograph courtesy of the Madain Project, https://madainproject.com/cradle_of_jesus.

## *VII. Journey to Egypt*

Juniper berries page number ornament: YevgeniyDr/Shutterstock.com.

p. 125 *The Flight into Egypt* by Meister des Maréchal de Boucicaut: The Yorck Project (2002) 10.000 Meisterwerke der Malerei (DVD-ROM), distributed by DIRECTMEDIA Publishing GmbH. ISBN: 3936122202., Public Domain, https://commons.wikimedia.org/w/index.php?curid=155298.

p. 135 "*Ashtiname* (Book of Peace) of Muhammad": By Mohammed (?), Public Domain, https://commons.wikimedia.org/w/index.php?curid=50391967.

p. 137 Balsam Tree of Beloved Maryam in Matariyya: Photograph courtesy of Shangyun Shen.

p. 140 Juniper with Mary-blue Berries: YevgeniyDr/Shutterstock.com.

## *VIII. Losing and Finding Jesus: Calling the Beloved*

Forget-me-nots page number ornament by Cara Grace Chadwick, © 2021.

p. 145 *Mountain Under A Starry Sky In Timelapse Mode*: Photo by Şahin Sezer Dinçer from Pexels.

## *IX. Miracles of Nourishment and New Life*

Grapes page number ornament: Macrovector/Alamy Stock Vector.

p. 173 Mary Fountain: Antique postcard of fresco from Maaloula, Syria; collection of author. Floral border (added for this text) by Master of Jean Rolin II: This media file is from the collections of the Koninklijke Bibliotheek, part of which is available on Wikimedia Commons. Public Domain, https://commons.wikimedia.org/w/index.php?curid=66054512.

p. 181 *Angels Bow before Adam and Eve in Paradise*, detail from the *Falnama* ascribed to Jafar as-Sadiq, Iran (Tabriz or Qazwin) circa 1550 CE: Arthur M. Sackler Gallery, Smithsonian Institution, Washington, D.C.: Purchase — Smithsonian Unrestricted Trust Funds, Smithsonian Collections Acquisition Program, and Dr. Arthur M. Sackler, S1986.254 (Detail).

p. 193 Magdala Stone (top image): Mick Harper/Shutterstock.com.

p. 193 Magdala Stone (bottom image): Eddie Gerald/Alamy Stock Photo.

## *X. The Gathering to God: Death and Resurrection*

p. 217 *Noli Me Tangere* by Fra Angelico: Web Gallery of Art, Public Domain, https://commons.wikimedia.org/w/index.php?curid=15451028.

p. 222 The Virgin and Child (*Theotokos*) mosaic, in the apse of Hagia Sophia (Istanbul, Turkey): Photograph by Myrabella, own work, Public Domain, https://commons.wikimedia.org/w/index.php?curid=23970627.

p. 224 *Our Lady of Czestochowa (Hodegetria)*: By Kancelaria Sejmu/Krzysztof Kurek - 31. Pielgrzymka Parlamentarzystów na Jasną Górę, CC BY 2.0, https://commons.wikimedia.org/w/index.php?curid=87143103.

p. 234 Spikenard (also used as page number ornament throughout chapter): Foxyliam/Shutterstock.com.

p. 251 *Blue Flag Iris* by Lee Adams, #11 of 50 Wildflower Identification Card set, all of which were painted by Lee Adams in 1970 for the National Audubon Society. Reprinted "Courtesy of the National Audubon Society."

p. 251 Madonna lily illustration from *Les liliacées* (1805) by Pierre Joseph Redouté (1759–1840): By Rawpixel, own work, CC BY-SA 4.0, https://commons.wikimedia.org/w/index.php?curid=75326154.

p. 252 Lotus: Tieu Bao Truong/Shutterstock.com.

p. 270 *Kaff Maryam* (Resurrection Plant): Science History Images/Alamy Stock Photo.

## *XI. Teaching Journeys*

Fig page number ornament: Anna L. e Marina Durante/Shutterstock.com.

p. 277 House of the Virgin Mary statue: Photograph by Dennis Jarvis. Wikimedia Commons: https://commons.wikimedia.org/wiki/File:House_of_Virgin_Mary3.jpg.

p. 279 *The Holy Family with a Palm Tree* by Raphael (1483–1520): The Yorck Project (2002) 10.000 Meisterwerke der Malerei (DVD-ROM), distributed by DIRECTMEDIA Publishing GmbH. ISBN: 3936122202, Public Domain, https://commons.wikimedia.org/w/index.php?curid=157680.

p. 301 Chinese Madonna scroll: © The Field Museum, Image No. A114604_02d, Cat. No. 116027, Photographer John Weinstein.

p. 310 Ancient Christian Caves of Maaloula near Damascus, Syria: Photograph by Camille Hamilton Adams Helminski.

p. 311 Cave of the Hebrew Prophet Elijah on Mt. Horeb. Photograph courtesy of Doubting Thomas Research Foundation, https://doubtingthomasresearch.com/elijah-cave-mount-sinai/.

p. 313 Jabal an-Nur (Mountain of Light): Nurlan Mammadzada/Shutterstock.com.

p. 329 *The Ascent of Muhammad to Heaven (Miraj)* from an illustrated *Khamseh* of Nizami. Ascribed to the court painter Sultan Muhammad, this version was created for the Persian Shah Tahmasp I. (Gouache and ink on paper.) Collection of the British Library. http://www.mirror.org/greg.roberts/MirajB1.jpg, Public Domain, https://commons.wikimedia.org/w/index.php?curid=4137203.

p. 330 Madonna of Tenderness (*Eleusa*), painted within the "flame" of the bodhi leaf of light, India: gift of a dear friend, George Witterschein; collection of author.

p. 342 *Meryem Ana Evi*, the Holy Virgin's House (rendering drawn of it when discovered by P. Eugene Poulin): Sourced from the completion page of P. Eugene Poulin, *The Holy Virgin's House, the True Story of Its Discovery*, translated by Ivi Richichi (Istanbul: Arıkan Yayınları, 1999).

p. 348 Ephesus, Virgin Mary's house: By Rita1234, own work, CC BY-SA 3.0, https://commons.wikimedia.org/w/index.php?curid=8325181.

## *XII. Tranquility of Spirit*

Hildesheim rose page number ornament: By Kauk0r, own work, CC BY-SA 3.0, https://commons.wikimedia.org/w/index.php?curid=6878611.

p. 351 Mary of the Stars: "The Virgin Praying," antique postcard from Maaloula, Syria; collection of author.

p. 359 Our Lady of Guadalupe Tilma, 1531 CE: By unknown (1531 presented by Juan Diego), Nueva Basílica de Nuestra Señora de Guadalupe, Public Domain, https://commons.wikimedia.org/w/index.php?curid=30578416.

p. 361 Fleur-de-lys detail, Sainte-Chapelle, Paris: Photograph by Camille Hamilton Adams Helminski.

p. 367 Statue of Our Lady of Immaculate Conception with a rosary in the Grotto of Massabielle in Lourdes: DyziO/Shutterstock.com.

p. 373 *The Virgin* by Joseph Stella: https://www.wikiart.org/en/joseph-stella, Public Domain, https://commons.wikimedia.org/w/index.php?curid=65283660.

p. 375 Our Lady of Fátima: ceramic tile painting, Mission of San Juan Capistrano, San Juan Capistrano, California. Photograph by Camille Hamilton Adams Helminski.

p. 380 Hand of Fatima: Illustration 80243895 © Elena Matveeva | Dreamstime.com.

p. 384 *Our Lady of Rocamadour* wooden statue: Hemis/Alamy Stock Photo.

p. 385 *Miroku (Maitreya) in Meditation*, gilt bronze, Japanese, Asuka period, seventh century CE. Photograph courtesy of the Cleveland Museum of Art.

p. 390 Rose and illuminated windows amid starry heavens at Sainte-Chapelle, Paris: Photograph by Camille Hamilton Adams Helminski.

## *Rose Prayers*

p. 413 Hildesheim Rose of the Cathedral of the Assumption of Mary: By Kauk0r, own work, CC BY-SA 3.0, https://commons.wikimedia.org/w/index.php?curid=6878611.

p. 480 Camille with Father Tarcy: Photograph by Kabir Helminski.

Endpapers: Antique Italian decorative paper; collection of author.

Cover Design: Kabir and Camille Helminski.

# *Selected Bibliography*


Authorized King James Version: The Holy Bible, containing the Old and New Testaments, translated out of the original tongues and with the former translations diligently compared and revised (Cleveland, OH: The World Publishing Company [1611]).

Douay-Rheims 1899 The Holy Bible in English, Douay-Rheims American Edition of 1899, translated from the Latin Vulgate. Public Domain Language: English Dialect: archaic American.

The Holy Bible, English Standard Version® (ESV®), copyright © 2001 by Crossway, a publishing ministry of Good News Publishers. Used by permission. All rights reserved. Selections noted as "(ESV)" in text.

The Holy Bible, New International Version®, NIV® Copyright © 1973, 1978, 1984, 2011 by Biblica, Inc.® Used by permission. All rights reserved worldwide. Selections noted as "(NIV)" in text.

New American Standard Bible®, Copyright © 1960, 1971, 1977, 1995, 2020 by The Lockman Foundation. Used by permission. All rights reserved. www.lockman.org.

New King James Version®. Copyright © 1982 by Thomas Nelson. Used by permission. All rights reserved.

*Holy Bible*, New Living Translation, copyright © 1996, 2004, 2015 by Tyndale House Foundation. Used by permission of Tyndale House Publishers, Inc., Carol Stream, Illinois 60188. All rights reserved.

*The Song of Songs which Is Solomon's*, illustrated and illuminated by Valenti Angelo for the members of the Heritage Club (New York: The Heritage Press, limited edition, 1935).

*The Unvarnished Gospels, translated by Andy Gaus (Putney, VT: Threshold Books, 1999)*. Selections noted as "(UG)" in text.

*The Unvarnished New Testament,* translated by Andy Gaus (Grand Rapids, MI: Phanes Press, 1991). Selections noted as "(UNT)" in text.

*The Gospel of Mary Magdalene,* translation from the Coptic and commentary by Jean-Yves Leloup, English translation and notes by Joseph Rowe (Rochester, VT: Inner Traditions International, 2002).

*The Nag Hammadi Scriptures, the Revised and Updated Translation of Sacred Gnostic Texts,* (Complete in One Volume), edited by Marvin Meyer (New York: HarperCollins, 2008).

*Lost Gospel Q: The Original Sayings of Jesus,* edited by Marcus Borg, Mark Powelson, and Ray Riegert (Ulysses Press, 1996).

*The Gospel of the Beloved Companion, The Complete Gospel of Mary Magdalene,* translation and commentary by Jehanne de Quillan (Ariège, France: Éditions Athara, 2010).

*Asad, Muhammad. The Message of the Qur'an, The Full Account of the Revealed Arabic Text Accompanied by Parallel Transliteration,* translated and explained by Muhammad Asad (Bristol, England: The Book Foundation, 2003 [1980]).

*Roman Transliteration of the Quran with Full Arabic Text,* English translation by Abdullah Yusuf Ali, (Lahore: Sh. Muhammad Ashraf, 1991).

*The Light of Dawn, Daily Readings from the Holy Qur'an,* rendered by Camille Adams Helminski (Boston, MA: Shambhala Publications, 2000).

Adams, Hannah. *A Dictionary of All Religions and Religious Denominations* (Atlanta: Scholars Press (with The American Academy of Religion), 1992 [1817]).

Aflaki, Shamsuddin Ahmad. *Rumi and His Friends, Stories of the Lovers of God: Excerpts from the Manaqib al-'Arifin of Aflaki,* translated by Camille Adams Helminski with Susan Blaylock (Louisville, KY: Fons Vitae, 2013).

'Ali, Hadrat, *Living and Dying with Grace: Counsels of Hadrat 'Ali,* translated by Thomas Cleary (Boston, Massachusetts: Shambhala Publications, 1995).

Aquinas, St. Thomas. *Meditations*, selected by P. D. Mezard, O. P., adapted and translated by E. C. McEnery, O. P., new and revised ed. (Columbus, Ohio: College Book Co., 1941).

Armstrong, Karen. *Mohammad, A Biography* (New York: HarperCollins Publisher, 1992).

Barker, Margaret. *Temple Themes in Christian Worship* (London: Bloomsbury Publishing, 2008).

Bauman, Lynn C., Ward J. Bauman, and Cynthia Bourgeault, *The Luminous Gospels, Thomas, Mary Magdalene, and Philip* (Telephone, TX: Praxis Publishing, 2008).

Behari, Dr. Bankey. *Fariduddin 'Attar's Tadhkaratul-Auliya or Memoirs of Saints* (Lahore, Pakistan: Sh. Muhammad Ashraf, 1975).

Bielecki, Tessa. *Teresa of Avila, Mystical Writings* (New York: The Crossroad Publishing Co., 1997).

Blake, William. *Collected Poems* (New York: Penguin, 1991).

Bourgeault, Cynthia. *The Meaning of Mary Magdalene, Discovering the Woman at the Heart of Christianity* (Boulder: Shambhala Publications, 2010).

Brentano, Clemens. *The Life of Jesus Christ and Biblical Revelations: From the Visions of Venerable Anne Catherine Emmerich*, Vol. 1–4, translated by Sir Michael Palairet (Charlotte, NC: TAN Books).

Brown, Rachel Fulton. *Mary and the Art of Prayer, the Hours of the Virgin in Medieval Christian Life and Thought* (New York: Columbia University Press, 2018).

Byrne, Lavinia (ed.). *The Hidden tradition, Women's Spiritual Writings Rediscovered, An Anthology* (New York, NY: Crossroad Publishing Co., 1991).

Chryssavigis, John. *In the Heart of the Desert: the Spirituality of the Desert Fathers and Mothers*, revised ed. (Bloomington, IN: World Wisdom, 2008).

Cuneen, Sally. *In Search of Mary, the Woman and the Symbol* (New York: Ballantine Books, 1996).

Duquesne, Jacques. *Salve Regina, The Story of Mary* (Paris: Éditions Flammarion, 2006).

Durham, Michael S. *The Miracles of Mary, Apparitions, Legends, and Miraculous Works of the Blessed Virgin Mary* (New York, NY: HarperSanFrancisco, 1995).

Flinders, Carol Lee. *The Little Book of Women Mystics* (New York: HarperCollins Publishers, 1995).

Gendler, J. Ruth. *Changing Light, the Eternal Cycle of Night and Day* (New York: HarperCollins Publishers, 1991).

Al-Ghazali, Abu Hamid. *Al-Ghazali: On the Duties of Brotherhood*, translated from the Arabic by Muhtar Holland (Woodstock, NY: Overlook Press, 1979).

Al-Ghazali, Muhammad. *Remembrance and Prayer: The Way of the Prophet Muhammad*, translated by Yusuf Talal De Lorenzo (Leicester, UK: The Islamic Foundation, 1986).

Grant, Robert M. *Irenaeus of Lyons* (London: Routledge, 1997).

Helminski, Camille. *Women of Sufism, A Hidden Treasure: Writings and Stories of Mystic Poets, Scholars, and Saints* (Boston, MA: Shambhala Publications, 2003).

Helminski, Camille (ed.), *The Book of Character, Writings on Character and Virtue from Islamic and Other Sources* (Watsonville and Bristol: The Book Foundation, 2004).

Helminski, Camille (ed.), *The Book of Nature, A Sourcebook of Spiritual Perspectives on Nature and the Environment* (Bristol and Watsonville: The Book Foundation, 2006).

Helminski, Camille Hamilton Adam. *Words from the East* (Louisville, KY: Sweet Lady Press, 2016).

Helminski, Camille Hamilton Adams. *Exaltations* (forthcoming from Sweet Lady Press).

Helminski, Camille Hamilton Adams. *A New World* (forthcoming from Sweet Lady Press).

Helminski, Camille Hamilton Adams. *On the Way Home* (forthcoming from Sweet Lady Press).

Hennecke, Edgar. *New Testament Apocrypha*, 2 Vols. (Philadelphia: Westminster Press, 1963–1966).

Hildegard of Bingen. *Illuminations of Hildegard of Bingen*, commentary by Matthew Fox (Santa Fe, NM: Bear and Co.).

Hildegard von Bingen. *Writings of Medieval Women*, translated by Marcelle Thiebaux (New York: Garland Publishing, 1994).

Julian of Norwich, *Showings*, edited by Edmund Colledge, O. S. A., and James Walsh, S. J. (New York, Paulist Press, 1978).

Khaqani, *The Book of Khaqani*, translation and introduction by Paul Smith (New Humanity Books, 2014).

Lowden, John. *Early Christian and Byzantine Art* (London: Phaidon Press, 1997).

Mary of Agreda, Ven. *The Mystical City of God,* translated by Piscar Marison (Charlotte, NC: TAN Books, 2009).

Matt, Daniel C. *Zohar, Annotated and Explained* (Woodstock, VT: Skylight Paths Publishing, 2002).

Maximus the Confessor. *The Life of the Virgin—Maximus the Confessor*, translated by Stephen Shoemaker (New Haven: Yale University Press, 2012).

Merton, Thomas. *Conjectures of a Guilty Bystander* (New York: IMAGE, 2014).

Mitchell, Stephen. *A Book of Psalms: Selected and Adapted from the Hebrew* (New York, NY: HarperCollins Publishers, 1993).

Montfort, St. Louis-Marie de. *True Devotion to Mary* (London: Catholic Way Publishing, 2013).

Morrow, John Andrew. *The Covenants of the Prophet Muhammad with the Christians of the World* (Angelico Press, 2013).

Murata, Sachiko. *Chinese Gleams of Sufi Light, Wang Tai-yu's Great Learning of the Pure and Real and Liu Chih's Displaying the Concealment of the Real Realm* (Albany, NY: State University of New York Press, 2000).

Patterson, Stephen J., James M. Robinson, and Hans-Gebhard Bethge. *The Fifth Gospel: The Gospel of Thomas Comes of Age* (Harrisburg, PA: Trinity Press International, 1998).

Perry, Whitall. *A Treasury of Traditional Wisdom* (London, 1971).

Pez, B. *Thesaurus Anecdotorum Novissimus* (Augsburg: 1721).

Poulin, P. Eugene. *The Holy Virgin's House, the True Story of its Discovery* (Istanbul: Arikan Yayinlari, 1999).

Al-Qushayri, Abu'l-Qasim. *Principles of Sufism*, translated by B.R. von Schlegell (Berkeley, CA: Mizan Press, 1990).

Robson, James. *Mishkat al Masabih*, (Lahore, Pakistan: Sh. Muhammad Ashraf Publishers, 1991).

Rumi, Jalaluddin. *Kolliyaat-e Shams-e Tabrizi*, edited by Badiozzaman Forouzanfar (Tehran: Amir Kabir, 1988).

Rumi, Jalaluddin. *Jewels of Remembrance, A Daybook of Spiritual Guidance Containing 365 Selections from the Wisdom of Rumi*, selected and translated by Camille and Kabir Helminski (Putney, VT: Threshold Books, 1996).

Rumi, Jalaluddin. *Love is a Stranger*, translated by Kabir Edmund Helminski (Brattleboro, VT: Threshold Books, 1993).

Rumi, Jalalu'ddin. *The Mathnawi of Jalalu'ddin Rumi*, edited and translated by Reynold A. Nicholson (London, UK: Luzac and Company, 1982 [1930]).

Rumi, Jalaluddin. *The Pocket Rumi*, edited by Kabir Helminski, translations by Kabir and Camille Helminski (Boston, MA: Shambhala Publications, 2001).

Rumi, Jalaluddin. *The Rumi Collection*, selected and edited by Kabir Helminski (Boston, MA: Shambhala Publications, 1998).

Rumi, Jalaluddin. *The Rumi Daybook, 365 Poems and Teachings from the Beloved Sufi Master*, Selected and Translated by Kabir and Camille Helminski (Boston, MA: Shambhala Publications, 2012).

Rumi, Jalaluddin. *Rumi Daylight, A Daybook of Spiritual Guidance, Three Hundred and Sixty-Five Selections from Jalaluddin Rumi's Mathnawi*, Translated by Camille and Kabir Helminski (Putney, VT: Threshold Books, 1990).

Rumi, Jalaluddin. *Signs of the Unseen, The Discourses of Jalaluddin Rumi*, introduction and translation by W. M. Thackston, Jr. (Boulder, CO: Shambhala Publications, 1994).

Al-Sadiq, Jafar. *Spiritual Gems, The Mystical Commentary ascribed to Ja'far al-Sadiq as contained in Sulami's Haqa'iq al-Tafsir from the text of Paul Nwyia*, translated and annotated by Farhana Mayer (Louisville, KY: Fons Vitae, 2011).

Sakkakini, Widad El. *First Among Sufis, The Life and Thought of Rabi'a al-Adawiyya*, translated by Dr. Nabil Safwat (London, UK: The Octagon Press, 1982).

Sands, Kristin Zahra. *Sufi Commentaries on the Qur'an in Classical Islam* (New York: Routledge Studies in the Quran, 2000).

Schimmel, Annemarie. *Mystical Dimensions of Islam* (Chapel Hill: University of North Carolina Press, 1975).

Schleifer, Aliah. *Mary the Blessed Virgin of Islam* (Louisville, KY; Fons Vitae, 1997).

Shams of Tabriz. *Rumi's Sun, The Teachings of Shams of Tabriz*, translated by Refik Algan and Camille Adams Helminski (Louisville, KY: Threshold Books, 2017 [2008]).

Shapiro, Rabbi Rami. *The Divine Feminine in Biblical Wisdom Literature, Selections Annotated and Explained* (Woodstock, VT Skylight Paths Publishing, 2005).

Shushud, Hasan Lutfi. *The Masters of Wisdom of Central Asia* (Rochester, VT: Inner Traditions, 2014).

Smith, Margaret. *Rabi'a the Mystic and Her Fellow Saints in Islam* (Cambridge: Cambridge University Press, 1928; San Francisco: Rainbow Bridge, 1977).

Stewart, Dorothy (ed). *Women of Vision: An Anthology of Spiritual Words from Women Across the Centuries* (Chicago, IL: Loyola Press, 2000).

As-Sulami, Abu 'Abd ar-Rahman. *Early Sufi Women: Dhikr an-Niswa al-Muta'abbidat aç-Çufiyyat*, edited and translated from the Riyadh manuscript with introduction and notes by Rkia Elaroui Cornell (Louisville, KT: Fons Vitae, 1999).

Al-Sulami, Ibn al-Ausayn. *The Way of Sufi Chivalry*, an interpretation by Tosun Bayrak al-Jerrahi (Rochester, VT: Inner Traditions International, 1991 [1983]).

Taylor, John W. *The Coming of the Saints, The Story of the Lost Disciples* (Muskogee, OK: Artisan Publishers, 2011 [1906]).

Al-Tha'labi, Ahmad Ibn Muhammad. *Ara'is al-madjalis fi kisas al anbiya: Lives of the Prophets,* translation by William M. Brimmer, Brill Studies in Middle Eastern Literature (Boston and Leiden: Brill Academic Publishers, 2002).

Upton, Charles. *Doorkeeper of the Heart, Versions of Rabi'a* (Putney, VT: Threshold Books, 1988).

Verdun, Timothy and Melissa R. Katz, Amy G. Remensnyder, and Miri Rubin. *Picturing Mary: Woman, Mother, Idea* (New York: Scala Arts Publishers (in association with The National Museum of Women in the Arts, Washington, D.C.), 2014).

Wadud, Amina. *Qur'an and Woman* (New York: Oxford University Press, 1999).

Walsh, William Thomas. *Our Lady of Fátima* (New York: Image Books, Doubleday, 1990).

Walther, Wiebke. *Women in Islam: from Medieval to Modern Times,* translated from the German by C. S. V., revised edition (Salt. Princeton, NJ: Markus Wiener Publishing, 1993).

*Alim 6.0: The World's Most Useful Islamic Software* (Silver Spring, Maryland: ISL Software Corporation, www.alim.org, © 1986-2002).

*Cantigas de Santa Maria for Singers*, http://cantigasdesantamaria.com.

*Centre for the Study of the Cantigas de Santa Maria*, http://csm.mml.ox.ac.uk/.

"The enchantment of the Holy Girdle," *Museo di Palazzo Pretorio,* http://www.palazzopretorio.prato.it/en/museum/exhibition/enchantment-holy-girdle/.

*House of Mary—The Church and Fountains*, https://www.hzmeryemanaevi.com/en/monastery-water-supply-hiking/.

"Lectio Divina," *Contemplative Outreach*, https://www.contemplativeoutreach.org/lectio-divina-contemplation/ (accessed May 13, 2021).

*The Leon Levy Dead Sea Scrolls Digital Library*, https://www.deadseascrolls.org.il.

"Our Lady of Saydnaya Patriarchal Monastery," *Greek Orthodox Patriarchate of Antioch and All the East*, https://www.antiochpatriarchate.org/en/page/our-lady-of-saydnaya-patriarchal-monastery/146/.

"Our Lady's image on the Tilma," *Our Lady of Guadalupe*, https://olg.cc/about/about-our-patroness/our-ladys-image-on-the-tilma/.

*The Piacenza Pilgrim*, translation by Andrew Jacobs, from the critical edition of P. Geyer in *Itineraria et alia geographica*, http://andrewjacobs. org/translations/piacenzapilgrim.html.

Adonia, Beata. "Kathisma–A place of rest on the way to Bethlehem," *The Jerusalem Post*, January 31, 2013, https://www.jpost.com/Travel/Around-Israel/Kathisma-A-place-of-rest-on-the-way-to-Bethlehem.

Braybrooke, Marcus. "A Monk, Catholic and Hindu: Bede Griffiths—Interfaith's Interspiritual Pioneer," *The Interfaith Observer*, http://www.theinterfaithobserver.org/journal-articles/2017/10/4/bede-griffiths-interfaiths-interspiritual-pioneer.

Dioscorides. *De Materia Medica*, available at *World Digital Library*, https://www.wdl. org/en/item/10632/.

Loewen, Peter V. "Cantigas de Santa Maria," *Oxford Bibliographies*, https://www.oxfordbibliographies.com/view/document/obo-9780195396584/obo-9780195396584-0210.xml.

Lorenco, Fr. Ignacio. "Sixth Apparition of Our Lady," *One Hundred Years of Fatima*, https://www.ewtn.com/fatima/sixth-apparition-of-our-lady.asp.

Mary, Francis. "Miracle Of The Dancing Sun At Fatima & Eye Witness Accounts," *Catholics Online*, http://francismary.org/miracle-of-the-dancing-sun-at-fatima-eye-witness-accounts/.

Montfort, St Louis-Marie Grignion de. *Treatise on True Devotion to the Blessed Virgin*, translated from the original French by Reverend Frederick William Faber, D. D., *Catholic Treasury*, http://www.catholictreasury.info/books/true_devotion/index.php.

Ristine, Jennifer. "The Magdala Stone: The Jerusalem Temple Embodied," *Biblical Archaeology Society*, https://www.biblicalarchaeology.org/daily/ancient-cultures/ancient-israel/the-magdala-stone/.

Roach, John. "'Methuselah' Palm Grown From 2,000-Year-Old Seed Is a Father, " *National Geographic,* March 24, 2015, https://www.nationalgeographic.com/science/article/150324-ancient-methuselah-date-palm-sprout-science.

# Index

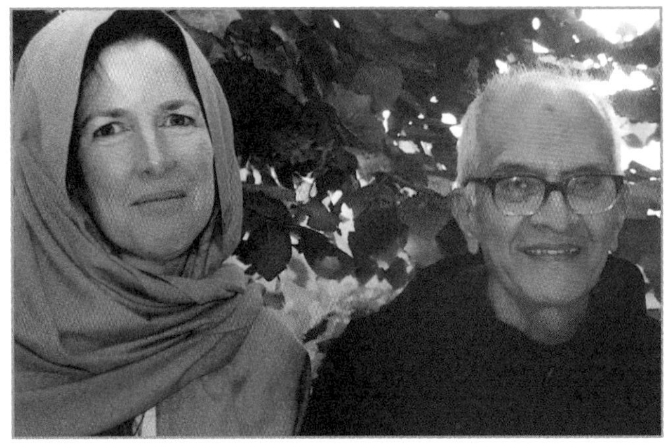

*Camille with Father Tarcy*
*(Mother Maryam's House [Meryem Ana Evi] near Ephesus, Turkey)*

## *Other Publications by Camille*

(www.sweetladypress.com; www.sufism.org)

*Ninety-Nine Names of the Beloved, Intimations of the Beauty and Power of the Divine*
Camille Hamilton Adams Helminski

*Words from the East*
Poetic reflections, first in the series of "Songs of the Soul"
Camille Hamilton Adams Helminski

*Ramadan Love Songs*
Poetic reflections, second in the series of "Songs of the Soul"
Camille Hamilton Adams Helminski

*The Light of Dawn, Daily Readings from the Holy Qur'an*
Selected and rendered by Camille Helminski

*Women of Sufism, A Hidden Treasure: Writings and Stories of Mystic Poets, Scholars, and Saints*
(which brought to light the integral contribution of women to the spiritual path of Islam)
Selected and introduced by Camille Helminski

*Rumi's Sun, The Teachings of Shams of Tabriz*
Excerpts from the *Maqalat* of Shams-i Tabriz
Translated by Refik Algan and Camille Helminski

*Rumi and His Friends, Stories of the Lovers of God, Excerpts from the Manaqib al-'Arifin of Aflaki*
Selected and translated by Camille Adams Helminski with Susan Blaylock

RUMI TRANSLATIONS with Kabir Helminski:

*The Rumi Daybook, 365 Poems and Teachings from the Beloved Sufi Master*
Selected and translated by Kabir Helminski and Camille Helminski

*Jewels of Remembrance, A Daybook of Spiritual Guidance from the Wisdom of Mevlana Jalaluddin Rumi*
Selected and translated by Kabir and Camille Helminski

*Rumi Daylight, A Daybook of Spiritual Guidance: Three Hundred and Sixty-Five Selections from the Mathnawi of Mevlana Jalaluddin Rumi*
Translated by Camille and Kabir Helminski

*The Pocket Rumi* (Shambhala Pocket Classics)
Edited by Kabir Helminski (translations by Kabir and Camille)

*Happiness without Death, Desert Hymns*
Assad Ali, translated by Camille Adams Helminski, Kabir Helminski, and Dr. Ibrahim Al-Shihabi

*Civilization of Paradise, Revelation Poems*
Asad Ali, translated by Kabir Helminski with Camille Helminski, Mahmoud Mostafa, and Ibrahim Shihabi

*The Book of Nature, A Sourcebook of Spiritual Perspectives on Nature and the Environment*
The Book Foundation Education Project Series, edited by Camille Helminski

*The Book of Character, An Anthology of Writings on Virtue from Islamic and Other Sources*
The Book Foundation Education Project Series, edited by Camille Helminski

*Awakened Dreams, Raji's Journeys with the Mirror Dede*
Ahmet Hilmi, translated by Refik Algan and Camille Helminski

*The Mevlevi Wird, The Prayers Recited Daily by Mevlevi Dervishes* (the tradition of Rumi)

RECORDINGS:

*Glorious Morning Light* (Quranic recitations by Camille)

*The Mevlevi Wird*

*Rumi's Sun, Excerpts from the Teachings of Shams of Tabriz*

*You Are Joy* (Rumi recitations by Kabir and Camille with Sufi music from around the world)

*Garden within the Flames* (*ilahis* sung by Kabir and Camille—Dost Quartet)

The "Songs of the Soul," books of poetic reflection, that began in 1990 with the inspiration of *Words from the East,* and continued with *Ramadan Love Songs*, is opening further through several forthcoming publications: *Exaltations*, *On the Way Home*, *Sketches from the Unseen,* and *A New World.* Also forthcoming is a volume of stories of ancestral grandmothers: *Tree of Grace: Troubadours, Patriots, Mystics and Lovers.*